BRITISH SOCIALIST FICTION, 1884–1914

CONTENTS OF THE EDITION

VOLUME 1
General Introduction
1884–1891

VOLUME 2
1892–1900

VOLUME 3
1901–1906

VOLUME 4
1907–1910

VOLUME 5
1911–1914

BRITISH SOCIALIST FICTION, 1884–1914

Volume 1
1884–1891

Edited by
Deborah Mutch

PICKERING & CHATTO
2013

Published by Pickering & Chatto (Publishers) Limited
21 Bloomsbury Way, London WC1A 2TH

2252 Ridge Road, Brookfield, Vermont 05036-9704, USA

www.pickeringchatto.com

BRITISH LIBRARY CATALOGUING IN PUBLICATION DATA

British socialist fiction, 1884–1914.
1. Political fiction, English – 19th century. 2. Political fiction, English – 20th
century. 3. Socialism – Fiction.
I. Mutch, Deborah, 1965– editor of compilation.
823.8'0803581-dc23

ISBN-13: 9781848933576

This publication is printed on acid-free paper that conforms to the American
National Standard for the Permanence of Paper for Printed Library Materials.

Typeset by Pickering & Chatto (Publishers) Limited
Printed and bound in the United Kingdom by Berforts Information Press

CONTENTS

General Introduction   vii
Acknowledgements   xxix
Bibliography   xxxi
Glossary of Dialect Terms   xli

Introduction   xlix

Bolton Trotter   1
    C. Allen Clarke, 'What a Christmas Carol Wrought' (1891)   3
    Teddy Ashton, 'Heaw Bill Spriggs Leet New Yer In' (1891)   11
Commonweal   15
    H. S. S., 'A Dream of Queer Fishes (A Modern Prose Idyll)' (1887)   17
    D., 'Scaring the Capitalists' (1888)   19
    Thomas Barclay, 'Master and Man in Heaven' (1891)   25
    Thomas Maubourg, 'A Mournful Fate' (1891)   27
Justice   31
    William Morris, 'An Old Fable Retold' (1884)   35
    'Utile Dulci', 'Fables for the Times – I: The Monkeys and the Nuts'
        (1884)   37
    Anon., 'Fables for the Times – II: The Political Economist and the
        Flowers' (1884)   39
    Anon., 'Archie Cameron's Success' (1885)   41
    D. F. Hannigan, 'Aristos and Demos' (1887)   47
    H. J. Bramsbury, 'A Working Class Tragedy' (1888–9)   51
Labour Elector   213
    Anon., 'A New "Labour" Paper' (1890)   215
To-Day   225
    Ivan Tourgeneff, 'Only a Dog' (1883)   227
    'Bauer und Dichter', 'Eros or Erin. A Tale of an Irish Conspiracy'
        (1886–7)   245
    Fabian Bland, 'Blood' (1886)   269

R. G. B., 'Birds of a Feather' (1886)   277
John Broadhouse, 'How He Lost his "Strad"' (1886)   283
A. Gilbert Katte, 'The Whip Hand. A Political Story – in Three Parts'
    (1888)   287
John Law, 'The Gospel of Getting On. (To Olive Schreiner.)' (1888)   305
H. Bellingham, 'Chips' (1888)   309

Editorial Notes   313
Silent Corrections   341

GENERAL INTRODUCTION

Of course, I don't pretend to known [*sic*] all about [socialism], but I have learnt all I can, and the same means of learning are open to you if you care to know anything about it. There's some pamphlets on the drawers there that you can read. They put the question in the most simple manner. Then we have a weekly paper and meetings and lectures.
> —H. J. Bramsbury, 'A Working Class Tragedy' (below, pp. 142–3)

Then you have books and pictures; you have been taught things that are interesting and good and beautiful. Are you trying to pass on that knowledge to others who have not had your chances, or does it merely make you hold yourself aloof from them?
> —Lilian Claxton, 'Nigel Grey (A Serial Story of Love and Effort)'
> (Volume 2, p. 142)

The variety and volume of fiction written and published by British socialists during the period 1884–1914 and the multiplicity of socialist periodicals, almost all of which included some form of creative literature, make obvious British socialists' appreciation of the written and printed word as a political tool. Their appreciation was not unique: earlier in the century the Chartist movement also had a strong literary impulse, and their periodicals carried imaginative literature by authors such as Ernest Jones and John Frost, while the Chartist activist, poet and author Thomas Cooper founded the Shakespearian Chartist Association in 1841.[1] A similarly strong literary thread runs through the socialist movement, and Raphael Samuel points to evidence of this in Tom Mann's formation of a Shakespeare Mutual Improvement Society some thirty years after Cooper's Association, and in Ramsay MacDonald's poetic oration at James Keir Hardie's funeral.[2] It is evident in Robert Blatchford's arguments on the necessity of culture in *Merrie England* and his use of literature to support his points, and in the astonishing range of literary references liberally threaded through the fiction. This literary literacy is not only evidence of the authors' range of reading but must also indicate an expectation of similar levels of literary knowledge in the general reader. The quotations, references and allusions make no distinction between 'high' and 'low' culture: the work of dialect poets Samuel Laycock and Edwin Waugh are recited as seriously as Shakespeare and Shelley; the music hall songs are as appreciated as the hymns. This is not cultural incontinence but a wide embrace of cultural production without socially imposed distinctions of hierarchy. Literature was not valued simply for the development of the individual intellect but was also expected to produce a material effect. How that effect was to be achieved, and to what ends, was the point where socialist authors and groups differed, but the cohering desire to broadcast socialist ideas through literature is illustrated in the opening quotations.

The quotations are taken from serializations published in the official periodicals of two of the most important socialist groups of the period covered by these volumes: the Social Democratic Federation's (SDF) *Justice* and the Independent Labour Party's (ILP) *Labour Leader*. There were significant differences between the founders and chairmen of these groups: the SDF's Henry Mayers Hyndman took a Marxist-Tory view of socialism,[3] while the ILP's James Keir Hardie filtered his socialism through his Liberal-trade union background; the SDF wanted a clear Marxist re-ordering of society, while the ILP aimed to draw the working-class voter away from ties with both Liberal and Tory politics. Nevertheless, both produced a periodical to promote their visions and arguments for socialism, both periodicals carried serializations, and both appreciated the political effects of reading. In H. J. Bramsbury's 'A Working Class Tragedy' (possibly a pseudonymous publication by Hyndman), the literature is placed firmly within the socialist movement as the character of the socialist Nobby Wright literally directs Frank, the political novice, to his education in the 'pamphlets on the drawers there'. By doing so he unintentionally reinforces the criticism made by ILP member John Bruce Glasier of the SDF's 'dry presentation of the socialist ideal'.[4] The ILP's less theoretical, more ethical approach to socialism is evident in the question socialist Nigel Grey puts to the Squire's daughter, Constance Compton: does she use her books to educate others, or does she use her literacy and knowledge to elevate herself above the undereducated masses? There is no suggestion that the patrician Constance is a collector or reader of socialist literature; rather, literature expands the reader's perception of the world and their place in it, leading to informed change. Both quotations illustrate the two functions of literature in promoting socialism: the encouragement of the neophyte-autodidact in the journey to political understanding, and the responsibility to disseminate literature, socialism and ideas.

In his essay on the serializations in *Justice* and the *Commonweal* in the 1880s and 1890s, Jack Mitchell states that 'it was not just a matter of socialism attracting people of a literary bent. In their activities the socialist societies laid tremendous weight on the word'.[5] This weight is evident in both the sheer volume of socialist periodicals and the proliferation of creative literature published in those socialist periodicals during the period 1884–1914.[6] Although the continuum of literary style and political ideas means that any imposition of a 'period' or 'era' is arbitrary, critics, readers and publishers need boundaries to ensure focus, interest and an end-page. These years have been selected as convenient start and end dates for this work because 1884 was the year *Justice*, the first avowedly socialist periodical, was published, and because the First World War, beginning in 1914, was to change the social and political landscape of Britain. The war did not cohere the British socialist groups nor did it dissolve them, but it changed the landscape of the debates.

The socialists' general recognition of the power of print did not mean all appreciated the political power of fiction. A look at the SDF's *Justice* reveals its low regard for fiction, particularly long serializations, as it published only four serial fictions between 1884 and 1914: James S. Borlase's 'Darker than Death: A Tale of Russia To-Day' (1885); H. J. Bramsbury's 'A Working Class Tragedy' (1888–9); Charles Allen Clarke's 'The Red Flag' (1909); and Henry Baxter's 'David Dexter, Socialist' (1909). On the other hand, the literary predispositions of *Clarion* editor Robert Blatchford and Charles Allen Clarke, editor of *Teddy Ashton's Journal* and its many titles, meant that both regularly included creative literature. Despite variations in the significance placed on creative writing in the socialist movement, the literary output between 1884 and 1914 constitutes an enormous body of work, much of which remains largely undiscovered and un-researched.

The aim of this collection is to give an overview of the fiction published in the longer-running and influential periodicals of the British socialist movement. And despite the collection running to five volumes, it is still only a flavour of the phenomenal socialist literary output. The difficulty with making any selection is the decision of what to exclude. The first decision was based on genre: the prevalence of poetry throughout the socialist periodicals during this period deserves its own collection in order to do justice to the genre as used by the socialists and to make socialist poetry as accessible as Chartist poetry.[7] The reader of these volumes will also be aware of the absence of some famous socialist names. Possibly the most noticeable omission is the work of William Morris, apart from 'An Old Fable Retold' in the *Justice* section of Volume 1. This tale is included here because it formed one of a short series of socialist fables, but for the rest of Morris's output, the reader is directed to Pickering & Chatto's forthcoming collection of his complete works. Morris's lasting fame has cast a long shadow over many socialist authors, so this collection has the opportunity to bring to light some of the fictions that have been overshadowed by Morris for more than a century. Copyright restrictions prevent the inclusion of long-lived famous names: many of the works of George Bernard Shaw (d. 1950) and H. G. Wells (d. 1946) are already accessible, unlike most of the authors who published in the socialist press, but it is with regret that fiction by Hillaire Belloc (d. 1953), Adela Pankhurst (d. 1961), Ethel Carnie Holdsworth (d. 1962) and Upton Sinclair (d. 1968) must remain buried in the pages of the periodical press for the time being. The fiction chosen for inclusion has been selected to give as broad a view as possible of the publication of creative literature in the socialist press. Some periodicals such as *Justice* had long periods when no fiction was published, and so there is more bunching of short stories for these than there is for periodicals such as the *Clarion*, which published fiction regularly. Similarly, prolific authors such as Charles Allen Clarke (under this name and his many pseudonyms) and A. Neil Lyons have multiple inclusions because of their output; for instance, in 1912 there was very little fiction published in the *Clarion* that was not written by Lyons. While the volumes themselves cover distinct time periods, there are some serializations that straddle the divide – Blatchford's The Sorcery Shop' (1906–7) has been included in Volume 4 – while other stories fall just outside the specific years – for instance, Quinbus Flestrin's 'A Tale of a Turnip', featured in Volume 2, was published on 26 December 1891, a few days short of the following year.

Each of the five volumes of this collection organizes the fiction under the selected periodicals. These periodicals have been chosen because of their longevity (*Justice*, 1884–1933; *Clarion*, 1891–1935; *Labour Leader*, 1894–1987; *Social Democrat*, 1897–1913), influence (*Labour Elector* for its investigative journalism and its role in the London dock strike in 1889; *Workman's Times* for its role in developing the Independent Labour Party), popularity (*Clarion*, *Teddy Ashton's Journal/Northern Weekly*), readership (*To-Day* and *Social Democrat* took a more theoretical approach to socialism) or role within the socialist movement (*Commonweal* for its challenge to *Justice*; *Labour Prophet* as the organ of the Labour Church). Each volume presents a selection of both short stories and serializations published in the periodicals, and the Volume Introductions take a more detailed look at some of the fiction in the specific volume, while this General Introduction takes a broader view of the socialist uses of fiction, form and the periodical.

Fiction

The *fin de siècle* and the early decades of the twentieth century was a period of change in the publication of the novel. The popularity of the three-decker novel was waning, and single-volume fiction was the rising new form. Nevertheless, the form was still 'the novel', albeit now with the story cohered for immediate purchase and consumption. The novel has long been associated with the rise of the middle class, as increasing wealth and literacy in the eighteenth century 'must have increased the relative importance of those who desired an easier form of literary entertainment, even if it had little prestige among the literati'.[8] It was not only in Britain that class and literary form were interwoven; the popularity of French novelists 'occurred only after the French Revolution had placed the French middle class in a position of social and literary power'.[9] Raymond Williams has argued that this association created a more nuanced categorization, expanding the broad feudal distinctions of verse and prose to include '"historical" or "philosophical" or "descriptive" or "didactic" or even "instructional" writing, as well as ... "imaginative" or "dramatic" or "fictional" or "personal" writing experience'.[10] The relation of genres to social groupings, Williams states, maintained both 'clear social and historical relations between particular literary forms and the societies and periods in which they were originated or practised', though the dominant form did not disappear when the social hierarchy shifted across periods.[11] The period associated with a particular literary form may end, according to Williams, but the form, or aspects of it, remain and are integrated into the literature of a new era.

The periodical was a useful vehicle for developing new modes of fiction, being free from the constraints of conservative publishers who were themselves restricted by the economic power of libraries such as Mudies and national booksellers like W. H. Smith. Periodicals gave authors the freedom to experiment, giving, for instance, Joseph Conrad a platform for *Heart of Darkness* and *Lord Jim* in *Blackwoods*, and for the fiction of the decadents and the New Woman in the *Yellow Book*. Nevertheless, periodicals did not allow a free reign on serialization, as Thomas Hardy found when he was forced to bowdlerize *Tess of the D'Urbervilles* for the *Graphic* after rejections from *Murray's Magazine* and *Macmillan's*.[12] Questions of 'taste' and 'decency' aside, socialist editors and proprietors were free to create and give space to what they understood to be 'socialist' fiction.

The question that should be asked at this point is, what *is* 'socialist' fiction? The close association between the middle classes and the novel meant that this form was not a useful vehicle for the socialist experience. This had long been an issue, as Ian Haywood argues: 'By the time Chartist authors turned their hands to fiction, the British novel was deeply biased against reflecting a working-class perspective on society'.[13] One caveat to the definition of 'socialist' fiction has been raised by Nicholas Daly's work on popular fiction and the impossibility of reclaiming 'authentic' literature. Daly dispels the myth of authenticity:

> We cannot identify, therefore, a set of practices or texts that is always essentially popular, or oppositional; the dominant culture can assimilate the artefacts of an oppositional culture, and indeed, aspects of the dominant culture can be given an oppositional edge. It follows that from this perspective there is no possibility of 'rescuing' some authentic, fully autonomous essence of the popular; rather the popular inhabits that grey area where the less powerful confront, adopt, adapt, or even reject the ideologies of a more powerful group.[14]

The same difficulties of separation and authenticity are evident in the fiction produced by socialist authors. In the movement itself there is no clear division between dominant and opposing groups, particularly along class lines: the wealthy upper-class Hyndman had a long and close working relationship with the former unskilled labourer and *Justice* editor Harry Quelch; upper-class Henry Hyde Champion worked closely with former engineers Tom Mann and John Burns while organizing the 1889 London dock strike. And like the boundaries of class, socialists similarly dismantled the boundaries of genre.

Both the serials and the short stories published by the socialist movement during this period hybridized the sub-generic content in ways similar to the fiction produced by mid-nineteenth-century Chartist authors. Ian Haywood notes the necessity of the hybrid form in the production of working-class political fiction: 'Whereas Chartist poets could draw on a solid heritage of radical plebian verse stretching back to the 1790s, there was no equivalent tradition of radical plebian fiction'.[15] This patchwork of genres, the basis of Chartist political fiction, has been seen as a levelling literary form, doing in fiction what the Chartists aimed to do in fact. Rob Breton argues that '[w]ith the clash of popular, simplifying genres and intellectualizing or politicizing ones came a specific aesthetic amenable and familiar to working classes. Chartist leaders such as Feargus O'Connor, Thomas Martin Wheeler, and Thomas Cooper acquiesced to popular forms because doing so was inherently democratic and thus in keeping with their political objectives'.[16] The same claim could be made of socialist fiction, as many of the fictions – both short and long – layer genre to create a socialist form that simultaneously entertains and educates.

The favoured genre for socialist authors was realism, despite its historical associations with the rise of the middle classes. In 1888 Engels had outlined his ideas on the usefulness of realism to the socialist cause in his letter to Margaret Harkness, responding to her novel *A City Girl*, explaining that realism was not tied to ideology:

> That Balzac thus was compelled to go against his own class sympathies and political prejudices, that he saw the necessity of the downfall of his favourite nobles, and described them as people deserving no better fate; and that he saw the real men of the future where, for the time being, they alone were to be found – that I consider one of the greatest triumphs of Realism, and one of the grandest features in old Balzac.[17]

For Engels, an objective representation of life under capitalism could not fail to expose the problems and contradictions of capitalist society. Lenin later took the same approach to Tolstoy's literary depiction of the 1906 Russian revolution: 'If we have before us a *really* great *artist*, he must have *reflected* in his work *at least some of the essential aspects* of the revolution'.[18] However, the term 'Socialist Realism', which was defined at the Congress of Soviet Writers in 1932, took a party approach and declared that while '[s]ocialist realism ... demands of the artist a truthful historically concrete depiction of reality in its revolutionary development', the depiction 'must be combined with the task of the ideological molding and education of the working people in the spirit of socialism'.[19] For the later Soviet authors, reality must be combined with conscious didacticism.

However, this dual aim of having both 'truthfulness' and 'ideology' at the heart of socialist realism is contradictory: realism is, and can only be, selective and bound by its contemporary publishing values; an ideological lens is a literary construct that refocuses 'reality'. Blatchford discussed the difficulties of writing 'realism' when he considered the praise and disgust heaped onto Arthur Morrison's *A Child of the Jago* (1896):

> What is a Realist? At first thought one would reply that a realist is an author who portrays things as they really are. But how *are* they? No landscape is exactly the same thing to any two artists. No idea, character, act, consequence, scene, or moral produces exactly the same impression upon any two authors. Suppose, then, a place or person to be described by a dozen novelists, from as many different points of view, with as many different results, who is to decide which of the twelve is the faithful witness – the Realist?[20]

Blatchford concluded that a realist is 'one who describes things as they actually appear to *him*',[21] and if the authors writing for a socialist periodical see life through the prism of socialist ideology, then there is no need for a diktat imposing an ideological didacticism on fiction. The ideological perspective is evident even in the apparently 'neutral' omniscient narrative, which does not necessarily remove or dilute the revolutionary content of socialist fiction. As Paul Cobley argues, the selection process is itself political, but the prevalence of realism means that 'readers have become so used to "classic realism" that they "forget" that [the narrative voice] is there, manipulating, framing and presenting its own version of "events"'.[22] The socialist predilection for realism meant that the alternative perspectives raised in the fiction were as 'naturalized' as they were in mainstream fiction.

The genre of realism draws a number of common themes into the fiction that are presented in similar ways, regardless of periodicals' different approaches to socialism. One of the primary issues dealt with in the fiction is the devastating effect of homelessness, eviction or its threat. The prevalence of this issue is evident in its depiction throughout this collection: in Bramsbury's 'A Working Class Tragedy' (*Justice*, Volume 1), where Frank Wilson's wife and mother are evicted after his imprisonment; in 'Citizen's' 'The Blackleg' (*Workman's Times*, Volume 2), when the women attack the rent collector; in Harry Beswick's 'Brother Eli on Tramps' (*Clarion*, Volume 3), where Eli discusses homelessness; in F. J. Maynard's 'Unemployment: A Tragedy in Little' (*Social Democrat*, Volume 4), where the rent is paid by drastic means; and in Eileen Hynes's 'Barky: A Sketch' (*Socialist Review*, Volume 5), which depicts the desolation of homelessness. The issue of homelessness is inextricably tied to the issue of unemployment, underemployment or low wages. Again, this issue is addressed throughout the period: again in Bramsbury's fiction; in Isabella Fyvie Mayo's 'A Bit of a Tragedy' (*Labour Leader*, Volume 2); in M. Winchersky's 'He, She and It' (*Social Democrat*, Volume 3); in Arthur Laycock's 'The "Retired" Street Sweeper' (*Labour Leader*, Volume 4); and in J. Zimmerman's 'Stitch, Stitch, Stitch' (*Labour Leader*, Volume 5). These and many other real pressures on the poor, including the effect of poverty on children, are woven throughout the fiction published by socialist authors.

The unflinching depiction of the hardships caused by poverty might lead to the conclusion that socialist authors were taking a naturalist position in their fiction. The early years of British socialism were also the years when British naturalism was developing, and authors were taking poverty as their central theme. In the period covered by the first two volumes of this collection, George Gissing published *The Nether World* (1889), Arthur Morrison published *Tales of Mean Streets* (1892–4) and *A Child of the Jago*, and George Moore published *Esther Waters* (1894). Generally, British naturalism differed from the French original in a variety of ways. Practical constraints were imposed by the demands of publishers and the potential of prosecution for obscenity. Therefore Bramsbury makes the cleanliness of the socialist's wife's scrubbed kitchen table the focus for his description of working-class housing (p. 140), while Émile Zola's *Germinal* shows us Maheu having sex with his wife on theirs. It was not merely the restrictions placed on authors that separated British and French naturalism, but also the attitude British authors had towards their work. Peter Keating has noted that although British naturalist authors were reacting against the overt moralizing of Charles Dickens, their '[m]oral purpose, though veiled, never disappears entirely; the finer qualities of human personality are not ruthlessly and inevitably destroyed by environment or heredity; and the personal feelings of the author, if not so obvious as in Dickens, are everywhere apparent'.[23] Keating is referring to authors of working-class stories; his point is even more relevant to the socialist authors. For them, the point of producing fiction (and the printed word generally) was to initiate change and to create an effect in reality. If the closed vision of French naturalism on the inevitable effects of heredity and environment had been a part of the socialist ideology and drawn into the fiction, then change could be neither imagined nor effected.

In *The Haunted Study*, Keating has argued that the manipulation of the novel's sub-genres during this period can be read as a reaction against mid-Victorian hypocrisy in the rejection of realism and its morals.[24] The socialist critique of society presents the devastating effects of poverty through a realism swirled with other genres to differentiate socialist morality from liberal/bourgeois morality. This combination of genre, in the manner noted by Haywood and Breton in Chartist fiction, is most evident in the long serializations. All the serials included in this collection have an element of romance running through them as a cohering element that works towards a conclusion, as lovers either achieve union (for instance, Charles Allen Clarke's 'The Cotton Panic' in *Teddy Ashton's Northern Weekly*, Volume 3, and 'The Red Flag' in *Justice*, Volume 4) or are divided for ever (H. J. Bramsbury's 'A Working Class Tragedy' in *Justice*, Volume 1). The presentation of the balance of power under capitalism draws on the genre of melodrama, which is manipulated to critique capitalist rather than aristocratic force. 'Power' might be embodied in a particular character or set of characters (for instance, Cranston the factory owner in Bramsbury's 'A Working Class Tragedy'; the dock owner Crushem in 'Citizen's' 'The Blackleg', *Workman's Times*, Volume 2; the newspaper proprietor Archibald Lodden in Hugh Derrick's 'The Making of a Red', *Daily Citizen*, Volume 5) or in a more abstract form through the general difficulties of obtaining employment under capitalism (again, Clarke's 'The Cotton Panic' and 'The Red Flag'). Socialist realist fiction might also draw on non-literary genres such as history (Clarke's 'The Cotton Panic' weaves through the fiction a detailed historical account of both the Lancashire cotton famine and its origins in the American Civil War), reportage (Bramsbury's 'A Working Class Tragedy' presents a different perspective on the West End Riots of 1886 to that given in mainstream newspapers) and social investigation (Clarke's 'The Red Flag' draws on Mary Higgs's undercover investigation into homelessness, *Five Days and Five Nights as a Tramp among Tramps* (1904)). This inclusion of non-literary 'factual' genres in the fiction amplifies the 'real' in realism, despite being themselves narratives of selection and specific focus. The critique of capitalism was also projected through non-realist genres, and the first to be discussed here – the utopian – had more than a literary connection to reality.

Although the political theories of Marx and Engels distinguished between 'utopian' and 'scientific' socialism, utopian fiction has been criticized for 'the construction of blueprints to a future society that are incapable of realisation'.[25] Practical attempts to found a utopian socialist society in the midst of capitalism proved this criticism of utopian fiction true: Charles Allen Clarke's Daisy Colony in Lancashire, organized through his periodical *Teddy Ashton's Northern Weekly*, was founded in hope in 1905, but infighting, jealousy and greed brought its collapse in 1907; and Upton Sinclair's Helicon Home Colony in New Jersey, founded in 1906, was destroyed by fire in a suspected arson attack in 1907. Despite the methodology of securing the utopian society being, at best, obscure to the socialist visionary under capitalism, the use of the literary genre as a critique of present-day society was appreciated for the way it 'fundamentally interrogates the present, piercing through existing societies' defensive mechanisms – common sense, realism, positivism and scientism'.[26]

There are two ways utopian ideals are presented in socialist fiction. The first is the awakening of the narrator after a long period of sleep into an unknown future, the technique used by Edward Bellamy in *Looking Backward* (1888), William Morris in *News from Nowhere* (1890) and H. G. Wells in *When the Sleeper Awakes* (1899). All of these novels (and many others) present a culmination of socialist striving, an end of history, and a reward for those working towards the socialist millennia. The literary vision of utopia acts as a motivation for continuing the work of socialism: Blatchford's 'What They Thought: A Vision' (*Clarion*, Volume 2), published under the pseudonym M'Ginnis (sometimes given as McGinnis), and Optimus's 'The May-Day Festival in the Year 1970' (*Social Democrat*, Volume 5) are both set in an idyllic future. Sometimes the route to the idyllic future is not linear but circular, as William Morris's *A Dream of John Ball* (1888) takes the reader back to a historical utopia that may be used as a template for the future idyll. The second technique is that of removing the narrator from capitalism by a spatial shift: Wells takes the narrator and his botanist companion into utopia as they cross the Alps in *A Modern Utopia* (1905), and Blatchford's Fry, Storm and Jorkle travel out of the capitalist world through the inkwell and back by balloon in 'The Sorcery Shop' (*Clarion*, Volume 4).[27]

Regardless of whether the utopia is reached by shifts in space or time, the result is a moment of peace created by removal from the busy route to socialism and modernity, what Thomas Linehan describes as 'a suspended moment of time outside of normal time ... a moment of constructive contemplation ripped out of the narrative of Enlightenment-modernist or historical time'.[28] This vision of a peaceful haven, however, is not intended to create a sense of comfort and rest for the reader; in fact, quite the opposite. Literary utopias generally have a direct relationship with their surrounding reality as they resonate with implicit criticism through the presentation of a better alternative. As Barbara Goodwin and Keith Taylor explain, 'The relationship between a hypothetical model and present society also introduces a dynamic element into the conceptualization, justification and criticism of the present with reference to past, future or "lateral" possibilities'.[29] And the point of revealing these possibilities is to motivate readers to enact change in the material world to bring the imagined into reality. The intention of utopian fiction is action.

Utopian fiction was not as widely used as realism by socialist authors publishing in the periodicals, and there are a number of possible reasons for this preference. As Blatchford tells the reader in the 'Explanatory Notes' appended to 'The Sorcery Shop': 'The Utopian romance may at first sight appear to be an easy form of political exposition, but it has many difficulties' (Volume 4, p. 103). The imagination of the author must create a completely new society; it must remove the fictional world from capitalist reality but make it 'real' enough to be recognizable to avoid alienating the reader; and it must be desirable in order to motivate change. It is this sense of movement and change that also locates socialist fiction, with its patchwork of genres, within the modernist genre.

In his study of realism and naturalism, Richard Daniel Lehan notes the literary continuum that runs from realism to modernism: 'naturalism evolved out of realism and that naturalism eventually gave way to modernism'.[30] While this may be true, modernism as a literary genre is only part of the phenomena of 'modernism', and Linehan also takes what he terms a 'maximalist' view of modernism, expanding it 'beyond that realm usually cited in the scholarship – art, literature and the avant-garde – to embrace social and political phenomena and movements'.[31] It is through this 'maximalist' view that he locates the British socialist movement in modernism as both a part and a symptom of the flux of modernization in the movement towards modernity. The fiction produced by socialist authors would not be categorized as 'modernist' despite the genre's roots in the late nineteenth century. The shift of focus to interiority and a psychological perspective by authors such as Henry James and Joseph Conrad[32] are not to be found in socialist fiction, which promotes the necessity of collective political action and unification and where the successful, utopian society is built on a network of individuals working for the common good. Linehan notes the literariness of socialist politics and polemics during this period as the necessity of socialism, and the socialist future was evoked 'not through conventional political declarations or detailed policy formulations but through aesthetics, myth, Christian symbolism and idioms, metaphor and other forms of literary embellishment, dreams and various kinds of utopian imagining'.[33] The presence of symbolism, metaphor and myth in socialist fiction simultaneously looks forward to the disruptions of realism by the modernists and back to the ancient literary form of the fable.

The fable is useful and historically relevant for oppositional political fiction – most famously used by George Orwell in *Animal Farm* (1945) – as a form that can trace its roots back to Aesop the slave. The necessity for the disempowered to encode their criticisms of the surrounding society was not relevant in the nineteenth and early twentieth centuries, but the role of metaphor to take human consciousness down to the most basic level, often 'by rejoining the animals',[34] strips away extraneous narrative and social matter to reveal the heart of the problem. The fable, sometimes called the Christian parable, has a variety of uses: to criticize capitalist economics ('Utile Dulci's' 'The Monkeys and the Nuts' and 'The Political Economist and the Flowers' by Anon., both *Justice*, Volume 1), to describe the arbitrariness of hierarchy (Dan Baxter's 'A Monkey Story', *Justice*, Volume 2) and to juxtapose the social hierarchies (Frank Starr's 'The Doll Shop', *Labour Leader*, Volume 3; Glanville Maidstone's 'Nightmare Bridge', *Clarion*, Volume 4). The didacticism of the fable was a useful political tool, and H. Gustav Klaus notes the Chartist Thomas Cooper's use of the form to 'debate about the pros and cons of the "physical" and the "moral" force positions in the Chartist movement'.[35] Later in the nineteenth and early in the twentieth centuries, the use of fable, metaphor, symbol and other non-realist forms were popular with modernist authors such as Katherine Mansfield, James Joyce and Henry James and were used to create the modernist short story.

Form I: The Short Story

The short story is a much older form than the novel; it is evident, as noted above, in Biblical parables, the fables of Aesop, the *exempla* and *novellae* of the late Middle Ages (most famously Boccaccio's *Decameron* and Chaucer's *Canterbury Tales*) and on through the influence of the eighteenth-century periodical narrative essay, to become the form we recognize today as the 'short story' in the nineteenth century with the work of Nathaniel Hawthorne, Edgar Allen Poe in the United States and Nikolai Gogol in Russia.[36] This lengthy history, as Dominic Head has argued, means that a reductive definition of 'short story' is both impossible and undesirable, and the form is certainly not defined merely by length.[37] The sense of a changing world at the end of the nineteenth century meant that different literary forms were necessary to express the changing human condition. The *Yellow Book* published short stories by New Woman writers such as George Egerton, who 'recognized the necessity of experimenting with narrative techniques in order to provide a more complete representation of women's inner lives'.[38] The short story's dense form makes demands on the attention of the reader because of the 'two key elements of the short story: its intensity and its exaggerated artifice'.[39] This is evident as the short story collapses fictional time and exaggerates and intensifies single issues or events, often (but not always) omitting backstory, sub-plot and extraneous matter. Thus the condensed form 'exhibited characteristic structures where metaphoric relationships subverted linearity and built to epiphanies'.[40] These structures, according to Dominic Head, are the signifiers of the short story rather than a novel in brief. He argues that 'the length question must be secondary to a consideration of *technique*'.[41]

Frank O'Connor's theory of the short story set it alongside the 'bourgeois' novel and argued 'that the short story is characterized by its treatment of "submerged population groups", of those lonely people who live on the fringes of society because of spiritual emptiness or material deprivation'.[42] The New Woman and the socialist author grasped the short story as a useful form in the articulation of both the female and the working-class condition. It was also a useful form for the periodical: a complete work of fiction within a single issue, a sharp focus on a particular matter and the flexibility for a wide range of genres carrying the socialist message. Although some short stories, as Mary Rohrberger states, require the reader to 'put the extensional world out of mind and deal in and with a kind of underworld, a world of inexplicable strange loops, a mystical world of paradox and ambiguity, of shadows and shifting perspectives governed not by rational order but by intuition and dream logic',[43] the range of socialist short fiction is so much more than this alone. Taking Volume 3 as an example, there is the fable (Frank Starr's 'The Doll Shop', *Labour Leader*), the ghost story (John

Bruce Glasier's 'Andrew Carnegie's Ghost', *Labour Leader*), the army tale (Robert Blatchford's 'Dismal Dan's Story', *Clarion*), comedy (Teddy Ashton's 'The Female Fister', *Teddy Ashton's Northern Weekly*) and realism (R. B. Cunninghame Graham's 'A Fisherman', *Justice*). Thus the genre of the short story allows socialist authors to present a contained argument for, or vision of, socialism in a variety of ways and through a variety of sub-genres to create a variety of perspectives.

Socialist fiction has been given little academic attention, but its short fiction has been given even less attention than its novels. Both the brevity of the short story and the proliferation of the form and authors exacerbate the difficulties of locating periodical fiction. Even the most prolific author of short stories in the British socialist movement during this period, Charles Allen Clarke under the pseudonym Teddy Ashton, has generally been recorded in literary history through his long fiction rather than his short stories, which include the phenomenally popular 'Bill Spriggs' dialect series.[44] Clarke was unusual in that his short stories – as well as some of his longer fiction – transcended the periodical and were published in pamphlet form. The multiplicity of stories, authors and sub-genres within the fiction, published across a multiplicity of periodicals, makes anthologizing this form difficult at best. Nevertheless, as this was the preferred form for many socialist periodicals and there were more short stories published across more periodicals than there was serialized fiction, it deserves more critical attention than has previously been given.

Form II: Serialization

The serialization of fiction in the nineteenth century was a popular method of publishing long works prior to book publication. Charles Dickens, Elizabeth Gaskell, Wilkie Collins, Thomas Hardy, Henry James, Joseph Conrad and many others initially serialized their fiction, but while serialization was a lucrative method of publishing fiction, it was not considered to be conducive to artistic quality. Rachel Ihara notes Henry James's conflicting attitudes to serial publication: he simultaneously sought to place his work in journals and magazines because it was 'a mode of publication that sustained [him] economically throughout his career ... but denounced [the serial] as an impediment to artistic freedom'.[45] But while the novelist-as-artist worried about his or her work's critical reception and aesthetic form, the novelist-as-propagandist was more concerned about the effect of the work on the reader and the world. The serial, as Linda Hughes and Michael Lund have recognized, gave time for considered deliberation and interpretation of the literary text: '[r]eaders and reviewers engaged in provisional assumptions and interpretations about the literary world, which then shaped the evolving understanding of works as they continued to unfold part by part. And a work's extended duration meant that serials could become entwined with readers' own sense of lived experience and passing time'.[46] The longevity and regular periodicity of the serial could be a useful persuasive tool.

The point of socialist fiction – of any length – was to encourage change. Michael Hanne opens his study of the political uses of fiction with a question for the reader to consider: 'Can a novel start a war, free serfs, break up marriages, drive readers to suicide, close factories, bring about a law change, swing an election or serve as a weapon in a national or international struggle?'[47] Regardless of the answer to this question, readers and authors *want* it to be true that the written word can have a material effect on the world. There is no better illustration of this desire to see the power of fiction made evident in reality than the apocryphal story of Abraham Lincoln's meeting with Harriet Beecher Stowe, author of *Uncle Tom's Cabin*. According to legend, on meeting Stowe, Lincoln grasped her hand and exclaimed, 'Is this the little woman who made the great war?'[48] Daniel R. Vollaro's article on the sources of this anecdote urges scepticism when considering the claims made for Stowe's impact on the abolition movement, but what is important is that the anecdote has survived, not simply as an illustration of the dovetailing of literature and politics but as 'evidence' of the power of literature. Nevertheless, the response to Upton Sinclair's *The Jungle*, which was serialized in the American socialist periodical *Appeal to Reason* in 1905, proved that fiction could make a material difference to the world. Sinclair's story of the Chicago meat trade so horrified its readers that '[i]t had a very direct consequence: the passage of federal legislation (the Pure Food and Drug Act) *within a year* which transformed working practices in the food industry'.[49] The results of Sinclair's fiction were unusual in having such a direct and material impact on the world, but the aim to change opinions and the world was at the heart of both the socialist periodical and its fiction.

Volumes 1 to 4 contain two or three serializations while Volume 5 has only one, the lengthy 'The Making of a Red' by Hugh Derrick. Previous studies of socialist fiction have tended to gravitate towards the book versions of socialist literary output rather than the serialization. For instance, J. M. Rignall's 1987 study of historiography in socialist fiction takes James Haslam's 1904 novel *The Handloom Weaver's Daughter* rather than the story's original form as a serial (1898–9) in Clarke's periodical *Teddy Ashton's Northern Weekly* under the title 'The Mill on the Moor'.[50] Nor is the preference for bound print limited to the older study. Elizabeth Carolyn Miller's *Slow Print* (2013) notes the serialization of 'Connie' by 'John Law' (Margaret Harkness) in Champion's *Labour Elector* but chooses to analyse the author's bound publications *A City Girl*, *Captain Lobe* and *A Manchester Shirtmaker*. The same book refers to Blatchford's *A Son of the Forge* as serial fiction, using the book title to refer to the serial published as 'No. 66'.[51] Studies of socialist authors such as Margaret Harkness, Clementina Black and William Morris have also generally focused on their book publications.[52]

Where the serial form is used for critical studies, there is a tendency to hone in on certain texts, most often Morris's serialization of 'News from Nowhere' in the *Commonweal* and Bramsbury's 'A Working Class Tragedy' in *Justice*,[53] presumably because their existence is recorded in literary criticism.

Inevitably the book form will be more visible through library cataloguing and more conveniently accessible for the researcher than the serial buried among the pages of the periodical, but there is also a sense of literary hierarchy in the separation. The elevation of the novel in book form over that of the serial is clear in the structure of some serials as books-in-waiting where 'the three-decker-volume structure was evident despite publication in individual numbers'.[54] This hierarchy of publication illustrates David Payne's separation of the 'ephemeral' and 'permanent' forms of serialization and book respectively, and a further hierarchy is classified within serial publication as 'the Dickensian monthly "part" was the sought-after exception rather than the workaday rule in Victorian serial publishing'.[55] The critical focus on book publication simultaneously removes the text from its original context and presents the work as a complete and autonomous piece of literature; taking the fiction out of its context may have a significant effect on the story or its form.[56] This collection of fictions published in the British socialist periodical also necessarily lifts the literary text out of its periodical context, therefore creating a new reading experience; but rather than presenting the longer fiction as a complete piece, the breaks formed by each periodical issue are recorded so the reader can at least see the lines of fragmentation, which were not always in line with the chapter breaks.

The Periodical

The hierarchy of fiction discussed above is one part of the separation of fiction from the 'hack work' of journalism. Literature was revered while journalism was deemed a lower intellectual form; the rising popularity of journals and periodicals with the working-class reader through the New Journalism was perceived to have denigrated a previously elite form through its new class associations. In *Subjugated Knowledges*, Laurel Brake charts the separation of journalism and literature: the timelessness and gentlemanly intellectualism of the complete piece of literature was deemed art, whereas journalism was neither timeless (rather being considered ephemeral through its immediate relation to the moment) nor complete (in terms of the mode of constant serial production).[57] But regardless of literary hierarchy, the power of the press had created in Britain what Thomas Carlyle termed the 'fourth estate', expanding democratic power through the act of writing as both 'the *purest* embodiment a thought of man can have' and 'the activest and noblest'.[58] It was the printed word as spur to activity that created the so-called 'Taxes on Knowledge', taxing paper, advertising and newspaper publication to limit access to the press. After the final tax was lifted in 1855, the radical press, which had never been eradicated, flourished, especially in the socialist movement.

The relationship between print and the material world is most visible in the rise of investigative journalism in the last third of the nineteenth century. Investigative journalism was not created in the nineteenth century; it is a journalistic tradition that, according to Hugo de Burgh, can be traced back to AD 700 in China.[59] From the mid-nineteenth century onward, investigative and undercover journalists reported on conditions in workhouses (James Greenwood's 'A Night in a Workhouse' (1866)), in prison (Henry Labouchere's 'Inside Newgate' (1872)) and in working-class homes (G. R. Sims's 'How the Poor Live' (1883)).[60] But the investigative journalism with the most significant impact in Britain was that of W. T. Stead in the *Pall Mall Gazette*. His campaigns established a Royal Commission on Housing (*The Bitter Cry of Outcast London* (1883)), forced the government to reverse cuts to the naval budget (*The Responsibility for the Navy* (1884)) and raised the age of consent from thirteen to sixteen (*The Maiden Tribute* (1885)).

This kind of impact on the world – and more – was also the aim of the socialist movement as they conducted their own investigations into working-class life; the earliest investigation, by the SDF in 1885 on poverty in London, was published in *Justice*. The study was later claimed by Hyndman to be the inspiration for Charles Booth's *Life and Labour of the People in London*: 'Mr Booth ... assured me that he felt quite certain we were wrong, and then told me that he himself intended to make, at his own expense, an elaborate inquiry into the condition of the workers of London'.[61] Between 1888 and 1889 Champion's *Labour Elector* exposed the vast wealth of the owners at the Brunner Mond chemical plant in Cheshire and gathered evidence of poor working conditions through the trade union organized by Champion and Tom Mann, and through Mann's undercover employment at the plant under the name 'Joe Miller'.[62] The investigation successfully reduced the working hours at the plant from twelve or thirteen hours per day to eight hours, which also had the effect of reducing fatalities. Similarly, in 1899 Keir Hardie's *Labour Leader* exposed harsh conditions at Lord Overtoun's chemical plant near Rutherglen, South Lanarkshire, which imposed long days and a seven-day working week. The latter, for Hardie, was particularly hypocritical, as Overtoun promoted himself as both a philanthropist and a Sabbatarian. Hardie's campaign reduced the working day and ended Sunday work. Thus socialist periodicals worked not just as educative material on behalf of socialism, but also as a tool for change and a method for cohering the community.

This community would be, like Benedict Anderson's definition of the nation, 'imagined': the national community is imagined 'because the members of even the smallest nation will never know most of their fellow-members, meet them, or even hear of them, yet in the minds of each lives the image of their communion'.[63] While the smaller and regionally based socialist groups, such as the Bristol Socialist Society, might have the opportunity to become familiar with most members, the national membership of the larger socialist groups would need to rely on the periodical as a forum. For example, the SDF was originally founded in London but had its strongest membership in Lancashire, where Tom Mann organized branches in Bolton, Blackburn and Darwen.[64] The ILP had no such regional centre and was even more reliant on periodicals such as the *Labour Leader*, *Workman's Times* and *Clarion* to attract and unite supporters. Even the *Clarion*, the most sociable of the British socialist groups, could not hope to create a single, physical community of members despite encouraging and supporting social activities under the *Clarion* banner. There was a vast range of *Clarion* clubs, including cycling (and later motorcycling) clubs, glee clubs, vocal unions, Cinderella clubs for children and handicraft guilds, which took *Clarion* socialism across the country as 'Clarion clubs sprang up in Scotland and the North and Midlands'.[65] The most popular was the cycling club that was founded in 1894, and '[w]ithin three years the membership grew to 7,000. Five club houses in Cheshire, Lancashire, Yorkshire, Essex, and Warwickshire, provided district quarters'.[66] Nevertheless, these clubs could only create a space for sections of the British socialist movement to physically come together at one time. The national scale of British socialism meant that the printed word was the site where socialists developed what Raymond Williams terms their 'knowable community'.[67] Just as Williams recognizes the selection and identification at the heart of a community (he uses Jane Austen's fictional communities of class as an example), so the members of the British socialist movement would align with a specific group, feel at liberty to criticize other groups and change allegiance when groups or personal identification changed.

The periodical was essential to this identification; the *Clarion* was taken across the country by means of the *Clarion* scouts and propaganda vans, the latter being a scheme initiated by Julia Dawson (the pseudonym of Mrs D. J. Myddleton-Worrall), while other periodicals would include a weekly list of meetings where members could meet face to face. But even without a physical form of meeting, the act of reading created a sense of community. As James Mussell argues, 'publications cohered groups by offering the same reading to people distributed in space at similar intervals of time. Their periodicity created moments, allowing readers to feel as if they occupied the same space and time while providing the mechanisms through which it could be remembered in similar ways by all'.[68] The fiction serialized in socialist periodicals would be an important method of creating a community; as Graham Law notes, periodicals aimed to attract readers through serialized fiction.[69] The purchase of the next issue was encouraged by the inclusion of serialized fiction; as Margaret Beetham has argued of periodicals generally, 'the consumer ... is not so much satisfied as stimulated to return at regular intervals to buy the next number'.[70] And so they did, in increasing numbers. The *Commonweal* had weekly sales of between 2,000 and 3,000 copies,[71] and *Justice* had reached its peak of 4,000 issues per week in 1887,[72] but by the 1890s sales of the *Labour Leader* were around 13,000 per week, *Teddy Ashton's Journal* between 25,000 and 35,000 copies per week,[73] and the *Clarion* between 35,000 and 50,000 copies per week, reaching a peak of 83,000 in 1910.[74]

For the twenty-first-century researcher, the fiction published in these periodicals has three distinct benefits. First, its distinction from journalism allows us to appreciate and understand the group's attitudes towards the balance of entertainment and education, aesthetics and pragmatics, evident in the periodical's use of fiction. Second, it is a political document through which we can better understand the nuances of the group's distinct socialist ideas. And third, it is a historical document giving us another position of insight into the period in the manner of Raymond Williams's 'structures of feeling'. For all of these reasons, the fiction of the socialist periodicals should not be judged by canonical criteria of 'good' and 'bad' art but recognized for the multidimensional document it was then and remains so now.

Notes

1.   J. Rose, *The Intellectual Life of the British Working Classes* (New Haven, CT and London: Yale University Press, 2001), p. 123.

2.   R. Samuel, 'Theatre and Socialism in Britain (1880–1935)', in R. Samuel, E. MacColl and S. Cosgrove (eds), *Theatres of the Left 1880–1935: Workers' Theatre Movements in Britain and America* (London: Routledge and Kegan Paul, 1985), pp. 3–77.

3.   See M. Bevir, *The Making of British Socialism* (Princeton, NJ: Princeton University Press, 2011) for a detailed explanation of Hyndman's socialism.

4.   M. Bevir, 'H. M. Hyndman: A Rereading and a Reassessment', *History of Political Thought*, 12:1 (1991), pp. 125–46, on p. 125.

5.   J. Mitchell, 'Tendencies in Narrative Fiction in the London-Based Socialist Press of the 1880s and 1890s', in H. G. Klaus (ed.), *The Rise of Socialist Fiction* (Brighton: Harvester Press, 1987), pp. 49–72, on p. 51.

6.   For the prolific literary and journalistic output of the British socialist movement between 1880 and 1900, see D. Mutch, *English Socialist Periodicals, 1880–1900: A Reference Source* (Aldershot: Ashgate, 2005).

7.   See, for instance, P. Scheckner, *An Anthology of Chartist Poetry: Poetry of the British Working Class* (Cranbury, NJ, London and Ontario: Associated University Presses, 1989); B. Maidment, *The Poorhouse Fugitives* (Manchester: Carcenet, 1992); M. Sanders, *Chartist Literary Landmarks* (London: Pickering & Chatto, 2014); and I. Parks, *The Voice of the People: Chartist Poetry 1838–1848* (Leeds: Flux Gallery Press, 2013).

8.   I. Watt, *The Rise of the Novel* (London: Hogarth, 1987), p. 48.

9.   Ibid., p. 300.

10. R. Williams, *Marxism and Literature* (Oxford: Oxford University Press, 1977), p. 147.

11. Ibid., pp. 182–3.

12. P. J. Keating, *The Haunted Study: A Social History of the English Novel, 1875–1914* (London: Faber and Faber, 2008), p. 261.

13. I. Haywood, *Working-Class Fiction from Chartism to Trainspotting* (Plymouth: Northcote House, 1997), p. 3.

14. N. Daly, *Modernism, Romance and the Fin de Siècle: Popular Fiction and British Culture, 1880–1914* (Cambridge: Cambridge University Press, 2004), p. 5.

15. I. Haywood, *The Revolution in Popular Literature: Print, Politics and the People, 1790–1860* (Cambridge: Cambridge University Press, 2004), p. 145.

16. R. Breton, 'Genre in the Chartist Periodical', in A. Krishnamurthy (ed.), *The Working-Class Intellectual in Eighteenth- and Nineteenth-Century Britain* (Farnham: Ashgate, 2009), pp. 109–28, on p. 110.

17. F. Engels to M. Harkness, April 1888, in *Selected Correspondence* (Moscow, 1953), transcribed by D. McNeill (2000), *Marxist Internet Archive*, at http://www.marxists.org/archive/marx/works/1888/letters/88_04_15.htm [accessed 29 January 2013].

18. Quoted in E. A. Dobrenko, *Political Economy of Socialist Realism* (New Haven, CT: Yale University Press, 2007), p. 236; italics in original.

19. H. Ermovlaev, quoted in L. Herman, *Concepts of Realism* (Columbia, SC: Camden House, 1996), p. 86.

20. R. Blatchford, *My Favourite Books* (London: Walter Scott, 1900), pp. 222–3.

21. Ibid., p. 223.

22. P. Cobley, *Narrative* (London: Routledge, 2001), pp. 92–3.

23. P. J. Keating, *Working-Class: Stories of the 1890s* (London: Routledge and Kegan Paul, 1971), p. x.

24. Keating, *The Haunted Study*, p. 160.

25. R. Levitas, *'The' Concept of Utopia* (London: Philip Allan, 1990), p. 42.

26. V. Geoghegan, *Utopianism and Marxism* (Bern: Peter Lang, 2008), p. 16.

27. See the Introduction to Volume 4 for a more detailed examination of Blatchford and utopia.

28. T. Linehan, *Modernism and British Socialism* (Basingstoke: Palgrave Macmillan, 2012), p. 47.

29. B. Goodwin and K. Taylor, *The Politics of Utopia: A Study in Theory and Practice* (London: Hutchinson and Co., 1982), p. 11.

30. R. D. Lehan, *Realism and Naturalism: The Novel in an Age of Transition* (Madison, WI: University of Wisconsin Press, 2005), p. xx.

31. Linehan, *Modernism and British Socialism*, p. 17.

32. R. Stevenson, *Modernist Fiction: An Introduction* (Lexington, KY: University Press of Kentucky, 1992), p. 2.

33. Linehan, *Modernism and British Socialism*, p. 14.

34. A. Patterson, *Fables of Power, Aesopian Writing and Political History* (Durham, NC: Duke University Press, 1991), p. 16.

35. H. G. Klaus, 'Mrs Rochester and Mr Cooper: Alternative Visions of Class, History and Rebellion in the "Hungry Forties"', *Literature and History*, 14:1 (2005), pp. 1–13, on p. 5.

36. R. C. Feddersen, 'Introduction: A Glance at the History of the Short Story in English', in E. Fallon et al. (eds), *A Reader's Companion to the Short Story in English* (Westport, CT: Greenwood Press, 2001), pp. xv–xxxiv, on pp. xvi–ii.

37. D. Head, *The Modernist Short Story: A Study in Theory and Practice* (Cambridge: Cambridge University Press, 1992) pp. 1–9.

38. M. A. Gillies and A. D. Mahood, *Modernist Literature: An Introduction* (Edinburgh: Edinburgh University Press, 2007), p. 27.

39. Head, *The Modernist Short Story*, p. 2.

40. M. Rohrberger, 'Origins, Development, Substance and Design of the Short Story', in P. Winther, J. Lothe and I. H. Skei (eds), *The Art of Brevity: Excursions in Short Fiction Theory and Analysis* (Columbia, SC: University of South Carolina Press, 2004), pp. 1–13, on p. 7.

41. Head, *The Modernist Short Story*, p. 4.

42. D. Kiberd, *The Irish Writer and the World* (Cambridge: Cambridge University Press, 2005), p. 48.

43. Rohrberger, 'Origins', p. 6.

44. See, for instance, J. Sutherland, *The Stanford Companion to Victorian Fiction* (Stanford, CA: Stanford University Press, 1989), p. 128; and P. Salveson, 'Allen Clarke and the Lancashire School', in H. G. Klaus, *The Rise of Socialist Fiction* (Brighton: Harvester Press, 1987), pp. 172–202; although Salveson's biography of Clarke, *Lancashire's Romantic Radical: The Life and Writings of Allen Clarke/Teddy Ashton* (Huddersfield: Little Northern Books, 2009) gives a chapter to the Bill Spriggs/Tum Fowt dialect series; see ch. 8, pp. 74–9.

45. R. Ihara, '"Rather Rude Jolts": Henry James, Serial Novels, and the Art of Fiction', *Henry James Review*, 31:2 (Spring 2010), pp.188–206, on p. 189.

46. L. K. Hughes and M. Lund, *The Victorian Serial* (Charlottesville, VA and London: University Press of Virginia, 1991), p. 8.

47. M. Hanne, *The Power of the Story, Fiction and Political Change* (Providence, RI: Berghahn Books, 1996), p. 1.

48. See D. R. Vollaro, 'Lincoln, Stowe, and the "Little Woman/Great War" Story: The Making, and Breaking, of a Great American Anecdote', *Journal of the Abraham Lincoln Association*, 30:1 (2009) http://hdl.handle.net/2027/spo.2629860.0030.104 [accessed 7 March 2013], for a comprehensive discussion of this quotation.

49. S. Ingle, *Narratives of British Socialism* (Basingstoke: Palgrave Macmillan, 2002), p. 133.

50. See the Introduction in Mutch, *English Socialist Periodicals*, for further discussion.

51. E. C. Miller, *Slow Print, Literary Radicalism and Late Victorian Print Culture* (Stanford, CA: Stanford University Press, 2013), pp. 94–102.

52. For instance, L. Hapgood, 'The Novel and Political Agency: Socialism and the Work of Margaret Harkness, Constance Howell and Clementina Black: 1888–1896', *Literature and History*, 3:5 (1996), pp. 37–52; J. Goode, 'Margaret Harkness and the Socialist Novel', in H. G. Klaus (ed.), *The Socialist Novel in Britain* (Brighton: Harvester Press, 1982); and F. and W. Boos, '*News from Nowhere* and Victorian Socialist Feminism', *Nineteenth Century Contexts*, 14:1 (1990), pp. 3–52; but also see Mitchell, 'Tendencies in Narrative Fiction', for his study of H. J. Bramsbury's 'A Working Class Tragedy' as serialized in *Justice*.

53. See, for instance, Keating, *The Haunted Study*; Mitchell, 'Tendencies in Narrative Fiction'; J. Mitchell, 'The Ragged Trousered Philanthropists', *Marxism Today* (May 1961), pp. 154–9; M. Vicinus, *The Industrial Muse* (London: Croom Helm, 1974); and C. Jia, *A History of English Literature, Volume 1* (Beijing: Commercial Press, 1986).

54. J. Mussell, *The Nineteenth-Century Press in the Digital Age* (Basingstoke: Palgrave, 2012), p. 54.

55. D. Payne, *The Reenchantment of Nineteenth-Century Fiction* (Basingstoke: Palgrave Macmillan, 2005), p.10.

56. See D. Mutch, 'The Merrie England Triptych: Robert Blatchford, Edward Fay and the Didactic Use of Clarion Fiction', *Victorian Periodicals Review*, 38:1 (2005), pp. 83–103, on the changes made by Blatchford to the *Merrie England* text for the pamphlet publication.

57. L. Brake, *Subjugated Knowledges: Journalism, Gender and Literature in the Nineteenth Century* (London: Macmillan 1994), p. 67.

58. T. Carlyle, 'Lecture V. The Hero as Man of Letters. Johnson, Rousseau, Burns', in T. Carlyle, *On Heroes, Hero-Worship, and the Heroic in History*, ed. M. K. Goldberg, J. J. Brattin and M. Engel (1841; Berkeley, CA and Los Angeles, CA: University of California Press, 1993), pp. 133–67, on p. 141.

59. H. de Burgh, 'The Emergence of Investigative Journalism', in H. de Burgh (ed.), *Investigative Journalism* (Abingdon and New York: Routledge, 2008), pp. 32–53, on p. 33.

60. See S. Donovan and M. Rubery, *Secret Commissions, An Anthology of Victorian Investigative Journalism* (Ontario, London and Moorebank: Broadview Press, 2012) for a flavour of Victorian investigative journalism.

61. H. M. Hyndman, *The Record of an Adventurous Life* (London: Macmillan and Co., 1911), p. 331. Hyndman's claim has been questioned by some historians – see, for example, J. Harris's entry 'Charles Booth' in the *Oxford Dictionary of National Biography*, and A. Lees, *Cities Perceived: Urban Society in European and American Thought, 1820–1940* (Manchester: Manchester University Press, 1985), p. 112 – but is accepted in Booth's biography on the London School of Economics' *Charles Booth Online Archive*, at http://booth.lse.ac.uk/static/a/2.html#viii [accessed 14 March 2013].

62. T. Mann, *Tom Mann's Memoirs* (1923; Nottingham: Spokesman, 2008), p. 57.

63. B. Anderson, *Imagined Communities* (London: Verso, 2006), p. 6.

64. M. Crick, *The History of the Social-Democratic Federation* (Keele: Keele University Press, 1994), pp. 52–3.

65. R. Blatchford, *My Eighty Years* (London: Cassell and Co., 1931), p. 202.

66. A. M. Thompson, *Here I Lie* (London: George Routledge and Sons, 1937), p. 138.

67. R. Williams, *The Country and the City* (Oxford: Oxford University Press, 1975), p. 165.

68. Mussell, *The Nineteenth-Century Press in the Digital Age*, p. 49.

69. G. Law, *Serializing Fiction in the Victorian Press* (Basingstoke: Palgrave, 2000), p. 13.

70. M. Beetham, 'Towards a Theory of the Periodical as a Publishing Genre', in L. Brake, A. Jones and L. Madden (eds), *Investigating Victorian Journalism* (London: Macmillan, 1999), pp. 19–32, on p. 21.

71. E. P. Thompson, *William Morris, Romantic to Revolutionary* (London: Lawrence and Wishart, 1955), p. 488.

72. C. Tsuzuki, *H. M. Hyndman and British Socialism* (Oxford: Oxford University Press, 1961), p. 108.

73. M. Espinasse, '(Charles) Allen Clarke', in J. M. Bellamy and J. Saville (eds), *Dictionary of Labour Biography, Volume 5* (London: Macmillan, 1979), pp. 64–70; P. Joyce, *Visions of the People: Industrial England and the Question of Class, c.1848–1914* (Cambridge: Cambridge University Press, 1991), p. 264.

74. Thompson, *Here I Lie*, p. 100; C. Levy, 'Education and Self-Education: Staffing the Early ILP', in C. Levy (ed.), *Socialism and the Intelligentsia: 1880–1914* (London: Routledge and Kegan Paul, 1987), pp. 135–210, on p. 149.

ACKNOWLEDGEMENTS

The beginning and end of this project have benefited from invaluable academic support. An award of a British Academy Small Grant for travel and research enabled me to carry out the primary research, and the faculty research leave granted to me by De Montfort University made the timely completion of the project possible. A project of this nature would be impossible to undertake without the help and advice of librarians and archivists across the country. The primary research and transcriptions were completed with the aid of the friendly, accommodating and patient staff at the Bishopsgate Institute, the British Library, the BL Newspaper Library at Colindale, the Bodleian Library of Oxford University, the Bolton Local Studies Library, the Manchester Central Library and the Working Class Movement Library in Salford. Felicity Monckton, Elizabeth Penner and Kathryn Shipman have helped with the proofreading, but responsibility for the accuracy of the content is mine alone. The members of the VICTORIA listserv, run by Patrick Leary, have proven to be a fount of wisdom and an enormous help with many of the more obscure references. As ever, none of this would have been possible without the support and patience of my family, particularly my husband, Dave Ellis, who probably thinks the door of my study has been wedged shut.

BIBLIOGRAPHY

Anderson, B., *Imagined Communities* (London: Verso, 2006).

Anon., 'Charles Booth (1840–1916)', *Charles Booth Online Archive*, at http://booth.lse. ac.uk/static/a/2.html#viii [accessed 14 March 2013].

Baguley, D., *Naturalist Fiction: The Entropic Vision* (Cambridge: Cambridge University Press, 1990).

Barnes, J., *Socialist Champion: Portrait of the Gentleman as Crusader* (Melbourne: Australian Scholarly Publishing, 2006).

Bax, E. B., and J. L. Joynes, 'Preface', *To-Day*, 14 April 1883, p. 4.

Beetham, M., *A Magazine of her Own? Domesticity and Desire in the Woman's Magazine, 1800–1914* (London: Routledge, 1996).

—, 'Towards a Theory of the Periodical as a Publishing Genre', in L. Brake, A. Jones and L. Madden (eds), *Investigating Victorian Journalism* (London: Macmillan, 1999), pp. 19–32.

Bevir, M., 'H. M. Hyndman: A Rereading and a Reassessment', *History of Political Thought*, 12:1 (1991), pp. 125–46.

—, *The Making of British Socialism* (Princeton, NJ and Oxford: Princeton University Press, 2011).

Blatchford, R., Editorial, *Clarion*, 12 December 1891, p. 4.

—, *My Favourite Books* (London: Walter Scott, 1900).

—, *The Sorcery Shop* (London: Clarion Press, 1907).

—, *My Eighty Years* (London: Cassell and Co., 1931).

Boos, F., and W. Boos, '*News from Nowhere* and Victorian Socialist Feminism', *Nineteenth Century Contexts*, 14:1 (1990), pp. 3–52.

Boulton, J. T. (ed.), *The Letters of D. H. Lawrence*, 8 vols (Cambridge: Cambridge University Press, 2000).

Bourke, J., *Working Class Cultures in Britain, 1890–1960: Gender, Class and Ethnicity* (London: Routledge, 1994).

Brake, L., *Subjugated Knowledges: Journalism, Gender and Literature in the Nineteenth Century* (London: Macmillan 1994).

Breton, R., 'Ghost in the Machina: Plotting in Chartist and Working-Class Fiction', *Victorian Studies* (2005), pp. 557–75.

—, 'Genre in the Chartist Periodical', in A. Krishnamurthy (ed.), *The Working-Class Intellectual in Eighteenth- and Nineteenth-Century Britain* (Farnham: Ashgate, 2009), pp. 109–28.

Briggs, J., 'Bland, Hubert (1855–1914)', *Oxford Dictionary of National Biography* (Oxford: Oxford University Press, 2004), online edn at http://www.oxforddnb.com/view/article/47683 [accessed 12 December 2012].

Burgh, H. de, 'The Emergence of Investigative Journalism', in H. de Burgh (ed.), *Investigative Journalism* (Abingdon and New York: Routledge, 2008), pp. 32–53.

Cain, P. J., 'Railways 1870–1914', in M. J. Freeman (ed.), *Transport in Victorian Britain* (Manchester: Manchester University Press, 1988), pp. 92–133.

Cannadine, D., *The Decline and Fall of the British Aristocracy* (London: Macmillan, 1996).

Carlyle, T., 'Lecture V. The Hero as Man of Letters. Johnson, Rousseau, Burns', in T. Carlyle, *On Heroes, Hero-Worship, and the Heroic in History*, ed. M. K. Goldberg, J. J. Brattin and M. Engel (1841; Berkeley, CA and Los Angeles, CA: University of California Press, 1993), pp. 133–67.

Cobley, P., *Narrative* (London: Routledge, 2001).

Cowman, K., *Mrs. Brown is a Man and a Brother: Women in Merseyside's Political Organisations, 1890–1920* (Liverpool: Liverpool University Press, 2004).

—, 'Martyn, Caroline Eliza Derecourt (1867–1896)', *Oxford Dictionary of National Biography* (Oxford: Oxford University Press, 2004), online edn at http://www.oxforddnb.com/view/article/45476 [accessed 17 March 2013].

Crick, M., *The History of the Social-Democratic Federation* (Keele: Keele University Press, 1994).

Daly, N., *Modernism, Romance and the Fin de Siècle: Popular Fiction and British Culture, 1880–1914* (Cambridge: Cambridge University Press, 2004).

Denton, S., *American Massacre* (New York: Vintage, 2004).

Dickenson, J., *Renegades and Rats: Betrayal and the Remaking of Radical Organisations in Britain and Australia* (Melbourne: Melbourne University Press, 2006).

Dictionary of the Scots Language, at http://www.dsl.ac.uk/index.html [accessed 7 February 2013].

Dobrenko, E. A., *Political Economy of Socialist Realism* (New Haven, CT: Yale University Press, 2007).

Donovan, S., and M. Rubery, *Secret Commissions: An Anthology of Victorian Investigative Journalism* (Ontario, London and Moorebank: Broadview Press, 2012).

Engels, F., *Selected Correspondence* (Moscow, 1953), transcribed by D. McNeill (2000), *Marxist Internet Archive*, at http://www.marxists.org/archive/marx/works/1888/letters/88_04_15.htm [accessed 29 January 2013].

Ensor, R. C. K., 'Blatchford, Robert Peel Glanville (1851–1943)', rev. H. C. G. Matthew, *Oxford Dictionary of National Biography* (Oxford: Oxford University Press, 2004), online edn at http://www.oxforddnb.com/view/article/31924 [accessed 16 December 2012].

Espinasse, M., '(Charles) Allen Clarke', in J. M. Bellamy and J. Saville (eds), *Dictionary of Labour Biography: Volume 5* (London: Macmillan, 1979), pp. 64–70.

Feddersen, R. C., 'Introduction: A Glance at the History of the Short Story in English', in E. Fallon et al. (eds), *A Reader's Companion to the Short Story in English* (Westport, CT: Greenwood Press, 2001), pp. xv–xxxiv.

Feldman, J. R., *Victorian Modernism: Pragmatism and the Varieties of Aesthetic Experience* (Cambridge: Cambridge University Press, 2002).

Forster, J., *The Life of Charles Dickens*, 2 vols (London: Chapman and Hall, 1876).

Fox, P., *Class Fictions: Shame and Resistance in the British Working-Class Novel* (Durham, NC: Duke University Press, 1994).

Frow, R., and E. Frow, 'C. Allen Clarke, Lancashire Author', Eccles and District Historical Society, 1971–2, unpublished lecture, Working Class Movement Library, Salford.

Fumerton, P., A. Guerrini and K. McAbee, *Ballads and Broadsides in Britain, 1500–1800* (Farnham: Ashgate, 2010).

Fyfe, A., *Steam-Powered Knowledge, William Chambers and the Business of Publishing, 1820–1860* (Chicago, IL: University of Chicago Press, 2012).

Gammond, P., *Music Hall Songbook* (London: EMI Publishing, 1975).

Geoghegan, V., *Utopianism and Marxism* (Bern: Peter Lang, 2008).

Gillies, M. A., and A. D. Mahood, *Modernist Literature: An Introduction* (Edinburgh: Edinburgh University Press, 2007).

Goode, J., 'Margaret Harkness and the Socialist Novel', in H. G. Klaus (ed.), *The Socialist Novel in Britain* (Brighton: Harvester Press, 1982), pp. 45–67.

Goodwin, B., and K. Taylor, *The Politics of Utopia: A Study in Theory and Practice* (London: Hutchinson and Co., 1982).

Gould, R. T., *Oddities: A Book of Unexplained Facts* (London: Philip Allen, 1928).

Griffiths, T., 'Clarke, (Charles) Allen (1863–1935)', *Oxford Dictionary of National Biography* (Oxford: Oxford University Press, 2004), online edn at http://www.oxforddnb.com/view/article/92482 [accessed 15 April 2013].

Hannam, J., *Isabella Ford, 1855–1924* (London: Basil Blackwell, 1989).

—, 'Ford, Isabella Ormston (1855–1924)', *Oxford Dictionary of National Biography* (Oxford: Oxford University Press, 2004), online edn at http://www.oxforddnb.com/view/article/39084 [accessed 7 February 2013].

—, and K. Hunt, *Socialist Women: Britain, 1880s to 1920s* (London and New York: Routledge, 2002).

Hanne, M., *The Power of the Story, Fiction and Political Change* (Providence, RI: Berghahn Books, 1996).

Hapgood, L., 'The Novel and Political Agency: Socialism and the Work of Margaret Harkness, Constance Howell and Clementina Black: 1888–1896', *Literature and History*, 3:5 (1996) pp. 37–52.

Harker, D., *Tressell: The Real Story of the Ragged Trousered Philanthropists* (London and New York: Zed Books, 2003).

Harris, J., 'Booth, Charles (1840–1916)', *Oxford Dictionary of National Biography* (Oxford: Oxford University Press, 2004), online edn at http://www.oxforddnb.com/view/article/31966 [accessed 12 December 2012].

Harrison, B., 'Turner, Richard (1790–1846)', *Oxford Dictionary of National Biography* (Oxford: Oxford University Press, 2004), online edn at http://www.oxforddnb.com/view/article/38081 [accessed 6 July 2012].

Harrison, R., G. B. Woolven and R. Duncan (eds), *Warwick Guide to British Labour Periodicals 1790–1970* (Brighton: Harvester Press, 1977).

Haywood, I., *Working-Class Fiction from Chartism to Trainspotting* (Plymouth: Northcote House, 1997).

—, *The Revolution in Popular Literature: Print, Politics and the People, 1790–1860* (Cambridge: Cambridge University Press, 2004).

Head, D., *The Modernist Short Story: A Study in Theory and Practice* (Cambridge: Cambridge University Press, 1992).

Hepburn, J. G., *A Book of Scattered Leaves* (Cranbury, NJ, London and Mississauga: Associated University Presses, 2000).

Herman, L., *Concepts of Realism* (Columbia, SC: Camden House, 1996).

Hough, W. E., *The Wellesley Index to Victorian Periodicals, 1824–1900: Volume 2* (Toronto and Buffalo, NY: University of Toronto Press, Routledge and Kegan Paul, 1972).

Howell, D., *British Workers and the Independent Labour Party, 1888–1906* (Manchester: Manchester University Press, 1983).

—, 'Grayson, (Albert) Victor (b. 1881)', *Oxford Dictionary of National Biography* (Oxford: Oxford University Press, 2004), online edn at http://www.oxforddnb.com/view/article/38338 [accessed 27 March 2013].

—, 'Morrison, Herbert Stanley, Baron Morrison of Lambeth (1888–1965)', *Oxford Dictionary of National Biography* (Oxford: Oxford University Press, 2004), online edn at http://www.oxforddnb.com/view/article/35121 [accessed 7 February 2013].

Hughes, L. K., and M. Lund, *The Victorian Serial* (Charlottesville, VA and London: University Press of Virginia, 1991).

Hunt, K., *Equivocal Feminists: The Social Democratic Federation and the Woman Question, 1884–1911* (Cambridge: Cambridge University Press, 1996).

Hyndman, H. M., *England for All* (London: E. W. Allen, 1881), transcribed by T. Crawford, *Marxist Internet Archive*, at http://www.marxists.org/archive/hyndman/1881/england/chap01.html [accessed 1 November 2012].

—, *The Record of an Adventurous Life* (London: Macmillan and Co., 1911).

—, *Further Reminiscences* (London, 1912), transcribed by E. O'Callaghan, *Marxist Internet Archive*, at http://www.marxists.org/archive/hyndman/1912/further/index.html [accessed 6 April 2013].

Ihara, R., "'Rather Rude Jolts": Henry James, Serial Novels, and the Art of Fiction', *Henry James Review*, 31:2 (Spring 2010), pp. 188–206.

Ingle, S., *Narratives of British Socialism* (Basingstoke: Palgrave Macmillan, 2002).

Jackson, K., 'The *Tit-bits* Phenomenon: George Newnes, New Journalism and the Periodical Texts', *Victorian Periodicals Review*, 30 (1997), pp. 201–6.

Jameson, F., *The Political Unconscious: Narrative as a Socially Symbolic Act* (London: Methuen, 1981).

Jia, C., *A History of English Literature, Volume 1* (Beijing: Commercial Press, 1986).

Jones, G. S., *Languages of Class* (Cambridge: Cambridge University Press, 1983).

Jones, P., 'A. Neil Lyons, "Arthur's"', *London Fictions*, at http://www.londonfictions.com/a-neil-lyons-arthurs.html [accessed 29 October 2012].

Joyce, P., *Work, Society and Politics: The Culture of the Factory in Later Victorian England* (London: Methuen, 1982).

—, *Visions of the People: Industrial England and the Question of Class, c.1848–1914* (Cambridge: Cambridge University Press, 1991).

—, *Democratic Subjects: The Self and the Social in Nineteenth-Century England* (Cambridge: Cambridge University Press, 1994).

Kahan, J., *The Cult of Kean* (Aldershot: Ashgate, 2006).

Keating, P. J., *The Working Classes in Victorian Fiction* (London: Routledge and Kegan Paul, 1971).

—, *Working-Class: Stories of the 1890s* (London: Routledge and Kegan Paul, 1971).

—, *The Haunted Study: A Social History of the Novel, 1875–1914* (London: Faber and Faber, 2008).

Kellett, J. R., *The Impact of Railways on Victorian Cities* (1969; Abingdon: Routledge, 2007).

Kiberd, D., *The Irish Writer and the World* (Cambridge: Cambridge University Press, 2005).

Klaus, H. G., *The Literature of Labour: 200 Years of Working Class Writing* (Brighton: Harvester Press, 1985).

—, 'Mrs Rochester and Mr Cooper: Alternative Visions of Class, History and Rebellion in the "Hungry Forties"', *Literature and History*, 14:1 (2005), pp. 1–13.

Krakauer, J., *Under the Banner of Heaven* (New York: Anchor, 2004).

'Lady, A' [M. Higgs], 'Five Days and Five Nights as a Tramp among Tramps' (1904), *The Workhouse, The Story of an Institution*, at http://www.workhouses.org.uk/Higgs/TrampAmongTramps.shtml [accessed 7 February 2013].

Laite, J., *Common Prostitutes and Ordinary Citizens: Commercial Sex in London, 1885–1960* (Basingstoke: Palgrave Macmillan, 2012).

Law, G., *Serializing Fiction in the Victorian Press* (Basingstoke: Palgrave, 2000).

—, '"Nothing but a Newspaper"': The Contested Space of Serial Fiction in the 1840s Press', in L. Brake and J. Codell (eds), *Encounters in the Victorian Press: Editors, Authors, Readers* (London: Palgrave, 2005), pp. 29–49.

Lawrence, D. H., *The Letters of D. H. Lawrence*, ed. J. T. Boulton, 8 vols (Cambridge: Cambridge University Press, 2000).

Lees, A., *Cities Perceived: Urban Society in European and American Thought, 1820–1940* (Manchester: Manchester University Press, 1985).

Lehan, R. D., *Realism and Naturalism: The Novel in an Age of Transition* (Madison, WI: University of Wisconsin Press, 2005).

Levitas, R., *'The' Concept of Utopia* (London: Philip Allan, 1990).

Levy, C., 'Education and Self-Education: Staffing the Early ILP', in C. Levy (ed.), *Socialism and the Intelligentsia: 1880–1914* (London: Routledge and Kegan Paul, 1987), pp. 135–210.

Lewis, J. E., *The English Fable: Aesop and Literary Culture, 1651–1740* (Cambridge: Cambridge University Press, 1996).

Linehan, T., *Modernism and British Socialism* (Basingstoke: Palgrave Macmillan, 2012).

Loewen, J. W., and E. H. Sebesta (eds), *The Confederate and Neo-Confederate Reader* (Jackson, MS: University Press of Mississippi, 2010).

Longford, E., 'Blunt, Wilfrid Scawen (1840–1922)', *Oxford Dictionary of National Biography* (Oxford: Oxford University Press, 2004), online edn at http://www.oxforddnb.com/view/article/31938 [accessed 1 April 2013].

Lucas, J., 'Harkness, Margaret Elise (1854–1923)', *Oxford Dictionary of National Biography* (Oxford: Oxford University Press, 2004), online edn at http://www.oxforddnb.com/view/article/56894 [accessed 9 April 2013].

MacCarthy, F., 'Morris, William (1834–1896)', *Oxford Dictionary of National Biography* (Oxford: Oxford University Press, 2004), online edn at http://www.oxforddnb.com/view/article/19322 [accessed 12 April 2013].

Machrey, R., *Night Side of London* (Philadelphia, PA: Lippincott, 1902).

Maidment, B., *The Poorhouse Fugitives* (Manchester: Carcenet, 1992).

Malchow, L. *Gothic Images of Race in Nineteenth-Century Britain* (Stanford, CA: Stanford University Press, 1996).

Malone, C., 'Campaigning Journalism: *Clarion*, the *Daily Citizen*, and the Protection of Women Workers, 1898–1912', *Labour History Review*, 67:3 (2002), pp. 281–97.

Manchester Literary Club, *The Dialect of Lancashire*, Internet Archive, at http://archive.org/details/glossaryoflancas00nodauoft [accessed 7 February 2013].

Mann, T., *Tom Mann's Memoirs* (1923; Nottingham: Spokesman, 2008).

Marx, K., and F. Engels, *Selected Correspondence* (Moscow, 1953), transcribed by D. McNeill (2000), *Marxist Internet Archive*, at http://www.marxists.org/archive/marx/works/1888/letters/88_04_15.htm [accessed 29 January 2013].

Masterman, C. F. G., *The Condition of England*, ed. J. T. Boulton (1909; London: Faber and Faber, 2012).

McPhillips, K., *Joseph Burgess (1853–1934) and the Founding of the Independent Labour Party* (Lewiston, NY: Edwin Mellen Press, 2005).

McWilliam, R., 'Barrie, Michael Maltman (1842–1909)', *Oxford Dictionary of National Biography* (Oxford: Oxford University Press, 2004), online edn at http://www.oxforddnb.com/view/article/42331 [accessed 1 April 2013].

Miller, E. C., *Slow Print, Literary Radicalism and Late Victorian Print Culture* (Stanford, CA: Stanford University Press, 2013).

Mitchell, J., 'The Ragged Trousered Philanthropists', *Marxism Today* (May 1961), pp. 154–9.

—, 'Tendencies in Narrative Fiction in the London-Based Socialist Press of the 1880s and 1890s', in H. G. Klaus (ed.), *The Rise of Socialist Fiction* (Brighton: Harvester Press, 1987), pp. 49–72.

Montmorency, J. E. G. de, 'Barnes, John Gorell, first Baron Gorell (1848–1913)', rev. H. Mooney, *Oxford Dictionary of National Biography* (Oxford: Oxford University Press, 2004), online edn at http://www.oxforddnb.com/view/article/30604 [accessed 17 October 2012].

Moran, M., *Victorian Literature and Culture* (London: Continuum, 2006).

Morris, W., and H. M. Hyndman, *A Summary of the Principles of Socialism* (1884), *Marxist Internet Archive*, at http://www.marxists.org/archive/morris/works/1884/principles/flippy.htm#page/48/mode/2up [accessed 24 January 2013].

Mussell, J., *The Nineteenth-Century Press in the Digital Age* (Basingstoke: Palgrave, 2012).

Mutch, D., *English Socialist Periodicals, 1880–1900: A Reference Source* (Aldershot: Ashgate, 2005).

—, 'The Merrie England Triptych: Robert Blatchford, Edward Fay and the Didactic Use of Clarion Fiction', *Victorian Periodicals Review*, 38:1 (2005), pp. 83–103.

—, '"A Working Class Tragedy": The Fiction of Henry Hyndman', *Nineteenth Century Studies*, 20 (2007), pp. 99–112.

—, 'Intemperate Narratives: Tory Tipplers, Liberal Abstainers and Nineteenth-Century British Socialist Fiction', *Victorian Literature and Culture*, 36:2 (2008), pp. 471–87.

—, 'Robert Blatchford', 'Joseph Burgess', 'Henry Hyde Champion', '*Clarion*', 'Charles Allen Clarke', '*Commonweal*', 'Henry Mayers Hyndman', '*Justice*', '*Labour Elector*', 'William Morris', 'Harry Quelch', '*Workman's Times*', in L. Brake and M. Demoor (eds), *Dictionary of Nineteenth-Century Journalism* (Gent: Academia Press, 2009).

—, 'Re-Humanising Marx: Theory and Fiction in the *Fin de Siècle* British Socialist Periodical', in A. Mousley (ed.), *Towards a New Literary Humanism* (Basingstoke: Palgrave, 2011), pp. 197–212.

Nash, A., *Kailyard and Scottish Literature* (Amsterdam and New York: Rodopi, 2007).

Nodal, J. H., and G. Milner, *A Glossary of the Lancashire Dialect* (London: Trübner, 1875).

Olson, L., *Modernism and the Ordinary* (Oxford: Oxford University Press, 2009).

Oxbury, H. F., 'Salt, Henry Shakespear Stephens (1851–1939)', *Oxford Dictionary of National Biography* (Oxford: Oxford University Press, 2004), online edn at http://www.oxforddnb.com/view/article/37932 [accessed 23 January 2013].

Parks, I., *The Voice of the People: Chartist Poetry 1838–1848* (Leeds: Flux Gallery Press, 2013).

Parsons, D., 'Whirlpools of Modernity: European Naturalism and the Urban Phantasmagoria', in M. Ryle and J. Bourne Taylor (eds), *George Gissing: Voices of the Unclassed* (Aldershot: Ashgate, 2005), pp. 107–18.

Pascoe, C. E., *London of To-Day: An Illustrated Handbook for the Season* (Boston, MA: Roberts Brothers, 1890).

Patterson, A., *Fables of Power, Aesopian Writing and Political History* (Durham, NC: Duke University Press, 1991).

Payne, D., *The Reenchantment of Nineteenth-Century Fiction* (Basingstoke: Palgrave Macmillan, 2005).

Pelling H., and A. J. Reid, *A Short History of the Labour Party* (Basingstoke: Macmillan, 1996).

Phillips, G. A., 'Sexton, Sir James (1856–1938)', *Oxford Dictionary of National Biography* (Oxford: Oxford University Press, 2004), online edn at http://www.oxforddnb.com/view/article/36030 [accessed 16 August 2012].

Plaskitt, E., 'Mayo, Isabella (1843–1914)', *Oxford Dictionary of National Biography* (Oxford: Oxford University Press, 2004), online edn at http://www.oxforddnb.com/view/article/55957 [accessed 5 April 2013].

Pugh, M., *Speak for Britain! A New History of the Labour Party* (London: Vintage, 2011).

Pullen, K., *Actresses and Whores: On Stage and in Society* (Cambridge: Cambridge University Press, 2005).

Rowbotham, S., *Dreamers of a New Day: Women who Invented the Twentieth Century* (London: Verso, 2011).

Rohrberger, M., 'Origins, Development, Substance and Design of the Short Story', in P. Winther, J. Lothe and I. H. Skei (eds), *The Art of Brevity: Excursions in Short Fiction Theory and Analysis* (Columbia, SC: University of South Carolina Press, 2004), pp. 1–13.

Rose, J., *The Intellectual Life of the British Working Classes* (New Haven, CT and London: Yale University Press, 2001).

Rubery, M., *The Novelty of Newspapers: Victorian Fiction after the Invention of the News* (Oxford: Oxford University Press, 2009).

Salmon, E. G., 'What the Working Classes Read', *Nineteenth Century*, 65 (1886), pp. 108–17.

Salveson, P., 'Allen Clarke and the Lancashire School', in H. G. Klaus (ed.), *The Rise of Socialist Fiction* (Brighton: Harvester Press, 1987), pp. 172–202.

—, *Lancashire's Romantic Radical: The Life and Writings of Allen Clarke/Teddy Ashton* (Huddersfield: Little Northern Books, 2009).

Samuel, R., 'Theatre and Socialism in Britain (1880–1935)', in R. Samuel, E. MacColl and S. Cosgrove (eds), *Theatres of the Left 1880–1935: Workers' Theatre Movements in Britain and America* (London: Routledge and Kegan Paul, 1985), pp. 3–77.

Sanders, M., *Chartist Literary Landmarks* (London: Pickering & Chatto, 2014).

Saville, J., 'Quelch, Henry [Harry] (1858–1913)', *Oxford Dictionary of National Biography* (Oxford: Oxford University Press, 2004), online edn at http://www.oxforddnb.com/view/article/37874 [accessed 21 January 2013].

Schapiro, L. B., *Turgenev: His Life and Times* (New York: Random House, 1978).

Scheckner, P., *An Anthology of Chartist Poetry: Poetry of the British Working Class* (Cranbury, NJ, London and Ontario: Associated University Presses, 1989).

Seccombe, W., *Weathering the Storm: Working-Class Families from the Industrial Revolution to the Fertility Decline* (London: Verso, 1995).

'Shaw, Bernard – Henry Hyndman – Annie Besant – 1887. Exchange of Letters on Value Theory in Marx', transcribed by T. Crawford, *Marxist Internet Archive*, at http://www.marxists.org/subject/economy/authors/fabians/earlyenglishvalue/lettersonvalue.htm [accessed 17 November 2012].

Shaw, D., and I. Petticrew, *Gerald Massey: Chartist, Poet, Radical and Freethinker* (1995/2009), *Minor Victorian Poets and Authors*, at http://gerald-massey.org.uk/massey/biog_contents.htm [accessed 25 February 2013].

Smith, L., 'Religion and the ILP', in D. James, T. Jowitt and K. Laybourne (eds), *The Centennial History of the Independent Labour Party* (Halifax: Ryburn, 1992), pp. 259–76.

Stead, W. T., 'Government by Journalism', *Contemporary Review*, 49 (1886), pp. 653–74, online edn *W. T. Stead Resource Site*, at http://www.attackingthedevil.co.uk/steadworks/gov.php [accessed 8 March 2013].

Steedman, C., 'McMillan, Margaret (1860–1931)', *Oxford Dictionary of National Biography* (Oxford: Oxford University Press, 2004), online edn at http://www.oxforddnb.com/view/article/34801 [accessed 13 March 2013].

Stevenson, R., *Modernist Fiction: An Introduction* (Lexington, KY: University Press of Kentucky, 1992).

Stoddart, J., *Ruskin's Culture Wars: Fors Clavigera and the Crisis of Victorian Liberalism* (Charlottesville, VA: University of Virginia Press, 1998).

Sumpter, C. R., '*Labour Leader*', '*Labour Prophet*', in L. Brake and M. Demoor (eds), *Dictionary of Nineteenth-Century Journalism* (Gent: Academia Press, 2009).

Sutherland, J., *The Stanford Companion to Victorian Fiction* (Stanford, CA: Stanford University Press, 1989).

The Dialect Dictionary, at http://www.thedialectdictionary.com/view/letter/Lancashire [accessed 7 February 2013].

Thompson, A. M., *Here I Lie* (London: George Routledge and Sons, 1937).

Thompson, E. P., *William Morris, Romantic to Revolutionary* (London: Lawrence and Wishart, 1955).

Thompson, L., *Robert Blatchford: Portrait of an Englishman* (London: Victor Gollancz, 1951).

Tressell, R., *The Ragged Trousered Philanthropists* (1914, 1955; London: HarperCollins, 1993).

Trotter, D., 'The Avoidance of Naturalism: Gissing, Moore, Grand, Bennett, and Others', in H. Bloom (ed.), *Edwardian and Georgian Fiction* (New York: Chelsea House, 2005), pp. 309–30.

Tsuzuki, C., *H. M. Hyndman and British Socialism* (Oxford: Oxford University Press, 1961).

Vaninskaya, A., *William Morris and the Idea of Community: Romance, History and Propaganda* (Edinburgh: Edinburgh University Press, 2010).

Vicinus, M., *The Industrial Muse* (London: Croom Helm, 1974).

Villanueva, D., *Theories of Literary Realism* (Albany, NY: State University of New York Press, 1997).

Vollaro, D. R., 'Lincoln, Stowe, and the "Little Woman/Great War" Story: The Making, and Breaking, of a Great American Anecdote', *Journal of the Abraham Lincoln Association*, 30:1 (2009), at http://hdl.handle.net/2027/spo.2629860.0030.104 [accessed 7 March 2013].

Walker, R. W., R. E. Turley and G. M. Leonard, *Massacre at Mountain Meadows* (Oxford: Oxford University Press, 2008).

Walkowitz, J. R., *City of Dreadful Delight: Narratives of Sexual Danger in Late Victorian London* (London: Virago, 1992).

Ward, P., *Red Flag and Union Jack: Englishness, Patriotism, and the British Left, 1881–1924* (Woodbridge: Boydell Press, 1998).

Waters, C., *British Socialists and the Politics of Popular Culture, 1884–1914* (Manchester: Manchester University Press, 1990).

Watt, I., *The Rise of the Novel* (London: Hogarth, 1987).

Watts, C., 'Graham, Robert Bontine Cunninghame (1852–1936)', *Oxford Dictionary of National Biography* (Oxford: Oxford University Press, 2004), online edn at http://www.oxforddnb.com/view/article/33504 [accessed 9 February 2013].

Williams, K., *Read All About It! A History of the British Newspaper* (London and New York: Routledge, 2010).

Williams, R., *The Country and the City* (Oxford: Oxford University Press, 1975).

—, *Marxism and Literature* (Oxford: Oxford University Press, 1977).

—, *Writing in Society* (London and New York: Verso, 1991).

—, *Modern Tragedy* (Toronto: Broadview, 2006).

Wir Ain Leed: An Innin tae Modern Scots (An Introduction to Modern Scots), at http://www.scots-online.org/grammar/index.asp [accessed 7 February 2013].

Wise, S., *The Blackest Streets* (London: Vintage, 2008).

Wrigley, C., 'Glasier, John Bruce (1859–1920)', *Oxford Dictionary of National Biography* (Oxford: Oxford University Press, 2004), online edn at http://www.oxforddnb.com/view/article/38468 [accessed 9 January 2013].

Woolf, V., 'Mr. Bennett and Mrs. Brown', in M. J. Hoffman and P. D. Murphy (eds), *Essentials of the Theory of Fiction* (Durham, NC: Duke University Press, 2005), pp. 21–34.

GLOSSARY OF DIALECT TERMS

abeaut (Lancs.)	about
abune (Scots.)	above
addle (Lancs.)	get
afore (Lancs.)	before
agate (Lancs.)	starting, underway, afoot
ain (Scots.)	own, my own
aince (Scots.)	once
alung (Lancs.)	along
allus (Lancs.)	always
ane (Scots.)	one
auld (Scots.)	old
Aw'd (Lancs.)	I would, I should
awhum (Lancs.)	at home
axed (Lancs.)	asked
babby (Lancs.)	baby
bailies (Lancs.)	bailiffs
bairns (Scots.)	babies or children
beaut (Lancs.)	without
beigh (Lancs.)	buy
bellywarch (Lancs.)	belly ache, stomach ache, stomach pains
bewk (Lancs.)	book
bigod (Lancs.)	by God
boggart (Lancs.)	an evil or mischievous spirit
borne/bourne/boyrn (Lancs.)	to swill, to wash; from burne, a stream
brast (Lancs.)	burst, broken
braw (Scots.)	fine
brid/s (Lancs.)	bird/s
brunt (Lancs.)	burnt
buzzes (Lancs.)	humour, wit or gossip
ceaw (Lancs.)	cow
cheer (Lancs.)	chair
chep (Lancs.)	cheap
clarty (Scots.)	dirty, filthy

clugs (Lancs.)	clogs
cracked (Lancs.)	foolish, wrong-headed
clamming/clemming (Lancs.)	starving
clash (Scots.)	idle chatter, gossip
cop/coppin (Lancs.)	to catch or to get
corbie (Scots.)	crow
co's (Lancs.)	calls
cowd (Lancs.)	cold
creawd (Lancs.)	crowd
cudno (Lancs.)	could not
dacent (Lancs.)	decent
darst (Lancs.)	dare not
daun (Scots.)	done
daunder (Scots.)	stroll
deawn (Lancs.)	down
dee (Lancs./Scots.)	die
deid (Scots.)	dead
dinna (Scots.)	do not, did not
divvle/s (Lancs.)	devils
divvy (Lancs.)	possibly a truncation of divulskin, meaning a mischievous person (the devil's kin)
doup/s (Norse/Scots.)	behind or buttocks
drouth (Scots.)	thirst
dur (Lancs.)	door
durn't (Lancs.)	don't, do not
eaut/eawt (Lancs.)	out
een (Lancs.)	eyes
eitin (Lancs.)	eating
etten (Lancs.)	eaten
ettle (Scots.)	intend, plan
fain (Lancs.)	glad, to rejoice
fause/fawse (Lancs.)	cunning, sly
favvour (Lancs.)	to resemble, to look like
faw/fawin (Lancs.)	fall, falling
feart (Lancs.)	afraid
feaw (Lancs.)	ugly
feawnt'in (Lancs.)	fountain
fecht/fechtin (Scots.)	fight, fighting
feck (Scots.)	amount, most
felly (Lancs.)	fellow
fettle (Lancs.)	condition
fleawer (Lancs.)	flour or flower
fley/ed (Scots.)	to be put to flight, frightened
flunter (Lancs.)	in a hurry, to hurry out of something

forrud (Lancs.)	forward
fot (Lancs.)	fetched. Usually meaning 'to give' as in 'I fot him a clip round the ear'
fower (Scots.)	four
fowt (Lancs.)	fold
freeten/freetent (Lancs.)	frighten, frightened
fun (Lancs.)	found
fust (Lancs.)	first
gam (Lancs.)	sport or fun
gan (Scots.)	go, gone
gar (Scots.)	compel, cause
gate (Lancs.)	a road or a rate of movement; also meaning a manner or fashion
geet/geeten (Lancs.)	get, got
gie/gied (Scots.)	give, gave
gey (Scots.)	goodly, considerably, greatly
gleg (Scots.)	nimble, swift, smart
gloppent/gloppend (Lancs.)	frightened, stunned, thunder-struck
gobbin (Lancs.)	an ignorant or foolish person
goo/gooin (Lancs.)	go, going
gootn (Lancs.)	gotten, have got
gow (Lancs.)	God, usually 'by gow'
graft (Lancs.)	work, to labour
greit/greyt (Lancs.)	great
guid (Scots.)	good
haars (Scots.)	cold easterly winds
hae (Scots.)	have
han (Lancs.)	have
heaw (Lancs.)	how
heid (Scots.)	head
henpeck/ed (Lancs.)	to be bullied by one's wife
Hinglishmon (Lancs.)	Englishman
hobble (Lancs.)	an awkward or difficult situation
hoo (Lancs.)	she
hond/s (Lancs.)	hands
hutch/ing (Lancs.)	to sit closely together, to huddle
hyam (Scots.)	home
intil (Scots.)	into, inside
iver (Scots.)	ever
jannock (Lancs.)	straightforward, honest or thorough; term taken from a loaf made of oatmeal or coarse wheat meal
jein/in (Lancs.)	join/ing
keepit (Scots.)	kept

ken/kent (Scots.)	know, knew
kirk (Scots.)	church
kilt (Lancs.)	killed
kist (Scots.)	chest, wooden box
lake (Lancs.)	to play
larnin (Lancs.)	learning
lat (Lancs.)	a staff or a pole
lauch/laucht (Scots.)	laugh, laughed
leatheryed (Lancs.)	a blockhead, a stupid person
leif (Lancs.)	rather, as soon as
Losh (Scots.)	Lord save us, an oath
lowf/lowfin (Lancs.)	laugh, laughing
lung (Lancs.)	long
mair (Scots.)	more
mak (Lancs.)	make
marlocks (Lancs.)	fun or mischief
maun (Scots.)	must
meauth (Lancs.)	mouth
meither/moider/moither (Lancs.)	to confuse, perplex, pester
'Meriky (Lancs.)	America, USA
mestur (Lancs.)	master
met (Lancs.)	might
misc'ed (Scots.)	miscalled, decried
mon (Lancs.)	man or men
motter (Lancs.)	motto
murn't (Lancs.)	mustn't, must not
mun (Lancs.)	must
nae (Scots.)	no, none
navvyin' (Lancs.)	manual labour, often digging and constructing roads, railways or canals; term comes from 'navigation' and was used most frequently in the north of England and the Midlands
neaw (Lancs.)	now or no
neet (Lancs./Scots.)	night
ner (Lancs.)	near
neuk (Scots.)	nook
niver (Lancs.)	never
noan (Lancs.)	not
noather (Lancs.)	neither
nobbut (Lancs.)	nothing but, only
noo (Scots.)	now
nowt (Lancs.)	nothing

o' (Lancs.)	of, on, all
oather (Lancs.)	either
onnyone (Lancs.)	anyone
ony (Lancs.)	any
oor (Scots.)	hour
oppen (Lancs.)	open
oss (Lancs.)	offer, to attempt, to try
ostid (Lancs.)	instead
outern (Lancs.)	out of
owd (Lancs.)	old
owder (Lancs.)	older
ower (Lancs.)	over
owt (Lancs.)	anything
peaun/peawnd	pound, either as a measurement of weight or a unit of currency
peawder (Lancs.)	powder
peil/peyl (Lancs.)	to beat severely
peint (Lancs.)	point
pike/piking (Lancs.)	a dialect word with different meanings depending on context; often used as a term meaning to go away or to make one's way (possibly a variation of 'peg' below), or to choose or select something (to 'pick')
peg (Lancs.)	walk, to walk determinedly, quickly
pobbies (Lancs.)	a meal of milk and water, often given to small children, the sick or the elderly as an easily digestible meal
pow (Lancs.)	to cut hair
poo/pood (Lancs.)	pull, pulled
pouch (Scots.)	pocket
prato (Lancs.)	potato
puir (Scots.)	poor
punce (Lancs.)	punch
purr (Lancs.)	kick
puir (Scots.)	poor
pusson (Lancs.)	person
quare (Lancs.)	queer, odd, strange
quicksticks (Lancs.)	quickly, in a short space of time
reet (Lancs./Scots.)	right
reyther (Lancs.)	rather
ricin' (Scots.)	a beating, to be beaten
roon (Scots.)	round

scrappin (Lancs.)	fighting
scrat (Lancs.)	scratched, scratching
seechin (Lancs.)	searching
Setterday (Scots.)	Saturday
shoon (Lancs.)	shoes
shoot (Scots.)	shout
shunt (Lancs.)	move
sithi (Lancs.)	see thee? Do you see?
sken (Lancs.)	squint
skinny (Lancs.)	tight-fisted, mean with money or any other form of material goods
skrike/strikin (Lancs.)	to shriek, shout, make an outcry
skule (Scots.)	school
slutch (Lancs.)	sludge, mud
smook (Lancs.)	smoke
smoor (Scots.)	smother, suffocate
snaw (Scots.)	snow
splores (Scots.)	frolics
steilin' (Lancs.)	stealing
steyl (Lancs.)	handle
stirk (Scots.)	heifer, bull, ox
stoo (Lancs.)	stool
sud (Lancs.)	should
summat (Lancs.)	something
syne (Scots.)	since, since that time
tallygraf (Lancs.)	telegraph
tan (Lancs.)	taken
tay (Lancs.)	tea, meaning either the hot beverage or the meal at the end of the day
threap (Scots.)	to argue persistently
theau't (Lancs.)	thou art, you are
thisel (Lancs.)	thyself, yourself
thowt (Lancs.)	thought
throng (Lancs.)	busy, with a heavy work-load; or pressed
throstle (Lancs.)	song-bird, singer, poet, balladeer
thrutch/ed (Lancs.)	to be pressed, either literally (for instance, in a crowd) or figuratively as in troubled by others or circumstances
Tommy/Tommie/s (British)	Tommy Atkins, a colloquial name for a soldier in the British Army
tort (Lancs.)	towards
towd (Lancs.)	told
twal (Scots.)	twelve

two-three (Lancs.)	two or three; not to be taken literally but meaning 'for a while' if in a context of time, or 'a few' if in a context of numbers
vittles (Lancs.)	food and drink
wark/warkin (Lancs.)	to work, working
warld (Lancs.)	world
weel (Lancs.)	well
welly (Lancs.)	well nigh, nearly
wersh (Scots.)	tasteless
weyn't (Lancs.)	will not, won't
wheer (Lancs.)	where
whet (Lancs.)	what
worrit (Lancs.)	worry
wrang (Scots.)	wrong
wreyt (Lancs.)	write
wrocht (Scots.)	work, worked
wur (Lancs.)	were
yance (Scots)	once, formerly, previously
yeard/yed (Lancs.)	head
yer (Lancs.)	ear or hear
yerd (Lancs.)	heard
yo (Lancs.)	you
yowes (Scots.)	ewes
yure (Lancs.)	hair

INTRODUCTION

This volume presents a selection of literature published in socialist periodicals during the early period of the British socialist movement. Like the Chartists before them, socialists appreciated the use of literature as an important vehicle for political discourse. All of the early socialist groups drew on literature to reinforce their political polemic and to provide depth to their ideology. The most striking aspect of this volume, when set beside the others, is the seriousness of the fiction in the early days of the British socialist revival. Apart from Charles Allen Clarke's humorous dialect story 'Bill Spriggs', the fiction in this volume is mostly didactic and ponderous, with a general theme of tragedy. There was no intention to draw out the tragic genre when selecting samples for this volume; rather, this seems to have been the general inclination of the literature published in the early periodicals. This may have been a symptom of the early socialist authors' earnestness and of the seriousness with which they viewed their task and the necessity of social, political and economic change. It may also be a symptom of class horror and guilt.

In the early years the British socialist movement was predominantly driven by socialists from the upper and middle classes: people such as Hyndman, Morris, Champion and Shaw came from backgrounds of wealth or faded gentry and had reached socialism through study rather than experience. This class basis is also evident in the literature published in the early periodicals. In the selection presented in this volume, there are fictions published by the Eton-educated Henry S. Salt (H. S. S.) and James Leigh Joynes, who both worked as Eton masters before resigning to focus on socialism; by Edith Nesbit (under the pseudonym Fabian Bland she used when writing with her husband, Hubert Bland), whose father owned an agricultural college; by William Morris, son of a wealthy City financier; by Margaret Harkness (under the pseudonym John Law), daughter of a Worcestershire clergyman; and by Henry Mayers Hyndman (under the pseudonym John Broadhouse and also, possibly, H. J. Bramsbury), son of a wealthy West India merchant. Their sense of horror at the conditions experienced by the poor may have impacted on their choice of genre for their literature, and the two most popular genres used by socialist authors during this period are the didactic fable and realism/naturalism.

There is a much greater sense in this volume of the reader being directed to
an 'acceptable' conclusion to their reading than there is in the following volumes.
This didacticism is most evident in the *Justice* trilogy 'Fables for the Times', all
published in 1884, which draws on the traditional fable genre to explain une-
qual distribution under capitalism ('Utile Dulci', 'The Monkeys and the Nuts'),
the socialist critique of Liberal *laissez-faire* economics (Anon., 'The Political
Economist and the Flowers') and the difficulty of dissent against established
party politics (William Morris, 'An Old Fable Retold').

Morris and 'Utile Dulci' draw on the tradition of the animal fable to make
their socialist points, as Morris's poultry squabble over the issue of 'with what
sauce shall we be eaten?' (p. 35) and 'Utile Dulci's' wise monkeys divide the
community through greed. All three authors direct the reader to the 'right' conclusion from the literature: that capitalism is unjust and disempowering to the
worker and that socialism is the best and only response. In the 'Utile Dulci' fable
this conclusion is ensured by a single-sentence postscript to the short fable that
explains the 'moral' for any reader who may not have realized the point. The
fable was a popular genre in *Justice* at this period, and D. F. Hannigan also uti-
lizes it in 'Aristos and Demos' to illustrate the division of power within capitalist
society, as 'Aristos' holds sway over the people until the arrival of 'Demos' to lead
them out of his power.

All these authors use the genre of fable as a means of creating both a unity
within their stories and a hope of creating the same in their readership; the genre
presents a call to join with the socialists and to change the world for the better.
However, as Jayne Elizabeth Lewis recognizes, this goal of unity is established on
a concept of disunity: 'we are reminded that fables finally forge unity around a
common center only through a more insidious kind of fragmentation. For they
split the field of symbolic action into acceptable and unacceptable halves, with
different groups firmly distributed between the two'.[1] Thus in order to create
socialist unity, the socialist author has to illustrate the divisions in society before
healing can begin. The disunity shown through the fable is not only social but
also political, as illustrated in Henry Salt's animal fable 'A Dream of Queer Fishes
(A Modern Prose Idyll)' (*Commonweal*, 1887). Here Salt tells the story of 'Joe,
the Commissioner of Fisheries' and his dream about the 'Public Meeting of sea-
fish' (p. 17), but unlike 'Utile Dulci's' *Justice* fable, where the message is spelled
out for the reader, Salt's fable expects that the reader will be aware of political
and current affairs. References to 'Joe', the 'fishy business of Salisbury and Co.'
and Joe's offer to the enraged fish of 'three acres of good submarine pasturage
and a sea-cow' clearly situate this fable as a critical satire on the political volte-
face of Joseph Chamberlain over Irish Home Rule, and the reader is expected to
understand the references without authorial explanation. Thus the *Justice* and

Commonweal fables reveal a significant difference in the intended reader, their cognitive ability and their political knowledge.

While the fable was a popular genre, it was not the only one used by socialist authors to carry their visions and arguments. The ancient form of the fable, with its strong moral force, was reinforced by vivid realism as the contemporary literary atmosphere influenced the socialist authors. However, this volume opens with two stories that eschew both genres of fable and realism. The organization of these volumes in alphabetical order by periodical title means that this volume opens with the stories of Charles Allen Clarke when, chronologically, his fiction is the latest. The two short stories from the *Bolton Trotter* are written in two different genres: 'Heaw Bill Spriggs Leet New Yer In' (1891) is a humorous dialect story and is discussed later in this Introduction. The second, 'What a Christmas Carol Wrought' (1891), is a story of dire poverty and fantastic escape. It could be criticized for presenting an unrealistic sense of relief as the poverty-stricken, fatherless family is revealed as the estranged family of the local Squire who are reunited on Christmas Eve. Nevertheless, as Rob Breton has argued, the *deus ex machina* has been used for political purposes by both Chartist and socialist authors, and Clarke 'continued to practice the Chartist stratagem of oscillating between representations of hard luck and luck in order to expose capitalism's uneven playing field'.[2] Like Chartist fiction, Clarke's 'salvation' for his working-class characters does not come from divine intervention but from material, earthly coincidence and good fortune. Clarke's revelation is similar to that of John Frost's *The Secret* (1850), where the seduced 'working-class' protagonist is revealed to be the daughter of the Duke of Belgrave. Breton argues that a 'realistic' happy ending cannot be envisaged under the pressures and restrictions imposed on the working classes under capitalist economics. Of *The Secret*, he claims that 'the story reinforces class differences, insisting on a distinct working-class moral character; and again, the dramatic turn of fate presents change as impossible within the economic and social status quo'.[3]

The longest fiction in this volume, H. J. Bramsbury's 'A Working Class Tragedy' (*Justice*, 1888–9), is constructed through the patchwork of genres discussed in the General Introduction and recognized by critics as favoured by the working-class author. Although there is some evidence that 'H. J. Bramsbury' might be a pseudonym for Henry Mayers Hyndman, the upper-class leader of the SDF, this does not undermine the argument that realism cannot present the working-class experience. Quite the opposite: if the author is Hyndman, then the multiple genres used to create 'A Working Class Tragedy' show the necessity of creating a new form of fiction to tell the working-class story, regardless of the class background of the author.

One of the most visible genres in Bramsbury's fiction is that of journalistic reportage, particularly in Chapter XXXIV (published in the issue for 26 January

1889), when protagonist Frank Wilson attends a meeting in Trafalgar Square. In 1886 the SDF organized a counter-demonstration to a Fair Trade meeting in Trafalgar Square that descended into riot and looting after the socialist platform was asked to move elsewhere. Subsequently Hyndman, Henry Hyde Champion, John Burns and Jack Williams were arrested, tried and acquitted of sedition.[4] The meeting Frank attends is a fictional representation of what became known as the West End Riots and serves as an account of the disturbances from the participant's perspective. Frank is aware the meeting has attracted 'roughs' and is approached by an *agent provocateur* who advocates 'a little dynamite' instead of 'all their spoutin'' (p. 175). Not only is the socialist side of the story projected through socialist journalism, that reportage is similarly incorporated into the fiction to reiterate the experience.

Bramsbury's serial has also been read as pessimistically naturalist, an interpretation that undermines the socialist vision. The fiction follows the trials of Frank, who is hounded from work by his employer, wrongfully charged with murder, escapes custody and lives on the run in London, returns to his home town after falling in love with the local landowner's daughter, and sacrifices himself to save her husband. The most recent critic to tackle Bramsbury's work, Elizabeth Carolyn Miller, labels the fiction as 'socialist-naturalist' and argues that 'working-class violence turns inward in the form of suicide, rather than outward, and ultimately Wilson represents a passive victim of the class system who never really converts to the socialist doctrine the novel promotes'.[5] While this is a valid argument for an initial reading of the fiction, it is one that is undermined by further investigation into both the fiction and the genre of naturalism. Bramsbury's fiction does have a political 'subterranean and disruptive ... universe of force',[6] but the presence of the socialist movement in the fiction resists accusations of passivity. As Jack Mitchell argues, '[t]he handling of the hero also runs directly counter to naturalism. Far from being a passive victim of circumstance he develops, through contact with socialist theory combined with what he learns from experience, from a traditional Radical into the class-conscious socialist'.[7]

My own reading of the fiction[8] leans towards Mitchell's comment on the tragedy of the fiction being Frank's isolation from the collective, but I would argue that Frank does not become a 'class-conscious socialist'. His attempts to practise socialist farming techniques on the Colonel's land align him with the fading patrician class rather than with his own emerging social group. Frank's death may be read as the worker's only escape from capitalist society (naturalism) and as the punishment for isolation from the collective (tragedy), but if Raymond Williams's definition of tragedy is applied, Bramsbury's fiction becomes much more positive. Williams asks us to widen our response to tragedy, to stop 'confin[ing] our attention to the hero' and therefore 'confining ourselves to one kind of experience', and instead to see beyond the single vision of the hero.

That life carries on 'after so important a death' is seen as part of the tragedy, but, Williams argues, '[w]hat is involved, of course, is not a simple forgetting, or a picking-up for the new day. The life that is continued is informed by the death; has indeed, in a sense, been created by it'.[9] By taking this perspective, the fiction is now a positive argument for collective action which leads the way out of the tragedy of the working-class condition under capitalism. The life that is continued and informed by Frank's death is that of the reader who has invested time and money in the story and who, on the same page as the final instalment, is provided with a list of SDF lectures and meetings where they might help advance the socialist cause and avoid Frank's fate.

The fiction of the socialist movement had been affected by the rise of naturalism in Europe, which shocked the British establishment with its direct look at the grimier side of Western life: 'Naturalist fiction projects a rational, scientific stance through its detached, clinical voice; careful observation of detail; dispassionate analysis of the human condition, including the sleazy, the degrading and the taboo; and use of natural and social laws to explain behaviour'.[10] Generally agreed to have begun with Jules and Edmond Goncourt's *Germinie Lacerteaux* (1864), Zola's Rougon-Macquart cycle (1871–93) brought the genre to Britain. Henry Vizetelly, who published seventeen translations of Zola's fiction between 1884 and 1889,[11] was imprisoned for publishing obscene literature, and the outcry against literary naturalism provoked George Moore's scathing response in his article 'A New Censorship of Literature' (*Pall Mall Gazette*, 1884) and his pamphlet *Literature at Nurse, or Circulating Morals* (1885), which was also published by Vizetelly.

While detailed depictions of poverty and sexuality were generally responsible for giving the establishment an attack of the vapours (antagonistic reviewers are referred to by Robert Blatchford as 'respectable old ladies of both sexes'[12]), the anti-capitalist sentiments of naturalism would be just as offensive to the establishment but not so easy to whip up a panic around. Deborah Parsons describes the political underpinning of literary naturalism: 'Images of the unstable energies of bourgeois modernity abound throughout naturalist fiction; financial speculation and the scramble for the spoils of expansion, the profusion of goods and equally abundant refuse of consumerism, the inflation of monetary value, fortunes and desires'.[13] The entrapment of the poor and working class under capitalism was strengthened by the inescapable effects of heredity. The sociological basis of naturalism, especially in Zola's work, emphasized the degeneration of the Western human being and human society through the hereditary flaw; Zola's novels 'described the effects of heredity and environment on the members of a single family, tracing the passage of a genetic "flaw" down the legitimate line of the Rougons and the illegitimate line of the Macquarts'.[14] This sense of pessimism about the possibility of change is also found in the fiction of George

Gissing, Henry Nevinson, Rudyard Kipling and others. Although not all took the theme of heredity into their work, there was a general sense of the inescapability from poverty, destitution and slum life.

While there was no recourse to the 'effects of heredity' in the socialist fiction – which would give little hope for immediate social improvement – there was a strong critique of 'environment', where improvements could be made immediately through the implementation of socialist policies. Some authors found it difficult to see the possibility of improvement in the capitalist world, and H. Bellingham's 'Chips' (*To-Day*, 1888) takes the same approach to escape for his destitute child as Arthur Morrison would later take for Dicky Perrott in *A Child of the Jago* (1896): death. Bellingham's pessimism (or, perhaps, optimism for the afterlife) was not a perspective held by others, as is most clearly shown in the translation of Ivan Turgenev's 'Only a Dog' (*To-Day*, 1883). Turgenev's story had been published in 1852 under the title 'Mumu', and the *To-Day* translation is largely faithful to the original story of Gerassim, a large, deaf and mute Russian peasant, who is sent to work for a wealthy urban woman. The power his mistress holds over him robs him both of the woman he loved and of his faithful dog; the latter he is ordered to destroy by drowning in the lake. However, where Turgenev's original ending had anticipated the pessimism of naturalism by having Gerassim return to his mistress after carrying out her order and serve her for the rest of his life, the *To-Day* version returns Gerassim to his village, his family and his useful labour. Gerassim takes control of his life, releases himself from servitude and retrieves his freedom, and thus the translation instils a sense of hope and autonomy in the fiction that was absent from the original.

The naturalist presentation of grim reality and heredity included a relatively more open representation of sexual relationships. While authors such as George Gissing, Arthur Morrison and George Moore depicted the less restrictive attitudes of the working classes towards sex, A. Gilbert Katte uses this openness to criticize both the hypocritical veneer of 'respectability' in the upper classes and the absurdity of that veneer, which could ruin a reputation and career because of a mistaken emotional decision. In 'The Whip Hand' (*To-Day*, 1888), the reader is presented with Sir Reginald Hastie's dysfunctional marriage, his loving relationship with his mistress, Kate, and the devastating choice he faces between his love and his career. Strangely prophetic of the divorce scandal that destroyed Charles Stewart Parnell through his affair with the separated Catherine O'Shea, Hastie faces losing the position he has been offered as Prime Minister when his wife threatens to expose his affair. Kate's knowledge of Lady Hastie's own infidelities creates a balance of power in the marriage, and both agree to present a united front and a semblance of marriage for the public. The story was published seven years before Thomas Hardy's *Jude the Obscure* (1895) tackled the breakdown of marriage and extramarital sex, and Katte is straightforward in his description of the sexual nature of Hastie and Kate's relationship. This is indicated in the ease by which she greets him while in a state of relative undress:

> A couple of hours later she was sitting at her toilet table, half undressed, looking through a little pile of letters, when she heard a sharp hurried rat-tat at the front door. The sound seemed familiar, for she rose, went swiftly to the wardrobe, scrambled into a grey dressing-gown and was making for the door when it burst open, almost striking her in the face, and Sir Reginald Hastie, his hat still on his head and umbrella in hand, came into the room. (pp. 298–9)

That Hastie also walks directly into her bedroom also indicates a familiar and intimate relationship. While Hardy's novel was bowdlerized for serialization in *Harper's New Monthly Magazine* (1894–5), Katte's more explicit fiction is 'safely' buried in the socialist periodical and therefore either unknown or felt not to be a threat to the sensibilities and respectability of the reading public. Nevertheless, such sexual frankness chimed with the discussions surrounding marriage and cohabitation that flowed through the socialist movement.[15] Marriage is not a crucial part of the happy-ever-after, as evidenced by socialist women such as Eleanor Marx and Edith Lanchester, who lived unmarried with their partners. Nevertheless, the sexual directness is the only aspect of naturalism in Katte's fiction; the upper-class Kate and Hastie have the power of control over their lives, and their unmarried cohabitation is their happy ending.

Katte's fiction is one of the few in this volume with a happy ending, and it is interesting that the happiness of Hastie and Kate is achieved by their power as upper-class people to control their lives; the authors do not generally present working-class characters as having that luxury under capitalism. As discussed above, this tendency to perceive or present only the direst situations for the working classes might be a product of the middle- or upper-class author's distress at the horrors of poverty. Nevertheless, the working-class Thomas Barclay imagines the equality of employer and worker in 'Master and Man in Heaven' (*Commonweal*, 1891), but only after death, again giving the sense that equality cannot be achieved under current social and economic conditions. The same sense is evident in Charles Allen Clarke's 'What a Christmas Carol Wrought' and his use of the *deus ex machina*, as discussed earlier. But what we also see in the working-class Clarke's fiction is a different approach to the working-class condition. Like the upper- and middle-class authors in this volume, Clarke does not shy away from descriptions of poverty and deprivation, but his stories have a sense of hope and optimism that is either absent or downplayed in the other fictions. The Bill Spriggs story, one of a long series of very popular short stories about the feckless Spriggs and his harridan wife, Bet, is a humorous celebration of working-class life in the dialect tradition. Unlike earlier Lancashire dialect authors such as Tim Bobbin, Ben Brierley and Edwin Waugh, Clarke gives a more rounded vision of working-class life in Lancashire. He recognizes and presents the struggles for money and work faced by the workers, but the Spriggs series (as well as his other dialect fiction) balances a depiction of life which is not relentlessly dire but which has moments of humour, love and hope. Clarke's fiction included in this volume gives an indication of the changes in tone in the following volumes as working-class socialists join their middle- and upper-class comrades in depicting socialist arguments through fiction.

Notes

1. J. E. Lewis, *The English Fable: Aesop and Literary Culture, 1651-1740* (Cambridge: Cambridge University Press, 1996), p. 69.
2. R. Breton, 'Ghost in the Machina', *Victorian Studies* (2005), pp. 557–75, on p. 569.
3. Ibid., p. 562.
4. Hyndman, *The Record of an Adventurous Life*, pp. 403–4.
5. Miller, *Slow Print*, pp. 103–4.
6. Lehan, *Realism and Naturalism*, pp. xx–i.
7. Mitchell, 'Tendencies in Narrative Fiction', p. 61.
8. D. Mutch, '"A Working Class Tragedy": The Fiction of Henry Hyndman', *Nineteenth Century Studies*, 20 (2007), pp. 99–112.
9. R. Williams, *Modern Tragedy* (Toronto: Broadview, 2006), p.79.
10. M. Moran, *Victorian Literature and Culture* (London: Continuum, 2006), p. 145.
11. D. Baguley, *Naturalist Fiction: The Entropic Vision* (Cambridge: Cambridge University Press, 1990), p. 32.
12. Blatchford, *My Favourite Books*, p. 228.
13. D. Parsons, 'Whirlpools of Modernity: European Naturalism and the Urban Phantasmagoria', in M. Ryle and J. Bourne Taylor (eds), *George Gissing: Voices of the Unclassed* (Aldershot: Ashgate, 2005), pp. 107–18, on p. 107.
14. D. Trotter, 'The Avoidance of Naturalism: Gissing, Moore, Grand, Bennett, and Others', in H. Bloom (ed.), *Edwardian and Georgian Fiction* (New York: Chelsea House, 2005), pp. 309–30, on p. 310.
15. See, for instance, K. Hunt, *Equivocal Feminists: The Social Democratic Federation and the Woman Question, 1884–1911* (Cambridge: Cambridge University Press, 1996); and J. Hannam and K. Hunt, *Socialist Women: Britain, 1880s to 1920s* (London and New York: Routledge, 2002).

BOLTON TROTTER

C. Allen Clarke, 'What a Christmas Carol Wrought', *Bolton Trotter*, 25 December 1891, pp. 2–3.

Teddy Ashton, 'Heaw Bill Spriggs Leet New Yer In', *Bolton Trotter*, 16 January 1891, p. 6.

The *Bolton Trotter* (1891–3) was founded and edited by Charles Allen Clarke (1863–1935) and was published as the *Bolton Trotter* between 9 January 1891 and 22 April 1892. It was renamed the *Trotter* in the issue of 29 April 1892 and was published under this name until the final issue on 23 June 1893. Issued weekly, it was published first in Manchester and then in Blackpool, and it sold for a halfpenny under both titles. The paper followed Clarke's first periodical, the *Labour Light*, first published in March 1890, which had failed through poor sales. The *Bolton Trotter* was a more light-hearted periodical than the *Light*, and the word 'trotter' was a reference to the nickname for the inhabitants of Bolton. One of the reasons for the popularity of the paper was Clarke's dialect 'Tum Fowt' (Tonge Fold) sketches – comedy tales about the feckless Bill Spriggs, his harridan wife, Bet, and Bill's equally feckless friends.

    Clarke was born in Bolton, Lancashire, to cotton mill workers. He became a 'half timer' (a child worker who worked for the first half of the day and spent the latter half in school) at the age of eleven and a little piecer at the age of thirteen. He escaped the usual path into full-time millwork, a path followed by many working-class Lancastrians, by becoming a pupil-teacher at the age of fourteen. In 1885 he left teaching and began work as a journalist for the *Bolton Evening News*. After discovering socialism in 1887 and joining the Bolton Social Democratic Federation, he resigned from the *Bolton Evening News* in 1890 to begin the *Labour Light*. The *Labour Light* was claimed by Clarke to be the first socialist periodical in Lancashire, but it was short-lived. After the *Light* folded, Clarke earned money by publishing articles for the *Cotton Factory Times* and the *Bolton Evening News* before starting his next paper, the *Bolton Trotter*, in 1891. The *Trotter* folded in 1893, and Clarke took a post as journalist for the *Cotton Factory Times*, which at this point was being edited by Joseph Burgess. In 1896 he left the *Cotton Factory Times* to begin *Teddy Ashton's Journal*, which continued, under a variety of names, until 1908. Clarke was a talented dialectician, and his dialect fiction, especially the 'Bill Spriggs' stories, were incredibly popular. He wrote most of the inclusions in the *Bolton Trotter* and in his subsequent periodical, *Teddy Ashton's Journal/Northern Weekly and Teddy Ashton's Journal*, under a multitude of pseudonyms: Teddy Ashton was his dialect pseudonym, while he published poetry under the name 'Capanbells', children's stories and poetry under 'Grandad Grey', and work under the names Allen-a-Dale and Ben Adhem, as well as under his own name.

C. Allen Clarke, 'What a Christmas Carol Wrought' (1891)

"Shut the door, sharp!" That is what you say as I enter the house for, as I open the door, the bitter wind blows in from the street, and the sleet rushes in, and the bright fire roars excitedly as the air flies up the chimney. I shut the door as you bid me, and the wind, mad at being shut out, shakes the latch, and leaps about so frantically that the scared sleet trembles as it beats against the windows. You bid me draw a chair near the fire, and join in the chat that is going on, and also to partake of the warm supper. But I decline, with all respect to your hospitality, for I want to show you something outside, and ask you to accompany me. You seem reluctant to quit the smiling fire for the purpose of braving the December storm, and would rather spend the Christmas Eve at home. For, as you know, it is Christmas Eve; and as *I* know, the Christmas dinner is stowed away somewhere awaiting the morrow. "It's such a wild night!" you protest as I urge you to come out; but at last you consent. So you put on your great coat, and button it up tightly; then leave the hot comfortable fire, open the door, and we are out in the dark wet street. Hear how the breeze wails! The ghostly sleet goes whirling down the road. You can hardly see for it. How it tries to penetrate to your skin through every unguarded way. It seeks out every weak place in your apparel, and sends its sharp sting there, pricking you with a point of ice. It is very sloppy underfoot; the slush splashes about the feet at every step.

Come along, down here. Every door is shut, but the gaslight shows on the blinds in the windows. Did you hear the children singing in that house as we passed? For the moment their voices rose above the tumult. Look at that poor fellow; some outcast tramp, trudging along, hatless and shoeless and but scantily attired! See how the cruel sleet beats on his breast! How he shivers! God help him! Here, give him that copper, poor fellow! Charity is the most practicable creed, after all. Ah, see that rich man's coach dashing along; the horses are better protected than that poor tramp we saw just now. The coach is out of sight now; the carriage and the trap are both lost in the grey indistinction and confusion of the swirling, eddying sleet. Here, follow me. Now we are right in the heart of the town. Gas-lit shops, magnificent and many, are on either hand; but their brilliant windows are dim with the damp and the mist. Few people are abroad though it is Christmas Eve. There stands the policeman in a corner; he has not a nice time of it just now. But still, he is much better prepared to face the night than a very, very many houseless waifs, old and young, tender and tough. O God help them to-night. Ah, one or two smile as if they doubted God could help them and I detect that they are skeptically inclined. Well maybe you are right. No man should contradict another about what neither of them knows; yet, 'tis often done. The sky is full of wrath and winter and death tonight, and it seems hard to think there is a loving God above it, who will not help the starving, frozen, miserable things who have no home but that under the open heavens on a night like this, and who will have to share their bed-chamber with soaking sleet, cold freezing air, tyrannic winds, and not even a star to light them to bed. But still I say God help them! And maybe He will – for who understands all things?

Look at that poor little lad! Wretched little streetling.[1] He is selling matches; his frozen hands can hardly hold the boxes; his hoarse voice sounds like a mockery of childhood. Will he ever – should he live to grow old, which is improbable – will he ever look back with yearning joy to the days of his childhood, as poets would have us believe all men do? Mistaken poets! What does the canary sinking in luxury know of the sparrow perishing in the frost? Poor little matchboy! There is nothing on his feet; there is nothing on his head; and worst of all there is nothing in his stomach. How longingly he eyes the pies – old and uninviting though they are – in the shop window. Ah, see; a foppish young swell condescendingly stops to buy a box of fusees;[2] then he lights his cigar, and puffs away in careless content, while the little match-boy is dying inch by inch, murdered by relentless winter and the fate that had him born.

But come along. How you tremble! What! Are *you* cold; *you*, so well-garbed and warm-clothed; do *you* feel the icy chill? Oh, what then must it be to those who are only half-clothed and half-fed? Stop here. We are at the junction of four of the main streets in the town, or rather at the place where two principal streets cross at right angles. Look around. There is a fruit shop; there a grocer's; there a newsagent's; here a big clothier's. In the middle of the crossing stands the policeman. Let us stand by this big window. Why, the wind makes you stagger, it blows in such force. Stand against the wall and you will be sheltered a little. Now see! I want you to look at that little girl standing alone at the corner. She is shouting – what a sad tone! Listen. She shouts, "Evening News! Evening News! Last edition! Awful account of a starving family! Evening News! Evening News!" She is aged about eight. Her feet are almost bare for the old shoes she has on are a lot too big, and the water fills them; her stockings are full of holes; and she has an old hat on her head. Her arms are partly uncovered. The sleet beats in her eyes, and trickles down her face mixed with tears. Poor little thing. See how the wind whirls her rags about, and almost knocks her down. Look at her blue wet fingers;

her pale cheeks, and staring wet eyes. How the rain and snow strikes on her bare neck, as if the terrible wind were trying to cut her throat with a sharp knife of icy sleet! How she shivers and crouches! 'It's a shame!" you exclaim, "a great evil shame! That such children should be sent out on nights like this. Why can't the law stop it? Why do men let such things be! Oh, ye who dwell in palaces help those who dwell in hovels. Help them. Help them! It will do you good to be kind; just try, and see how great is the pleasure of making others happy. You who have a little too much give to those who have much too little! Charity gratifies both giver and taker.

Look; a big strong man comes along. He wears a thick overcoat, and his neck is muffled up well. Waterproof shoes are on his feet, and warm gloves on his hands. He is of middle age. He hears the girl shouting "Evening News!" and sees she is crying bitterly too. He stops. Is he rubbing the sleet out of his eyes, for he dashes his hands hastily across them? Now he feels in his pocket. He gives the girl half-a-crown; "Here, lass, hasten home, and" – his voice is choked, and he hurries on, once more dashing his hand across his face. He is out of view now. The girl looks at the half-crown, and thinks, "Should I go home? No, I'll not. I'll try to sell the papers too; that will be so much more for mother and little Joe; I know he would like something good at Christmas; yes, I'll stay, but it's very, very cold!" Still the wind blows, and the sleet stings; they care nought for the self-denial of the brave little newsgirl.

Ah, a carriage is coming up. It stops at the fruiterer's. An old gentleman gets out and enters the shop. Now the shopman puts a goose and some other articles in the carriage; and the old gentleman is re-entering. As he is stepping in, the little newsgirl runs to him, and says, "Evening News, sir?" He looks at her and frowns; "No, no!" he says gruffly, "What do I want with 'Evening News'?" and the little repulsed lass springs back as the carriage drives off, while the old man inside mutters, "Good God! Can it be? I'm sure that is Philip's child. How like him! It is horrible to think it! How deathly cold she was! Good heavens! Are they so poor? But Philip's gone abroad to make his fortune, so folks say. And his child starving! But it was his own fault. He should have done as I wished him, and married the rich one. What's beauty of itself? Pah!" And the carriage rolls on, but that old man cannot help thinking of the beseeching eyes of the newsgirl; and he thinks how odd it is for her to be freezing out there, while a dead goose – a dead goose – is reposing so snugly on the cushions inside his coach. And his eyes close in a reverie; see, he falls in a doze; he dreams. Suddenly the goose on the seat in front of him sits up, and, fixing its eyes right on his, sings this song in a weird voice, while a host of ghostly geese wail the refrain: –

SONG OF THE CHRISTMAS GOOSE.

A little while just listen to me,
    For, though I'm but a goose,
I'll hold up wisdom for you to see: –
    Which now I'll introduce;
And if you cannot read it right,
    And take the intimation,
Why, then, if not of my family quite,
    You're a very near relation.
Chorus of Ghosts of Christmas Geese: – A very near relation.

Now Christmastide is a time for love,
    Good-will, and peace, you know,
Which is true, for the angels in heaven above,
    Sang that fact long ago.
With all that have offended you,
    And all that you've offended,
Shake hands and be friends; and, if you do,
    Your Christmas will be splendid.
Chorus: – Christmas will be splendid!

Now, if you don't do as I've told
    (Though I don't like to threaten)
In horrid dream you shall behold
    The night that I am eaten!
So my advice at once accept,
    Shut out all bitter bother;
For Christmas is by those best kept,
    Who all love one another.
Chorus: – All love one another.

The song ceased, all the geese faded away, and he woke up. But he had almost resolved on something, – almost, for a pride crept in and delayed his resolution, like a traitor advising one to wait and wait while he stealthily is obtaining his own object. And still the coach rolls homeward.

Come down in the town again. It is fine now. The streets are wet, but the storm has ceased, and in the dark-blue sky of night the stars are shining with a wintry sparkle. The little newsgirl is going home, her wet clothes making her shiver as they cling to her skin. That half-crown brought her luck. She sold her papers so rapidly that she was astonished; and several good folks gave her silver and told her to keep the change; and one or two patted her gently on the head, which made her almost cry, it was so unusual.

See, folks, are crowding the streets. The beauty of the night after the storm lures them out; and, as the streets are filling, the newsgirl hurries homeward. Scarcely has she left the spot where she was accustomed to stand, than the man who gave her the half-crown hastens up. He is talking to himself, "I'm sure it was my own little Maggie! Oh God! And out on such a night. It's heart-rending, – something urged me to return, – I feel strange – full of a great emotion, like one just making a great discovery, – can my wife have become so poor? I've only been gone a year, and I've made a fortune. Oh they shall know want no more! Where do they live? I've sought all over the town, and can't find them! And I felt irresistibly drawn to this place; – and now, oh God! She's gone! – How cold she was! How she cried! My child, oh, my child! Starving while I've plenty! They say my father forced my wife to remove – said he wouldn't have her living in one of his cottages – may his conscience forgive him for it. Oh God – where is she? They may die wile I'm seeking them; my poor lost family!"

See, he rushes off. Let us hope he finds them. He hardly knows where he is going scarcely knows what he's doing. Let us follow him.

He is off up that dark alley. Black walls, gloomy as night, frown upon either side. He passes that house with the broken window through which the wind is blowing strongly. Let us go in this house, while he runs on, looking for those he loves.

Now we are inside. There is a small fire, – very small, and dull, and a woman kneeling by it. A little boy is in her arms; she is trying to warm him. "Wait a bit, Joe," she says, soothingly yet sorrowfully, "Maggie will be home soon, and perhaps she'll have sold all her papers, and we'll buy some coal, and you shall sit before a big fire, and have a nice Christmas dinner!" Then she goes on to herself, "Poor Maggie! I was wrong to let her go and sell papers. God bless the child! She wanted to go, wanted to be useful, she said, "Why can't I do it if other children do?" And on such a night as this has been. She shall not go any more; not if I starve; not if I work all the flesh off my bones – (alas! there was very little to work off!) – she shall not go any more, for it will kill her; and that's a murder I will not do!"

Hark! The door opens gently, and Maggie enters. "Oh mother, I've sold all my papers, every one! And many told me to keep the change, and one gentleman gave me half-a-crown, and after that I had such luck! I wish I could see him again to thank him; he went away before I could speak." The mother starts. She hears "Glad tidings." Maggie gives her the money. How quickly then does the joyful mother go out to purchase eatables, and soon there is a supper for them all. Little Joe's heart fairly jumps in delight; and the kiss he gives Maggie fully makes up in warmth for all the cold she had suffered through that evening. As they eat, how content they are! What a happy thing it is to feel satisfied!

Hark! a knock at the door. A party of a dozen then come in, noisily and merrily. "Oh Mrs. Grove!" shouts one, "we're going out carol-singing; you'll let Maggie come? – they'll think it's a real angel will those who hear her – just one of them that sang to the shepherds on the first Christmas Eve that ever was; we can't do without her; you shan't refuse; she must come."

"Yes, yes," cry the others.

"But," says Mrs. Grove, "she's been out in all the storm, and is wet through and cold. You see what a poor fire we have."

"Oh," cries one, "she can have my cloak!" "And my big scarf," says the bass singer. "And I'll take her to our house and give her some hot coffee and toast," says the tenor. "Yes, let her come, and we'll make her right," exclaim they all; and Mrs. Grove cannot say no, and there are tears in her eyes too, glad tears, to find that still there are kind hearts in the world, and that charitable souls are not an extinct race.

It is eleven o'clock now. The carol-singers are abroad. Little Maggie is out with the choir of the chapel she attends. It is quite calm now, but cold. Bright stars glitter above, and the shadows of night flit about restlessly. Let us go with these singers.

Now we are out in the country. Still fields and farms are all about us; and on the horizon everything fades and grows dim in that hazy indistinction peculiar to things at a distance in the darkness.

Come down this lane. Now we are close by a large villa; and the carolers are assembled on the lawn in front of it. The singers know whose house it is, but they do not tell Maggie. Now they are all ready; and the silence which precedes the music, which sounds all the sweeter after it, is over all things. Hark! the melody flows forth. Beautiful tones are in the air, harmonious combinations that have a thrilling effect; eccentric discords that sound in the right place, lending that charm to music which shading does to painting; delicious chords are rising to the sky, and spreading over the earth.

How strangely sweet does the song of a chorus of singers, or the music of a band, sound to one who is lying awake in bed in the silence of midnight! How rapturing thus to be awaked! Have you never been gently roused from slumber by the delicate touch of music on your ears on some Christmas Eve, when lying in bed you could look into the night beyond your window, and dream in a pleasant reverie; and then, faintly, you could hear far off in the still night, the strains of some homely Christmas Carol sung by soft subdued voices? And how indefinably delicious were your feelings at such a time! Indeed, if you have once experienced it, you will never forget it till you forget heaven.

I wonder what old Squire Grove will say when he finds Maggie here, thinks the tenor, who knows all about the old Squire driving his son Philip from home for marrying the girl he loved; how Philip, reduced to great extremity, had bidden good-bye to his wife and children, and gone abroad to seek his fortune, promising to return soon; and how little Maggie was Philip's child, and Squire Grove's granddaughter.

But Maggie knows nothing. She sings on. Listen; it is a solo. Her voice seems everywhere. It enters the bedroom of Squire Grove. He awakes. Never before had he such a joyful awakening. He rubs his eyes and listens, in a semi-dazed way, wondering wherever such marvellous music is coming from. Still Maggie sings on, unconscious of the charm in her voice, and the change that it is effecting. "What a splendid singer!" you exclaim as you gaze at her in admiration, which soon becomes pity as you notice her thin form. Now the chorus rings out; and you strain your ears to catch the fullness of harmony that is gathering round you.

Up in his bedroom Squire Grove lies listening. The child's voice penetrates him. The words, "Peace on earth, good will to men," are pricking his heart. The song of the Christmas Goose is in his mind too, and he thinks of the dream in his carriage as he rode home from town. Now the hymn-notes sink ebbingly low, and the voices sound curiously far away, like unseen angels singing in the skies. Floods of thought overwhelm the man, and he struggles in them confused and bewildered. He sits up in bed. "I will!" he cries, "I will! I will forgive him, or rather ask him to forgive me. How that child's voice fills me. I shall have her inside; I'll have them all inside; and they shall have a good feast, and a Christmas gift too. I will *not* be a Christmas goose, nor yet a very near relation." He jumps from the bed; he rings the bell; orders his servant to bring the carolers in and take them into the kitchen; and then prepares to see them himself.

Still the singers are on the lawn. Little Maggie has gone very pale. Ah! look; two persons are advancing up one side of the lawn. Why, it is the stranger who gave little Maggie the half-crown, and of whom we lost sight while he was searching for her. And who is this with him? Why, bless us! How glad I am! It's Mrs. Grove; he has found his wife! How happy they both are, "O Philip," she whispers, as they stealthily make their way toward the singers, "there is our Maggie. Can you not hear her voice? Let us wait till they have done."

But Philip Grove is intently looking about him.

"What!" he cries, as he ceased scrutinizing the objects round him, "what fiend has led me here! This is my father's! Let us go, or I shall be wild! Let me fetch Maggie, and we'll leave this cursed place."

The wife stares, speechless, as he drags her along. He reaches the carol-singers. As he joins the group the song is done. See! Maggie is falling; he darts quickly forward and catches her in his arms; she has fainted; the trials she has lately gone through have been too much for her; and now Philip Grove holds his child in his hands; helpless, ill, – and in such a condition before his father's house. "O little Maggie! Look up! Speak to me!" – and he kisses her. The singers in astonishment watch the scene.

The door of the house opens. Squire Grove comes out, and bids all the carollists enter and welcome. "And bring that angel-voiced little one in," he said "and she shall have something too – the best and daintiest I can give, but not so dainty as her singing; not so good as that had been to me. No, oh –"

Then the Squire starts in surprise. Silently the tenor points to Maggie in her father's arms. The Squire rushes forward. "Oh heaven! What's the matter? She's not ill, is she? – tell –" See! He stops abruptly and slowly steps backward, staring wildly and his body trembling, as his eyes meet those of the man holding the girl in his arms – his son!

"O Philip! – you are here! Forgive me! And your –" and the old Squire falls in a swoon on the lawn; and Philip's tears fall on his daughter's face as he lays her in her mother's arms while he attends to his father.

* * *

Hark how the Christmas bells are ringing! Over all the land; out from the gloom of the old belfry of the church comes the stirring sound, telling to all its story. Peal away! The child listens, the wife, the husband, the lover, the old man, all listen. How the stars shine now! Merrily ring the bells; merrily twinkle the stars.

Come in Squire Grove's house. The carollists are enjoying themselves in the kitchen, chatting, joking, laughing, and eating. "A Merry Christmas to Little Maggie!" cries the tenor, and everyone repeats it. Let us leave these gay souls, and look into the old Squire's snug parlor. What a rich repast is there! and look, little Maggie, and lesser Joe too – (for the tenor had been for him – his mother had left him asleep in bed); and Philip Grove and his wife, and the old Squire, all chatting and eating together. Little Joe is on the Squire's knee, and is amusing the old man immensely. It's quite certain that the Christmas Goose will not haunt the Squire now; he'll have no scaring dreams or awful nightmare after such a reunion. His soul is full of the peace of reconciliation; and he feels what a good thing it is to love and be loved; and he and all the party, are quite sure that this Christmas will be the happiest Merriest Christmas that ever was.

Teddy Ashton, 'Heaw Bill Spriggs Leet New Yer In' (1891)

"Neaw Bill," said Bet Spriggs to her husband, "theau's geet a black yed, an' theau mun let eaur new yer in. Black yeds are lucky. That's why ah allus had my fayther for t' let eaur new yer in, but neaw as he's deeod there's nobody else but thee for it."

It wur New Yer's Eve an abeaut hauve past ten at neet, i' Tum Fowt, at onny rate when the above konversashun took place betwixt Bet Sprigs an' her beluvved spouse, which is French fur dada.

"Neaw," hur went on, "ah's let thee goo eaut deaun t' teawn for t' bring a bit o' pork up ut I've ordered, an' theau mun get back bi about five minutes past twelve, an let t' new yer in, same as my feyther used t' do."

"But thi feyther used allus come drunk; mun ah do t' same?" axt Bill.

"Bill;" hoo says, coppin him a slap o' t' yerhole wi' t' dishcleaut as lay just on t' taybull near, "durn't thee slander t' deeod, wots in their grave an cornt defend theirsels. If theau says a word agen my feyther aw'll make thee wish theau wor deeod too."

"Ah doo as it is," sed Bill, but very low; for he daren't let hur yer him.

Well, Bill seet eaut, at abeaut a quarter to eleven. When he geet i' Deansgate[1] he dropped across some pals o' his, members o' t' Tum Fowt Debatin Menociashun, to which he belunged, an' to which aw have the onher o' bein' sackretarry.

Of coarse they had a drink, an' then another after that to kee t' fust drink kumpany.

"Wot are yo dooin deaun here?" axed Bill.

"Oh we'n cum o' seein' t' New Yer in, that's aw," said Ben Roke.

"Wheer does it cum in?" axed Bill, who's rayther simpler than he met be.

"On t' Teaun Haw Square," said one.

"An heaw do they let it in?" inkwired Bill.

"I dunno," replied t' other, "but it comes in just at midneet an' t' band plays, an' –"

"Let's goo i' t' Wild Beast Show,"[2] cried Ben Roke.

"Agreed," yelled Joe Lung. He has a wooden leg, yo know.

Well they persuaded Bill t' goo in wi' 'em, an' wouldn't tak nay, so in they aw went.

"Wot's them?" sed Bill, as soon as they geet in', "them things wi' bustles[3] o' their backs, sithi?"

"Oh, them's camels; them things wot goes throo the eye of a needle, i' scripter," sed Ben.

"That's aw my eye," sed Bill, "aw'st noan swallow that, – Hello," – an he gan o' jump eaut o' t' road o' th' elefant wot were just comin reaund wi' hauve a dozen kids on its back.

"By gum," he sed, "that's a big un. What do they caw that?"

"A helefant," answered Ben.

"A hell-what?" sed Bill, "no cussin, en; that's noan it I know, theau'rt tryin t' have me."

"I tell thee it's a helefant, an' it is."

"Well it's a quare beast, for sure, wi a' arm on its face isted of a nose, an' yers like parashoots."[4]

Then they proceeded for t' examine t' monkeys which amused 'em very much, only Bill wur a bit astonisht becos ther wur no Italian organ grinders wi' 'em, as he thowt they allus went together.

Just as they were gooin t' look at wolves performin, there was a sheawt, "Lion loase! Lion's escaped!"

Then they were a roosh for t' dur. Bill were knockt deawn, an' his yed went slap in a bucket o' whitewash wot they'd bin usin in t' menadghery.[5] He nearly fainted for he thowt as one o' t' wild beasts had owt on him. His mates pick't him up, an' hurried eawt o' show. When they get eawtside they fun it wur a fawse alarm.

Bill wur trembling aw o'er. "Aw'm gooin whoam," he sed, but he could hardly ston up, an th' ale he'd had were beginning to tell. "Aw'm gooin whoam," he repeated, "while it's safe, before they caw t' millinarry eawt,"(he meant military).

Then there wur a lowf as the seed his yed, for he just poo'd his hat off for t' scratch it.

"By gum," said Ben Roke seriously, "it's turned Bill's hair grey."

"So it has," exclaimed t' others.

Bill felt ill. He felt at his yed too, an some o' t' whitewash coom off on his hond."

"An it's made him swet white too," said Joe Lung. "Theau mun have had a terrible freet, Bill. It would be wuss than yore Bet maulin thee."

"Aw'm gooin whoam," said Bill, an off he seet i' mortal terror un suspense. Beein abeaut three parts gone it took him aw his time t' get alung. He let o' one of his pals, an were trated to another drink.

"Wot's do wi' th' yed, Bill," axed his companion in a bit o' surprise.

"Why,' sed Bill, "we were in't wild beast show, an' a fawse alarm geet loase eawt o' its cage, and knocked me deawn, an' mi face turnt grey wi' it."

"A fawse alarm geet loase! That mun be a new addition to t' show. Ah never yert o' sich a beast before. But theau'd better get whoam an' see somebody abeaut it fust thing i' t' morning," said t' other.

Bill seet off agen. Once or twice he narrowly escaped bein' lockt up, he were so unstiddy, but he manig'd keep on his feet. He lost his hat, though.

It was abeaut one o'clock in' t' morning when he reached whoam. His wife had bin waitin', "nussin her wrath to keep it warm,"[6] and Bill were in for it.

He knock'd at t' dur.

"Is that thee?" sheauted Bet.

"Oi," he replied, "its'h me."

Hoo oppen't dur, but when hoo seed a fellay theer wi' a wite yed, there wur a catastrofy for that felly. Hoo landed eawt wi' her fist, un' fotched blood fro' his nose – fust smack, – hoo's a big lump is Bet Spriggs. Then hoo pummell'd him, screamin' aw't time, "I'll teach thee come here wi' a white yed, for t' let New Yer in, theau scamp, so hoo theau art. Theau seed mi husband goo eawt, so theau thowt they'd come and attack a defenceless woman, theau villain, theau burglar, theau."

"Howd on, Bet," yelled Bill, "I'm no burglar; I'm thi' husband, wot wed thee i' t' church."

"Eawr Bill has a black yed, an thoine's wite, theaw wretch. Dunnot think theau con desave me," an' her thump'd away.

"But I'm thi' husand. Didn't to send me eawt for t' let New Yer in? How'd on Bet; I'll tell thi' wot's made mi' hair wite. Aw've been freekunt. Wild beeasts geet eawt, a savage beggar, cawd a fawse alarm, knockt mi deawn, an' –"

"Oh, it *is* thee, then," hoo exclaimed, lookin at him.

"Ay, an theau owt thank God as aw'm saved, for –"

"So it is," hoo went on, interruptin him, "an' a bonny foo theau's bin makin o' thy sel, letting somebody daub thi' yed wi' lime, they greight gobbin. An wheer's t' pork, wha?"

"Aw forgeet it," faltered Bill.

"Aw'll forgeet thee! Thou's bin on t' spree. Come inside, an I'll tawk to thee."

Hoo dragged him in bi' t' yure o' t' yed, an' then hoo tawked to him wi' t' rowlin pin an' her tung combined, for a good bit. He look't pitiful when ah seed him t' day after. Bill says he'll never let New Yer in agen.

COMMONWEAL

H. S. S., 'A Dream of Queer Fishes (A Modern Prose Idyll)', *Commonweal*, 19 November 1887, pp. 372–3.

D., 'Scaring the Capitalists', *Commonweal*, 17 March 1888, pp. 84–5.

Thomas Barclay, 'Master and Man in Heaven', *Commonweal*, 23 May 1891, pp. 45–6.

Thomas Maubourg, 'A Mournful Fate', *Commonweal*, 3 October 1891, p. 123.

The *Commonweal* (1885–92) was founded by William Morris (1834–96) and first published as *Commonweal: The Official Journal of the Socialist League* in February 1885. It was published monthly until 1 May 1886, when it became a weekly publication. Its title changed to *Commonweal: A Journal of Revolutionary Socialism* in December 1890, when it reverted to monthly issues. It was edited by Morris between 1885 and 1890, during which time Edward Aveling (1849–98), Ernest Belfort Bax (1854–1926) and Morris's son-in-law Henry Halliday Sparling (1860–1924) consecutively acted as sub-editors. Frank Kitz (1849–1923) and David Nicholl (n.d.) edited the periodical from November 1889 until January 1891, when C. W. Mowbray (d. 1910) took over. Both the Socialist League and the *Commonweal* were gradually taken over by the anarchist faction of the group. The *Commonweal* returned to weekly issues from May 1891, again changing its subtitle to *A Revolutionary Journal of Anarchist Communism*. H. B. Samuels (d. 1933) was the final editor from May 1892 until it folded. Priced at one penny, it was published in London throughout its run. The first issue sold 5,000 copies, but subsequently it averaged sales of 2,000 to 3,000 during the mid-1880s.

The *Commonweal* published articles by many of the leading socialists of the period, including Ernest Belfort Bax, Eleanor Marx (1855–98), George Bernard Shaw (1856–1950) and Friedrich Engels (1820–95), as well as Morris and Aveling. Morris first published *A Dream of John Ball* (1886–7) and *News from Nowhere* (1890) as serials in the periodical. In the selection of stories presented in this volume, Thomas Barclay (b. 1852) was a Leicester socialist and a member of the SDF, ILP, Socialist League and the Anarchists at different periods of his activism, and he published his autobiography, *Memoirs and Medleys: The Autobiography of a Bottle Washer*, in 1923; H. S. S. (Henry Shakespear Stephens Salt, 1851–1939) was a humanitarian, vegetarian and Fabian whose pamphlet *The Logic of Vegetarianism* (1897) was claimed by M. K. Gandhi to have converted him to vegetarianism; Jean Maubourg was a pseudonym for Joseph-Eugene Fourniere (1857–1914), the French author, socialist and Possibilist; and the identity of 'D.' has not been discovered.

H. S. S., 'A Dream of Queer Fishes (A Modern Prose Idyll)' (1887)

"As the sleeping hound dreams of the chase, so the fisherman dreams of fishes." Thus says the old Greek poet Theocritus;[1] and that the same thing is true even to the present day may be seen from the strange dream dreamed by Joe, the Commissioner of Fisheries, as he was on his way to America to manage the fishy business of the firm of Salisbury and Co.,[2] whose service he had lately entered. Now Joe was thoroughly familiar with every kind of bait and fishing-tackle, having been apprenticed as a youth to a grand old fisherman, a regular old piscatorial hand, who carried on certain deep-sea fisheries, in which Joe soon became very expert, and was regarded by his master as his right-hand man. But unfortunately Joe had been always on the look-out for bettering himself, until at last he and the old man had words, and Joe rashly gave a month's notice and left the service in which he was doing so well. After this Joe had set up service on his own account, but finding it did not prosper, and being still very bitter against his old employer, he had become commercial traveller to the rival firm above-mentioned – a post for which he was specially qualified, through his proficiency in the piscatorial language usually known as "Billingsgate."[3]

So Joe was now in mid-voyage for America; and it happened that one night, after thinking a great deal by day of the fishy business on which he was embarked, he dreamed that he had fallen overboard and was surrounded by a vast multitude of fishes. Herring, mackerel, mullet, whiting, turbot, cod, haddock, soles, eels, oysters – every fish, great and small, was there, from a whale to a sprat. It was, in fact, a Public Meeting of sea-fish into which Joe had suddenly entered and just at that very moment the chair (a relic of a sunken vessel) was being taken by the Old Man of the Sea. It was a great annoyance to Joe in his dream to find that there was an Old Man even in this submarine assembly, especially as he seemed to detect in his features a lurking resemblance to his old employer; but what alarmed him still more was the hostile feeling which evidently animated the scaly meeting against himself. Each fish as he sailed round to his seat rolled a glassy eye on Joe with a very sinister expression; but Joe, smart fellow that he was, cocked his eyeglass in return and did his best to stare them out of countenance. Now fish, as we all know, are dumb; so in this Public Meeting there could not, on their part at least, be any delivery of speeches; yet, strange to say, Joe's conscience told him clearly enough what was the object of the meeting and how he himself was concerned with it. These fish were met for the purpose of demanding Home Rule, which he, as Commissioner of Fisheries, had the power of giving them – nay, more, which he had formerly pledged himself to give them (such was the extraordinary conviction by which he was possessed in his nightmare) and had since broken his promise.

Every eye now turned on Joe, and there was a twinkle on the features of the Old Man of the Sea as he invited him by a courteous gesture to reply to the complaints which, though unspoken, were plainly understood. What was Joe to say, and in what language could he address a company of fishes? Suddenly the happy thought occurred to him that he might address them in Billingsgate; so, leaping on an old fragment of a wreck, he poured out one of his vigorous harangues. The upshot of his speech, as far as it could afterwards be remembered – for, as is the way in dreams, it was rather vague and illogical – was that the Home Rule he had once promised them was not what they now demanded, but *Canadian* Home Rule, and that as they were a shoal of rascally, gaping, cold-blooded conspirators, he was now determined not to give them any Home Rule at all. He further managed to recommend them, in choicest Billingsgate, one and all to go about their business – the herrings to be cured, the mackerel to be pickled, the oysters to be scalloped, the cod to be crimped, the lobsters to be potted, and the eels to be skinned alive. Such was Joe's spirited oration; but if the truth be told, he soon repented of it, for he quickly found that he had got a pretty kettle of fish on his hands. So far from knocking under to Joe's bluster, the fish had one and all got their backs – or rather, their dorsal fins – up, and came round him in vast numbers, with the evident intent of making him food for fishes. In vain poor Joe, who now inwardly cursed himself for his temerity, entreated them to shake fins and be friends again, promising to use his influence with his new employer to obtain for each one of them three acres of good submarine pasturage and a sea-cow.[4] But they would have none of it – nothing but Home Rule would satisfy them, and it seemed even that was now to be preceded by the execution of Joe. For at a signal from the Old Man of the Sea, whose face wore a stern yet half-amused expression, a sword-fish appeared on the scene, while two large eels, even more slippery than Joe himself, began to pinch Joe and lead him towards a block of water-logged timber which lay on the ocean floor. It was a fearful moment; for, as is usual in nightmare, Joe could stir neither hand nor foot, and even his voice failed him as he tried to call aloud to his old pals to come to his assistance. However, just as the sword-fish was about to strike, Joe woke with a cry and found himself once more in his comfortable cabin.

Such was Joe's dream, which he remembered for a long time afterwards, the thing which dwelt longest in his memory being perhaps the sort of pitying half-smile on the face of the Old Man of the Sea when poor Joe, in the extremity of his despair, offered three acres and a sea-cow as a substitute for Home Rule which he had first promised and afterwards refused.

D., 'Scaring the Capitalists' (1888)

I was not long ago at a Socialist lecture, where I heard the wrongs of the workers explained and the tyranny of the capitalist fiercely denounced. From my own experience, I knew that the workman's portion is by no means a pleasant one. I, though as well educated as the best of workmen, receive very low wages, and often am on short time; and most of my companions are in the same state. But I thought it was just possible that if the Socialists denounced the capitalists too much, that these last would leave the country and take their capital with them, and so make our position worse than it is to-day; so I put a question to the lecturer, asking him whether it was not unwise to frighten capitalists, as if they got alarmed they would leave the country and take their capital with them. The lecturer replied very vigorously that it would be a good thing if the capitalists would go, and take with them what little ready money they had; but as for taking their capital, it was impossible. How could they ship a railway, a tunnel, a cotton or woollen mill, or a coal mine or a blast furnace? Let them go, by all means, said he; they are so many mouths whose hands won't work and whom we have to support. I was not convinced just at the moment, but thought carefully over the matter as I went home; and when I fell asleep I had a remarkable dream, which I very vividly remembered in the morning. The workmen had been continually holding meetings in Lancaster – the town where I work – and all over the country they seem to have been doing the same, to such an extent that the capitalists were alarmed and called a conference at Lancaster to consider the position. I was at work in the hall where they met and had an opportunity of seeing the whole performance. As usual, there was a great dinner, to which some five or six hundred of the richest men in England sat down. The conference went on over the dinner, and the idea was that the best way to teach the men a lesson was for a few of the largest employers to leave the country for time. "No doubt," said one fat old fellow with a red nose, most likely a City of London alderman, "the men will soon want us back, and we will be able to make our own terms."

"Oh, but," objected one, "what is to become of my mills in the meantime suppose I go?"

"Oh, you must take your capital with you."

"Confound it! I can't ship bricks and mortar, and the machinery. Why, taking it down, shipping, and fitting it up again would cost more than it's worth. I can't see that would do at all."

"Well," said another, "so far as I can see, we are quite at the mercy of these fellows of ours. It's that confounded education. I always said that was a bad thing. I knew that the people would find out at last, if we gave them anything of an education, that they could do without us. I think we'll have to give in and do our share of the work."

"That's all humbug," said a hook-nosed, dapper little man. "The workmen's committee have sent a deputation to confer with us; we can humbug them a little longer."

"They are not such fools as you think."

"Leave them to me."

In came the deputation. The men had an independent air, as if they were masters of the situation, and did not intend to be trifled with. The capitalists drew themselves up and looked in their most imposing manner at the members of the deputation, hoping no doubt to frighten them as they had often done before. However, little impression was made on the men, so at last the little hook-nosed man opened the proceedings.

"Well, men, I understand you have come to a better state of mind."

"Exactly," said the deputation.

"You now understand what our position is?"

"We do."

"And consequently are ready to accept our terms?"

"Oh no, we understand your position now."

"Well, so you see you can't do without us?"

"Not at all. We have discovered that we can not only do without you, but have found out that you are a useless burden, which we don't intend to be troubled with any longer."

"What, you blockhead!" roared a pursey-mouthed old blow-hard, whom I noticed a little while before stuffing himself at an alarming rate with venison in aspic, from Lewis deer-forest very likely. "What would you do without us? Who would employ you? Why, my dinner gives employment to half a dozen men every day: what would they do if I were to go?"

"They would have more time to prepare their own."

"Where would they get the money from?"

"From their labour."

"But if I go I will take all my capital with me. I have my portmanteau with me, and if you are not prepared to submit to my terms I shall leave the country."

"All right, old boy, you hook it, and take your portmanteau with you."

"I certainly will, if you continue so impudent; but I will show you what is in it, so that you may understand what my going really means." The fussy old gent opened his portmanteau, which was full of deeds, mortgages, consol certificates. "See," he said, "I'll take these with me."

"Very well, sir, they'll do to light the fire with."

"What!" roared the old swell, "they are worth half a million."

"Oh, I would not give half a crown for the lot mister. If you are only going to take these old papers with you, we won't raise any objections."

"Why, man, you must be mad," said the old usurer, holding up a piece of parchment; "do you see that? Why, that represents the largest coal mine in Durham."

"Oh, you can't get much coal out of it, though. You are not going to take the mine with you, are you?"

"What? But I'll shut it up."

"Oh, you will. Are you going to do it yourself?"

"Me do it! Of course not; I'll pay someone to attend to that."

"Oh," interrupted the capitalist that had previously advised the company to submit to the workers' term, "don't you know that you can't hire men in Durham to obey your orders?"

"Can't I?" he retorted, incredulously.

"No, of course not. You don't seem to understand, sir, how extremely serious the crisis is. The workers absolutely decline to support us any longer; they ignore all our orders, and treat our parchments as so much waste paper."

"You have described the position exactly," said the spokesman of the workmen's delegation.

"What about the Government?" roared the corpulent gentleman; "are they going to do nothing to protect our property?"

"What can they do? Half the soldiers have taken sides with the people, the other half are by no means anxious to risk their lives, and the police are all under the order of the municipalities, and won't carry out any Government instructions. Besides I hear that elections are going on, and a Socialist government in process of formation."

"Well, in that case I'll certainly leave the country." "And I, too," "I, too," was shouted from all parts of the hall.

"Well, you can go if you like, gentlemen," said a delegate, "if you can get any one to carry you across the ocean, but I may say we will be glad if you will stay with us and earn your living. We don't intend swindling you as you swindled us."

"I never swindled a man in my life," said the stout man, evidently much hurt.

"We won't quarrel about words. You made what you called a profit out of us, which comes to the same thing. Now if you like to stay with us you will get all you earn for yourself; all we propose doing is to prevent you taking any of our earnings."

"Now, sir, I won't be trifled with any longer. Do you know whom you are addressing? Do you know that I am the largest mine-owner in the North?"

"No, I don't. You were, but that you know, Sir Jabez, is all over now."

"My mines confiscated, you mean. By what authority? The Government will deal with you and those like you very severely –"

"We won't waste time, Sir Jabez, discussing about our authority. The people have resumed, so I prefer to phrase it, possession of their mines, mills, lands, etc., and have resolved that all able-bodied adults shall earn their living. Are you an able-bodied man, Sir Jabez?

"I am; of course you see I am."

"Well, then our ultimatum is that you and those like you must earn your living if you are to remain in England."

"I shall leave the country!"

"Well, gentlemen, are you all going to follow Sir Jabez's example?"

Loud cries of "Yes! Yes!" "No! No!" "We will, of course; we'll follow Sir Jabez!"

The din was indescribable, very like a row in the Stock Exchange I once saw when I was repairing the roof at a time when the market was excited; no one could judge what the feeling of the majority was; so a member of the conference suggested that some one should propose a motion to the meeting.

It was a long time before this person could get the meeting to proceed in an orderly manner, but at last Sir Jabez moved "that the propertied classes should leave the country." The Hon. Auberon Herbert moved, and the Rt. Hon. Charles Bradlaugh[1] seconded an amendment to the effect "that they should stay and organise to defend their property." One of the intending emigrants asked the movers of the amendment what forces they could command. Mr. Bradlaugh stated that on a previous occasion at a demonstration in Hyde Park he had armed the N.S.S. with cudgels, and could do it again; but on further enquiry the information was elicited that the Rt. Hon. Gent. had had his cudgel taken from him on that occasion, and was rather maltreated with his own weapon. Another treatment found more supporters, "That the terms of the men should be accepted;" but there was a large number of dissentients. Amendment after amendment was proposed, until it became evident that the capitalists were hopelessly divided, and that no common basis for action could be found. The delegates were highly amused at the antics of their recent bosses, but the time had come for them to take action.

"Gentlemen," said the spokesman peremptorily, "you must immediately come to a decision, and in order that you may have full information I may tell you that news has just been received of strong risings of the people in the large cities of the United States and France, so that if you go there you will be treated just the same as if you remain here."

By far the greater number agreed to the second amendment, but a small group were seen in one corner frantically gesticulating about the rights of property, among whom I noticed the Earl of Wemyss, A. J. Balfour, Auberon Herbert, George Howell, and Mr. Bradlaugh.[2] The idea of Mr. Bradlaugh being in such odd company made me laugh so much that my dream came to an abrupt conclusion. I was very sorry, because I should have liked to have been able to have followed the tactics of this queer group in its war against the Commonweal.

Altogether, the dream was an interesting psychological study. I often attended meetings, and sometimes dreamed of them. Evidently it was the curious turn given to my thoughts by reflecting on the differences between capitalists and capital caused by the Socialist lecturer's speech, together with the alarming state of the country, that caused me to have such a strange dream. Now that I am quite awake, I feel that my ideas regarding capitalists have materially altered; I no longer see them to be so *essential for the production of wealth* as I used to, and I have little doubt that a careful enquiry will induce me to accept many more of the Socialist's positions when I get to understand them, and I venture to urge on my fellow workmen the necessity of looking themselves into these matters, and not leaving all their thinking to be done by money-bags and scheming agitators, who have done and are doing the country so much harm.

Thomas Barclay, 'Master and Man in Heaven' (1891)

Employer (*Mr. De Tompkins*) and Workman (*Jack Smith*) *meet for the first time since shuffling off this mortal coil.*

Jack Smith. Hallo, Mr. De Tompkins! *Is* it Mr. De Tompkins? How are you, sir? You're looking younger and, and, not so proud as when I used to work for you down on earth.

    De Tompkins. Mr. Smith, isn't it? (*Reddening and confused*).

    J. S. I'm the man, sir.

    De T. Ah, Mr. Smith, I don't *feel* proud now. We're all equals here as you know. How much stouter and better you're looking!

    J. S. Yes, I didn't look as well when I worked for you, because we used to run so short; why some parts o' the year I hadn't enough to eat. It was hard nuts for me and the old woman, I can tell you; we couldn't let the kids go without grub.

    De. T. No, I suppose not.

    J. S. It was very hard that time as your overlooker sacked me 'cos I was thought to be the leader in asking for that advance. I went months without a job; and everything went out o' the house, to the bed as was under us.

    De. T. O well, let bygones *be* bygones, my dear fellow. I never expected we were going to pass eternity together, or you shouldn't have had a life of that sort – I'd have looked into the thing.

    J. S. You didn't think us hands were goin' to be damned in *this* life as well as upon earth, did you?

    De. T. No, no; I never thought anything about it at all.

    J. S. Ah, if ye only knowed how we hated that overlooker o' yours, and you too for listenin' to him and never listenin' to us! I can't forget it. Of course, I've got no bad feelin' now – I *can't* have in Heaven – but you didn't look on me as a man, now did you, Mr. De Tompkins?

    De. T. I didn't look on you as an equal, anyhow – but, if you knew all, Mr. Smith, you would not think so hard of me; and if, as I said a minute ago, I'd thought of the fact of us being companions up here, why – well, I'd have gone round to other rich men and entreated them to put their goods along with mine, and to throw the lot into a common fund, and we'd have shared with you, and stopped robbing you. I'd got a hundred – aye, a thousand times more than was good for *me*.

J. S. And the want of some of that nearly lost me Heaven. Poverty made me sometimes mean and grasping, and sometimes hopeless and careless. I used to doubt whether there *was* a God as made me slave and suffer, while them as never worked could all'us enjoy themselves and never had to fret nor trouble about nought. I don't understand it even now.

De T. Ah, well, I went nearer losing Heaven through possessing the money than you did for the want of it. It made me think I must the favourite of God, because he permitted me to *be* rich; and I thought I was generous when I built that wing of St. Michael's Church with some of the money made out of the labour of the poor. You've no notion how corrupting riches *are*, how vain, and selfish, and thoughtless they make a man. I don't want to talk about the reason why God took pity on me, but I tell you it was a miracle that I got in here at all.

J. S. Ah, well, it's all over, but it's very funny we should be equals.

De T. I'm not so sure about being equals. I hear that in the third Heaven an agitator has just been making a proposition that those who served and suffered in the last world should be masters, and the former masters their servants, not for all eternity, of course, but for some years. For my own part I don't deny that there does need to be some compensation.

J. S. O, I shan't agree to that. As you said, let bygones *be* bygones. I shouldn't like anybody to wait on me, I've never been used to it. If there's anything to do let's all take a hand in it. If it wasn't right for us to be under you, neither would it be for you to be under us. Let's go towards the thrones of the Cherubim and get to know whether the Almighty's likely to favour such a proposal. I don't think He will. I can't bear the notion of anybody polishing my crown; I should fly from it while I'd got a feather left me. If God's pardoned some o' you rich men, I should think we can be as generous as Him. Besides, if he hadn't allowed you to *be* rich you never could ha' been. I shall be at the next meeting in number three Heaven and have something to say; meanwhile, unsling your harp, old fellow, and let's have a tune.

Thomas Maubourg, 'A Mournful Fate' (1891)

"What Dos't Thou, Labourer?"

— "I rise at dawn, when the cocks are crowing their last watches; when the horizon has hardly tinged the slopes. I join my big red oxen, and go to till the soil which is hardened by a torrid summer. My hard feet are cut and blood-stained from the sharp stubble, into the furrows so painfully traced, and at the bottom of which sleeps the scattered and hidden manure, I pitch the wheat, the oats, the barley, and the rye. When winter comes the north wind bites, and my hands chap till they are as knotty as the trunk of an old maple, while I trim the vine for ever in the fields; from winter which strips hill and plain, to summer which covers them with harvest. From summer to winter, from early dawn till night sets in, I work almost without intermission. I eat black bread and salt pork. Sometimes – very rarely – on holidays, I taste a little fresh meat."

— "And whither goest thou?"

— "To ruin. The phylloxera has devoured my vines, and the wheat which I am obliged to sell at a low price, I must buy back at a high price. My land is mortgaged. I am tracked by creditors, sometimes as unfortunate as myself; and by the tax-collector who demands that which I cannot pay him. I am going to destitution and to ruin after having laboured hard all my life."

* *

*

— "What dos't thou, slum-dweller?"

— "What do I do? I am astir with the light. I shuffle hastily into my poor duds,[1] and with tired frames, the wife and myself set out for the body of the town, confounded by the multitude of early risers swinging along with heavy tread, rushing to be engulfed in the factories from which shriek the whistles of the greasy, well-fed, well-cared-for engines. From morning to night I toil hard and fast for a mere pittance, and these times of toil are my happiest. When the stoppage throws me on the streets, I suffer hunger; and hear the wife and little ones asking for bread."

— "And whither goes't thu?"

— "To miserable old age. My wages hardly suffice for daily sustenance. In times of crisis, I pawn my watch, the counterpane, everything. Sometimes also, I go with bursting heart to lay in the cemetery a child dead from famine-fever. I am going where all the other workers like me go, to misery, after having toiled continuously."

* *
*

— "What dos't thou, little workwoman, frail darling seamstress with the large eyes whose pupils are dilated by anemia, with the frizzy golden locks that make an aureole round the pale chlorotic face?"

— "What do I do? The same as my companion, the sweetheart, my brother, and my father; I hasten to the centre of Paris – Paris, which laughs, and shouts, and dazzles. Shortly after day-break I draw on my down-at-heel boots, put on coquettishly my old dress, which is nevertheless always in the latest fashion. I confine my rebellious ringlets in the hat trimmed during the spare hours of Sunday. Then I trot off to the workshop. Where, from twelve to fourteen hours, without sun or fresh air, my little hands ply the needle; sewing costly stuffs, making artificial flowers into brilliant wreaths, burnishing gold and silver, helping to turn the fly-wheel of the machinery that is slowly killing me. At midday there is a poor and hurried meal that does not make rich blood."

— "Where am I going? When the hard day's work is done, home with my companions through the streets and boulevards sparking with light; and merry or sad, I am pursued and beset by young and old who make me tempting offers. I hurry towards the faubourg,[2] towards my garret. My companions, alas! are separated from me. In time of stoppage, some go to the hospitable to cough away their lungs and sleep upon the dissecting table; others go to furnished mansions ... Who can say where?"

— "Where am I going? Where do we daughters of the workers go to? Some to the streets! ... The majority, where their fellows go: to work, to suffer, to listen in bad times to the wailing of little children."

— "Where am I going? Where do poor wretches like me go to, but to misery, having laboured and suffered?"

* *
*

— "What dos't thou, solider?"

— "I live in the barracks and hear the rude words of the officer, I perform my exercise and like a passive machine, I must obey, I think low and I speak still lower, I have no money and gloomily I tramp the streets of the garrison towns, I handle the tools that kill, and I regret the tools that give life. Every bugle-call reminds me that my will is dead."

— "Whither go you?"

— "Whither? Whithersoever they drive me, to exercise, to drudgery. To a military march. At a signal, to the frontier. Perhaps some evening I shall lie stretched on a plain moaning with fever; or it may be, stiff, my face imbedded in a pool of blood. Whither am I going? If I escape, to the workshop, to the fields, where my brothers are; and like them, to misery, after having worked and suffered."

* *
*

— "Whither go ye – all who have neither land nor houses, nor money, nor tools?"

— "Whither go we? Whence we came; to labour and to misery! We are the immense multitude who have created everything – produced all; yet possess nothing, and reap only misfortune, though we cry but for a little less fatigue and a little more bread."

(Translated from "La Révolte.")

JUSTICE

William Morris, 'An Old Fable Retold', *Justice*, 19 January 1884, p. 2.

'Utile Dulci', 'Fables for the Times – I: The Monkeys and the Nuts', *Justice*, 11 October 1884, p. 2.

Anon., 'Fables for the Times – II: The Political Economist and the Flowers', *Justice*, 18 October 1884, p. 2.

Anon., 'Archie Cameron's Success', *Justice*, 14 November 1885, p. 6.

D. F. Hannigan, 'Aristos and Demos', *Justice*, 30 April 1887, pp. 2–3.

H. J. Bramsbury, 'A Working Class Tragedy', *Justice*, Chapter I, 9 June 1888, pp. 2–3; Chapter II, 16 June 1888, pp. 2–3; Chapter III, 23 June 1888, pp. 2–3; Chapter IV, 30 June 1888, pp. 2–3; Chapter V, 7 June 1888, pp. 2–3; Chapter VI, 14 July 1888, pp. 2–3; Chapter VII, 21 July 1888, pp. 2–3; Chapter VIII, 28 July 1888, pp. 2–3; Chapter IX, 4 August 1888, pp. 2–3; Chapter X, 11 August 1888, pp. 2–3; Chapter XI, 18 August 1888, pp. 2–3; Chapter XII, 25 August 1888, pp. 2–3; Chapter XIII, 1 September 1888, pp. 2–3; Chapter XIV, 8 September 1888, pp. 2–3; Chapter XV, 15 September 1888, pp. 2–3; Chapter XVI, 22 September 1888, pp. 2–3; Chapter XVII, 29 September 1888, pp. 2–3; Chapter XVIII, 5 October 1888, pp. 2–3; Chapter XIX, 13 October 1888, pp. 2–3; Chapter XX, 20 October 1888, pp. 2–3; Chapter XXI, 27 October 1888, pp. 2–3; Chapter XXII, 3 November 1888, pp. 2–3; Chapter XXIII, 10 November 1888, pp. 2–3; Chapter XXIV, 17 November 1888, pp. 2–3; Chapter XXV, 24 November 1888, pp. 2–3; Chapter XXVI, 1 December 1888, pp. 2–3; Chapter XXVII, 8 December 1888, pp. 2–3; Chapter XXVIII, 15 December 1888, pp. 2–3; Chapter XXIX, 22 December 1888, p. 4; Chapter XXX, 29 December 1888, p. 4; Chapter XXXI, 6 January 1889, p. 4; Chapter XXXII, 12 January 1889, p. 4; Chapter XXXIII, 19 January 1889, p. 4; Chapter XXXIV, 26 January 1889, p. 4; Chapter XXXV, 2 February 1889, p. 4; Chapter XXXVI, 9 February 1889, p. 4; Chapter XXXVII, 16 February 1889, p. 4; Chapter XXXVIII, 23 February 1889, p. 4; Chapter XXXIX, 2 March 1889, p. 4; 9 Chapter XL, 9 March 1889, p. 4; Chapter XLI, 16 March 1889, p. 4; Chapter XLII, 23 March 1889, p. 4; Chapter XLIII, 30 March 1889, p. 4; Chapter XLIV, 6 April 1889, p. 4; Chapter XLV, 13 April 1889, p. 4.

Justice: The Organ of the Social Democracy (1884–1925) was the weekly official periodical of the Social Democratic Federation, founded by a donation of £300 from Edward Carpenter (1844–1929) and published by Henry Hyde Champion's (1859–1928) Modern Press. For the first few weeks Charles Fitzgerald (n.d.) was editor, until SDF chairman Henry Mayers Hyndman (1842–1921) took editorial control. Hyndman handed the editorial responsibilities to Harry Quelch (1858–1913) in 1886, after many on the SDF's executive board demanded a more democratic organization for the group and its periodical. *Justice* was initially priced at twopence, but complaints about the cost forced a reduction to one penny after the second issue. Sales reached peaks of between 3,000 and 4,000 during the Trafalgar Square demonstrations in 1887, falling to around 1,300 by the end of the 1880s. It did not have a high literary content in comparison to some of the other socialist periodicals of this era, and short stories and poetry were published on a more regular basis than longer serializations. Although it was criticized for its dry presentation, it published work by many of the leading socialists, including Annie Besant (1847–1933), George Bernard Shaw, John Burns (1858–1943), Ernest Belfort Bax and William Morris.

This volume reprints for the first time H. J. Bramsbury's 'A Working Class Tragedy', which was the second of only four serialized fictions published in *Justice* between 1884 and 1914. The first serialization was 'Darker than Death: A Tale of the Russia of To-Day' by James Skipp Borlase (1839–1902), published between 27 June and 14 November 1885. Borlase was a fairly prolific writer of newspaper and periodical serial fiction, but there is no evidence he had any involvement in the SDF; therefore his serial was probably purchased for *Justice*. There is some evidence to suggest that 'H. J. Bramsbury' might have been a pseudonym for Hyndman,[1] and so this serial was selected for inclusion in this volume. There was a greater tendency for authors publishing in early issues of *Justice* to publish either anonymously or under a pseudonym than in other or later periodicals. This is evident from the selection included in this volume: of the six pieces of fiction, two short stories were published anonymously and the authors are unidentified; two were published pseudonymously (H. J. Bramsbury and 'Utile Dulci'; the latter pseudonym, taken from *utile et dulci*, meaning useful and pleasant, is by an unidentified author whose story Hyndman commends in *The Record of an Adventurous Life* but states 'I have forgotten the name of the writer'[2]); and two are published under the author's name.

William Morris had achieved fame through the publication and popularity of his poetry, including *The Defence of Guinevere, and Other Poems* (1858), *The Earthy Paradise* (1866–70) and *Sigurd the Volsung and the Fall of the Niblungs* (1876), before he joined the SDF in 1883. His interest and involvement in architecture and design, through the firm Morris & Co., dovetailed with his socialist politics, as he believed all design should be both beautiful and functional. Morris began to move away from Hyndman's parliamentary vision of change, and in December 1884 he and nine other members of the SDF executive board left to form the Socialist League, publishing the first edition of the *Commonweal* in February 1885. All of his famous socialist fiction and poetry were published through the *Commonweal*, including *A Dream of John Ball* (1886–7) and *News from Nowhere* (1890). The Socialist League and the *Commonweal* were gradually taken over by the Anarchist faction of the group, and before his death Morris began working on a project to unite all British socialist groups. The final named author, Denis F. Hannigan (n.d.), was a reviewer and translator of (among other works) Gustave Flaubert's (1821–80) *Sentimental Education* (1898) and *Boubard and Pecuchet* (n.d.) and Honoré de Balzac's (1799–1850) *The Love Letters* (1901).

Notes
1. See Mutch, "'A Working Class Tragedy'" for further discussion on Hyndman as author.
2. Hyndman, *The Record of an Adventurous Life*, p. 335.

William Morris, 'An Old Fable Retold' (1884)

In the days before man had completely established his domination over the animal world, the poultry of a certain country, unnamed in my record, met in solemn conference in the largest hall they could hire for their money: the period was serious, for it was drawing near Christmas, and the question in the debate partook of the gravity of the times; for, in short, various resolutions, the wording of which has not come down to us were to be moved on the all important subject, '*with what sauce shall we be eaten?*'

Needless to say that the hall was crowded to suffocation, or that an overflow meeting (presided over by working-class leaders) was held on the neighbouring dung-hill.

All went smoothly; the meeting was apparently unanimous and certainly enthusiastic, abundant wisdom was poured out on the all-important question, and the hearts of all glowed with satisfaction at the progress of the race of – poultry. The very bantam-*hens* were made happy by the assurance that their claims to cackling were seriously considered.

But when the hands of the clock were pointing to ten minutes to ten the excited audience, as they recovered from the enthusiasm produced by one of the great speeches of the evening, saw on the platform beside the chairman a battered looking and middle-aged barn-door cock, who they perceived was holding forth in a lugubrious voice, praising the career and motives of every advanced politician of the poultry yard. This bored the audience a good deal, but being used to it they stood it with patience for some time, till at last the orator's voice got rather clearer and louder, and he spoke somewhat as follows: – "Sir, I know I have little right to air my own theories (cheers) after the remarkably and clear exposition of the rights of poultry, which has been delivered in various ways on this platform to-night (loud cheers), but I am free to confess that one idea has occurred to me which seems to have escaped the more educated minds of our leaders to-night; (cries of Oh, Oh) – the idea is this!" Here he stopped dead, and amid ironical cheers tried nervously to help himself to water from the long-ago emptied decanter, then at last blurted out in a trembling, shrieking voice not without a suspicion of tears in it; "In short *I don't want to be eaten at all*: is it poss—"

But here a storm of disapproving cries broke out, amongst which could be heard loudest the words 'practical politics!' 'county franchise,' 'great liberal party,' 'municipal government for – Coxstead!' which at last all *calmed* themselves down into a steady howl of 'question, question!' in the midst of which the ragged, middle-aged cock withdrew, apparently not much more depressed than when he first stood up.

After his departure the meeting ended in all harmony, and a resolution was passed with great enthusiasm that the conclusions come to as embodied in the foregoing resolutions should be engrossed and forwarded to the farmer's wife (or widow was it?) and the head poulterer.

A rumour has reached us that while there were doubts as to the sauce to be used in the serving up, slow stewing was settled on as the least revolutionary form of cookery.

Moral: Citizens, pray draw it for yourselves.

'Utile Dulci', 'Fables for the Times – I: The Monkeys and the Nuts' (1884)

A colony of monkeys, having gathered a store of nuts for the winter, begged their Wise Ones to distribute them. The Wise Ones reserved a good half for themselves, and distributed the remainder amongst the rest of the community, giving to some twenty nuts, to others ten, to others five, and to a considerable number none. Now, when those to whom twenty had been given complained that the Wise Ones had kept so many for themselves, the Wise Ones answered, "Peace, foolish ones, are ye not much better off than those who have ten?" And they were pacified, and to those who objected, having only ten, they said, "Be satisfied, are there not many who have but five?" and they kept silence. And they answered those who had five, saying, "Nay, but see ye not the number who have none?" Now when these last made complaint of the unjust division and demanded a share, the Wise Ones stepped forward and exclaimed to those who had twenty, and ten, and five, "Behold the wickedness of these monkeys! Because they have no nuts they are dissatisfied, and would fain rob you of those which are yours!" And they all fell on the portionless monkeys and beat them sorely.

Moral. – The selfishness of the moderately well-to-do blinds them to the rapacity of the rich.

Anon., 'Fables for the Times – II: The Political Economist and the Flowers' (1884)

A Political Economist, grown tired of writing books, bought a garden and resolved to devote himself to growing flowers on economic principles. The soil was very poor, but he sowed seeds and planted flowers, and bade them grow. They did their best; but in the summer they were but a sorry spectacle compared with those of the Ignorant Man in the next garden. The Ignorant Man, looking over the fence one day, and seeing a heap of manure in the Professor's garden, said to him, "Sir, why do you not improve the soil of your garden by spreading over it that manure in order that your flowers may have strength and beauty?" "My good fellow," responded the Professor, "you are a most immoral and unscientific gardener, though I forgive you on account of your ignorance. What! Would you treat all the plants alike, the strong and the weak, the good and the bad? Nay, but let them contend among themselves for the soil which they have, and when I see plainly which of them flourish best in this poor soil, to them will I shortly give more manure than they will know what to do with!"

Moral. – It was the Ignorant Man who took the prize at the Flower Show.

Anon., 'Archie Cameron's Success' (1885)

Archie Cameron was one of the best fellows in the world personally; but his face bore the terrible word "failure" stamped upon it as plainly as though it were printed therein in letters of Brobdingnagian[1] type.

Whatever Archie "turned his hand to" or was connected with was bound to be a failure; he had dabbled in every profession under the sun and failed ignominiously in one and all. I had lost sight of him for some years, when I ran against him casually in a large manufacturing town, where to my intense astonishment he communicated to me the astounding fact that he had turned actor.

"Well," I said in reply, "with your education and appearance" – he was a tall handsome-looking fellow, standing over six feet high – "you ought to make a big success at it."

His reply was a sigh: it was the old story, it was not in Archie to make a success in anything. He had entered the theatrical profession as a last resource, possessing the enthusiasm and ambition which aspirants to histrionic honours generally possess, and with every hope that by means of application and hard study he might ultimately reach the top of the tree.

And he did study with a vengeance. Not content with the trivial "utility" characters which fell to his portion, he worked hard at the principal parts in the higher walks of the drama, and before he had been in the profession two year there was scarcely a leading character in legitimate tragedy or comedy which Archie was not thoroughly "up" in.

"For," he argued to himself, "I'm bound to get my chance in these parts some day, and it's as well to be prepared. I shall apply for leading business in a twelvemonth's time, and the previous study of the characters will be a wonderful help to me."

And Archie did apply for leading business; but to no purpose. He did not get it, for somehow theatrical managers, like the rest of the world, did not believe in him. His compeers distanced him quickly and rose to first-class positions, but poor Archie had to be content with his general utility, his miserable pittance and degrading surroundings, with no prospect of rising, no chance of fame. "Hope deferred maketh the heart grow sick,"[2] says the adage; but, though Archie's hope had been deferred for a whole life-time, his heart was too healthy to grow sick or despair, and he plodded on anxiously, hopefully, for he declared:

"If they would only give me one chance – just one – I know, I feel assured I should make a success."

But poor Archie never had a shadow of a chance to cheer him on his desolate journey; even his love-making was a failure, and after courting and being accepted by a pretty little girl in his own profession for upwards of two years, he learned that she had run away and married another fellow just a fortnight before the day appointed for his own wedding.

As time wore on, and the fates still proved unkind, hope grew fainter within him, and he had also ceased to pray for his "chance," as he termed it. Then, by a freak of fortune, it came to him when least expected.

He was fulfilling an engagement as "general utility" at a wretched little theatre in the North of England. Manager after manager had tried this house, but with the same results – bankruptcy; and its owners were undecided whether to pull it down or dispose of it to a body of religious enthusiasts, when an enterprising caterer – one Mr. Sharpleigh Beck, who was already the proprietor of two or three similar establishments in the same locality – offered them a nominal figure for the building as it stood, which the proprietors were only too glad to accept.

This man was noted for paying the lowest salaries, engaging the worst company, and being the most successful manager for many a mile; he was as arrant a rogue as ever breathed and an impudent scoundrel into the bargain; the lying announcements he would resort to in order to induce the public to patronize his theatre being really marvels of effrontery in their way.

It was at this theatre that Archie Cameron found himself fulfilling an engagement under the banner of this man, when one fine morning the town was startled by the appearance of some glaring posters which intimated to the public that Mr. Sharpleigh Beck had, at an enormous expense, entered into an arrangement with the eminent tragedienne Miss Constantia Leroy, of the principal London theatres, who would appear the following Monday in her favourite character of *Pauline*, in "The Lady of Lyons."[3]

The visit of a London star of such magnitude to so unimportant a town and theatre was an event of no little importance, and caused considerable excitement, not only among the townspeople, but also among the members of Mr. Sharpleigh Beck's "stock company," who were to have the honour of supporting the lady in question; and great was the anxiety to know how the parts would be allotted in the play in which she made her first appearance.

As usual, Archie found himself cast for the Second Officer, a part of some ten or dozen lines, which he had played for the past seven years, and which seemed likely to stick to him, limpet-like, until the end of the chapter. "Ah," he sighed, as he gazed ruefully upon the dirty little piece of paper called a "cast" pinned against the green-room wall, "if – if they had only given me *Claude*[4] for a change – but no matter!"

But *Claude Melnotte* was of course cast to the "leading man" of the company, one Mr. Horace Bowdler,[5] a gentleman to whom the fates had been much kinder than to Archie. He had had his chances, but had wilfully neglected them by reason of an "infirmity," which accounted for his being under the management of such a fourth-rate manager as Mr. Sharpleigh Beck.

The eventful morning at last arrived when the "star," attended by her maid and her secretary, walked into the theatre for rehearsal with all the arrogance and pomposity of a royal potentate. She was a large, showily dressed woman, with a haughty, imperious manner, and looked down upon her less fortunate brethren with a withering contempt, directing them in their duties in a cruelly offensive manner, to which they meekly submitted, with the exception of Mr. Horace Bowdler. He might have held as good a position as the "star " herself, had it not been for his "infirmity": and he felt that for a man of his calibre to be thus dictated to was lowering both to his personal and professional dignity. There were skirmishes betwixt *Claude* and *Pauline* respecting the arrangement of the stage business; as sure as ever Mr. Bowdler rehearsed his dialogue on the right hand side of the stage, the "star" would insist upon his rehearsing it all over again on the left. If Mr. Bowdler delivered a speech in one tone of voice, she would insist upon his delivering it again in another. Thus, during the rehearsal, there were many little passages of arms between them, which skirmishes ultimately led to a very serious catastrophe.

Mr. Bowdler's "infirmity" was not an uncommon one – in fact, it arose from a weakness for strong spirits. He had been remarkably sober for the past ten weeks, his standard beverage during that time having been claret and soda-water; but on this eventful morning he became so incensed that, at the termination of each disagreement, he deliberately betook himself to the bar of the Golden Lion, to find solace for his wounded dignity; and, as by the time the rehearsal was ended the said "disagreements" numbered about fourteen, it soon became evident that Bowdler was decidedly the worse for his frequent libations.

About six o'clock that evening a message was brought to the horror-stricken manager to the effect that his *Claude Melnotte* was helplessly intoxicated in the bar of the Golden Lion, and unable to perform!

Here was a pretty dilemma! The company had all arrived to dress for their respective parts, the street was already filled by an anxious crowd waiting to do homage to Miss Constantia Leroy and sympathise with the sorrows of *Pauline*, and there was no *Claude Melnotte* to support her!

Mr. Sharpleigh Beck was at his wits end, and as he stood upon the stage surrounded by his company, looked the very picture of helpless despair. What was to be done? To close the theatre and disappoint the public would be ruin. *Pauline* could not possibly appear without a *Claude*, and he did not dare to deceive them by substituting another piece with his ordinary stock company. For once his fertile imagination failed to assist him, and he was, to use his own words, "in a terrible hole, and no mistake."

"I'll play *Claude*, if you like, Mr. Beck."

It was a quiet, deep voice which spoke close at his elbow that made the manager turn quickly on his heel.

"Eh, what? Why, bless my soul, who's that? What, you – you, Cameron, a utility man, attempt *Claude Melnotte*? Absurd – nonsense, you couldn't do it."

But, after a few minutes' conversation and explanation, the "utility man" succeeded in convincing Mr. Beck that he could do it. He was perfect in the words, and, with half an hour's rehearsal with the "star," might possibly be coached in the "business"; so the lady was abruptly summoned from the dressing-room and informed of the change in the cast.

At first she flew into a violent passion, refused to it at all, considered it an unwarrantable insult on Mr. Beck's part even to dream of playing *Pauline* to a "utility man's" *Claude*, threatened to return to her hotel, pack up her trunks, and depart by the next train for London, and eyed Archie Cameron up and down with a withering glance of scorn and contempt. But the play-goers of the last town not having appreciated the abilities of Miss Constantia Leroy as highly as she had anticipated, and her pockets thus not being so well filled as they ought to have been, she was ultimately induced to see things in a different light.

Awfully nervous the poor fellow was when, arrayed in his peasant's blouse, with gun in hand,[6] he rushed on for his first entrance and saw the packed audience in front of him; and still more so when he stalked on in his prince's costume with the great London "star" hanging on his arm, the "star" who snubbed him so unmercifully at the wings. Before the act has half over, however, Archie forgot himself, his poverty, and his troubles, and became for the time being the enthusiastic lover the playwright had created. He forgot the painted, powdered representative beside him, with all her miserable little pomps and vanities, and saw only the poet's creation, *Pauline*, the worshipped idol of the peasant's dream, delivering his speeches with such fervour and making love so naturally that, when the act-drop descended and the "star" took her call before it on one side of the stage, Archie was summoned forth to receive the enthusiastic applause of the audience on the other.

His next act was even more favourably received; and, when he made his appearance on his return from the battle-field, looking supremely handsome in his military garb, his reception was so warm that even the "star" condescended to unbend, and went so far as to admit that he was "not so bad."

When the curtain finally descended that night, and two or three representatives of the press and some of the principal inhabitants came behind the scenes and congratulated him, Archie Campbell[7] was so bewildered and excited with his success that he declared he scarcely knew whether he stood on his head or on his heels.

"To think I have waited all these years for this," he muttered as he buttoned his seedy paletot[8] over this chest and made his way home to his homely lodgings;

"and it has come at last. I knew I should make a success some day, and, by Jove, now I've done it."

And when he laid his head upon his pillow that night, he slept with his mind full of glorious visions of the future.

There was an early rehearsal called the next morning to perfect Archie in the minor details of the piece, which, owing to its great success, was to be repeated that night; and, punctually at the hour directed, his grimy old landlady clambered up the dilapidated staircase to rouse him from his slumbers. In vain her bony knuckles rapped upon the door of his chamber; there was no response. She knocked and knocked again with the same result; at length, thinking her lodger had been over-fatigued by his exertions of the previous night, she gave up her task in despair, and resolved to let him enjoy an extra half-hour's slumber.

"For heaven knows," the good dame muttered as she descended, "the poor fellow deeds it sorely!"

So the morning wore on, until the time arrived when Archie was due at the theatre; the company, manager, and star were all assembled on the dirty little stage, but still he came not. At length the manager grew uneasy at his absence, and Miss Constantia Leroy angry.

"I am not in the habit of visiting such places to be kept waiting for a parcel of utility people," she remarked. "Perhaps the young man is ill; you had better send a messenger and ascertain."

So a messenger started, in the person of Jack Powell, a sturdy young fellow of some six-and-twenty years, who was a grateful friend to Archie by reason of the many hints the latter had given him on his entrance into the profession three years before.

Jack passed the landlady of Archie's lodgings without a word. Ascending the staircase he knocked loudly at the door of his attic; then, receiving no reply, he knocked louder.

"Dear heart alive!" exclaimed the woman below, as she heard the sound of Jack's manly fist upon the panels of the door, "how soundly that lad do sleep! He mun[9] be mortal tired."

Then, still receiving no response, Jack turned the handle of the door, and, finding it locked, with one kick of his foot sent it crashing forward and burst into the room.

Archie Cameron did sleep soundly, for it was the sleep that knew no awakening in this world. The rays of the bright morning sun were streaming brilliantly through the dirty little skylight which was the only window the room boasted, and fell straight upon the worn, weary, stricken face now calm, peaceful, dead.

For he had passed away in his sleep in the very hour of his success.

D. F. Hannigan, 'Aristos and Demos' (1887)

Once upon a time there lived a mighty monarch whose name was Aristos. He ruled over millions of subjects by whose labour he acquired enormous wealth. He dwelt in a gorgeous palace, where hundreds of white slaves attended on him, and the honour of men and the chastity of women were sacrificed to his all-devouring passions. Though in his life he ignored every moral law, Aristos considered it indispensable to have an established religion in order to awe and intimidate the multitude by impressing on their minds the belief that there was a connection between monarchy and the divine government of the world. A crowd of obsequious priests paid homage to the sovereign, and urged upon the people the necessity of blind obedience. The monarch's authority was further strengthened by the intrigues and sophistries of cunning lawyers, who invented a number of false maxims calculated to deceive the credulous masses, and to bewilder even the wise and virtuous. Amongst other things they laid down that "the king can do no wrong"; and that even to conceive the idea of dethroning the reigning sovereign was an offence more heinous than murder, to punish which the most horrible form of death should be devised.

By this system of monopoly and self-deification, Aristos kept the toiling millions down, and it was only when some terrible calamity, such as famine or pestilence, aroused the people to a sense of their miserable condition that anyone dared to question the right of the monarch to oppress, tax, murder and degrade his subjects. So strong is the influence of custom that many of the poor and weak who were ground down to the earth by tyranny of Aristos looked upon him as something more than a man: else (they asked themselves) how could he have such unlimited power? A curious notion took possession of some minds as to the very colour of the royal blood. Inasmuch as the blood of common people was red, they assumed that the blood of a king must be blue, though they might as readily have assumed that it was yellow or black. A privileged class sprung up in the course of time which owed its social eminence to the favour of Aristos. This class consisted mainly of persons who devoted themselves to upholding the royal authority. Titles of nobility were conferred upon these persons and they were known as the aristocracy. Though they possessed no great or noble qualities and were, as a body, ignorant, cowardly and sensual, the aristocracy looked down on the rest of the king's subjects as their inferiors, and only addressed them in terms of opprobrium or contempt. As the greater portion of the population was kept necessarily in a condition of abject poverty in order that Aristos and his parasites might live in luxury and splendour, all who did not belong to the privileged class had to earn a wretched livelihood by work of the most distasteful and exhausting description. Some of them were employed in sweeping the streets of large cities; others worked as miners in the bowels of the earth; many had to become the hired slaves of the aristocracy, who treated them worse than horses or dogs. Gradually a few of the toiling multitude yearned for some change in their condition, and, in the effort to emancipate themselves from the thraldom of the aristocracy, they were sometimes driven into acts of violence. These manifestations of discontent were punished as crimes, and the toilers who indulged in them were either put to death or immured in prison for the rest of their lives. The result of this repression was to strike a temporary dread of the law into the hearts of the masses who lived, or tried to live, by menial work. The king had a large army for the maintenance of which he taxed his subjects, exacting payment from the poor as well as the rich. He also employed many thousands of police and gaolers to enforce the criminal code, by means of which he had succeeded, for a time at least, in intimidating the discontented workers. To the latter, under these circumstances, the struggle to free themselves from the misery of their lot seemed a hopeless one. Many of them in despair abandoned their ordinary occupations and enlisted as soldiers in the king's army, deeming it better to die on the field of battle than to perish by disease or starvation. If they had not been plunged in the densest ignorance, the masses would, no doubt, long ere this, have risen up in revolt against the system which enslaved and degraded them. To educate them would have been the first step towards freedom. For this reason, Aristos and the aristocracy made education such an expensive luxury that no poor man's child could afford to learn anything except merely to read and write. Even this scanty modicum of knowledge was shut out from most of them. Finding no other means of softening the bitter hardness of their lives, the toilers, in a wretched fashion, began to imitate the vices of the aristocracy, and too often lowered themselves to a greater depth than poverty could ever lower them to by drunkenness and debauchery. Thus arose a trade by which intoxicating liquors were supplied to the unhappy beings who could only procure those vile stimulates by depriving themselves and their families of food. Other trades sprang up, too, in the course of time, through the exigencies of the toiler's lot, such as that of the petty usurer, the pawnbroker, and the auctioneer. The extravagant tastes of the aristocracy gave rise to other departments of commerce such as the sale of jewellery and lace. Most of these traders were a hybrid race consisting of persons who had made some money by pandering to the aristocracy, while a few of them were members of the privileged class, who had from some cause or another become impoverished. The growth of a commercial class instead of improving the condition of the toilers made it much worse, for the traders imitated the vices of the aristocracy, and compelling those who were poorest in the community to work for them, ground them down until life became perfectly intolerable. Suicides amongst the toilers or their children were common occurrences; and when the aristocracy read of such things in the newspapers they only laughed.

It happened, however, that in spite of evil laws, young men amongst the toiling masses learned some of the truths of science almost starving themselves to procure books; and at length a few of them had the courage to publish their thoughts and to denounce the oppression of the privileged class. These young men were prosecuted and severely punished, but the seed they had sown bore fruit. The people's hearts had been stirred and they thirsted for liberty.

The time arrived when an emancipator was born in the midst of the struggling, starving multitude. His name was Demos. He was poor and apparently helpless, but a spirit of divine energy inspired him. He was strong, courageous, intelligent, loving and indomitable. Some people said he was an archangel and compared him to St. Michael,[1] but this was an idle superstition. He was only a man, but ah how much there is in that! Because he was a man he had no fear of Aristos and his myrmidons.[2] He defied and despised them. He saw that the vile monarch who had kept his brethren so long in bondage had relied altogether on the power of money. With money Aristos had hired soldiers and police to terrify and coerce the millions whom he called his subjects; with money he had bought the support of his parasites, the aristocracy; and by monopolising all forms of wealth he had left the multitude no resource but slavery or death. There was one thing, however, that Aristos had forgotten, namely that labour is the origin of all wealth, and that without it no wealth, however enormous, can be preserved. This great fact flashed on the clear brain of Demos. He grasped the whole problem with his far-seeing intellect, and he saw the true remedy for all the evil wrought during the long reign of Aristos. He called some of the other young men around him and spoke to them earnestly.

"My friends," he said, "let us organise labour! That is the lever which moves the world! No king, no tyrant, no capitalist, can compete with organised labour. Let these wealthy despots coop themselves up in their palaces and their mansions, without us they cannot exist; their luxuries, their food, their lives depend on us. They have trampled on us for years. They have treated us as if we were inferior animals. They shall do so no more! We are men; we are workers; we inherit as men this earth and its produce. Let us crush this fabric under which we have groaned! Down with Aristos and his minions!"

Those who heard him cheered, and soon a great multitude had assembled. Demos showed them how by organisation they might destroy the artificial structure which, as if in mockery, had been called "society," and he taught them, in simple but eloquent language, that until now they had lived in the vilest slavery, because they knew nothing of the rights of man.

No apostle in olden days had ever more enthusiastic followers. The millions raised a mighty shout of exultation. They knew their power at last, and they resolved to level Aristos to the dust. Demos, who was as prudent as he was brave, saw the necessity for caution as well as courage. He had already prepared his plans. He had provided money and arms by agencies known only to himself and his trusted confederates. The multitude were undisciplined, but what are a few thousand soldiers and police against millions with arms in their hands.

The struggle was short lived. The aristocracy, most of whom were large landowners, feebly cried out to the police to help them. The police laughed and after firing into the air surrendered to the revolutionists at discretion. Not many lives were lost. Aristos shut himself up in his palace, but the people, in spite of the bayonets of the soldiery, forced their way in. They found him lying on a luxurious couch, stone dead. The system had perished along with it.

"Let us burn his vile body!" cried the people wildly.

"No comrades," said Demos solemnly. "Remember he was a man like each of ourselves, and if he trampled on his fellow men he will do so no more."

Some of those who followed Demos grumbled at these words, and the more fiery spirits suggested, as a sort of compensation for this disappointment, that all the aristocracy should be massacred.

"What?" burst out Demos with flaming eyes, "would you commit murder the very day you have gained your freedom?"

"They murdered our kith and kin," shouted several hoarse voices together.

"True," said Demos, "but we have destroyed the system. Is not that enough? If they submit to human laws we will pardon them; and they like us shall honourably toil. The goods of the earth are for all. Those only shall suffer who refuse to work for the good of all. The happiness of the whole community must be our only aim and object. The tyrant has passed away, and it now becomes our duty to erect upon the ruins of tyranny the Republic of Man."

H. J. Bramsbury, 'A Working Class Tragedy' (1888–9)

[9 June 1888]

Chapter I.

"Now my lads, the guv'nor wants to speak to you in the moulders' shop."

The speaker was Sam Crosbie, foreman of Cranston and Son's ironworks, Benton, and the "lads" addressed were the workmen in the fitters' shop.

Benton is one of those quaint, quiet little towns which are studded about in rural England, where, in spite of telegraphs and railways, life flows monotonously and calmly, unruffled by the social and political storms that rage in big cities. It is, in fact, the centre of an agricultural district. Cranston's ironworks had given the place an importance which it otherwise would not have possessed. It was here that the farmers and landlords for miles round came for the tools and appliances to be used in agriculture. The firm had been the first to introduce the steam plough into the district; they hired out thrashing and reaping machines; and they had gained a reputation which had made their name well known throughout the country.[1]

Sam was a bluff sort of fellow, whose cheery manner had won for him the good will of every one of the men under his charge, but the abrupt tone in which these words were uttered and the unusual character of the message, caused a murmur of excitement as the men threw down their tools and proceeded to obey.

The "guv'nor" seldom condescended even to notice his "hands," much less to speak to them. Everyone was, therefore, asking his neighbour what could be the meaning of this summons. When they reached the moulders' shop the men from the other shops had already assembled – the moulders, fresh from groping in the sand, their white overalls smirched and blackened; the smiths, with their shirt-sleeves rolled up above their elbows, their faces and arms black and damp with perspiration; the pattern-makers and wheelwrights looking clean and cool by the side of the grimy sons of Vulcan; and the fitters themselves, in their jean jackets and overalls, bearing greasy traces of their work at the bench and the lathe.

Mr. Cranston was excitedly pacing up and down, after the manner of a tiger in the Zoo just before feeding time. He was a short, podgy little man, with sandy hair and a very red face, and a well-fed and withal sanctimonious appearance that suggested a cross between an alderman and a Methodist parson. He presented a marked contrast to the other occupants of the shop – they in their white dress blackened with toil, he in faultless broadcloth, the pink of respectability; they pale from the heat and confinement of the factory, he florid and wheezy from idleness and overfeeding.

When the men had all collected he turned and confronted them.

"Now, look here men," said he, "I have called you here to tell you plainly that I'll stand no more of the kind of thing that has been going on in this establishment. I find that morning after morning some one or other of you is absent until after breakfast time. There is scarcely one of you who does not lose one or more quarters in a week, and this in spite of the fact that the hooter blows every morning at a quarter to six. The fines, too, for loss of time have been doubled in order to ensure punctuality; every time one of you loses a quarter he is stopped nearly half a day's wages, and yet you will persist in going on in this disgraceful way. You are all too well paid I know, that is the long and short of it; but if you can afford to go on in this way I can't and won't. Fuel is being burnt in waste, and machinery standing idle every morning in consequence of some lazy scamp or the other not turning up to time. Besides the work is falling into arrear and orders are accumulating, although we are working overtime, when by rights you ought to be on three-quarter time. I'll have no more if it. Mark my words, the next man who loses a quarter will be instantly dismissed."

"I beg your pardon, sir," said a young fitter, stepping forward as his employer turned to go, "I think there's something to be said on our side. It isn't to our interest to lose time, we have quite enough of that when things are slack. We are none of us so well off as to want to be fined every week. It's like this; if we get down to the gate two or three minutes after six we are shut out till after breakfast. Don't you think, sir, you could arrange to have the gate opened again at half-past six, so that anyone a few minutes late could be stopped half an hour instead of having to lose a quarter?"

"That will do, Wilson, that will do," yelled Mr. Cranston, turning fiercely upon his questioner, his face purple with rage. "Do you think I am going to be dictated to by my hands as to how this establishment is to be conducted?"

"I tell you," said he, again addressing the men, "I am master here, and mean to be obeyed. You work here on my terms or you don't work here at all. As for you, Wilson, you had better go at once. I won't have discontented men about the place. In fact you can all go if you like. Crosbie, you had better come up to the office for Wilson's money, and if any other man shows signs of insubordination I will pay him off too. I will have discipline and obedience."

"Surely, sir, you don't mean to turn me off in this way, merely for speaking. What have I done? I've only put the matter to you fairly. I don't think I've shown any discontent or insubordination. I only proposed what seemed to me a reasonable and fair way out of the difficulty which you called us here to talk about. If we hadn't got to say anything about it what was the use of calling us here. You might have stuck up a notice on the gate to say all that you have told us. I –"

"I won't have it I tell you, that's all about it. I didn't come here to argue with you. I simply called you here to tell you the rule I mean to have carried out and my reasons for making that rule. I will not be dictated to by you or anyone else who works for me."

"I don't want to dictate but surely I've got a right to speak to you. I've always done my work properly. I've always earned all I've had from you. You've no more right to bully me than I have to speak to you. We're not slaves, are we?"

"I've heard about you before, Wilson. Your notions are altogether too high for me. You seem to forget that you are only a workman. You must be taught your place. I won't have you here any longer so there's an end of it."

As their employer bounced out of the shop, followed at a respectful distance by Crosbie, the men were voluble in their expressions of disgust.

"Curse the old swine," said one old fellow, "I have been here this three and twenty year, and never see such a go as this before. I wonder what things are coming to now!"

"Well," chimed a younger and more impulsive man, "I vote we take the old beggar at his word. Wilson's got to go, and you may depend upon it we shall all get shoved off one by one, we had better all go together at once."

"No, no," said Wilson, as the men began to prepare to follow the advice of the last speaker. "Look here chaps, what's the use of running your heads against a brick wall? Things aint so lively that you that have got a job can afford to chuck it up. We are pretty busy here, because Cranston's is the only place in this district. But ask Bill Smith here what work is like in the big centres and he'll tell you there's thousands of men who'd be glad to take your place. Old Cranston knows this and that's what makes him so cocky. It's bad enough for me to be out of collar, but I'm only a youngster; it 'ud be a sight worse for some of you others."[2]

"What's the good of talking in that way; why should we be bullied about like a lot of dogs? What would he be without us? If he wears a fine coat and lives in a mansion it's through our work he does it. I'd like to hang the old reprobate. If we let him bounce over us this time he'll make the place a perfect hell for us."

"You're right Jack," growled a burly blacksmith, "I've had very near enough of his infernal nigger-driving. If it wasn't for the missus and the kids I'd tell him to go to the devil with his job."

"Besides," said another, "harvest time will be here directly, and everybody'll be busy. 'Tisn't as if it was winter time. We've got the best part of the year before us."

"Yes, that's all very well, but things are very different now to what they used to be. The harvest doesn't make as much work as it used to. We ought to know that, seeing the new machines we've been turning out. There'll be hardly enough work in the fields for the chaps that are idling about the town now, and as for anything at any other place, as I said just now, work is not to be had. Besides after all, masters are very much alike, go where you will. It's only a question of choosing between the devil you do know and the devil you don't. And then, as Joe said, there's the missus and the kids to be considered. You haven't only got yourselves to think of. I tell you I'm sorry to have to go. It's not a very cheerful prospect to look forward to. I should certainly advise all of you to hang on as long as you can."

The force of this reasoning was not lost upon the men, and by the time Crosbie returned they had sullenly resumed their work.

"Frank, my boy," said he, handing Wilson the fifteen shillings which represented his three days' wages, "this is a deuced bad business. I did the best I could for you; I pointed out that you were one of the best workmen in the shop, that you were always steady and punctual. He didn't care, he said, he'd show them he could do without any of them, even the best."

Frank folded up his things and put on his coat, like a man in a dream. In the same dazed state he walked out of the shop, the burr and rattle of the machinery, again set in motion, in his ears.

[16 June 1888]

Chapter II.

Cranston's ironworks stood on the outskirts of the town, by the London coach road, which stretched away like a thin white ribbon as far as the eye could reach, through field and heath and wood. A cluster of low-roofed rusty sheds with a tall chimney shaft belching black sulphurous smoke into the clear sky, the works were a black, unsightly blot in a beautiful landscape. The surrounding fields glowed with the tints of approaching harvest, the woods were glorious in the deep green of the closing summer, the cool river gleamed and sparkled in the sun like a sheet of silver as Frank Wilson left the factory gate and turned homeward. But neither golden field, green wood nor silver river attracted his attention; there was a feeling of bitterness at his heart that made even the bright landscape look gloomy, and the stillness of that summer noon seemed hot, stifling and depressing.

It was a new experience for him to be out of work, and the very words as they shaped themselves in his mind conveyed an indefinable feeling of dread, of loneliness and isolation. He had worked at Cranston's from a lad and had come to regard himself as part and parcel of the place. Young, energetic and sanguine, work was to him a pleasure, he never lost time, and always availed himself of the opportunity of working overtime. By frugality, thrift and industry he had hoped to win a better position than that of a mere journeyman, even perhaps in time to become a capitalist.[3] During his apprenticeship he had saved a little money. He had married directly he was out of his time[4] and the possession of a wife and a home had given him the necessary incentive of an object in life, and to work and save, therefore, were to him the pleasurable means to that success he had set himself to attain.

Now he was out of work. The words kept running through his mind as he slowly and mechanically crossed the greystone bridge that spanned the river, and turned into the broad high street of the little town. Dull as it ever was, it had never seemed so dull to him before; there was no stir of life in this the principal street of the place, its wide whiteness glistening in the sun. The hammering of some carpenters at work sounded far away and unreal.

The dismissal from the factory was the heaviest blow that had yet fallen upon him since the death of his father. It was so unexpected, so unjust. His bright hopes for the future had all been crushed by a word from his master.

There would be great difficulty in obtaining employment in any other place. As Cranston's was the only works in the district he would have to seek work in places where he was entirely unknown, and there, as he knew, the prejudice against "yokels" would prevent his being employed, even if work was brisk. Unfortunately it was very slack all round, as he knew by the number of men on tramp who had called at he works.

The prospect was certainly not encouraging. Frank almost regretted the advice he had given to the other men. He began to think he had been rather foolish and quixotic in playing the scapegoat and opposing them in their proposal to all come out together. Supposing they had done so, wouldn't old Cranston have had to give way? He couldn't carry on the works himself and it could take him some time to fill up all their places while one vacancy presented no difficulty. Frank thought he would talk it over with the others in the evening.

At the corner of the street in which he lived a little knot of men were gathered.

"Hullo, Mr. Wilson," said one of them, "Where are you off to at this time of day? It ain't dinner time yet you know."

"I'm coming to join you fellows, Ben," said he, with an attempt at a smile; "I've got the sack."

"Go on, don't you come any of that sort of gammon. I know old Crosbie better than that."

"Oh, it isn't Crosbie, my boy, it's the guv'nor. He came and read us a lecture, and because I ventured to speak to him he turned me off there and then."

"Well, I'm sorry for you, Mr. Wilson," said Ben, "there's enough of us walking about now; and what with the steam ploughs and reaping machines cutting us out of the fields, and Sergeant Gripper and his two bullies circumventing our little game at night, things is precious rough. However, if we get a few of you toffs from the works among us, he'll be taking us for the swell mob."

"You don't like the Sergeant much Ben?"

"No, and I don't see as you have any particular call to; he's no great friend of yours if all I've heard is true."

Frank's brow darkened, but he said as he turned to go, –

"We hear a good deal more than is true, Ben, very often, and we mustn't judge too harshly."

To this general remark Ben nodded assent as he growled, –

"You'll walk a good many miles before you'll hear any labouring man say a good word for Sergeant Gripper all the same. You know what the immortal bard says about men 'Drest in a little brief authority.' Maybe he knew something about the Sergeant Grippers of his time. Will Shakespeare by all accounts did a bit of moonlighting himself sometimes,[5] Mr. Wilson."

This last was a parting shot at Frank, who shared Ben's love for Shakespeare, while he frequently lectured him on the immorality of "moonlighting" as Ben facetiously termed poaching.

Ben Green was one of those original characters that are frequently to be met within country towns and villages. Half gipsy, half labourer, and all vagabond, he could turn his hand to almost anything, and possessed such an amount of knowledge on every conceivable subject as to cause him to be regarded as an oracle by the simple country folk. He could sing a song, break a horse, mow a field or snare a hare with anyone. His predilection for the latter performance prevented him securing a permanent situation and led the neighbouring gentry to regard him as a dangerous character; and though the local tradespeople frequently availed themselves of Ben's services in this direction, they were very severe in their condemnation of such practices. A policeman was Ben's pet aversion.

Frank Wilson's home was one of a row of thatched cottages standing near the church. A pretty little place enough in the summer time with roses growing over the front and a small patch of garden at the back. The front door opened direct onto the one room, which took up the whole of the ground floor and served as kitchen and living room.

As Frank opened the door and stepped inside, his wife, a comely young woman of about twenty, who was busily engaged peeling potatoes, looked up with a start.

"Why Frank," said she, "you are home early. It isn't nearly one o'clock, and I haven't got the dinner ready yet. How is it you are here so soon?"

"You needn't be in a hurry, Polly," he replied, looking around ruefully on the simple home which loving hands had made so bright and dear to him. "I haven't got to go back."

"Oh you have taken a holiday for the rest of the day. I'm so glad. I'll make haste and get dinner, and then we'll go out on the common you and mother and I. That will be a treat, it's such a lovely day and the sunshine and fresh air will do you good. Oh, and couldn't we have a row on the river? We haven't been on the river for ever so long. I am glad you aren't going back any more to-day. You want a holiday badly, I'm sure; being shut up so much in that factory is making you look quite ill."

"Well, I shan't be shut up there any more Polly, I've got the sack."

"Oh dear! Frank, you don't mean it. Surely you and Mr. Crosbie haven't been falling out?"

"It isn't Crosbie, my girl, Crosbie's all right. I believe he's as sorry as I am for the matter of that, it's the old man himself."

Frank then narrated the occurrences of the morning, bitterly denouncing the tyrannical behaviour of his late employer.

"Well," said his wife when he had finished, "it's a very bad job that you should be thrown out of work just now, when we seem to be getting along so nicely. We have already got a couple of pounds in the savings bank, and if you had kept your job you would in a few years be able to start for yourself. However, it's no use being down-hearted, something's sure to turn up before long. Perhaps old Cranston might send for you back again to-morrow, or there might be the chance of a job up at the Park."

"Hullo Frank, what's brought you home so soon?" said his mother who had just come in with a basket which she placed upon a chair by the door. "You ought to be at work. I never see what's come to young people nowadays, always idling around."

"Can't help it this time mother; I've got the sack."

"Oh, I'm not surprised at that. I wonder you've gone on so long as you have without something happening. I'm sure it makes me shudder to think of it; ploughing the fields by steam, and reaping and mowing by machinery, a regular flying in the face of Providence I call it."

"You're always talking like that. What's machinery got to do with it?"

"What's machinery got to do with it? A good deal I should think. Look at the men there are out of work, and all through these new-fangled devil's tools doing the work that Providence provided for men to do."

"Oh well, if machinery throws men out of work in one direction it finds them work in another. I can earn more money as an engineer than working on a farm."

"Yes, but you wouldn't have had to work on a farm. You might have been head keeper at the Park by this time if you had followed in your poor father's footsteps and done as I wanted you to."

"I can fall back on that at any time. I fancy I know as much about the coverts at the Park[6] as any of the fellows that are there. I think I shall try for a job there if I don't soon get something to do in my own line, and what I don't know about it I can get Ben Green to teach me."

"Ben Green, he's no good to you; always loafing about the place. A regular bad lot he is."

"Oh, he ain't a bad sort. He's a good deal better than some of the folks that are so down on him. It was through that infernal scoundrel Gripper that Ben got into trouble in the first place, telling a parcel of lies about him."

"Dinner's ready," said Polly, and the announcement stopped all further argument between mother and son.

The dinner consisted of boiled bacon, greens and potatoes, a rather superior fare to that generally falling to the lot of the average country workman. But they all felt too depressed to thoroughly enjoy it. Nothing more was said about going for a walk on the common or a row on the river.

The afternoon Frank spent in pottering about his patch of garden; there were some potatoes to be dug up and some plants to set. He felt unsettled and restless, and about seven o'clock he left home, saying to his wife, –

"I think I'll take a walk down to the Red Lion[7] and see what the chaps are talking about."

[23 June 1888]

Chapter III.

Denmere, the residence of Mr. Cranston, was pleasantly situated about a mile and a half from the works, near the river which ran by the town. It was a handsome mansion of Elizabethan construction, surrounded by a spacious lawn, which was intersected by a gravelled carriage drive and pathways leading to the entrance. There was a garden at the back of the house, in the cultivation of which, and the trimness of his stable and coachhouse, Mr. Cranston took a special interest. Beyond the garden the lawn sloped down to the river by the side of which was a boathouse suggestive of water parties, picnics, and flirtations. In the summer the river at this spot presented a brilliant appearance; passing pleasure boats, containing parties of gaily dressed ladies with their flannel-clad swains, giving life and colour to a naturally beautiful scene and making the neighbouring woods echo with snatches of song and joyous laughter.

It was six o'clock on the evening of the day on which Frank Wilson had been discharged from his employment. In the drawing-room at Denmere there were gathered the members of Mr. Cranston's family, his wife and children, and a couple of visitors, trying as best they could to pass away the short time which would have to elapse before Mr. Cranston arrived from the works and dinner would be served.

"Charming, my dear Miss Louisa, charming," said the Vicar of Benton, the Rev. Mr. Gray, a flabby-faced individual of middle age, who looked as though he was perfectly satisfied with himself and quite ready to agree with the fads and fancies of his wealthy parishioners.

He was speaking to a young lady of about eighteen who had just finished playing a selection form "Il Trovatore"[8] on the piano. Louisa, although not exactly beautiful was pretty, with brown eyes and hair, a tip-tilted nose, a well formed figure and a fresh complexion.

By her side was a young naval officer, Lieutenant Vernon, who had been engaged in turning over her music, and, now that she had ceased playing was gazing admiringly into her face.

"Are you really sincere, Mr. Gray?" she interrogated.

"Decidedly, my dear child, I have seldom or never heard anyone play in so brilliant a manner as yourself."

"Have you ever heard Lizst,[9] Mr. Gray?"

"No, but I have heard many of the best London performers when I've gone to the metropolis to the May meetings."

"Ah, by the way, you haven't told us anything about the gatherings in Exeter Hall[10] this year. Was there anything particularly interesting going on?"

"Well, we had some interesting particulars about the missions in the South Seas, but unfortunately the sums subscribed for carrying on this good work are not nearly sufficient to do all we might do out there. One of the East London clergymen brought up the condition of the poor in the East End, but we had so many more important matters to attend to that we didn't discuss that very much."

"What did he say?"

"Oh, he talked about the matchbox-makers living in garrets[11] and gave us a lot of unsavoury details about tailors and bakers. But really, after all, what was the good of telling us? We could do nothing. It is their own fault. If they will be drunken and thriftless they must bear the consequences."

At this moment Mr. Cranston entered the room.

"But here is your father," the Vicar went on. "My dear Mr. Cranston how do you do. You have thrown off the cares of your business for the day I suppose."

"Yes, yes. But I've had a very troublesome day, Mr. Gray. You would scarcely believe how my hands impose upon my good nature. I have treated the scamps too well."

"Dear me, what have they been doing, might I ask?"

"Why, they come late to their work every morning, and this morning I told them I would have it no longer. One of them, a talkative, discontented fellow, answered me back, and I discharged him at once. And I'll get rid of them all if they're not more obedient."

"And quite right too, sir," replied the Vicar. "There are plenty of men out of work now who would be glad to fill their places, and for lower wages. They are too well paid, I really believe. Working men knew their places better when I was a young man. They become unbearable nowadays."

"A set of ignorant conceited rascals," broke in George Cranston, the capitalist's son, a well-dressed young fop, with reddish hair and an incipient moustache, the cultivation of which seemed to be his one object in life. "Some of them believe, I fancy, that we are dependent upon them, instead of their being indebted to father for their bread."

"Why really, you know," said Lieutenant Vernon, "it's a pity you can't put some of them in irons. They don't know how to appreciate the advantages of living in Christian England. Only the other day, during my recent cruise, we captured a slave dhow and rescued some niggers who had been taken from their homes by the piratical slave traders. How delighted they were to stand free upon the deck of an English frigate, and how different were their expressions of gratitude to the continual grumblings of these working men of ours here at home. Instead of being glad to live in so great a country, where everyone is free, these discontented wretches are continually growling and complaining. I'm hanged if I don't think they'll want to live in the houses of their masters directly, and eat as good food, drink as good wine and wear as good clothes as we do."[12]

"After all, perhaps we ought rather to pity than to blame them," said Mrs. Cranston, a fussy little woman about forty-five. "It's their stupidity that's to blame. They don't consider that anyone can do their work, and that we're paying them more than they are really worth now."[13]

"That is so," said Mr. Cranston. "I could get men to work for half I'm paying them. I consider I make them a present of half their wages every week. And this is the gratitude I get."

"Yes my dear Mr. Cranston, it's always so," said the representative of the Church who was drawing £900 a year for looking after the spiritual welfare of the good folk of Benton. "Some of them are even beginning to lose their respect for the Church. They don't touch their hats to me now, and actually the other day, when I was visiting them in their homes, giving them that spiritual advice of which they are so much in need, and teaching them to be contented with their lot, one of them told me that he could get all the religion he wanted out of the Bible and hadn't time to waste listening to musty sermons. His name, I think, is Wilson; an engineer, I believe, who works at your place. He lives in one of Mr. Brown's cottages at the top of Brook Street."

"Oh, Wilson was it? Yes, he's a discontented, stuck up sort of fellow. He's the one I've dismissed to-day."

At this point in the conversation, a plump, rosy-faced young girl, possessed of a pair of intelligent eyes, and dressed in the coloured calico which forms the livery of the domestic, came in and announced that dinner was ready.

They went into the dining room – Lieutenant Vernon escorting Louisa, Mr. Gray taking the arm of Mrs. Cranston and the father and son bringing up the rear.

The dinner was an excellent one, and showed that Mr. Cranston was as particular in the selection of his cook as in enforcing discipline amongst his workpeople. The gusto with which he ate his food and the solicitude with which he pressed the claims of each dish upon his friends proved that neither his appetite nor his power of appreciating the pleasures of dining had suffered by the little contretemps of the morning. The conversation, as far as Mr. Cranston and the Vicar were concerned, ran on the fall of prices in the iron market, the prospects of the coming harvest, and Mr. Gladstone's latest speech on the Irish question, the capitalist concurring with Mr. Gray in his opinion that almost all recent Irish troubles were due to the disestablishment of the Irish church.

Young George was volubly explaining the points of a bull terrier he had recently acquired, and the merits of the trout-fishing in the river to Lieutenant Vernon, whose attention, however, he only partially succeeded in gaining. Vernon was apparently more interested in ogling the fair Louisa, and endeavouring to engage her in conversation by pressing her foot with his own under the table.

"I suppose you'll stay at the Park for some little time after having been away so long, Mr. Vernon?" said she for want of something better to say.

"Well," he replied, "I don't think I shall outstay my welcome. My uncle, Colonel Ashville, was very pleased to see me, and most anxious that I should spend the whole of my leave with him, but I have so many friends to call upon in town that I fear I shall be unable to prolong my stay in this charming neighbourhood beyond a fortnight."

"Eva is growing to be quite a woman now. I suppose you'll be falling in love with her directly?"

"No, I don't think that's at all likely. At present I think I can boast that I'm quite heartwhole, in that direction at any rate. Eva, as my cousin, I regard more as a younger sister. Besides though quite a child she seems to have picked up some absurd notions with which I don't at all agree."

"Only a fortnight!" remarked George, "Why you won't have much time for the fishing."

"Oh, I shall run down occasionally for a day or so while I'm staying in town, if only for the pleasure of a day on the water with Miss Louisa and yourself."

"Oh, yes," said Louisa, "that will be jolly. We must arrange for a water party to go down to the Paddock, and invite Eva and the Colonel. And you might bring down some of your town friends, too, Mr. Vernon."

When the ladies had retired to the drawing room, and the gentlemen had lighted their cigars, Polly, the servant, found an opportunity to say to George,

"If you please, Mr. George, a young man wants to speak to you in the garden."

George went out. Standing at the door was a man whom he recognised as Jim, the ostler from the Red Lion.

"Hullo Jim, what do you want?"

"I've brought you this note, sir."

"Oh, you might as well have given that to the servant."

"Oh, ay, but then perhaps you'd have forgotten to pay the postman."

"Don't be too cheeky, Jim. Here's a tanner for you. But next time you bring a letter give it to the servant and wait for the pay."

Turning round he opened the letter and said, "Ah, this is from Alice. I must go down and see her."

Five minutes later he was walking in the direction of the Red Lion.

[30 June 1888]

Chapter IV.

There was a considerable company assembled in the Red Lion. Many of the men from the adjacent ironworks had dropped in to talk over the unexpected occurrence of the morning. Such an incident was quite an event in the monotony of their lives and formed matter for more serious consideration than the most important affair of state. In the taproom, besides Cranston's men, were several labourers from neighbouring farms who lived in the town, who were stolidly discussing, over a couple of quarts of ale, the prospects of the coming harvest and the latest innovations of machinery.

They, in their smock frocks and billycock hats, looked fresher and more healthful than the mechanics, though scarcely so well developed in stature.

"I tell ye what it is Bill," said one, "these yer engineer chaps be the fellows as does it for we. Wi' their darned machinery there soon won't be a chance for honest folk to earn a living at all."

This was said loudly enough, and purposely, to attract the attention of the ironworkers.

"D'ye mean to say that we aint honest folk, then?" demanded the burly blacksmith.

"I don't say what you be and I don't keer; all's I know is that you be taking the grub out of the mouths of such as we."

Some of the other men now joined in, and the altercation was developing into a general row. The ironworkers abusing the agriculturalists as "straw yard savages" and one of the latter offering to fight the best man among his opponents for a quart.

The blacksmith pulled off his coat in acceptance of the challenge, and they were about to adjourn to have it out, as Frank Wilson entered the taproom.

"Hullo Joe," said he, addressing the blacksmith, "who are you going to fight now?"

"Why these infernal clodhoppers have been pitching into us, saying that we are taking the bread out of their mouths, and this fellow here is offering to fight the best man in the company for a quart."

"You're a modest man, Joe, to accept such a challenge; put on your coat man, these poor fools don't know what they are talking about, or else they'd know that we are their best friends."

"Good evening, Frank," said Mr. Steggles, just then entering with a jug of ale, "You're quite a stranger here, you hardly ever give us a look in now you're married. I'm glad you have come in now for I was afraid we were going to have a row and I don't want any disturbance in my house."

Mr. Steggles was a typical publican. He liked to be on good terms with everybody, and tried, with considerable success, to be all things to all men. If he had any opinions of his own on any subject no one knew what they were, as he entirely agreed with the views expressed by anyone with whom he happened to come in contact, though these might be exactly opposite to those he was championing but a minute or two before. He didn't object to controversy among his customers, as that generally involved an increased consumption of liquor, but he disliked rows, which might bring his house into disrepute and would certainly lose him a customer or two. To his taproom customers he was urbane and condescending, to those of the bar parlour he was effusively obsequious, and to the bar loungers he was the soul of affability and good humour.

Frank returned his salutation shortly, sat down on one of the deal forms which were ranged round the room and began conversing with his late shopmates.

He found that the feeling with regard to his dismissal had considerably cooled down. They had come to accept the position as an accomplished fact and his half-suggested idea of a general turn-out found no favour.

The question raised by the agriculturists as to the effects of the introduction of machinery was still being warmly discussed by several, and they at length appealed to Frank for his opinion. He had always been looked up to in his workshop as being an authority on political or social problems. Being fond of reading he had acquired an amount of miscellaneous information which gave him a kind of superiority over his fellows, and which had won him the dislike of those superior persons, like Mr. Gray, who believed in keeping the working man in his proper place. In short he was a Radical and had a Radical's contempt for the pretensions of the Church and old nobility people, and all a Radical's respect for the self-made man, the capitalist and the money-grubber – so long as the money-grubber was not a landlord. He held the orthodox Radical view as to the effect of machinery, that although it tended to displace labour in one direction it made work at higher wages in others, and generally effected an improvement in the position of the workman.

This view he proceeded to put with some success. The farm hands, however, were not to be convinced.

"Why look at our farm," said the man who had offered to fight, "there used to be ten of us on all the year round, and work for extra hands at harvest time. Now there's only five and hardly any extra labour wanted. Where's the other five? Well, they aint in the engineer's shops anyhow. No, I'll tell ye where they be. Let's see. There was Bill Stubbs, he and his wife and kids, they had to go in the work'us. Their eldest gal, her what used to help in the kitchen, she had no home to go to when she warn't wanted at the farm any more and went to the bad. Then there was Joe Stiles; he hung about here a bit arter he got the sack and then he had a job of beating up at the Park. One of the keepers caught un wi' a rabbit in his pocket, and there was a row and the end of it was that Joe got seven year for knocking the keeper about. Jim Marne drowned hisself, Ike Scott went to Canady, and Reube Stevens was killed on the line; some says 'twas an accident, but I aint so sure. That's improvement for you if you like, and all through your darn machinery."

"Well, no doubt it was a bad thing for the men you have mentioned, but then I daresay it has been better for others and you have got to consider the greatest good of the greatest number,"[14] said Frank sententiously.

"I don't know nothing about that, but I do know that machinery is making us wus off, and that you can't find work in your shops for the men as you drives out of the fields. Why I met a man on the road yesterday; he said he had tramped from Birmingham, he was something in your line too, and he said that work was so slack he'd be glad to take a job at field work if he could get it. I reckon he stands a poor chance."

This was not particularly cheering for Frank, who began to think it was no use arguing with these thick-headed louts, and he was on the point of saying so when the blacksmith, who was getting tired of the dry discussion, and had recovered his wonted good humour proposed a game of coddem.[15]

About a dozen assented to this proposition and the fighting ploughman and Joe proceeded to choose sides. The blacksmith's first choice fell on Frank.

"No," said he. "I shan't play. I'll be waiter and here goes for the first quart."

When he entered the bar to fetch the beer young Cranston was leaning over the counter talking to Alice Steggles. He scowled at Frank as Alice turned to serve him.

"Good evening Mr. Wilson," said she, as she handed him his beer, "you seem to have quite forgotten old friends since you have been married."

"Why *Mr.* Wilson, Alice? Surely I have given you no cause for offence. And as for forgetting old friends, they are none so many that I am likely to forget any of them."

"Neither must I forget that you are married now," she retorted.

Frank was rather puzzled by her manner. He had always liked Alice Steggles and had frequently dropped into the Red Lion merely for the sake of a chat with her, but since his marriage he had given up this intercourse, and he had never imagined she had entertained any regard for him. Now her manner suggested pleasure at seeing him again and pique at his past neglect, pique which could only spring from affection.

He took the beer from her and returned to the taproom.

Alice resumed her conversation with young Cranston.

He on his part was deeply smitten with this pretty barmaid. Her rustic beauty was of the kind to appeal to the susceptibilities of a young middle-class lounger. Rather fair, of medium height, rosy sunburnt cheeks, laughing blue eyes, full red lips suggesting kisses, with a touch of firmness about the chin which redeemed the otherwise sensual appearance of the mouth, a well developed bosom, full rounded limbs and a wealth of dark brown hair gathered in a coquettish coil at the back of her heard, Alice Steggles was the picture of a young English country-woman at her best.

Her originality, boldness and vivacity presented a marked contrast to the inane conventionalism of the young ladies George Cranston was in the habit of meeting at the houses of his friends.

She cared as little for him as for any of the numerous customers she waited on daily, but she was flattered by his attention.

"I wonder," he was saying, "that you condescend to notice a fellow like that Wilson."

"Surely, George, you are not so silly as to be jealous of Frank, you know he is a kind of relation of mine since he married my cousin. Besides, I must be civil to customers. I thought you were only jealous of Sergeant Gripper."

George cursed Gripper under his breath and protested against the absurdity of being jealous of Frank, adding that he hated the fellow for a stuck-up jacka-napes.

In the taproom the game of coddem was progressing merrily. The blacksmith had won the first game and the ploughman the second. They were finishing the third when someone remarked that it was a wonder they had not seen Ben Green.

"Why here he is," retorted another as Ben entered.

"Thou speak'st aright, I am that merry wanderer of the night."[16]

"Why we were just wanting you to come to liven us up a bit with a song," said one of the coddem players, "we have just finished our game."

"All right, my boy, wait while I get a jug of old Steggles' nectar to stimulate my vocal powers," said Ben as he turned towards the bar.

George Cranston was still lounging over the counter leisurely sipping his brandy and water as Ben called for his beer.

"Who's the swell this time, Alice?" Ben asked with a look towards Cranston, whose back was towards him.

As he was opening the door to re-enter the taproom Ben accidentally knocked the hand with which young Cranston was raising his glass to his lips, causing him to spill a small quantity of the liquor.

Ben turned to apologise.

"Curse you for a clumsy, dirty, drunken clodhopper," said the young swell, as he dashed the contents of his glass full in Ben's face.

This was too much. Ben's gipsy blood was up, and, setting his pot on the counter he dealt young Cranston a blow between the eyes with his clenched fist that sent him reeling against the half-opened door. His head caught the edge of the door as he went backwards and he sank down in a heap.

Alice Steggles screamed and the men rushed in from the taproom.

[7 July 1888]

Chapter V.

Mr. Steggles was alarmed, and despatched Jim, the ostler, in all haste to fetch the police. A few yards from the door Jim met Sergeant Gripper, who was very leisurely walking down the High Street, with the air of superiority so well befitting a man of his stature and station. The sergeant was a young man, at least six feet in height, of broad proportions and semi-military bearing. Towards the poorer villagers he assumed an authoritative manner, and the well-to-do he endeavoured to impress with the idea that their property was quite safe while he was on his rounds.

"Oh, please sergeant, there's been a row at the Lion, and the guv'nor has sent me to fetch you," said Jim, deferentially.

"Why, what's the matter, Jim?"

"That fellow Ben Green has been and hit Mr. George Cranston and half killed him, I believe."

"Oh, Ben Green, is it?" said the sergeant. "He's always up to something. He'll come to a bad end one of these days. You'd better run up to the station and tell constable Warren to come down at once, and I'll go on and see into it."

When the sergeant arrived young Cranston was just recovering consciousness. Ben had raised his head from the floor and was supporting him on one knee, while Alice, looking pale and terrified, was bathing his forehead and staunching the blood that flowed from a nasty-looking wound at the back of his head. Mr. Steggles was inwardly cursing the untoward incident which interfered with the night's business, and was soothing his ruffled feelings with a tumbler of cold brandy-and-water. Frank was moodily looking on with the rest of the working men who were gathered round.

"Hullo, landlord," said Sergeant Gripper, as he pushed his way through the little group to where the injured man was reclining, in a half-sitting position, "this is a nice piece of business, aint it?"

Mr. Steggles hastily gulped down the remainder of his brandy-and-water and approached the sergeant. Laying his hand on his arm, he said,

"My dear sergeant, this is very unfortunate. You know I always like to keep my house respectable, but I can't always keep quarrelsome people out. It seems that Mr. Cranston here was quietly drinking his liquor when that fellow, Green, struck him a violent blow, which knocked him senseless – But won't you take some refreshment, sergeant?"

"Thank you, landlord; but duty first. Does Mr. Cranston charge Green with this assault?"

Cranston, who had struggled to his feet, and was holding himself up by the partition, sullenly answered "Yes."

"Very well, then," said Gripper. "Ben Green, you are my prisoner. I shall detain you here until constable Warren arrives."

"All right," said Ben. "But you'd better detain another prisoner also. I charge Mr. Cranston here with committing an unprovoked assault upon me in the first instance. He threw a glass of liquor full into my face before I touched him."

"Yes," said Frank; "that's quite true. I saw him do it."

Young Cranston smiled contemptuously.

"Oh, well," said he. "You can take me too, if you like to believe such an absurd charge, sergeant. But you know what Green is and Wilson, of course, would say anything against me after having been discharged by my father for misconduct."

"I know my duty, sir," said the sergeant. "I shall arrest Green, as there is clear evidence of his having committed an assault. If he wishes to charge you with assault, he must apply for a summons."

Frank indignantly remonstrated against the unfairness of the sergeant's conduct, pointing out that Ben's face still bore traces of the liquor that had been thrown in it.

"Oh, I don't want to have any argument with you, Wilson. I know what you are. You're no better than Green, and will probably be in the same position, before long. A nice sort of fellow you are to teach me my duty. You've gone and lost a good situation now through your beastly Radical notions, and you'll drag everybody belonging to you down to your own level."

Alice, who had somewhat recovered from her fright, and was surprised at the conduct of the sergeant, attempted to explain the origin of the affair, but was prevented by Mr. Steggles, who called her to attend upon a customer at the other end of the bar.

On the arrival of his subordinate, Sergeant Gripper handed Ben over to his charge, while he himself entered into a most animated conversation with Alice, who counted the sergeant among the most ardent of her many admirers. At the present moment, however, she was not inclined to show him much favour. Her woman's instinct resented the official injustice of which she had seen him guilty, and it was in vain that he endeavoured to allay her indignation. Mr. Steggles hovered around in the hope of having a quiet word with the sergeant on his own behalf; but Gripper was blind to his nods and winks, and very soon marched off, he and his subordinate, with Ben Green between them, being followed all the way to the station by a small crowd of men and youths who had gathered outside the tavern.

After the police had gone, and he had sent Mr. Cranston off in the trap under the charge of Jim, Mr. Steggles withdrew to the bar parlour, where, in company with one or two old cronies, he bemoaned the hard fate that had caused such a mishap in his house.

The taproom company had broken up, and Frank, shortly bidding Alice good night, leisurely made his way homewards. His reflections were not of the pleasantest. He had got the sack, and now to make matters worse, he had got himself mixed up in a publichouse brawl.

When he got home he found his wife anxiously awaiting him. The news, with variations, had got there before him, and she was much relieved at seeing him arrive safe. She had heard there had been a fight at the Lion between Frank and George Cranston; but whether Frank had killed Cranston, and had got locked up himself, or whether Cranston had killed him, her informant was unable to tell her.

The next day Frank went down town to see Ben Green brought before the magistrates. Some of the loungers outside the Corn Exchange, where the court was held, eyed him curiously, as though they expected to see the marks of the terrible struggle in which they had heard he had been engaged.

Frank made his way into the hall, where, among the more favoured of the audience who were provided with seats, he saw Mr. Steggles and his daughter. Alice smiled, and beckoned him to take a seat by her side; but her father frowned and shook his head, clearly giving Frank to understand that he did not want to be too intimate with him there.

There was a full bench of magistrates, among whom were old Cranston and the Rev Mr. Gray; the squire, Colonel Ashville, presiding. Ben was brought in in custody, and Sergeant Gripper stepped into the box to state the charge against him.

The sergeant kissed the book as though he liked it, and proceeded to narrate the circumstances under which he had been called into the Red Lion. There was a substratum of truth in the sergeant's narrative, indeed it would have been difficult to point out exactly what was untrue in it; but Frank was amazed at the heavy indictment made out against the prisoner. What was made clear to the audience was that Ben Green was a most desperate, bloodthirsty ruffian, and that it was only by the merciful interposition of Providence, in the person of the stalwart sergeant himself, that George Cranston was saved from being murdered, as well probably as one or two other inoffensive inhabitants of Benton. The sergeant also left no doubt in the minds of the Bench and of the audience that he was the most exemplary individual that ever wore the uniform of the County Constabulary. He called George Cranston.

Cranston presented a rather pitiable spectacle as he came forward, with a bandage round his head and a shade over his eyes to hide their discolouration.

He stated the facts as to the assault committed, leaving out, however, all mention of the provocation he had given his assailant. Ben put several questions to him with a view to supplying this omission, after which Mr. Steggles was called.

Mr. Steggles bowed to the Bench, to the prosecutor, to the policemen and to the audience. He would have bowed to the prisoner also if the law clerk[17] had not checked him by handing him the book to kiss, just as he was about to do so.

"Did you see the prisoner assault Mr. Cranston?" asked the clerk.

"Yes, sir;" answered Mr. Steggles, bowing again. "I am very sorry, sir, that anything of the kind should have taken place in my house. I have always tried to keep my place respectable, gentlemen (turning to the Bench and bowing again); but you see, gentlemen, you can't always keep bad characters out."

"Did you see any provocation given to the prisoner?" interrogated the clerk.

"No, sir,' (with another bow). "Mr. Cranston has always behaved as a gentleman whenever he has honoured my house with his presence –"

"Answer my questions, please, and don't make any further observations. Did you see or hear anything take place between Mr. Cranston and the prisoner before the blow was struck?"

"No, sir; nothing whatever. I never allow any rows in my house, and if I had seen or heard anything of the kind going on I should have sent for the police directly."

Ben declined to ask him any questions and he was ordered to stand down, which he did, with the air of a man who has done his duty and is prepared to face the consequences, be what they may.

In his defence Ben stated the provocation he had received and called Frank Wilson as a witness.

Frank simply corroborated Ben's own statement, after which the Sergeant gave a report on the prisoner's antecedents showing him to be a notorious poacher, and having served a month's imprisonment for snaring hares.[18]

Mr. Cranston was for sentencing the prisoner to seven years penal servitude.[19] On the clerk mildly suggesting that this was a little beyond the power of the magistrates, the Vicar proposed that the case should be sent for trial. Eventually a sentence of three months imprisonment with hard labour was imposed, the chairman in pronouncing his decision declaring that but for the alleged provocation the term would have been six months instead of three. At the same time he pointed out that no amount of provocation was sufficient justification for such a brutal assault as was shown to have been committed, and wound up by warmly eulogising the conduct of Sergeant Gripper.

Frank was expressing his indignation of some of the bystanders outside, standing on the steps of the building, when Sergeant Gripper came out.

"Now then, you Wilson," said he, "you'd better clear off, or I'll soon get you sent where your friend has gone."

[14 July 1888]

Chapter VI.

The hewers of wood and drawers of water, the worker with hand and brain, are generally but little troubled to know how to pass their leisure time, they have so little of it. With the well-to-do, however, it is a very different matter. How to pass the time is the great question of their existence. They are seldom addicted to mental pursuits, and, scorning manual work, they find this a rather difficult question to answer. Some of the capitalists, it is true, devote a considerable portion of their time to the management of their factories, and this was the case with the proprietor of the ironworks at Benton. But with their dependents the case is different. Having domestic servants to do the household work, as they have workmen to produce the luxuries they enjoy, there is little for the wives and children of the well-to-do classes to attend to in their homes. So they are forced to devise various methods of making the time pass pleasantly.

The Cranston household was no exception to the general rule. Mrs. Cranston's chief aim in life was to bully the servants, and servants were changed pretty often at Denmere; but this she varied by gossiping with the clergyman and his wife, the doctor's wife, and Mrs. Fleecem, a lawyer's widow. Louisa spent her time in strumming the piano, exercising her voice and visiting and chatting with her acquaintances, whilst George apparently found an outlet for the energy which was not expended in the paternal office in shooting, boating, fishing or attending race meetings. Taken altogether things were dull enough at Denmere, and the advent of a visitor from London, or the arranging of a pleasure excursion made quite a pleasant diversion.

When, therefore, at the end of August Lieutenant Vernon wrote to his friends, to say he was coming down to spend a day with them on the river, everybody was delighted.

Quite a party was gathered on the lawn by the river on the day appointed – Colonel Ashville and his daughter Eva, Lieutenant Vernon and his friend Jack Somers, George, Louisa, Mr. and Mrs. Cranston, and Mr. Gray's daughter Jane. George had quite recovered from the effects of his brawl with Ben Green at the Red Lion, and was making himself particularly attentive to Eva.

There was much giggling amongst the young people as they proceeded to take their seats in the boat. It was arranged that they should row up to the Paddock which was about three miles from Denmere, where they were to land and spend the afternoon. A hamper filled with the material for a substantial repast, was carefully placed in the stern.

A delightful picture presented itself to the view of the Cranston party as they rowed away from the edge of the lawn and turned a bend in the river. For a little distance on one side of them the river was bordered by meadow-lands, but beyond this and on the other side, as far as the eye could reach, dense masses of green wood grew right down to the water's edge. The river sparkled in the sunshine of the glorious summer day, and the sombre, many-tinted green of the over-hanging trees, was relieved by the bright-coloured dresses of the numerous boating parties gliding over the surface of the stream.

The Paddock was a grassy plateau, surrounded by deep woods, a place of great beauty, forming a kind of natural lawn running down to the river side, and was part of a small estate which Mr. Cranston had purchased. It was cut off from the other fields by a small stream, and formed a kind of peninsula, jutting out at a bend in the river. Adjoining was an orchard, the trees of which were laden with fast-ripening fruit.

In due course, and thanks to the propelling powers of the younger men in the boat, the Cranston party arrived at this charming place and made their preparations to spend the day.

"Might I ask," said Jack Somers to Miss Grey, "who is the lucky owner of the property surrounding us?"

"The greater part, I believe belongs to Colonel Ashville, and will eventually fall to the husband of Miss Eva."[20]

"She's a lucky girl, and I dare say is pestered with admirers already."

"Well, no. There are very few visitors at the Park, and she knows scarcely anybody except the Cranstons and the people in the town. You can see her almost any day, walking about amongst the cottages, paying visits to the work people, and leaving substantial remembrances of her visits behind her too. For she's a very good-hearted girl."

Meanwhile Eva and George were threading their way through the adjoining wood whilst Louisa and Lieutenant Vernon were helping to get luncheon ready.

George would have preferred the society of the pretty barmaid at the Red Lion, but Eva was too good a match for him to let her escape without an effort. Wealth, far greater than that possessed by his father, and influence of no mean description, would come to the fortunate suitor of the Colonel's daughter, and George as a practical man made the best of his opportunities.

In his conversation he was actually discussing the merits of books, paintings and music, instead of bull-dogs and racehorses. It is true he was by no means well posted on the former matters, but by appearing intensely interested in what Eva said, and throwing in a judicious "Yes," or "Quite so, I agree with you entirely," he displayed an amount of conversational ability which few who knew him better would have credited him with.

When they had done justice to the luncheon and were sipping their champagne, Colonel Ashville took occasion to remark –

"And how do you like the service, Lieutenant?"

"Infinitely better, Colonel, than the praying and preaching which my father wished me to do. Parsons are very good fellows in their way, but I prefer the glories of defending our empire and adding to her Majesties dominions."[21]

A violent rustling, as of twigs being broken down and trampled under foot, and the sound of voices in altercation created a break in the conversation.

The noise which had attracted their attention was caused by two men, one of whom was dragging the other through the trees, and at this moment they made their appearance.

They were Sergeant Gripper and Frank Wilson. Frank was saying –

"All right; you needn't pull my coat off my back, Gripper. That's unnecessary violence."[22]

"I'd give you violence, if I had my way. Six months is what you want."

"Yes, I dare say; but you are not a judge yet."

"What's the matter, sergeant," said the Colonel.

"The matter's this, your worship. I met this man, just now, walking along the road to Benton, carrying these cresses.[23] I asked him where he found them, and he said he found them. Then I told him to take them back where he got them, and he told me to mind my own business, using violent language at the same time. With that I said, Very well, if you won't take them back quietly, I shall take you back myself. Now he tells me that he got 'em from this stream here, which is on Mr. Cranston's property, and I want to know if Mr. Cranston is a-going to prosecute him for the trespass?"

"Now, my man; what have you to say for yourself?"

"That's quite right, sir, as far as taking the cresses is concerned. I didn't use any violent language, but you can't expect a policeman to tell the truth."

"That's defamation of character," broke in Gripper.

"We are in want of food at home," said Frank dejectedly, paying little heed to Gripper's interruption, "and I took the cresses, but they were no good to Mr. Cranston. I have been out of work this last month, and I can't get a job anywhere. If he hadn't given me the sack I shouldn't have wanted his cresses."

"Do you want me to take him to the station, sir?" said Gripper addressing Mr. Cranston.

"Certainly, Gripper, you have done quite right," said the capitalist. "I cannot have such people prowling around my land. They must be taught a lesson, when they are caught at such things."

"You want to be taught a lesson, I think," said Frank, "it is your fault that I am out of work and in poverty. You are the cause of my home being destroyed and my wife and mother being reduced almost to starvation. And now you talk to me of lessons. Good God! haven't I been trying for the last month to get work, and haven't you been using all your influence to prevent my succeeding wherever I've gone for employment. And then you talk about teaching me a lesson. A nice sort of Christian you are! I've never asked you for any favours, and I aint going to, but I reckon I've got as much right to come and get watercresses here as anyone else has. I've done so before and shall do again without your permission."

"We'll see about that," replied Cranston, "whatever grows here is my property. If you take anything you will be committing a theft and must expect to suffer the consequences."

"I wonder you don't lay claim to the water in the river as well as the watercresses that grow in this stream."

"How dare you speak in that insolent manner to me. You trespass on my property and commit a barefaced robbery, and then you think to brazen it out with cool impudence – I have never heard such unmitigated insolence in all my life! I am surprised Sergeant, that you should have brought this man down here at all. You should have taken him to the station, and you'd better do so at once."

As the Sergeant turned to go, Eva, who had been a silent witness of the scene, turning to her father, said –

"Dear Papa, can't you do something to save this poor young man from being locked up. It may have been wrong for him to have taken these things but I know that he is very badly off. I saw his wife the other day when I was visiting in Benton. She seemed a nice, respectable young woman, and she told me that he'd always been very steady, industrious and thrifty. They were getting on very nicely until he got discharged from his work, but he's been out of work now for a month, and having his mother to support they have been reduced to absolute poverty."

"Why, really, my dear girl, its no affair of mine, I can't be taking up the cudgels on behalf of all your wretched protégés."

"My dear Miss Eva," interposed Jack Somers, "it's really no use troubling about these kind of people, a little prison discipline will no doubt do this fellow a deal of good, at any rate he'll be better off in gaol than he would be loafing about here, poaching, robbing orchards or stealing fowls. Don't stand staring there, Sergeant, like a stuffed scarecrow, walk him off to the station."

Frank quietly accompanied the Sergeant to the lock-up.

When his case came on before the magistrates he was sentenced to two months imprisonment on a charge of trespass and theft.

[21 July 1888]

Chapter VII.

It was a cold miserable day at the end of October when Frank Wilson and Ben Green were turned out of the county gaol. When they met outside the gates they shook hands. They had seen each other every day inside since Frank's incarceration, but although they had been able to furtively compare notes occasionally, the stern prison discipline seemed to separate them as effectively as time or distance could have done. And the time they had been there! What an age it seemed! Every day was like a month, every week a year.

Frank had received one letter from his wife during his imprisonment, but the cheerful tone in which it was written was so evidently assumed that it tended to increase rather than allay the anxiety he felt. Destitution was staring them in the face before his imprisonment. Was it not want that had driven him to go for those unfortunate watercresses, want that was making his wife look pale and thin, and the step of his poor old mother more infirm?

What had become of them? how had they managed to live during the two months he had been locked up?

These questions were harassing his mind, as, silently with his companion, he set out to walk the fifteen miles that lay between them and Benton.

A cold wind blew a thin drizzling rain into their faces and seemed to chill them to the bone. The prospect around was as cheerless as their thoughts.

"Lively this," remarked Ben, after they had trudged along for some time in silence.

"I wish it was night," said his companion, "I dread going into Benton in broad daylight, I am ashamed to be seen. I feel as if I had committed a murder or some other terrible crime."

"I feel as if I should like to commit one," returned Ben savagely, "I tell you what, my boy, *it'll be a cold morning for Gripper next time I meet him alone in the dark.*"

"Don't talk in that way, Ben, you make me shiver, and that's quite unnecessary with this cursed drizzle. After all, Gripper's very little to do with it."

"Oh, hasn't he? Look here, my boy, in my opinion, that infernal scoundrel is at the bottom of the whole mischief. He was never good friends with me, but ever since he found that you befriended me he has not given me a moment's peace. He has never forgiven you for robbing him of Polly Atherton, as he calls it, and he made up his mind to do you all the harm he can, and has done it."

"Well, but I don't see what that had to do with your being put away, if you hadn't struck young Cranston he couldn't have had a pull on you for that?"

"No, but wasn't it his evidence that convicted me? If it hadn't been for the way he put it, the provocation I received would have secured my acquittal in spite of old Cranston and that psalm-smiting old hypocrite, Gray. Colonel Ashville is a gentleman though he is a Tory, and he would have let me off with a caution, but Gripper did it for me, and he did it for you, too."

"Of course I know he collared me, but then if I hadn't been out of work and hard up he wouldn't have had the chance."

"Well, I believe he had something to do with your getting the sack. I know he's had his knife into you ever since you married Polly Atherton. He used to be very thick with young Cranston, and they used to be talking about you when they was drinking together in the bar at the Lion. I've heard 'em and you may depend they set the old un against you between 'em, and he only waited for an excuse to give you the chuck."

"But they aint very friendly now, are they?"

"No, Gripper still carneys[24] to young George, but George hates Gripper like the very devil now. You see your being at home so much you didn't see what was going on; but young George has been very sweet on Alice Steggles, and he's seen her talking to Gripper once or twice – you know the Sergeant always was a mark on the girls – and it has rather upset him, in fact the night that he had me locked up I heard that he had vowed vengeance on Gripper if he ever found him talking to her again. You know young George is a nasty sort of a cuss when he gets his monkey up."[25]

Frank felt in no mood for conversation and they relapsed into silence.

The rain continued to drizzle down on them till they were soaked to the skin. Wet, hungry, miserable, they slowly trudged along, the mud and water of the road soaking into their boots and increasing their discomfort. The trees and hedgerows were almost bare, there was scarcely a sign of life in the brown fields that skirted the road, except where one or two melancholy looking cows were vainly trying to shelter themselves from the rain by turning their tails to the hedgerows.

It was mid-day by the time they reached Benton and the men from the works were going home to dinner. Frank avoided them as much as possible, and pulled his cap down over his brow, as if by do doing he could escape observation.

They hurried by, however, without apparently noticing their quondam mate and his companion. They were all fearful of hurting his feelings, and therefore thought it best not to speak to him; except Crosbie who came face to face with him as he was crossing the bridge, and shook hands with him as if nothing had happened. Frank could scarcely trust himself to speak and hurried away as quickly as he could.

At the corner of Brook Street he parted with Ben and made his way homeward alone.

Inside the cottage was as cheerless as the prospect without. By the side of the fireless hearth sat his mother and opposite her his wife was bending over some needlework.

She turned towards him as he entered the room and the changed appearance of her pale, tear-stained face forced from him a cry of pain as he took her in his arms and kissed her pale lips. He was wet to the skin, the drizzling rain was still falling, and the dull monotonous drip, drip of the water from the eaves onto the stones outside added to the dreariness of the surroundings. The room had been denuded of most of the little ornaments which had made it bright and cheerful in the old days; he missed the ticking of the old dutch clock[26] that used to hang in the corner; there was no fire in the grate and the room seemed damp and cold; yet he felt far less miserable than he had done at any tine during the long weary weeks in gaol.

The agony of suspense was past. Standing there in the wreck of his home, hungry, cold and weary, he yet felt the unspeakable relief of at any rate knowing the worst, and being able to face it by the side of those he loved.

When his wife had kindled a fire with a few sticks and had set before him a cup of weak tea, with some bread and butter, and was relating to him all that had passed during his imprisonment, he felt almost happy.

They had done very well, she told him, though her looks belied her words; she had been able to get a little needlework, and Miss Ashville had been very good to send them things from the Park; indeed, if it had not been for her kindness, she really did not now what would have become of them.

"Yes," said Frank, "and if it had not been for that old scoundrel Cranston reporting about me as he did when Ashville sent to him for a reference, I should have got a job up there and we should have never been in this plight."

"As if he hadn't done us harm enough by giving you the sack, he goes and prevents you getting work elsewhere," continued his wife. "I do believe that he had something to do with your not getting a job at the other places where you tried; I can't understand else how it was you didn't succeed."

"And all because he thought I didn't humble myself enough to him; but, never mind, it may be his turn some day."

"I believe he'd like us to starve to death," said she, "I went to Hardman, the relieving officer,[27] after you had been away a month and had taken most of the things I could dispose of to Oldbury to pawn, to see if I could get some relief for mother. He told me I must go before the board, and I did so. Of course, Mr. Cranston was there, and you can guess what chance I had. He said that you were a-good-for-nothing scoundrel, and that you deserved to suffer, and the best thing we could do would be to go in the workhouse. I told him I would sooner starve first, and he said, of course we could do as we liked about it."

"Well, to-morrow is board day, and I'll go and see him myself," said Frank. "I never thought it would come to this. Good God," he exclaimed, starting up and excitedly pacing the room, "I'd sooner blow my brains out than I'd ask the curs for anything, if it was only myself; but what can I do? I can't seem to get work, and now it'll be harder than ever – now I'm a gaol-bird," he added bitterly; "and I can't see you and mother starve before my eyes."

"I don't want to be a burden on you, Frank, my poor boy," said his mother, beginning to cry; "but I'll starve under a hedge rather than go into the house.[28] It's bad enough to have parish relief, but it would kill me to go there. I wish, please God, he would take me out of it, there seems nothing but trouble for me since your poor father died."

"I only regret one thing," said Frank, pausing in his walk and looking into his wife's face, "and that is, that I ever asked you to marry me, to be dragged down to this. If you had married Gripper, you would have been better off, and I should have nothing to reproach myself with. It is hard for you. It is hard for mother, too, but for that I am not responsible; but I need not have brought it on you."

"Frank," said his wife, "do not talk so; I never cared for anyone but you, and we have been very happy together. The trouble that has come upon us is not of your bringing, and I do not and shall not reproach you with it. You have always done your best, but you cannot help misfortune. Do not let it make trouble between us, and we shall soon, let us hope, see brighter days. I wouldn't care if it wasn't for mother. We are young and strong, and can stand a little rough living; but she is getting old, and it is already beginning to tell upon her. She is getting weaker everyday. Do try and see if you can't get them to grant her something."

He did try, but unsuccessfully. The board of guardians was practically the bench of magistrates, with the addition of one or two local tradesmen, and when Frank presented himself he could see that the influence of his late employer had been used against him. He was told that the board were not prepared to grant out-door relief to his mother as that would be simply encouraging him to lead a life of idleness. She could go into the workhouse; they would give him the order for admission there and then if he liked, but that was all they would do. He pleaded and protested, but in vain. "Would either of them give him work?" he asked. That was no part of the business, they told him. He must find work, as other and better men had to do; and if he was so worthless that no one would employ him the best thing he could do would be to go into the house himself. Telling them he would see them damned first he withdrew.

[28 July 1888]

Chapter VIII.

The days passed slowly. The short autumn days spent in trudging from place to place vainly seeking for work; the long dark evenings passed in moody silence by the fireless hearth of the little cottage. The chilliness of the apartment was increased by the draughts which penetrated under the door and through the chinks of the window. When they used to have a fire, in the old days, they scarcely noticed these draughts, but now they seemed to pervade the place, and to penetrate to one's very marrow, and nothing seemed to exclude them.

They could not afford a fire now. They could not always have a light; indeed Frank preferred the darkness. The flickering lamp only served to illumine the gloom, to show up the bare walls and cheerless room and to make his wife's pale face look more pale and hollow and wan. She, indeed, was getting thinner and weaker day by day. He knew, in spite of her cheerful tone and words of encouragement, that the want and worry were making her ill, and the thought that he was dragging her down to the hell of a death by starvation worried him almost to madness. His mother, too, could scarcely get about for the rheumatics, for days together she was confined to her bed. Their little stock of money had long since gone as well as almost every article of furniture that could be disposed of.

Since he had come out of prison Frank had shunned all his old mates.

He never visited the Red Lion, for fear they should think he was sponging on them. He would hang around the market place on market days in hopes of getting an odd job, which sometimes happened, and on one occasion some of Cranston's men, seeing him, insisted on treating him to some bread and cheese and beer, and made up half-a-crown, which they gave him.

The food and drink seemed to choke him, and he was so overwhelmed with shame and humiliation at receiving the money that he carefully kept out of their way whenever he afterwards saw them approaching.

Crosbie once sent them five shillings, and the neighbours would sometimes bring them a home-made loaf, or some trifle; but then, as Frank said, what could any of these people do, who were almost as poor themselves. It was not likely they could keep them.

Sometimes Miss Ashville would call and leave them a shilling; but she only had her pocket-money, and altogether they only just managed to keep from starving.

One day, in the market, a gentleman gave him a job to take home a couple of greyhounds he had purchased.

The gentleman's residence was about five miles out and when Frank arrived there with his charges he was supplied with bread and cheese and beer, and two shillings for his trouble.

He was delighted. It was the largest sum of money he had earned since he had been out of work, and all the way home he was thinking what he should do with it to give his wife and mother a treat.

They would have some meat – it was weeks since he had tasted animal food – and they would have a fire and a cup of tea.

If there was any liver at the butcher's he would buy some, that would be cheapest, and after all bullock's liver would be a treat. It was not always that they could get it. Whenever the butcher had any liver it was quickly snapped up by the poorer townspeople, and was indeed almost the only kind of fresh meat they tasted.

It was dusk when he reached the butcher's shop, which was lighted up with flaring gas-jets, after the manner of butcher's shops.

Yes, there was the liver, lying, a dark red mass, on the block, under the flaring gas. He bought two-pennyworth, which he carried in his neckerchief.

Then, at another shop he bought a pennyworth of dripping, a loaf, and a pennyworth each of tea and sugar.

"Here my girl," said he, placing his purchases on the rickety round table, which stood I the centre of the apartment, "I've brought the materials for a feast. Just get a light while I run and fetch some wood and coal."

In a few minutes he returned with a quarter-hundredweight of coal in a bag over his shoulder, and a heavy faggot under his arm.

He soon had a fire burning, and when Polly had made the tea and the liver was merrily frizzling in the pan they seemed quite jolly.

While the meal was progressing he gave Polly the remaining shilling and told her how he had earnt it.

She was overjoyed at his success, and hoped that it was the forerunner of better fortune.

"But," she added, a shade passing over her face, "I know that you did it out of kindness, and I know that we must have food; but still, don't you think we ought to have kept the whole of the two shillings towards paying the rent? We owe six weeks now, and Mr. Brown says that we can't go on like this, and if we can't pay we must go out."

"It's no use worrying about that; Brown knows we shall pay him when we can, and I don't think he'll behave harshly. We always have paid him."

"Yes, that's what I said to him, but he seems to think we ought to pay, even if we starve to do it. It 'ud be a dreadful thing to be turned out in the street."

"Don't fear, Polly; we shan't be turned out. Once I can get work, we'll soon pull ourselves together a bit, and soon settle up with him."

But Frank did not get work very soon. He was always too late or too early wherever he went for a job; or business was slack; or for some reason or another they couldn't give him a job.

One week he tramped to Birmingham, only to return more heart-sick and hopeless than ever.

It was now November. There were a considerable number out of work, even in Benton, while in the large centres matters were even worse.

It was a dull, cold day. He had been vainly tramping round, looking for work. He returned home, only to find the same cheerless prospect, and he wandered forth again, not in the hope of finding work, but because he felt too restless to stay indoors. A little way from his door he met Ben Green.

"Well, you are a nice fellow," said Ben. "I thought you would have given me a look round now you are doing nothing, and yet I haven't seen you once since we came from the palace."

"Why haven't you been to give me a look?" queried Frank. "You know I don't care about going anywhere when I'm hard up."

"Neither do I; but that's no reason why we should keep apart, because we're both down on our luck. Anyhow, I've brought you a rabbit I picked up last night, if you like to have it."

"No, I'll not come in," said he, in reply to Frank's invitation, "I know your mother aint particularly fond of me, and I don't want to rile the old lady now things is rather gloomy."

Frank took the rabbit.

When he returned Ben said,

"I've got a job on to-night, and should be glad of your help."

"Oh, indeed, what sort of a job is it?"

"Well, it's more in my line than yours. I was down at the Lion last night, and Alice told me they were going to have a bit of a party there, and the old man 'ud be glad if I'd get him some birds."

"What!" interrupted Frank, "do you go to the Lion now?"

"Why, of course. It's a public-house. I don't bear any ill-will to old Steggles, nor he to me, as I know of. But that's not the question. The question is. Will you come with me to-night? If you like to meet me at Dyke's corner at nine o'clock, we can cut across the fir copse and there we shall be in the thick of it in about ten minutes. I'll bring a couple of sacks, and it won't take us long to fill both of 'em there."

"But suppose old Barton happens to drop on us?" queried Frank.

"Old Barton won't be around to-night, never fear. It's gong to be a wet night, and he knows that it's more comfortable in his house though it is but a keeper's hut, as they call it, than it is outside on a wet November night. I went over a bit of it last night, and I never heard anything of him."

"Well, you know it's the kind of thing I don't care about. I never have done any poaching, and it goes against the grain. Besides, 'Honesty is the best policy' after all."

"Yes, I know; you may be honest and starve. Be as honest as you can, that's my motto. I've never gone in for thieving. I couldn't do it; but poaching is another matter altogether.[29] There's nothing dishonest about that. If we can get a couple of bags, we can make up a hamper for the market, and we shall get about ten shillings each out of the business, and that's a consideration."

The thought of the ten shillings and what he might do with it for his starving wife and mother decided Frank, and he arranged to meet Ben that evening.

As they were parting Ben said, "You had better bring your gun with you. If we can't get enough birds we may knock over a rabbit or two to make up."

Frank spent the rest of the afternoon cleaning his gun. Not that this operation was necessary, but the thought of the poaching expedition made him restless and uneasy. He felt that he must be doing something, though he could not bestow any attention on anything that was unconnected with the project of the night.

He almost wished that he had not decided to go. The idea of poaching had always been repugnant to him; it seemed too much like stealing, and then it was so low. He had always possessed a sort of self-respect, and had refrained from doing anything which would injure him in the estimation of others. Though friendly with Ben Green, he had never been too intimately associated with him. To go poaching, was to his mind to sink to the level of the vagabond. Once he started up to go after Ben to tell him that he would not go that night; but a look round the miserable room kept him back. Could he sink any lower than he had already done? It was not his fault that they were hard up, and they must have food.

He had arranged to meet Ben at nine o'clock, so as soon as the town clock struck eight he set off, with his gun under his arm, and without giving any but the shortest answers to his wife's anxious questions.

A little distance from his home a footpath, leading through the churchyard, took him out into the main road, without passing through the town.

After following the road a short distance, and passing the turnpike-gate, he would come to another footpath, which, running across some fields and through a copse, led to Dyke's corner, where he had arranged to meet Ben. As he passed through the gate the gatekeeper, who was fastening his window shutter for the night, recognised him, and bade him good night.

Hurrying along in the darkness, his mind perturbed and full of foreboding, he had not noticed a man walking slowly in front of him until he was close by him. As Frank approached the other turned round. It was Sergeant Gripper.

[4 August 1888]

Chapter IX.

It was a black night. The stars and moon were obscured by heavy clouds, drifted by a gusty wind, which soughed mournfully through the trees and portended storm. Behind the lamps of Benton twinkled like tiny stars through the darkness, and made the immediate surroundings look blacker. In spite of the darkness the two men mutually recognised each other on the instant. An instinctive dislike caused Frank to draw back as soon as he saw who his companion was. But the other was too quick for him.

"So, my fine fellow, it has come to this, has it?" said he. "You're going from bad to worse. Thieving a little while ago, and now it's poaching. Oh, yes. I daresay you would," he added, roughly seizing Frank by the arm, as the latter turned to go. "You don't get off so easily, my man. I know what you are up to, and I shall make it my business to give you a night's lodging."

"Take care you don't drive me too far. I've never done anything wrong yet as you know. Even if you did get me two months, what I did was no crime, but I tell you I am getting desperate, and if you interfere with me I may do you a mischief."

"You! you scoundrel! You threaten me," yelled the sergeant, "you thieving scamp; to talk about having committed no crime, you ought to be ashamed to look anyone in the face."

"I am neither ashamed, nor afraid, to look you in the face," returned Frank, "nor to tell you that I know you to be a villain."

"Ashamed; no, damn you, you're ashamed of nothing, or you wouldn't dare to live as you are doing now on the earnings of your wife, the poor girl you have dragged down to poverty and starvation. A nice husband you have been to her."

"You liar!"

"Liar, am I? You thieving scamp. It's no lie, and you know it; you lazy, skulking rat."

"Let me go," said Frank, shaking off the grasp on his arm. "I don't want to have anything to do with you. I don't want to speak to you; you drive me to desperation."

He spoke quietly; but it was only by a violent effort that he could repress the rising torrent of his anger. All the misery that he and his had suffered for months past came vividly to his mind. The injustice which had been the cause of it all seemed impersonated in this policemen, who mocked, insulted and outraged him. He feared himself; he tried to escape.

"No, but I've got something to do with you, and something I want to say to you," said the Sergeant, again grasping him by the collar, and trying to shake him. "You thought yourself very smart, no doubt, when you cheated me of the girl I loved; but fortune hasn't favoured you so well since. A pretty object you are, skulking around the market after odd jobs; going to the workhouse for relief, like the mean, miserable cur you are; starving your wife and your poor old mother; lounging and loafing about till no one will employ you; and you look as despicable a vagabond as anyone could wish to see."

"You taunt me with my wretchedness, you who have been the main cause of it," said Frank hoarsely, his anger getting the complete mastery.

He wrenched himself free. His brain was on fire, and picking up his gun, which had slipped to the ground, he presented it at his opponent, when the latter sprang at him and seized him by the throat. He dropped his gun and closed with his assailant. For several minutes they struggled thus in the darkness, neither speaking, their lips and teeth set, their breath coming and going in quick gasps, each trying to force the other to the earth.

It was a strange sight, these two men, thus clutching each other by the throat. The one animated by the bitterest feelings of jealousy and hatred, the other enraged by a sense of wrong and injustice, but each experiencing a fierce joy in having his enemy in his grasp. They were on a slight elevation and all around them the wide expanse of country lay wrapped in darkness, except where, at a short distance below, the lamps of the town made a break in the gloom.

On either side of them was a bank, surmounted by a low hedge beyond which stretched the brown fields, on one side down to the river on the other to the plantations which formed part of the park grounds. The silence at night was only broken by their deep breathing, by the low moaning of the wind through the trees in the hedgerow, and by the beating of their feet on the hard ground as first one and then the other gave back a step.

Furious as the taunts of his enemy had made him, and in spite of the fierce gratification of at last grasping him by the throat, the idea of shaking him off, of getting clear away in order to keep his appointment with Ben, and get some food for those at home, was dominant in Frank's mind.[30]

Gripper, on the other hand, felt less desirous of capturing than of throttling his opponent. If he could only get him down! He felt as if he would tear his heart out. Their caps had fallen off, their hair was blown by the wind.

They were pretty equally matched. Though the sergeant was slightly heavier, Frank made up in muscle and agility for what he lacked in weight, and but for the privation he had undergone he would have made short work of his antagonist. As it was, desperation lent force to his arm, and suddenly loosing his hold on Gripper's throat, he brought his arm up under his chin with a jerk and forced him backwards to the ground. Flinging himself free, he picked up his gun, and dashed up the bank, as Gripper rose to his feet.

"If you're wise you'll stop where you are," he shouted, as he broke through the hedge, "for by God I'll blow your brains out if you come after me."

He broke into a run across the fields till he struck the path which led to the meeting place. Hurrying along the path he turned round one or twice, fancying he heard some one following him; perceiving no one he went on.

In the meantime, Sergeant Gripper having picked himself up, and looking over the hedge and seeing nothing of his antagonist, pursued his way till he came to a cross road, here he turned to the right. This road would take him past the point Frank Wilson would have to cross to get to Dyke's Corner, and by following this road along he could get back into Benton by a road which crossed it at a little distance beyond this point. This was his usual round of a night, between eight and ten o'clock, as it marked the town boundary which was on the border of the county.

The sergeant was no coward, although he was a bully, and he never shirked any part of his duty, however disagreeable it might be. Indeed the greatest fault that his humbler fellow citizens had to find with him was that he was altogether too officious and meddling.

The magistrates frequently eulogised him as a zealous and efficient officer. They, indeed, were often deeply indebted to him for exceeding his duty in frustrating the plans of Ben Green and his confreres of the gin and snare.[31] As an auxiliary gamekeeper he was invaluable, and neither dark nights nor bad weather ever prevented him from going his lonely rounds, or from even making them longer than necessary in order to capture or defeat a poacher.

Nevertheless on this particular occasion he almost wished himself back at the station. He was angry with himself for having let Wilson escape him, and the fall had given him a nasty shaking, not more calculated to steady his nerves than was the road he was then traversing on to raise his spirits, though he had trodden it many score of nights before.

It was a narrow lonely road. Even in the daytime it seemed dark and lonesome, with its tall hawthorn hedges on each side which were interspersed with huge elms and oaks, whose branches intertwined overhead and shut out the light.

The wind had freshened, and it was beginning to rain heavily. This did not trouble him much, however, as he was well clad and the trees afforded good shelter, but the wailing of the wind through their branches sounded dirge-like and mournful, and this, with the reaction, after the violent struggle in which he had been engaged, depressed and unnerved him, so that he started when he heard someone approaching from the opposite direction to that in which he was walking. He waited for the person, whoever it might be, to meet him. It was a woman. Turning on his lantern he recognised Alice Steggles.

The sight of her dispelled his gloomy feelings, though he was surprised to see her there at that hour.

Where could she have been? She might have gone to meet George Cranston, it was not very far from there to Denmere. The thought awakened alike his jealousy and his desire.

"Why, Alice, what are you doing here at this hour?" he asked.

"Don't ask impertinent questions, sir," she replied with a smile, "perhaps I came to meet you; and perhaps I didn't. Anyhow, now I have met you you had better walk back home with me, it's rather later than I care to be out alone."

"Just as if I wouldn't sooner walk back to the Lion with you than go all round the other way alone," he interjected.

"Oh no, you only say that," she rejoined. "If you meant it, you wouldn't talk about it at all. But, of course, you must attend to your *duty*. I suppose you are after some poor poacher to-night, or are you afraid that some one will set fire to old Brown's hayrick if you don't visit it every night? I passed a couple of little boys just up the road who scuttled off like scared rabbits when they saw me. Perhaps you had better go after them."

Gripper thought she had never seemed to charming as she did then, standing there saucily jeering him, and told her so as he advanced towards her, and seizing her round the waist attempted to kiss her.

"No, you don't Mr. Policeman," said she, administering him a vigorous slap with her right hand, while with the other she endeavoured to free herself from his embrace, "I am surprised at you."

"Hark, there is some one coming."

He reluctantly released her, and bidding her good-night, pursued his way.

The rain had ceased, but the sky was still clouded.

As he reached the point where the path to Dyke's Corner crossed the road, he fancied he heard some one on the other side of the hedge on his right.

"Surely," he said to himself, "it can't be that fellow Wilson lurking here waiting for me to pass before he goes on."

He clambered up the bank to where there was an opening in the hedge. "Now, my fine fellow, I'll have you if you're here," he murmured.

Forcing his way though, he uttered an exclamation of surprise as he came face to face with the man who was clambering towards him up the other side of the bank. He seized him by the collar, and for a moment they struggled on the summit. Suddenly the sergeant's foot slipped on the muddy bank, and, releasing his hold, he slid to the bottom. As he rose to his feet the light of the moon, breaking trough a rift in the clouds, shone full upon him; the instant after from out the darkness came a flash and a report. He threw up his arms and staggering back fell prone in the mud of the roadway with a gunshot wound in his breast from which his heart's blood was welling.

[11 August 1888]

Chapter X.

Benton was in a great state of excitement. In the extraordinary manner in which anything that happens in a small country town immediately seems to be known to everyone, the fact that Sergeant Gripper had been murdered seemed to have become known to all the inhabitants of Benton at once, as soon as they rose in the morning.

It was one of those bright balmy mornings which sometimes break the dullness of an English November with suggestions of returning Spring. The sun shone bright in a sky from which the clouds of the preceding night had all disappeared. The air was still and warm.

In Brook Street the women were gathered in little groups before their doors, talking, laughing, occasionally glancing up the street towards the dwelling from which Frank Wilson had been taken by the police early that morning. In the shops in the High Street, where some had gone to make their morning purchases, the murder of Sergeant Gripper formed an engrossing topic of conversation, and the probability of Wilson's guilt was freely discussed. In the market place there was an unusually large number of loungers, men and youths, several of whom had already been to view the scene of the murder. Most of these believed that Wilson was the murderer, they seemed to regard his arrest as conclusive evidence of his guilt.

As the hour approached for Wilson to be brought before the magistrates, the number of those in the market place, before the corn exchange, increased. The excitement became more intense. Women left their house work, shopkeepers closed their shops, many of the men from the ironworks had left off work, and all were there in this crowd, pushing, jostling, chattering, shouting, laughing, all eager, excited, waiting to catch a glimpse of the man whom they had known for years, whom they had passed unnoticed day by day, but who had suddenly become an object of interest to them through being arrested for murder.

In a group apart, Ben Green, with several of Frank's mates, were defending him against some shopkeepers who were strongly convinced of his guilt.

"When a man once starts you don't know where he'll stop," said one, "he started by stealing watercresses and he's ended by committing murder."

"It's very well to talk like that but you know that it wasn't stealing that he got sent to gaol for, and I daresay you would have bought some of his watercresses when he brought 'em round."

"What's that got to do with it? I might have done so out of kindness to him, but I didn't ask him to get them, of course he did that at his own risk and had to take the consequences."

"That don't show that he shot Gripper though."

"Who else could have done it? Turner sees them both go through the gate last night, one after the other, and then he hears a quarrel and some time after sees Wilson come back by himself. It seems pretty plain to me."

This was the general view, and in fact the feeling of the crowd was so strong against Frank that when his wife appeared, looking pale and ill, trembling with anxiety, they made way for her, shunning her as one stricken with the plague and regarding her with aversion, as though she too were guilty of murder.

She stood apart, grasping the railings of the building for support, feeling faint and ready to fall to the ground under the glances, almost menacing, that were occasionally turned towards her.

When Ben Green approached and spoke to her, the other good folks were even more offended.

"One sees the company they keep," they murmured, "it is not surprising if a man begins with poaching and ends with murder."

The crowd continued to grow. It seemed as if the whole town had turned out to see the miserable wretch who they believed to have committed this offence against the public peace.

As the time passed on the excitement increased. There was a constant murmur, low and indistinct, which grew into a roar as the culprit appeared between two policemen and guarded by four others, two in front and two behind.

Miserable and wretched he looked; his hair and beard unkempt and ragged, his face pale and haggard, his eyes heavy and bloodshot, like those of one who had been kept awake for a night by some terrible calamity. And old greasy cap on his head, collarless, his coat threadbare and ragged, his worn moleskin trousers, as well as his boots, soaked with mud; his appearance was certainly not calculated to prepossess anyone in his favour.

The crowd was not favourably disposed to him, and his miserable appearance increased their disfavour. The roar became menacing. As the police closed around him he cast a look round on the excited mob. They interpreted his look as one of defiance, and yelled, hurling foul epithets at him as the police forced a way through. If he had hung his head they would have regarded it as additional evidence of guilt; because he held his head upright they were shocked at his audacity.

Many of them had been on terms of the closest friendship with him; but with the exception of a few who pitied or sympathised with him they were ready to tear him to pieces. It was sufficient for them that he was down; they could well afford to kick him.

They pressed after him and his guard through the gate into the court room. The magistrates were already assembled, looking more than ordinarily solemn and severe. Their dignified appearance awed the crowd into silence, as the prisoner was placed before them.

Superintendent Williams, who had come from Oldbury to take charge of the police investigations, stated the charge against the prisoner of having murdered Sergeant Gripper.

Standing there between two policemen Frank felt as though he were passing through some horrid dream. He raised his manacled hands to his face, he wiped his clammy brow, and looked around. On the silent, angry crowd, all with upturned faces gazing scowlingly at him, on the bare whitewashed walls; on the windows, through which the bright sunlight was streaming; on the portly, sedate, well-fed, well-clad gentlemen, sitting there so calm and impassible, waiting to hear him charged with the terrible crime of murder.

It was a new experience for them, these comfortable country magnates, to have a murder case to deal with. The most important charges they had ever before had to deal with were poaching, turnip stealing and nutting. Now, it was murder, and they were correspondingly stern and severe. Frank gazed at them till each one of their faces seemed engraved on his mind; that of his late employer, red and sinister, seemed to glower at him like that of a mocking fiend. Again, his gaze wandered round till his eyes rested upon the face of his wife.

Shrinking away from the brutal crowd; shivering with fear and weakness, her eager anxiety to watch the result struggling with her timidity and her desire to escape observation; she stood cowering in a corner of the cold, bare, white-washed building, looking almost unearthly, with her white face peering out from beneath her black straw bonnet.

Police-constable Warren narrated the circumstances under which he had arrested the prisoner. The sergeant, he said, had gone his round as usual, leaving him on duty at the station. He usually returned about ten o'clock. That evening, however, he, the witness, waited till ten, and then he did not return. As the time passed on he became anxious, till at length, at midnight, he determined to go in search of him. He went in the opposite direction to that taken by the sergeant, thinking he might perhaps meet him. As he did not meet him he searched more carefully, and as he neared the corner of Marsh Road he saw him lying in the roadway. He spoke to him, but got no answer. He endeavoured to raise him up, and then found that he was quite dead. He came back towards Benton and roused the gatekeeper, telling him what he had seen. He afterwards returned to the town and knocked up the landlord of the Red Lion, with whom he returned, with a horse and cart, and fetched the body of his late superior. He afterwards walked to Oldbury, a distance of nine miles, to inform Superintendent Williams, who returned with him. In consequence of what the gatekeeper told him he afterwards with the superintendent arrested the prisoner at his own house.

James Turner, the gatekeeper, stated that he saw the sergeant pass through the gate on his rounds, about half-past eight on the preceding evening, and shortly afterwards he saw the prisoner. The latter was carrying a gun. He soon after heard the two men in altercation. He did not hear all that passed, as it was some little distance from his place; but after the quarrel had gone on for several minutes he distinctly heard the prisoner call out, "By God, if you come after me I'll blow your brains out!" About three hours after this the prisoner returned through the gate on his way home. He saw him, because he had some difficulty in opening the gate, and witness, who had not then retired, came out to let him through. It was some time after this when the constable knocked him up.

Superintendent Williams stated that he did not propose to submit any further evidence then. He had simply put forward what he thought would be sufficient to secure a remand,[32] and he asked that the prisoner should be remanded on this evidence until after the inquest.

The chairman asked if the prisoner had made any statement, to which the super-intendent replied that when arrested he had said, "Oh, I suppose this is Gripper's doing," and appeared very much startled when informed of the nature of the charge."

Frank was then asked if he had anything to say or if he wished to ask either of the witnesses any question. He said, "All I have to say, gentlemen, is that I am absolutely innocent of having caused the death of any man. More than that I can-not say. I have no question to ask either of the witnesses, as so far as I know, they have spoken the truth, except this, I would like to ask Mr. Turner if he saw anyone else pass through the gate towards Benton before I returned, and also if he heard any shots fired." Turner stated that he did not notice any firing, the place of the murder was some distance off, and only two persons, Alice Steggles and some time after, George Cranston had passed through the gate before Frank returned.

In reply to the magistrates Superintendent Williams said that both these persons were in attendance but he did not propose to call them until after the inquest, unless the magistrates wished to ask them any questions. He asked that the prisoner should be remanded.

This course was adopted, and Frank was removed; he and his escort being followed by a howling mob to the railway station, where they took train to the county gaol, some fifteen miles distant.

[18 August 1888]

Chapter XI.

It was four o'clock when Frank's wife returned home. As she opened the door she was surprised to see a man, a stranger, sitting by the empty fireplace smoking a clay pipe. As she entered, the mother, who was sitting by the table, her head on her hand, rose and came towards her.

"It's all over now, Polly," said she. "Brown has put this man in for the rent. We shall have to go to the workhouse, now."

"As if we hadn't got trouble enough," exclaimed her daughter-in-law, sinking into a chair and beginning to cry. "They have sent poor Frank back to prison for a week. Everybody seems to be against him. They all speak of him as a murderer; and now we are to be robbed of our home. Whatever shall we do?"

"Don't take on so, Missus," interposed the man, sympathetically. "These kind o' things will happen to the best on us, ye know. 'Taint very much, arter all; only a matter of a pound or so. I daresay you'll be able to raise that."

"Where can I go to get twenty shillings," said she, turning to the old woman, without noticing the speaker. "I don't know who would let us have as many pence, now. But I wouldn't care about that even, if poor Frank were safe. Oh, mother, mother! I know he is innocent, but they do not believe it. They will kill him."[33]

She bowed her head on the table and sobbed bitterly.

The mother sat silently gazing at her; her deeply lined face pale and set; her eyes dry and brilliant; her clasped hands, resting on the table, twitching nervously.

There was a knock at the door. No one stirred. It was repeated.

"Come in," said the old woman, in a dry, unnatural tone.

It was Ben Green. He had come straight there, after having had a warm discussion with some of the crowd who loitered about the Corn Exchange, after the examination had closed.

"What, crying?" exclaimed he, cheerily. "Don't go for to be downhearted, Missus. It'll be all right, by-and-by, don't you fear that."

"Well, Bill Jarvis, what be you up to here?" continued he, turning to the man who was still looking out of the window, quietly smoking his pipe.

"Oh, it's only a little matter o' rent, Ben. P'raps you'll settle it for the good lady, eh?"

"I'll damn soon settle you, if you don't make yourself scarce, my boy. Old Brown must be a mean old swine to put you in here just now; and you aint much better to lower yourself to do such dirty work."

"Easy, Ben, old fellow. I've got to get my living, and I only do what I'm ordered to do. The rights and wrongs on't is nothin' to do wi' me. That's all settled by our betters."

"Well, you'd better clear out, d'ye see? There's the door, and the word's walker. Go and get yourself a drink, and forget to come back."

"I'm here, and here I've got to stop till the money's paid or the goods is took. Not as there's much to take," he added with a glance round the almost empty room.

"If you don't go out I shall put you out, now then," said Ben, throwing open the door and advancing towards Jarvis in a threatening manner.

Jarvis placed his pipe on the window-sill, and stood on the defensive.

"You keep your hands off me or it'll be the worse for you," said he. "I don't see what it's got to do with you, anyhow."

"Don't you? Then I'll show you," said Ben, seizing him by the collar, and pushing him towards the door.

He was about the throw him out violently, when Mrs. Wilson interposed,

"No, no; what is the use? We shall have to go; you will only get yourself into trouble by interfering."

Ben desisted and turned to go. The old woman was standing upright, outraged, indignant, disgusted that she should have been brought to this, to witness such a scene in her home.

"I wanted to speak to you alone," said Ben, turning to the younger woman. She followed him outside.

"I've brought you ten shillings," said he, in a low voice, as soon as she had closed the door behind her. Then, as she made a gesture of refusal, he added,

"Oh, it's all right; I owe it to Frank; you needn't be afraid to take it. I know you want it bad enough, and I shall be going to work next week."

She took the money reluctantly, and re-entered the house.

The mother was still standing by the table.

"Things have come to a pretty pass," said she, "when you allow that man to come here and conduct himself in that way. To think that my boy should ever have had anything to do with such a low ruffian! It's time I was gone out of the way. There is only the workhouse or the grave for me now."

Her daughter-in-law made no reply, but set about some needlework.

Bill Jarvis resumed his pipe and his seat by the fireplace. Ben Green walked slowly down to the Red Lion.

This was a bad business, and no mistake. Frank Wilson had been a good friend to him, on more than one occasion; had once paid a fine for him to save him going to gaol; but this friendship had proved unfortunate for Frank. A pity he asked him to go with him last night. Well, if it came to the worst his course was clear – Anyway, now he would see if it were possible to do something to save the wife and mother from the workhouse.

With this idea in his mind he found himself at the Lion.

Mr. Steggles was beginning to be busy. It was six o'clock, and the men from the neighbouring ironworks were coming in. Contrary to his usual habit Crosbie came with them.

Ben beckoned him on one side, and informed him of what was taking place in Wilson's home. He asked him if it was possible to do anything amongst the men to save the wife and mother from the workhouse.

Crosbie shrugged his shoulders.

"No use; not a bit," said he. "They're on short time now, and some of 'em will be off this week, I couldn't ask 'em for anything. Besides, what good would it do? Suppose we paid the rent for her this time, in another week or two it would be just the same. It's only a question of a few weeks anyhow; you couldn't expect these men to keep 'em altogether."

"No, but I should have thought they might ha' done something. They may be hard up, as you say, but they manage to find something to come here with."

"I might say the same of you. You look pretty seedy, but you're very often here. Men must have something to drink and it's precious little they spend here, you know very well."

"That may be, but it wouldn't take much to keep them two women going. Half a pint o' beer a day for each man 'ud do it, with what his wife could earn herself."

"What's the good of talking," said the other, impatiently, "they won't do it. They want every penny they get. If they spend a penny in beer they have to go without something else. It isn't as it if was only for a short time. Wilson is sure to be convicted, and then his wife won't be able to get any work, even if she was able to do it, and she don't look fit for work now."

"You don't believe he's guilty, do you?"

"It's hard to say what a man'll do when he's drove into a corner. I pity him from the bottom of my heart, but I don't see what's to be done."

He emptied his glass and went out.

Mr. Steggles came to Ben when he saw him alone.

"I suppose you don't know anything about this, Ben?" said he curiously.

"No; and don't want. I was about your business last night as you know. And I'll tell you what, you'd better keep pretty mum about where you got them birds; and what's more, make much on 'em, for it'll be some time before I get you any more. I've just got a reg'lar job up at Apsted Farm, and am going to lead a respectable life on 'leven bob a week. After all, I believe it'll pay better'n t'other."

Going back to the bar he saw Alice, who had just come down. Her eyes were red, as thought she had been crying. As soon as the opportunity presented itself he told her of her cousin's trouble.

"Don't you think you could get the old man to do something for 'em?" he asked.

"I'm afraid not," she replied, sadly, "but I'll try."

"I suppose the inquest 'll be held here?" queried Ben.

"Yes, to-morrow, I believe. Isn't it dreadful? But I feel most sorry for poor Frank. I don't believe, and never shall believe that he did it. And to think I have got to go as a witness."

"But you didn't see Frank last night, did you?"

"No; but I saw the sergeant only a short time before he must have been shot. You don't think Frank did it, do you?"

"No," said Ben, as he turned to go.

Alice appealed to her father on behalf of the Wilsons. He was furious.

"Certainly not," said he, when she asked if he would pay their rent for them to keep them out of the workhouse. "That fellow had brought quite enough disgrace upon us. Let them go to the house, that's the proper place for them. We don't want to have anything to do with murderers."

"Oh, father! How can you speak in such a way of poor Frank!"

"Poor Frank, indeed! It would be more becoming of you to keep your pity for the poor fellow who lies dead in the other room. I hope you won't talk like that before customers. We want people to forget that he is any connection of ours."

The next day the inquest was held and the jury returned a verdict of wilful murder against Frank Wilson.

On the following day Frank's little remaining furniture was taken away to be sold.

When Ben Green called in the evening, he found the two women crouching on the bare brick floor. He offered to find them accommodation in his own house. The younger woman accepted his offer, but when she attempted to move, she found herself too weak and ill to walk, and it was necessary to get a cart to take her. The weather was cold, wet and miserable.

The old woman refused to accompany her; she would not be beholden to this poacher; she whose husband had been a gamekeeper to the lord of the manor. Her daughter-in-law, herself almost too weak to talk, begged her to accompany her, but without avail. She looked at Ben as though she did not comprehend what he was saying when he offered her the shelter of his roof, or as though every word he uttered were an insult which she could only meet with silent contempt. That night she cried herself to sleep, like a child, on the cold damp floor of the dismantled home. The next day she went into the workhouse.

[25 August 1888]

Chapter XII.

It was the evening of a raw cold day. A leaden sky overspread the bare brown landscape and threatened snow. A bleak north-east wind whistled through the bare branches of the trees which surrounded three sides of the residence of Mr. Cranston. The summer brightness had all disappeared and the scene was dull, mournful, deathlike. Cheerless as was the scene without, however, inside all was bright and cheerful enough. In the dining room a right fire burnt merrily, casting a ruddy glow on the rich brown and gold of the furniture and decorations. The heavy curtains close drawn, the massive candelabra, the costly mahogany, the soft velvety carpet, the glittering glass and silver on the table and sideboard, all betokened wealth and luxury, all breathed warmth and comfort, comfort rendered the more enjoyable by the bleak scene without.

It was the evening of the day after Frank Wilson's few remaining goods had been taken for rent, the evening of the day on which his poor old mother had betaken herself to the prison house which the Pecksniffian charity[34] of civilised Christian England constrains her to provide her worn-out or reserve workers – the workhouse.

The capitalist was in good spirits, the warmth and light, as well as the more material comfort of the good dinner he was eating, exhilarated him. This was not all however. He with his son George had just devised a scheme by which the works could be run more economically, which scheme he was just then explaining to the guest on his right, the Rev. Mr. Gray. For some few weeks work had been rather slack and the men had been working three quarter time. He now intended to discharge one fourth of the men and allow the others to work full time. This he thought would not only mean an economy of fuel, but the men whose services were retained would be grateful for being allowed to work full time, and would therefore be more industrious for fear of being discharged. "The same fear, too, will enable me to reduce their wages also," said he, his rubicund visage glowing with satisfaction at the idea of the increment to his income that would be thus effected. "And, indeed, it will really do the men themselves good, you know. They really have too much money to spend and it leads them into mischief. Intemperance and all the vices that spring from it are all due to workmen having more money than is really necessary to satisfy their reasonable requirements."

"I quite agree with you," said the reverend gentleman, calmly sipping his port, "how much of the crime which disgraces the working classes might be prevented if all employers of labour did but take the same wise view."

"That is a question in which I take a very deep interest," chimed in Jack Somers, from the other end of the table. "Working men are too independent, and I think employers are very much to blame for not keeping them down more. They ought to be kept down."

Jack Somers had been staying with the Cranstons for a few weeks for the shooting.

When the ladies had withdrawn and the men were smoking their cigars, Mr. Cranston renewed the subject –

"Without doubt," said he, "it will be rather a bad job for the men who will be discharged, but of course, that's their business, not mine. I've to look after my own interests and do the best I can with my business. But by and bye, when we get busy we shall be able to take them on again."

"Certainly," replied the clergyman, "I suppose they won't have gone away by the time you want them again?"

"Oh no, business it too slack all round for them to get work anywhere else."

"And, as you say," continued the clergyman, "it will be a good thing for them after all, it will teach them to be thrifty in the future if they have not been so in the past."

"Just so. Why these men might easily have saved sufficient to keep themselves all through the winter if they had only been careful with what they have earned. Drink and extravagance are the ruin of workmen. Look, for instance, at that fellow Wilson, who shot the police-sergeant. I don't know that he was a drunkard, but then he was so foolish as to get married and to keep his mother at home when she ought to have gone into the workhouse. It is such extravagance as that which drove him into the evil courses which have brought him to the gallows."

"You really believe that it was he who shot the sergeant, then?" queried Jack Somers.

"I have not the slightest doubt about it, my dear sir. The evidence is so clear, and besides who else could have done it?"

"Well, it's a mercy it was only the policeman," said Mr. Gray, "it might have been Mr. George here. Of course, those men have to undertake the risks of their calling, and there are plenty more to take their places if anything happens to them. But I really should like to know" – helping himself to another glass of port – "if this crime were in any way traceable to drink. It would considerably strengthen my hands in the crusade I am now carrying on against beer in the harvest field."

"Do you find it obtain much favour among the farmers, this new idea?"

"Well, not to such an extent as one might imagine. Farmers are strongly prejudiced in favour of the old methods, and it is with considerable difficulty that we can induce them to try anything new. The present agricultural depression however, is leading them to endeavour to carry on their business with greater economy and this of course helps the movement."

"Unfortunately," said the capitalist, "it seems to me that most agriculturalists are inclined to favour a return to protection. That the country will never stand. We depend upon our manufactures for our national prosperity, and protection, by increasing the cost of commodities, would simply kill our manufactures. We, sir," he continued, his red face becoming more red as he grew eloquent with his themes, "we, the men who represent the power, the wealth, and the influence of the great British nation, would be ruined, and the nation would be bankrupt."

"Exactly what I am constantly pointing out to the farmers. They are casting about for means to tide over this depression, to ward off the ruin which they see menacing them, I suggest that they should take advantage of the one thing to which they ascribe their depression – the universal cheapness, to avert misfortune. If they would but inculcate the principles of sobriety and thrift among their labourers, they would be able to get labour much cheaper, and it is in this direction that they should seek to economise."

"That is so," interjected Jack Somers. "They, like all employers, pay their workpeople too well; it makes them too independent; they should keep them down."

"And besides," resumed the rector, "it would be to the inestimable advantage of the labourers themselves. I was reading a little book the other day entitled, 'How to Live on Sixpence a Day.' It is a most excellent work, and should be widely circulated among our working population. If they would only follow its teachings, we should soon hear a great deal less of the rubbish which is now talked about 'starvation wages,' and should soon reap the advantage of greater thrift among our working people in a revival of trade, through being better able to compete with the foreigners. If we could only get our farmers to refuse any longer to give beer to their workpeople, a great deal would have been done in this direction, as well as effecting an improvement in the morals and general habits of the labourers. And their good is, after all, what one ought first to consider. Don't you think so, Mr. Somers?"

"Well, no; I can't say that I do; and I scarcely imagine anyone else does either, whatever one may get into the habit of saying about the matter. There they are, down; and it answers our purpose to keep them down; that's all that I think about it. Undoubtedly it is as well to make them believe that we do so for their good, but there can be no reason whatever for humbugging ourselves."

"But surely you don't suggest that they are treated unjustly, or that they are 'kept down,' as you term it, to their disadvantage? They are paid for their services, and need not accept what is offered them; they are perfectly free to reject it if they choose. There is no force or fraud about that."

"I never said there was. I only entered a mild protest against humbug. We get them to do all the dirty, disagreeable work which we don't care to do ourselves, and we pay them just as little as we can get them to take. They are fools enough to do the work, and to accept very little in return. This suits me, for one, admirably; and if we can humbug them into the idea that it is all for their good, in this world and the next, so much the better; but we shall succeed in humbugging them the better if we clearly understand what we are after, and don't attempt to deceive ourselves."

"After all, they seem happy and contented enough," said George, "and I don't see why they shouldn't be; they get a great deal more then they are worth, I know that."

"Oh, of course; I don't deny that, only I shouldn't care to change places with any of them, that's all I know my boy; now would you? Therefore I say keep them down."

The others thought it was time to change the conversation, and a move was made for the drawing room, where were Mrs. and Miss Cranston and the rector's daughter.

"Yes, I think it is very dreadful," the capitalist's wife was saying as they entered. "Just fancy; one poor creature, who used to have an income of twelve hundred a year, now only receives three hundred; they say she is in an almost destitute state, and all through that wicked Land League."[35]

"We were talking about the distressed Irish ladies, papa," explained Miss Gray. "The Lord Mayor of London has opened a fund for their relief, and Mrs. Cranston was suggesting that we might do something here to assist. What is your opinion?"

"I think it is a most laudable object, and shall be pleased to do all in my power to further it. I might, perhaps, preach a sermon with that object."

"I have already mentioned the matter to several," said Mr. Cranston, "and if my wife will start a list, as it is a ladies' question I have no doubt that a considerable amount will be subscribed. Among others, Mr. Brown has promised a pound in the event of a subscription being raised here."

"Oh, Brown ought to do something," said George. "He should have some sympathy with distressed landlords and ladies, seeing that he has just had some experience with one troublesome tenant, whose furniture he had to seize for rent."

"Yes; well that's the proper thing to do, anyhow," said Jack Somers. "If people won't pay their rent, sell them up or turn them out. Irish landlords have made the mistake of being too lenient, and it is that which has given rise to the present agitation.[36] It will be the same with our working-class if they are not kept down."

"The leniency of the landlords and the disestablishment of the Irish Church[37] are together the cause of most of the troubles at afflict Ireland," said Mr. Gray, rising to go. "However, it is for the respectable classes everywhere to stand together in a crisis like the present, and I trust that we in Benton shall not be wanting in our duty."

And with this very laudable aspiration the worthy clergyman departed with his daughter.

[1 September 1888]

Chapter XIII.

The following week Frank Wilson was again brought up for examination. Unlike the previous occasion the weather was dull and cold, and the chill north-east wind penetrated his ragged jacket and froze the blood in his veins. There was a crowd awaiting his arrival at the railway station, and another and larger crowd in the market place. The inclement weather had not sufficed to dispel the excitement, though the people were by no means so demonstrative as on the day after the murder. Many of them, indeed, could not help feeling a thrill of pity for the poor wretch as he passed, pale and shivering, with his escort, from the station to the corn exchange.

The silence of the crowd depressed him even more than their former loudly expressed hostility had done. He glanced round on the many familiar faces in the crowd till his gaze met that of Ben Green, who was standing, moody and silent, near the entrance. As their eyes met Ben's face lighted up, but it was only for a moment; he averted his face and passed into the hall.

The crowd inside was scarcely as large as on the former occasion. The novelty of having a murderer in their midst had worn off and the result of the examination, they felt, was a foregone conclusion. Still there were a good many present. Among others Frank caught sight of Mr. Steggles and Alice, the former, dressed in black and looking as solemn as an undertaker at a funeral, stared at Frank as though he had never seen him before in his life, while his daughter hung down her head, shading her face with her hand as though she was crying silently.

Frank would have liked to have spoken to her but that was impossible. He looked round anxiously to see if his wife was present. He could not see her; nor his mother. There was George Cranston, sitting by his father on the bench, prepared, as he understood, to give evidence against him; there was Turner, the gatekeeper, and Alice Steggles, both friends of his and both witnesses against him. For himself he had no witnesses, he scarcely comprehended the serious nature of the charge brought against him, its enormity had crushed and dazed him. It did not seem real. All that was clear and vivid to his mind was that he was in custody, forcibly detained from his home, that his wife and mother were ill, starving, perhaps dying, and he unable to assist them even by his presence, unable even to gain any tidings of them.

As soon a silence had been called, Superintendent Williams kissed the book and proceeded to state that since the previous examination the police had pursued their investigations with the result that they had found the prisoner's gun which had evidently been recently discharged. They also found that the pellets extracted from the murdered man's body were similar to a quantity of shot found in the possession of the prisoner.

The gun and pellets were here produced and created a marked impression upon the occupants of the bench and the audience.

The witness went on to say that he had also gone over the scene of the crime and had taken wax impressions, which he produced, of footmarks in the field behind the hedge and in the roadway. These impressions corresponded with the boots the prisoner was wearing on the night of the crime, which were peculiar, being odd ones, one having tips and hob nails and the other only tips.

Dr. Smart, a pompous individual, imbued with a strong sense of his own importance, deposed to having examined the body of Sergeant Gripper, and described the nature of the wound which had caused his death. The shot, he said, must have been fired point blank at him and within a short distance. Death must have been almost instantaneous.

Superintendent Williams stated that he had no further evidence to offer. Alice Steggles and Mr. George Cranston, both of whom had been seen by the witness Turner on the night in question shortly before or after the murder, were present and were willing to give evidence if the magistrates desired to hear their statement, but what they knew was of so little importance that he did not propose to call them unless the magistrates expressed such a desire. The evidence of Turner, and the additional proof that he himself had obtained, were, he submitted, quite sufficient to justify the magistrates in committing the prisoner for trial.[38]

"Well, for my part," said Mr. Cranston, "I have no doubt whatever as to the prisoner's guilt. He is a bad character, he has been loafing about out of work for months, he has been to gaol, where he was sent mainly on the evidence of the murdered man and that no doubt was the motive which prompted him to the diabolical crime. He could have been there at that time of night for no other purpose."

"It would be just as well, perhaps, to ask the prisoner if he has any explanation to offer, or any defence to make, before you express any opinion," mildly suggested the chairman, Colonel Ashville.

"No, sir, I have no explanation to offer," said Frank who had been stung out of his lethargy by the words of his old employer, "But why should I be asked to give any such explanation? I was there, I admit it. I had a gun, I saw the sergeant, I quarrelled with him and when he attempted to arrest me I threw him down and escaped. In a moment of anger I threatened him, but I declare to God that I am absolutely innocent of his death. I did not go there to seek him, I avoided him as much as possible, and have never seen him since I threw him down in the roadway. But why, I ask again, should I alone be asked to make such an explanation? Mr. George Cranston, it appears, was also near there. He too had a gun. One man is as good as another. Let him stand forward and explain what he was doing about there with a gun. I've got as much right to carry a gun around of a night as he has, or if I haven't I ought to have. As for you," he continued, turning to old Cranston, whose red face became purple under the look of scorn with which the speaker regarded him. "You who have done all in your power to deprive me of the means of earning a livelihood and now sit here as one of my judges; even if I had committed a crime it is you who would have been really guilty. But I am innocent, while you are guilty of a crime by the side of which that with which I stand charged sinks into insignificance. You have robbed me of my living, you have murdered my happiness and through your implacable hatred for the man you have injured the two helpless women depending on me who are being slowly murdered by starvation. But what am I saying? I am innocent. Let him stand up and explain why he was in the Marsh Road on the night Sergeant Gripper was shot."

There was a slight murmur of applause as Frank paused for breath, his eyes glaring fiercely on his persecutor, his face flushed, his manacled hands raised half threateningly, half imploringly.

The silence that followed was broken by Mr. Cranston, who in a voice betokening suppressed anger said, "Mr. George Cranston is perfectly willing to explain all that he knows with reference to that unhappy night, and I think it would be well if his evidence were taken."

This, however, the other magistrates regarded as unnecessary, and the prisoner was committed to trial.

Frank was conveyed back to the railway station, accompanied by a crowd of men and youths, though the demonstration was not so large or so noisy as on the former occasion.

Going along in the train, rapidly nearing the gaol, from whence he would be brought only to go through the form of a trial which it appeared to him would have but one termination, Frank reviewed in his mind all that had passed since he had left Cranston's.

The fresh north-east wind was blowing in at the carriage window, bearing the strong, indescribable odour of moss and dead leaves from the surrounding woodland. Daylight was declining, the sky was cold, leaden and threatening; the cold breeze seemed to stimulate his mental activity.

He regarded his case as hopeless. Appearances were all against him; there was only his bare word against all those tremendous links in the chain of evidence which was dragging him to a murderer's doom. He would be convicted, nay, was he not practically convicted already? He would be hanged. Horrible thought! The words burnt into his heart. Hanged! Strangled to death as a murderer inside the prison walls. Never more to see the bright fields and woods of his boyhood. Never more to indulge in those manly sports which had been the pleasure of his life, and in which he had excelled! What had he done to merit such a fate? And, then, what would become of his wife and poor old mother? What, indeed, had become of them even now? He had seen nor heard nothing of them since he saw his wife in the court-room the day of his arrest. He noticed how their neighbours shunned his wife then. Despised, contemned, hated as the relatives of a murderer they might have starved to death. The thought was maddening. He started to his feet, but was rudely forced back on the seat by one of his police-guards.

"You just keep still, young fellow," said he, "or it'll be the worse for you. You needn't think you're going to get away. We'll take good care you don't get the chance to kill any more policemen. You'll precious soon go where there are no police to trouble you if you are lucky."

Frank took no notice of this speech, but turning to another policeman he said, "Can you tell me anything of my wife and mother. I was thinking of them, and forgot myself. If you could tell me anything about them it would be a great relief to me, and I will pray with my latest breath that you may never know the agony I now suffer, may never have to beg for the favour I now ask."

"You needn't trouble your head about them," said the one who had first spoken. "They're all right. The old woman has gone to the workhouse, where she'll be well looked after and yer missus 'll most likely be in heaven before you to give you a welcome there. All murderers go to heaven nowadays, you know."

The others grinned at this brutal jest. Frank felt as if he had been stabbed. His mother in the workhouse, his wife dying! He would never see them again, they were parted for ever.

The train slackened speed, they were nearing the station. It stopped, and he and his escort alighted. As they were passing through the barrier where the tickets were being collected, a slight obstruction caused him to be momentarily separated from his guards. Like an electric flash the thought crossed his mind that here was a chance to escape, to see his wife once more before he was condemned to die. He took to his heels and ran, through the station, out into the street, down the street into the main road; tearing along as he had never raced before, sending flying every obstacle that impeded his progress, with a howling, cursing mob of policemen, clerks, men, women, and children at his heels. He was on the road to Benton. If he could keep up his present rate of speed he could out-distance his pursuers, but he was getting exhausted, the handcuffs prevented him from using his arms, and his strength was fast failing. Full in his course was a bridge over the river. If he attempted to cross the bridge his pursuers would be upon him before he reached the summit. It was getting dark, the lamps were lit. On one side of the bridge the road was open down to the towing-path which ran by the river. His pursuers were close upon him. He dashed down by the side of the bridge and plunged into the water.

[8 September 1888]

Chapter XIV.

The cottage in which Ben Green lived was one of a dozen which stood in a row at the upper end of the town. They were built with their backs to those of another row of cottages which faced the main road. These latter were of a better class, and had gardens in front, but the former were miserably poor and dilapidated. The passage in front of them was only wide enough to allow two persons to pass each other. It was paved with rough cobble stones and sloped down on one side to a gutter, which was generally full of the half solid filth that percolated from the cesspool attached to the one privy which was common to the whole dozen cottages. This privy, by the side of which was the well, stood in the centre of the row.

On the opposite and higher side of the passage, facing the cottages, was a high wall, that flanked some fields, which, however, could only be seen from the upstairs windows of the cottages. This passage was appropriately named Paradise Row.

The hovels were mainly inhabited by agricultural labourers; one, at the end of the row, was the home of an itinerant vendor of dried fish, who used to drive round the town and neighbouring villages with his fish in the daytime and block the passage with his donkey barrow at night. Another cottage, at the other end of the row, was occupied by a couple of loose women, who used occasionally, when they came home drunk with their men, to make night hideous with their yells and curses.

Paradise Row was the slum of Benton. Pale-faced, prematurely-aged women sat at the doors plying their needle and nursing puny infants. Stunted half-starved, weazen-faced children paddled in the mud of the filthy gutter, which impregnated the air with an overpowering pestiferous odour.

It was night. The cold north-east wind was vainly trying to purify the malodorous atmosphere of Paradise Row, which in spite of the cold retained its characteristic stench. Inside Ben Green's cottage the lamp was lit. They were having tea. Ben had just returned home from work, and was hungrily devouring huge slices of bread and "scrape," as he termed the very thin layer of butter with which the bread was garnished. This he occasionally helped down with a draught of weak warm tea from a basin. He was seated by the side of the fireplace in which a handful of coal was burning. On the opposite side of the fire sat his wife, a sallow, round-shouldered woman of twenty-seven, who looked forty. A round table stood between them, spread with a white, though much-worn cloth, on which were placed the materials of their frugal repast.

By the side of his wife, on a low stool, sat their two children, two little girls of four and five years of age. The woman was eating a herring, the smell of which mingled with the foul stench that forced its way into the apartment from without. The floor, which was lower than the pavement outside, was of brick, but in places where the bricks had broken away the ground appeared brown and muddy from the moisture which oozed in from the gutter, and which also marked the lower part of the inside of the front wall with a dark brown stain.

They huddled round the spare fire, for the night was cold, though the atmosphere of the little room was foul and oppressive.

"Don't joggle the table, Jenny," said the woman to the elder of the two little girls, who shook the table slightly as she shivered, gazing wistfully the while on the fish her mother was eating, "or you'll spill your father's tea."

"Gie me the herrin's head, please, mother," said the child, unable longer to avoid giving expression to her desire. "I be so hungry; and it makes me cold and shivery."

The mother shared the remainder of her fish between the two children, as she said, "I daresay you be hungry, but I don't know where we be going to get vittles from for the rest of the week. Here to-morrow's only Wednesday, and there's only two more loaves in the cupboard, and I've got but a shilling, and that poor gal upstairs ought to have something better'n we can get for her. The doctor's ordered her port wine and beef tea, but where be we to get it from, I should like to know; and the parish won't give her no 'lowance."

"Well, it's no use grumbling, my gal," said Ben. "That won't help things much; what can't be cured must be endured, as the saying is. After all, there's plenty worse off than what we be. We have got a shelter at any rate, and there's them as haven't got that; and then think of that poor fellow Wilson, in a police cell at the present minute for a crime he is as innocent of as that child is. I reckon he's worse off 'an we be; we have got a fire."

"Yes, it's all very well to say don't grumble, but who can help it? Here you go to work day after day, working early and late; you don't drink, neither do I; and yet it's as much as we can do to get vittles, not to mention clothes and boots. Here's the children going almost barefoot, and you'll be wanting a new pair o' boots as soon as the bad weather sets in. If it snows to-night, as I believe it will, you'll be working with wet feet all day to-morrow, and where we be going to get the money from to buy boots and things with I don't know."

"Well, we must hope for the best. 'Leven shillings a week aint much to do everything with I know; but there is them as has less."

"Yes, I know that; and how on earth they manage to live I can't make out. I used to grumble before; I thought that when you went 'moonlighting,' as you called it, that it was because you didn't lead a steady life that we was so bad off; but now you have got a reg'lar job, thing seem wus instead of better."

"Ah, virtue is too often its own reward," replied Ben. "However, we might as well economise as far as possible; and as the fire's going out, we'll go to bed. Early to bed and early to rise, you know."

"Well, I've risen early enough all my life, goodness knows," said his wife, as she began to undress the children, "whatever you have done but I don't get any wealthier. That old saying is like a good many more that are not over true. Like that about the early bird that catches the worm. Spects I've been the worm, though," she added, musingly.

There was a knock at the door.

"Come in," shouted Ben.

The door opened, and Frank Wilson entered. He presented a miserable appearance. His head was bare, and his hair, wet and matted, hung down over his forehead, from which a streak of blood was flowing which heightened the pallor of his face. His garments were saturated with water, and were dripping filth; his hand-cuffed hands were lacerated and bleeding.

Ben and his wife sprang to their feet, startled, as though they had seen a ghost; the children screamed and huddled closer to their mother.

Frank was the first to speak.

"Sorry to disturb you," said he, "but I didn't know where else to go. Reckon you were surprised to see me?"

"Well, I don't understand it at all," said Ben, "but I'm downright glad to see you. How did you get here? and how did you manage to get away? and how is it you're all wet?"

"Well, I can't answer all your questions at once, but I am here because I managed to escape from the police; I am wet because I did a dive into the river, and then to make matters worse I fell over the shafts of Ike Mooney's barrow at the end of the row here, and got a ducking in the gutter, which has by no means improved my personal appearance."

"Well, I never expected to see you here again. I thought you were in durance vile,[39] and am jolly glad to see that I was mistaken. However, we may as well deprive you of your jewellery first of all," saying which, Ben dived through a door leading into an adjoining apartment, and quickly reappeared with a file, with which he rapidly freed Frank's wrists from the handcuffs.

"Come, missus," he said, as first one and then the other of Frank's fetters fell to the ground, "put them kiddies to bed, and see if you can't find Mr. Wilson a dry tog or two to put on; and look here, Jenny and Sally," said he, turning to the two children, "don't you ever say a word about having seen Mr. Wilson, for if you do, I'll cut the life out of you." The youngsters were old and small for their years. They, unlike most children, knew how to hold their tongues. Privation had made them taciturn and thoughtful, and the father knew that their natural reserve, aided by the vague terror inspired by his threat, would prevent them saying anything about their present visitor.

Gazing at him for a moment the children silently turned away and clambered up the rude ladder that stood on one side of the apartment and did duty for a staircase.

"I've found you this old pair of trousers of Ben's," said Mrs. Green, as she descended the ladder, "but you'll have to put a sack round your shoulders while your other things is drying."

Frank took the trousers, and was proceeding to ascend the ladder, when Ben said, "I reckon you'd better change here, old man, your missus is up there, and I fancy you'd frighten her a bit if she saw you now of a sudden."

"Perhaps you're right," said Frank, hesitatingly, "but I wanted to see her. Is she very bad?"

"Well, the doctor comes to see her twice a week; and parish doctors don't do that for folks who've got nothing the matter with 'em. However, you just change yer things and the missus 'll give you a cup of tea and a bit of vittles, and then you can tell us how you managed to get here, and she'll prepare your wife to see you."

With Ben's old trousers on and a dry, warm sack round his shoulders, seated before the fire, which had been replenished with a couple of logs brought from the inner apartment, Frank began to feel a little more comfortable. Ben poured him out a basinful of an amber-coloured liquid which he called tea, and placed a couple of thick slices of bread and butter before him, and urged him to make himself at home. Frank drank the tea with avidity, but, hungry as he was, the almost dry bread seemed to choke him. It seemed to be impregnated with the evil odour which pervaded the apartment, and which the heat of the fire rendered still more pungent.

"I don't know how long I shall be safe, nor where I am to stop now I have given them leg-bail," he said presently.

"Oh, you get that grub down you, and don't you trouble about that. When you've had enough to eat, you can tell us how you managed to get away, and we'll then see what's to be done."

"I can't eat any more," said Frank, pushing the remaining slice away from him, "besides I shall eat you out of house and home if I'm not careful."

"Oh, we shall manage to get some vittles somewhere," said Ben, "we always have done. But I want to know how you managed to get here."

[15 September 1888]

Chapter XV.

Frank detailed the circumstances under which he had escaped from his escort. "As I neared the bridge," said he, "I felt my strength failing me. I felt half mad. I hardly knew what I was doing, except that I was being hunted, and that I wanted to escape from my pursuers; that anything, even death itself, would be preferable to falling into their hands again. The desire to escape, even by drowning if necessary, dominated me, and I rushed down by the side of the bridge and into the water. I thank the instinct which prompted me to this, it enabled me to escape to once more see you, my friend, and my poor wife, who is dying from the privation I have brought upon her. When I plunged into the water it was quite dark. By the side of the bridge where I struck, the water is rather deep, but I managed, in spite of my handcuffs, to swim under water with my feet, to a spot higher up the river, where by the side of the bank it is quite shallow. Here, among some reeds, I managed to keep my head above water, and I could see the dark forms of the policemen as they moved to and fro, anxiously watching for me to reappear in the deep water. I waited there for fully an hour, while they searched for me on both sides of the river with their lanterns, venting curses both loud and deep on my devoted head, and threatening what they would do to me when I was recaptured. I was almost perished with the cold, and believe I should have swooned right away and been drowned if I had to stay there much longer. At length, however one of them said, 'It's no use searching any further for him to-night. I reckon he's cheated the hangman by drowning himself. We may as well leave him here to-night and drag the river for his carcase to-morrow.' Cold, dispirited, and disappointed they took his advice and departed. As soon as I felt sure they had all gone, I scrambled out and started at a run along the towing-path. I thought I would stick to the river, which had proved such a good friend to me, thinking that if I should meet anyone as I came along I could easily plunge into the water again, and so get away. I ran all the way to escape pursuit, and to keep myself warm, for the cold water seemed to drive all the blood out of me."

"D'ye think there's any chance of the their finding your tracks?"

"No. It's beginning to snow fast, and if we have a heavy fall it'll cover up my footprints, and then when it thaws they will be washed away."

"Did anyone see you come here?"

"Not a soul. I was afraid when I fell over Ike's barrow that I should have roused up the whole row, but nobody stirred. I didn't know where else to go. It was either here or Crosbie's, and I didn't know how he would receive me; besides, my wife was here."

"You did quite right to come here. I am beholden to you for more than you know. Nobody knows you are here, and it'll be as well for you to stop here some time till the thing blows over a bit."

A feeble voice was heard from the room above, and Ben's wife ascended the ladder. Shorty after she returned, and told Frank that his wife knew he was there, and was anxious to see him. He took a candle and went up.

It was a low room in which Frank Wilson now found himself. The bare rafters of the roof sloped down to the side walls, where it was impossible to stand upright. The plaster between the rafters was brown and damp where the rain had soaked through the thatch, and the place appeared little better than the loft over a barn. This was the only room in the upper storey, and at the end nearest the ladder-head stood an old wooden bedstead, on which the children were lying, scantily furnished with a chaff bed[40] and patchwork counterpane. Across the centre of the room a line was stretched on which were hung a number of sacks so as to form a screen. On the other side of this screen, in a corner under the sloping roof, on a mattress formed of corn sacks stuffed with straw, with a sheet and two or three sacks for covering, Frank saw his wife. She had risen to a sitting position as he entered, and her pale, worn face bore a look of almost joyous expectation. As Frank looked on her hollow cheeks and sunken eyes he felt that hunger, privation, and gnawing care had done their work, that the wife he had sworn to love and cherish was dying there before him for want of that care which he would have been only too willing, but was powerless, to bestow. His heart seemed to swell to bursting, he could not speak a word, he threw himself on his knees beside her and kissed her passionately.

"My darling Frank," said his wife, placing her thin wasted arms round his neck, "I am so glad to have you with me again. It makes me feel quite happy. Do you know, dear, I was really afraid I should never see you again before I died."

"Don't talk like that, Polly. You mustn't think about dying now I've come back to you," said Frank, choking back a rising sob, "You must make haste and get well, and we'll go right away where nobody knows us, where we can start afresh."

"No, I shall never get well again Frank, I know it, but do not let that make you sad, dear. I feel so happy now that you are with me. I do not mind dying now that everybody knows you are innocent as well as myself. There will be no need for you to go away when I am gone; there are many here who love you and when you are free from all encumbrance you will be as happy in the future as you and I have been in the past."

Frank was silent. He dared not tell her the truth: That he was still regarded as a murderer, who had eluded the grasp of the law. The excitement of their meeting wearied her. He kissed her and soothed her to sleep. As soon as she was asleep he descended the ladder. Ben and his wife were still sitting by the fire.

"You may as well go to bed now," said Ben as Frank reappeared, "and I'll show Mr. Wilson to his apartment."

"Well, what do you think of our patient?" he asked, turning to Frank, when his wife had retired.

"I'm afraid to say anything, Ben, I fear it's useless hoping. No, they've killed her," he added in a hoarse voice, as he threw himself into a chair, "They're hunting me down as a murderer, but if my wife dies she will have been as surely murdered as ever was the man with whose death I am charged, and murdered in a more brutal manner than he was, too!"

"What has she done?" he went on, "that she should have to suffer in this way? Even if I had been guilty of all they charge me with, that is no reason why she and my poor old mother should be punished?"

"And how have you been getting on this last week?" he asked Ben, who sat silently and moodily regarding him, his elbow resting on the table and his chin in his hand.

"Oh, we're doing pretty well now, you know. I've got a job up at Apsted Farm there, reg'lar. Only things ain't as good as they used to be, there's nothing to be got now, and I was glad to drop into this. There's no chance of doing any moon-lighting now, the blessed peelers[41] are all over the shop. Last year, too, the missus and the kids picked up enough wheat to keep us in bread till over Christmas, but this year the farmers all round have put a stop to the leasing, and besides there'd be precious little to pick up if they hadn't, they rake it too devilish clean." [42]

"How did you manage to get this job up yonder?"

"Why, they're pretty busy, d'ye see; and they was a hand short. You know that chap as started rowing wi' some o' your fellows down at the Lion, the night I hit young Cranston?"

"Yes."

"Well, he got killed a day or two before our late lamented Mr. Gripper was shot. Of course you didn't hear much about it, because he wasn't shot, or any-thing like that. As I was saying, they're main busy up there; the crops have been pretty heavy, and they've been working early and late to get it threshed out, now they've got the thresher there, and this chap was carting. Of course they're short handed, and he was about done up, being about so many hours. He was walking along by his horses, half asleep in the darkness, when he stumbled and fell, and the wheels of the waggon passed over him. He wasn't dead when they picked him up, but was squished and mangled terribly. He lay for a day or two in awful agony before he died in the barn to which they carried him. They called it 'Acci-dental death' at the inquest, but to my mind it was murder, through overwork. Nobody made any fuss about his death, and yet look at the fuss they make just because a policeman has been shot."

"Well, I don't look at it in the same light as you do, Ben. If a man get killed by accident, that's one thing; but it is quite another for him to be murdered through the ill-will of others, as Gripper was shot, and as I contend my wife is being mur-dered now by those who have deprived me of the chance of earning a living. This chap needn't have done the work if he didn't like it."

"That's nonsense. If he didn't do it others would, and he'd have got the sack; you know that very well. I might as well say that you could be at work if you like. We workmen can only work when they like to let us, and then we have to accept their terms. Anyway, I reckon this chap was killed through overwork, and that's just as much murder in my opinion as the shooting of Gripper was."

"I hope, Ben, you don't think I shot the policeman, and are saying this to justify me?"

"Look here, my boy; I don't think anything about it; I know you didn't do it."

"You know?"

"Yes, of course. Wasn't you with me at the time?"

"Yes; but for all you know the sergeant was killed before I met you. How, then, do you *know* that I didn't shoot him?"

"Because I know the party as did."

"You know the party as did?" repeated Frank, eagerly, rising to his feet and gazing at his companion.

"Yes; or at any rate can form a pretty good guess."

"And yet you allowed me to lie under this suspicion – to be dragged to gaol! You could see my wife dying and my mother forced into the workhouse, because I was suspected, while you knew the real criminal, and did not even come forward to denounce him! Ben Green, I thought you were my friend!" he moaned as he sank back into his seat.

"What I did, I did for the best. I might have cleared you, of course; but I wasn't to know as you wouldn't get off. If it had come to the worst I could have stated what I know; but as it is you've got away, and there's no need to say anything. And why should I? Let the police find him if they can. For my part I wouldn't hang a dog for killing that scoundrel."

[22 September 1888]

Chapter XVI.

Frank was completely taken aback by his companion's words. He had always hoped that his friend Green, at any rate, believed in his innocence. Yet now he felt that he would far rather have him believe him guilty than to know that he had been assured of his innocence all along and yet had done nothing to bring the real criminal to justice. He could not understand the motive which had kept Ben silent. He felt that the only friend upon whom he had hitherto been able to count, had betrayed him. He appealed to him once more.

"After all that I have gone through don't you think it is only right that you should tell me who is the real criminal?"

"What! for you to go and inform upon him? to give him up? to have me called upon to help send this poor devil to the gallows?"

"Was it George Cranston?"

"Suppose I told you 'yes,' what would you do?"

"I should denounce him, certainly."

"But suppose it was someone else?"

"I should do exactly the same. Recollect I've got to clear my name; and even if I had not I should consider it my duty to bring the murderer to justice."

"Well, then, I'm not going to tell you. You have an exaggerated notion of the importance of this man's life. Who is to be hanged for the murder of the man I was speaking of a while ago? Who will be hanged for the murder, as you call it, of your wife, and the torture of your mother? No one. Why, then, should I or you help the law to hang anyone for an offence which I, for one, do not consider to be anything like as bad as either of those crimes. But perhaps I don't know anything about it. Anyway, it aint worth while arguing any further. I've got to get up early in the morning, and I reckon you're fagged out, so we'd better go to bed. You can sleep upstairs with your missus, if you like, only you'll have to come down pretty early in the morning, so's nobody sees you. I reckon you'd better doss here," he continued, leading the way to the adjoining apartment. "You'll be safe there."

This apartment was even more miserable than either of the two others. The floor was the bare damp earth, the brick walls were unplastered, and the bare thatch of the low roof was visible between the rafters. It was a mere outhouse opening onto the dwelling room of the cottage. On one side there was a window about a foot square, and beneath the window stood a washing stool, with one or two washing utensils. This was the whole of the furniture, if that could be called such.

In one corner stood a small stack of wood, and in another there was a heap of ashes, between the two was a bundle of straw.

"This is not exactly palatial," said Ben; "but the straw's clean, and it won't be much worse than the gaol, at any rate. You'd better keep pretty close here for a week or so, and then when the coast is clear you can get away."

Frank elected to stay there, and Ben gave him a couple of sacks for covering, and, bidding him good night, departed.

It was four o'clock in the morning when Ben called him, and asked if he would have a cup of tea.

"You'll have to take your breakfast pretty early, old fellow," said he, "so as to keep out of sight of the neighbours. The missus'll bring you your other meals; but you can go up and spend an hour or two with your wife after I'm gone as long as you don't make it too late."

"I wish you'd tell me what you know, Ben," said the other, "so that I could stand once more a free man in the face of the world, instead of hiding here a hunted murderer."

"A precious lot of good your freedom would be to you, wouldn't it now? What did the world care for you when you were free from the suspicion of crime that you should care for its good opinion? All that you would do would be to place some other poor devil in your own position. If you keep quiet you can get off without doing that."

The two men finished their basins of tea in silence, and Ben departed.

Frank spent the rest of the week and the greater part of the next in this hovel. The most of his time, day and night, was passed in the miserable apartment in which he slept, between the woodstack and ash heap. It was only half lighted in the day time by the dingy foot-square window.

It was damp and cold; the air reeked with the filthy smell from the gutter, while beetles, slugs and other creeping things crawled about the floor, and the bare brick walls. He dared not venture out for fear someone should see him.

Ben called him up every morning to have breakfast with him before he went to work.

One evening Ben went down to the Lion. It was the first time he had been there since the night he went on Frank Wilson's behalf. He did not see Alice Steggles, but the taproom company were delighted to see him.

"I'm getting on all right," said Ben in reply to their inquiries, "and daresay I shall be a farmer myself one of these days, when I've saved enough money out of my 'leven bob a week. But I'm thinking about the poor fellow as is gone, and his poor wife that's dying up at my crib."

"Well, for my part I don't believe as Wilson is drowned," said another, "and the police don't believe so either. I see they've offered a reward for him. They have dragged the river for several miles, and aint been able to find anything, so I reckon he's escaped, and I say good luck to him if he has."

"I wonder," said another, looking at Ben, "that if he has escaped, he didn't come to your place to see his wife."

"Well, he would be a fool to come back here, anyway," said the other. "I reckon if he ain't drowned he's made tracks for the smoke, and that 'ud be the wisest thing for him to do."

"If he has gone it is to be hoped the police won't catch him again."

"Catch him! Not if he's guilty they won't. You never hear of the police catching a murderer nowadays, do you?"

"Well, they've got his picter pasted about all over the country I hear."

"What o' that? this picter is from a photo that they took from his place; in this picter he wears a beard. Frank was rather proud of his beard you know. Well he's only got to shave off his beard and nobody'd know him."

"Well I do hear as how they've already collared two or three men that they have mistook for Wilson."

"I only hope he'll get clear away for my part. I'd be willing to give a trifle to help him to do so."

"Well, if you can't help him to get away," said Ben, "you can help him by giving me a trifle for his sick wife. She wants things as I can't get for her."

They collected five shillings which they gave to Ben, a half-a-crown of which he spent on his way home on little delicacies for the sick woman.

In the morning he related to Frank what he had heard at the Lion. "If they are after you, there's no telling how soon they may be on your track and the sooner you get away the better."

"Get away to the smoke, that's the best place. Here's half-a-crown out of what they gave me last night. I know it aint much, but it'll help you on the road and 'taint worth while to wait here to be copped."

"I don't much care if I am copped," returned the other moodily, "I don't care about always hiding away like a criminal while I know I am innocent and all because you don't choose to do your duty and tell the truth."

"Frank, my dear fellow," said Ben, "don't talk any more about it. If it's ever a question of saving your life, I'll speak out to some purpose, but I don't choose to do so as long as I know you're safe. But there's no need for you to be always hiding. Get right away where nobody knows you and you'll be all right."

"Well I shall stop here until the end," said Frank, significantly pointing to the ceiling, "or until I get copped."

"The end won't be far off now, I'm afraid, my boy. She's sinking fast. Anyway you will give me credit for doing my duty by her, Frank. Poor girl! she at any rate will die believing you innocent, and believing that you have been acquitted."

Frank was silent; he knew that his wife was dying, he knew that Ben Green had done all he could to alleviate the sufferings of her last days yet he could not get rid of the bitter resentment he felt towards him for his obstinate silence.

The end indeed was not far off. The poor woman was getting weaker every day. Frank would sit by her for hours holding her hand in his without either of them speaking. To Frank Wilson there was a bitter sweetness in these long, almost silent interviews with his dying wife. Sitting there by her bedside, gazing into her pallid face, holding her wasted, feverish hand in his, his thoughts would wander back to the old happy time, in the bright cheery cottage, where he, his wife and mother had been so happy and might have been so still if he had never been out of work.

It was towards the end of the second week. During the day his wife had seemed so much brighter and better that Frank almost began to hope she would recover.

Towards evening, however, there was a change for the worse, the poor woman became so ill that Mrs. Green sent one of the children for the doctor.

Frank heard him come in and when he had gone upstairs he crept to the foot of the ladder and listened. He had been there but a few minutes when he heard his wife call out in a terrified voice, "Frank, Frank, where are you?" For a moment again there was silence, then once more he heard, "Frank, my husband, come to me, I am dying, where are you? do not leave me to die alone?"

He could stand it no longer, he rushed up the ladder. As he drew aside the screen of sacks, Dr. Smart stared.

"What! you here, murderer," he shouted.

"Murderer! my husband is no murderer," shrieked the dying woman as Frank threw himself on his knees by her side, "he is innocent."

She fell back dead.

* * *

"Your wife is dead," said Dr. Smart turning to Frank, "and I shall make it my business to inform the authorities of your hiding place."

"Please to understand, sir, that neither Mr. nor Mrs. Green were aware of my being here before," cried Frank as the doctor disappeared down the ladder.

Ben came in as the doctor went out.

"You'll have to cut now, my boy," said he, when he heard that the doctor had seen Frank. "Hurry, wife, and shove him a thing or two into a bundle."

Frank kissed the cold dead face of his wife, took the small bundle Mrs. Green offered him and turned to go.

"Good bye, old fellow," said Ben, shaking his hand, "cut away for the smoke, let us know how you go on. We'll do our best by her that's gone. Good bye."

As Frank reached the end of Paradise Row nearest the London road two policemen arrived at the door of the house he had left.

[29 September 1888]

Chapter XVII.

Frank hurried quietly and rapidly along the road. It was a cold night, and there were but few people about, and whenever he saw anyone approaching he avoided them by dodging into a doorway. He would soon be clear of the houses.

At the extremity of the town he would have to pass the Red Lion, and beyond that the ironworks. Having passed these he would be clear of the town, and there would be less fear of anyone recognising him, though he fancied that, clean shaven as he was, he would be able to pass even an old acquaintance without being recognised in the darkness.

He had passed the Lion, and had just crossed the bridge over the river, when as he turned into the London road, he ran up against a woman. It was Alice Steggles. She gave a little scream of surprise. He saw she had recognised him.

"Alice," said he, seizing her hands, "don't tell anyone you have seen me. The police are on my track, and for all I know are close at my heels. I am going to London. I may be safe there. Good bye!"

She turned away her face without speaking.

"Surely you do not believe me guilty, Alice?"

"No, no, Frank," she murmured. "You may trust me. But it is dreadful. I was afraid you were drowned. And your poor wife – But I must not detain you."

"Polly is dead," he replied, sadly. "I have had to leave her to the care of others. My poor old mother is in the workhouse, and I am a hunted man. But I cannot give myself up to be hanged for what I did not do. Fate has been hard with me; I shall never look upon my dear wife's face again. I shall not even have the melancholy satisfaction of seeing her buried. But I shall at any rate have the comfort of knowing that at least one true heart in Benton believes in my innocence. It is hard for me to leave her thus, to be buried like a dog, by the parish."

"That she shall not," said Alice. "I will see that she has decent burial. For your sake," she added, in a lower tone.

"Thank you, Alice! For that kind promise I shall be ever grateful. Good bye!"

"Good bye," said she, looking up into his face, with her eyes full of tears.

Something in the tone in which she said the words arrested his attention. He kissed her upturned face, and, turning away, hurried along the road.

As he did so the sound of wheels, rapidly approaching from the town, broke on his ear.

He had got clear past the ironworks, and was on the high road, with a hedgerow on either side. On his right was a meadow, beyond which ran the river.

He broke through the hedge on this side, and stood still to listen. The vehicle, whatever it was, had stopped on the other side of the bridge. He could hear the sound of voices, one of which he thought he recognised as that of Warren, the policeman. In this he was correct.

Warren, who, since Gripper's death, had been promoted to the position of sergeant, was walking up the High Street when Dr. Smart met him and informed him that he had seen Wilson at Ben Green's place.

Warren lost no time in summoning one of his subordinates to accompany him, and they had both arrived at Green's cottage almost immediately after Frank had gone. They lost no time in following him and concluding that he would be most likely to take the London road, they had requisitioned a trap belonging to a publican in the High Street, thinking to over take him before he got clear of the town.

They had reached the bridge, however, without finding any trace of him. Seeing Alice Steggles walking rapidly homewards, Warren, who was driving, pulled up.

"Good evening, Miss," said he. "Did you meet a man as you were coming along the road?"

"I haven't come along the road," said she. "I've only come from Burton Mill," indicating a lane running off to the left at right angles with the road. "Why, are you after somebody?"

"Well, Wilson, the murderer, has been seen in the town, and I believe he has made his way down here on the road to London."

"Wilson the murderer?" she repeated. "How dreadful! I haven't seen any murderer."

Warren whipped up his horse.

Frank listened for the sound of the wheels.

The air was cold, still, and frosty. The moon had not yet risen, but the stars were shining brightly, and it was a clear night.

Down below him flowed the river, cold, clear and silent; to his left a black shadow showed where the greystone bridge crossed the river, that bridge over which he had passed two or three times every day, from the time he started work to the day he got the sack; the bridge by the side of which he had stood fishing in the cool of the summer evening, and from the parapet of which he had watched the gay boating parties rowing up to the woods beyond Denmere. Many a happy scene of his boyhood's days came back to his memory as he stood there behind the hedge, listening for the sound of approaching wheels.

He heard the crack of the whip as the horse was started afresh, and held his breath to listen.

Closer and closer came the vehicle. Did they know he was there? He felt as though he could see them in the trap, peering along the hedge till they discovered him.

The wheels were coming nearer. Would they pass him? The hedge was not thick enough, they would surely see him behind it. He threw himself down in the ditch.

Closer and closer they came; they were stopping. No, they had gone on; they had passed him. He had not been discovered.

What would they do now, when they did not find him on the road? Would they come back that way? At any rate, Frank decided to avoid the road, and struck across the meadow, till he reached the towpath by the side of the river.

For several miles he walked, or rather ran, as though he had determined on outdistancing those on the road.

When he had gone about six or seven miles, however, he slackened his speed a little. He had fifty miles to walk to London. He could not cover this distance that night, anyway. Still it would be best for him to get as far as possible before morning. With this idea he pushed on. In a short time he saw the lights of Oldbury, which was a rather more important place than Benton, and nine miles nearer the capital, and soon after was passing along the wharf of that place.

After he had left the lights of Oldbury behind him, he made his way out into the road again. He calculated that Warren, even if it were he who was after him in the trap, would not go further than Oldbury that night, and in that case he would be just as safe on the road as by the river, while he would save the extra distance caused by the serpentine course of the latter.

He had travelled some thirty miles by sunrise the next morning. He sat down by the roadside to rest. In a few minutes he fell asleep. When he awoke he could see by the sun that he had slept several hours. He got up and hurried on.

At a brook crossing the road he bathed his feet and washed his face and tidied his hair. He knew the advantage of appearing as clean and tidy as possible. With a wisp of straw borrowed from a neighbouring stack he brushed the dried mud from his trousers and boots, and anyone seeing him five minutes after would have never imagined that he had spent the night on the road.

Some three miles further on he came to a small village. He entered an alehouse that stood by the roadside and walked into the taproom. There were one or two men in it, lounging on the seats or leaning on the deal table that stood in the centre of the apartment. The brick floor was clean sanded. A fire burnt merrily in the huge fire-place over the mantelpiece hung a small looking-glass, on either side of which hung a pair of spurs, while the side walls were garnished with brilliantly coloured portraits of old-time Derby winners and heroes of the prize ring.

Frank called for half-a-pint of ale and two-pennyworth of bread and cheese. As he walked towards the fire-place he caught sight of his own face in the glass and smiled as he mentally compared it with the counterfeit presentment of himself which appeared on the bills that were pasted on the gateposts he had passed on the road.

"On the road betimes this mornin' mate," said one of the other occupants of the room in an enquiring tone. "Hev' you come fur?"

"Walked from Marsden," said Frank, naming a village he had passed some ten miles back on the road.

"On tramp, I s'pose, ye beant belonging to these parts, be ye?"

"No, I'm looking for a job."

"What line?"

"Farm hand," said Frank, fearful to disclose his trade lest that might betray him.

"You don't look much like a clodhopper, but I spose ye bin tending machinery?"

Frank, his mouth full of bread, nodded. This kind of cross-examination was getting wearisome to him, so as soon as he had finished his food and drunk his beer he paid the landlord out of the half-crown Ben had given him and departed.

One thing, however, pleased him: no-one there seemed to have the slightest suspicion as to his identity. When he had got some little distance from the village he looked round for a resting place. In an adjoining field he saw a haystack standing close by the gate. He climbed over the gate and threw himself down in the corner where the rick had been cut out, pulled a quantity of the loose hay over his feet and legs, and in a few minutes was fast asleep.

It was afternoon when he awoke. He sprang to his feet refreshed, shook off the loose hay and, clambering over the gate, regained the road.

He had not proceeded many yards when turning an angle in the road, he found himself face to face with a policeman who had just been perusing a bill affixed to the gatepost offering a reward for his capture.

He could not turn back, the policeman had seen him and there was nothing for it but to face it out. So looking the other boldly in the face, he was walking on when he was accosted with, –

"Have you come far?"

"About twenty miles," answered Frank.

"Ah! you haven't seen anything of anyone like that joker on the road, I s'pose?" asked the policeman touching the bill with his stick.

"No, I haven't, I reckon that fellow won't show himself much on the turnpike."

"That's what I think, but they seem to fancy that he's come this road. Anyway we are on the look out for him."

"'Tis to be hoped you'll catch him," returned Frank walking on. "If I'd seen him I should have given him up and claimed the reward."

He felt more secure after this rencontre. It was pretty evident that anyone who did not know him would be unable to recognise him as Frank Wilson.

He was relieved of the fear of capture, at any rate for the present. He had fifteen more miles to walk to London. Already he began to see signs, in the more minute character of the cultivation, of the contiguity of the great city, which, octopus like, is spreading its limbs over the surrounding country in all directions.

[5 October 1888]

Chapter XVIII.

Night had fallen when Frank Wilson entered the metropolis. As he walked up Piccadilly to the Circus he was smitten with wonder, not so much at the glare and glitter of the shops, but at the vast concourse of people, and the extraordinary bustle which was going on around him.

Everyone seemed busy; all hurrying here and there as if their very lives depended upon their haste. The rattle of the cabs and omnibuses, the shouts of the drivers and conductors – not a single word of which was intelligible to him – and the constant stream of pedestrians, all combined to make it the confusion of a veritable pandemonium.

He no longer breathed the clear frosty air of the country; the atmosphere was thick and humid; the pavement was damp and greasy with trampled mud. He was jostled this way and that. No one heeded him.

Each individual was intent on his own business, and all were apparently pursuing it with so much earnestness as to give their faces a careworn expression. All in this vast crowd seemed in too much hurry to be even pleased. One man pushed him out of the way, uttering an imprecation; he slipped, and would have fallen if he had not clutched at an iron pillar.

What troubled Frank most, however, was the sense of utter loneliness. Amid all these crowds of busy people he was a mere atom, isolated, unknown, and unnoticed; awaking neither interest, sympathy, nor suspicion. Of all these human beings around him not one knew him, or was known to him. He was indeed a stranger in a strange land.[43]

He had traversed some of the wildest parts of the country at midnight; during his wanderings in search of work he had often found himself belated when miles from any human habitation, yet he had never felt himself so lonely, so completely isolated, as he did at this moment, in the midst of the whirl and clatter of one of the most busy parts of the most populous city in the world. The very hurry and bustle depressed him. Every one of these people, hurrying along so eagerly, had an object in view – had something to attain, or at least something to do. He had nothing; he was out of work, and he felt that here at any rate, he was one too many.

To escape from the jostling he turned to the right, and walked mechanically down Waterloo Place. The mean and dirty appearance of the buildings surprised him. He would have imagined himself in a slum had not the width of the street and the size of the buildings as well as the appearance of the people he met, assured him that it was not so.

The damp heavy atmosphere seemed to cling about him, and he felt as though he were breathing a mixture of greasy mist and smoke. He wandered on across Trafalgar Square and was proceeding eastward when the roar of the Strand deterred him. Again he turned to the right, passed Whitehall and the Horse Guards, to Bridge Street.

Big Ben was chiming the quarter to eight. The sound attracted his attention to the clock tower, and he turned to a passer-by to enquire the name of the building.

The man answered him civilly, and passed on. Frank walked towards the bridge. He leaned on the parapet and gazed down into the cold dark water beneath. It was the same river he had known in his boyhood; but, like everything else, it was polluted by contact with the huge overgrown centre of commercialism. It possessed a strange fascination for him, this dark, muddy river, no longer pure and bright, flowing silently, sullenly, beneath the arches, beyond which, here and there, it reflected the light of the lamps on the embankment.

He had often sported on its surface, should he not now seek rest in its depths – so calm, so dark, so mysterious? Only one plunge, and then – oblivion. No more to work or to starve; no more to suffer; no more to be. The idea charmed and soothed him; and yet he could not take that plunge. It was not that he feared death, but the act of dying.

"No; I've not got pluck enough," he muttered to himself, with a sigh, and then turned and walked towards the south side.

He wandered on listlessly. He no longer felt any necessity for concealment. No one knew him; he was a stranger among strangers. He was tired, and began to look about him for a resting place. Several persons to whom he addressed himself directed him to the New Cut,[44] and there he wended his way.

Here a scene of even greater activity than that he had witnessed in Piccadilly, met his view. It was Saturday night; Saturday night in the New Cut! He had never seen anything like it in his life before. Not only the sidewalks but also the roadway was thronged with people. It was a very different kind of crowd to that which he had seen on the other side of the river. There the crowd was composed of well-dressed people, so intent upon their pleasure as to make a business of it; here it was composed of poorly-clad, meagre, pale-faced men and women, trying to get a little pleasure out of the most serious business, of their lives, that of laying out their weekly wages.

There were men and women of all ages, from the hobbledehoy[45] to the octogenarian, from the brazen-faced, loud-voiced, befeathered companion of the former to the broken-down, weazened, bent, draggle-tailed and decrepit old woman of three-score and ten.

It was indeed a motley crowd, shouting talking, laughing; many in more or less advanced stages of drunkenness. Some gathered round the outside stall of the butchers shops, haggling with the salesmen over the price of a few pounds of "cag mag"[46] for the next day's dinner; or driving a close bargain with the itinerant vendors of stale fruit and wilted vegetables, whose barrows were drawn up by the side of the kerb. Green oranges, for a penny; lozenges, warranted to cure all the ills that afflict mankind; toys, household utensils, and second-hand clothing; all these were being vended on the edge of the pavement by loquacious dealers, whose tongues never seemed to tire, and, around whom attentive and admiring crowds were gathered.

There were galvanic batteries, punching machines, and shooting galleries; where men and youths, animated with the natural instinct of destruction, banged away with air guns in the most ferocious manner at a harmless little sphere bobbing about on the top of a water jet.

Wandering along in this babel, Frank Wilson sought for some place where he could get a lodging for the night. In the country he would have gone to the first public-house. But he looked with dismay upon the gaudy, glittering gin-palaces, which were simply drinking bars, and were devoid of the comfort he had been accustomed to find in the country ale-house.

Eventually he noticed a dingy-looking building, the windows of which were garnished with an assortment of melancholy-looking herrings, ancient eggs, and stale chops. There was a lamp projecting in front on which was inscribed, "Good beds for single men, 6d. a night."

He walked in at the half-open door, and took his seat on one of the high-backed wooden benches, that were ranged transversely, with tables, on either side of the apartment. Of the slatternly-looking damsel who made her appearance five minutes after he had been seated he ordered a cup of tea, and bread and butter, and picked up a dirty, greasy, coffee-stained copy of a daily paper that was lying on the table.

The apartment was close and stuffy, and redolent with the aroma of broiled bloater and bad coffee. There were a number of other occupants; young men and youths drinking gingerette,[47] or some other vile compound, smoking cigarettes and playing dominoes.

Frank, after contemplating his surroundings for some time, turned listlessly to the paper he had picked up and began to read its contents. Suddenly a paragraph attracted his attention. It was headed "The Benton Murderer," and ran as follows:–

"The man Wilson, who was committed for trial for the murder of Sergeant Gripper, near Benton, and whose extraordinary escape from custody caused so much sensation little more than a week ago, was seen in Benton last evening. It appears that Dr. Smart, who was attending the murderer's wife in her last illness, was suddenly startled by the appearance of the culprit at the bedside of the dying woman. The woman died almost immediately after, and Dr. Smart hastened to give information to the police. When the police arrived on the scene, however, Wilson had decamped. It is believed that he is making his way to London, and as he is known to be almost destitute, the police are confident that he will be recaptured in a few days. The police are displaying the utmost vigilance, every railway station between Benton and the metropolis being carefully watched."

The girl brought his tea and bread and butter. The tea had been boiled, the bread was thick and dry, the butter was like tallow, but Frank was hungry and ate with avidity. When he had finished his repast he asked if he could have a bed. The girl looked at him with some surprise on hearing the question at so early an hour; however, she answered in the affirmative. He paid her for the food and the sixpence for the bed and asked to be shown to his room. The girl conducted him through the shop and up a staircase at the back. On the second floor, a large room extending the whole length of the shop, was furnished with a number of small beds, ranged along either side as in a hospital ward. The room was clean but stuffy, and impregnated with the odour of broiled bloater, which seemed to pervade the house. There was a gas jet hung in the room, but none of the beds were yet occupied. Frank selected the one nearest the window.

The next day, Sunday, he was awakened by the cries of the street hawkers. On opening his eyes he seemed thoroughly bewildered. He was so tired when he went to bed that he had not roused at all when his companions rolled into their quarters, one by one. Yet there must have been a deal of confusion, as some of them showed unmistakeable signs of debauch the night previously. He tumbled out of bed and made his way out into the street. The busy scene that met his view surprised him; there was scarcely less traffic than on the preceding evening, only the crowd appeared, if anything, more poverty-stricken. He would have been glad of a good breakfast, but his small stock of money must be economised. He went into a baker's shop and bought a pennyworth of bread, which he ate in the street.

He spent the rest of the day wandering about the streets and parks, returning to his coffee shop in the evening, when after having some tea and bread and butter he retired to rest.

He rose at an early hour on Monday, had a pennyworth of bread for break-fast, and afterwards visited all the engineers' shops he could find, in search of a job, but without success. Footsore and weary he found himself back at the coffee shop with but ninepence in his pocket.

On Tuesday morning he spent his last penny on bread, and found himself homeless, penniless and workless on the streets of London.

[13 October 1888]

Chapter XIX.

"And, Vive le Drapeau Rouge!"

The speaker was Jack Somers, who formed one of a merry party assembled in the drawing room at Benton Park, Colonel Ashville's residence.

He, with George Cranston, Lieutenant Vernon, and the Colonel had spent a lively day in the latter's coverts,[48] and were now enjoying the well-earned relaxa-tion of an evening in the company of the ladies.

His remark, which was uttered in an ironical tone, was addressed to Eva Ash-ville, who, with eyes sparkling and cheeks flushed, had been giving expression to some of the sentiments she had learnt in a French seminary from the daughter of a Parisian Communard.[49]

"Doubtless my fair cousin imagines herself the Madame Roland, or shall we say the Louise Michel?[50] of an English revolution," sneered Vernon, who seemed to imagine that one of the best means of winning the good opinions of Louisa Cranston was to ridicule the heterodox views of his young relative.

"I don't care about your sneers, cousin Charley; and you, Mr. Somers, can cry 'Vive le Drapeau Rouge' to your heart's content, but that does not alter the fact that the indifference of the wealthy to the misery of the poor is creating a danger of which we shall one day feel the consequences."

"But what would you have? There is the poor law; nobody can starve in this country. Even the most worthless, the most thriftless, is secured from absolute starvation."

This from George Cranston, who was too interested in winning the good-will of Miss Ashville to enter more than a mild protest against her subversive theories.

"Yes, everyone who cannot find the opportunity of living by his own labour is allowed to become a pauper, to subsist on charity, or to starve; but there is no rea-son why anyone should be forced to seek charity. If everyone were allowed to work, and received the full value of his labour, there would be no need of charity, and –"

"We should all have to work," interrupted Jack Somers. "It is extremely pretty, this Socialistic Utopia that young men and maidens are so fond of pictur-ing, in which all will live in fraternal co-operation, where refinement and culture will be common to all, where the tinker and the cobbler will recline on richly upholstered couches, and pursue their avocations to the sound of Beethoven's melodies, and where the man who paints your window shutters will also execute the masterpieces that adorn your drawing rooms. There are many, mostly poets and enthusiasts, who think that this would be a most desirable condition of things; but I fear that they have never regarded the other side of the question that this would involve the performance of menial tasks by those who, at present, in consequence of their superior social position, are relieved from the necessity of doing this degrading work."

"I don't think that a fear of the disagreeable consequences to ourselves ought to deter us from the performance of an act of justice," retorted Eva, warmly.

The Colonel and the elder Mr. Cranston were amusedly observing the war of words going on between the younger members of the party.

"That depends upon what you mean by justice," returned Somers. "If justice is only to be secured by every man or woman becoming his or her own butcher, baker or candlestick maker, you will pardon me, my dear Miss Ashville, for suggesting such a thing, but really, holding this view, it is a matter of some surprise that you yourself have not set the example."

"Yes," chimed in Vernon; "Eva, like the enthusiastic poets you have referred to, would doubtless like her housemaid to be as refined and cultured as she herself is, but she would scarcely care to step down and do the work of her servants."

"It is not what I care to do, but what good could I accomplish if I did it? Do you imagine that my servants would be benefitted if I did step down, as you phrase it, and do their work?"

"On the contrary," said Somers. "I imagine that it would materially injure them, and that they would most strongly resent this practical interpretation of your principles of justice."

"That demonstrates the absurdity of the whole thing," said Vernon.

"Not at all; it simply shows the helplessness of the individual, as such, to remedy the defects of an unjust social system," replied Eva.

"Still," continued Somers, "you might practice in your own household the equality you preach. If you cannot relieve your servants of their work without inflicting injury upon them, you might at any rate share their work and allow them to share your leisure. Place them on an equality with you yourself, let them have their meals with you, and associate with you and your friends in your drawing room."

"And what good would that do them? Would their lives be any the brighter or better for that?"

"All the brighter for your society and influence," remarked George Cranston, gallantly.

"But it is not of domestic servants that one is thinking generally in dealing with the wrongs of the workers," continued Eva, without apparently noticing the interruption. "They, after all, are a more or less useless class, the hanger-on of the parasites. Even in their case there is, of course, gross class injustice; but they are the product of a grosser class injustice, which it is impossible to remedy by pampering them. Neither can you improve their position much. Our servants, for instance, are as well fed as ourselves, are not overworked, have an abundance of leisure, are well and comfortably housed, and well paid.

"But treat them as equals, say you. That is impossible, so long as they are not equals. You cannot have equality between the slave and his owner; there cannot be social equality where there is not economic equality. If you attempt to treat servants as equals, they, knowing their dependent position, are either slavishly subservient or intolerably insolent. One girl upon whom I tried the experiment became so insolent as to threaten to slap my face, and I had to get rid of her; while another half starved herself through being afraid to eat in my presence, and I had to send her back to the servants' hall."

"Well, then, it seems our case is hopeless," said Vernon. "Society, according to your account, is hastening to destruction, and yet you do not tell us what we are to do to be saved."

"I suppose it's a case of selling all that one has and giving to the poor," remarked George Cranston, ruefully.

"I do not profess to know much about the remedy, or what we should do to be saved, but it does seems to me that no amount of giving will meet the case. What is wanted, as was pointed out by those much-maligned speakers at the unemployed meeting that was held on the Thames Embankment last year,[51] is not charity, but justice. Give to every man and woman the opportunity to work, and the full reward for their work when they have performed it, and there would be no social problem to solve."

"And then how about those who would toil not, and who would not spin?"

"Well, they would have to starve."

"Yourself included?"

"Oh, but I would work," said Eva, her blue eyes sparkling with the idea of doing something useful, as she pushed back with her hands the fair hair from her lovely forehead.

"What at? Would you take in washing?"

"I should have to do my own, I suppose, at any rate; but why not? Others every bit as good as I am have to do it, and why shouldn't I?"

"What should we have to do? Chop down trees, I suppose, like the Grand Old Agitator[52] who rules the destinies of this agitator-ridden country?"

"Why not? It would be just as healthful and far more useful than many of the pursuits you men follow now as pastimes."

"Well, I suppose one of these days, Colonel, we shall hear of your daughter marrying a bricklayer or a chimney-sweep?" queried Somers.

The Colonel shook his head with an amused smile.

"What do you think of this kind of talk?" asked Lieutenant Vernon of Louisa Cranston.

"I think it positively shocking for a lady to talk in the way Eva does. But of course she is to be pitied for having no mother. I cannot imagine why these questions cannot be left to men to settle."

"It is a matter of surprise to me, Colonel, that you have allowed your daughter to pick up such ideas," said old Cranston.

"Oh, as for that, they are only ideas, and can do no harm to anyone. Eva will be none the worse in the future for having conceived the idea of more perfect social arrangements than those which exist to-day. Youth is the time for enthusiasm, for high aspirations and bold ideals, and it seems to me a pity to destroy this youthful enthusiasm with the chilling frost of cold matter-of-fact reality. We get old and selfish all too soon," he added, with a sigh. "As for me," he continued, more gaily, "my youthful ambition was of a rather different kind. I sighed for a re-establishment of the old feudalism, with personal relations between all men, from the highest to the lowest. My motto was, "For God, Queen and Country."[53]

"Which is just as absurd a sentiment in this matter-of-fact age as those Miss Eva has been giving utterance to," said Jack Somers. "Your God, what is he? He simply furnishes a cloak for your mammon worship. Your Queen, well she simply protects you in your pursuit of profit; if she failed to do so you would as readily kick her crown into the Thames as our loyalist friends in Belfast would kick it into the Boyne under certain conditions.[54] And as for your Country, for all your profession of patriotism, your country is simply your happy hunting ground; if it wasn't, you'd repudiate it."

Both the Colonel and old Cranston were shocked at this outburst, and the former was about to speak when Somers interrupted him.

"Pardon me, Colonel. Of course, I did not refer to you personally, I was speaking generally, and that is my view, that all sentiment is mere humbug and hypocrisy. There is no room for it in this world of hard realities."

No one seemed inclined to dispute it, and Jack Somers accordingly rose to go.

"Well, good night, Colonel," said he, "I must be off."

"You're not going already, surely?" said George.

"Yes, I must get back to London to-night, and I want to make a call in the town."

"Shall I order the man to drive you down in the dogcart?" asked the Colonel.

"No thanks; I'll walk."

George offered to accompany him, which offer he cordially accepted, and their departure was the signal for the breaking up of the party, Colonel Ashville ordering the carriage to take the Cranstons home. There was an affectionate leave taking between Vernon and Louisa Cranston at the carriage door.

[20 October 1888]

Chapter XX.

George and Somers walked briskly along towards the town.

It was a clear frosty night, and their iron heels rung out on the hard road.

"Cursed cheerless about here at night," remarked Somers.

"Well, of course it isn't quite as lively as Regent Street," returned George.

"No, especially since that murder. Makes one imagine he sees a ghost behind every tree. Fancy! the fellow who shot Gripper may be waiting behind the hedge to drop us."

"Oh, dry up, old man, or change the subject."

"Well, how are you progressing with the fair Ashville?"

"It's all right, I think, though I haven't popped the question yet."

"She'll be rather a Tarter[55] to manage, I fancy, with those extraordinary views of hers."

"Oh, as for that, I don't think there'll be any difficulty. New duties, and so forth, will cause her to forget all that nonsense."[56]

"And how about the little Steggles?"

"Well, I thought she had a penchant towards me, but latterly she has been as cold as an iceberg. I thought we'd call in and see her."

"All right, I'm agreeable. I think she is a stunner. I've got an hour to spare before the last train."

They called at the Lion; Alice was in the bar. She was dressed in black.

It was the evening of the day on which Frank Wilson's wife had been buried. All the efforts of the young men to get her into conversation were ineffectual; she replied to them in monosyllables.

They passed nearly an hour drinking brandy and water, and chaffing her on her mournful appearance. George was slightly elevated when they emerged from the tavern.

"By Jove, she looks more beautiful than ever!" said Somers.

"Yes, but devilish cold," hiccupped his companion.

Somers bade him good night at the railway station.

It was eleven o'clock when Jack Somers reached Paddington Station. It was a cold, frosty night, and he felt chilly; so buttoning his coat up round his neck, and disdaining the offers of the numerous cabmen on the station rank, he set off on foot.

He had not proceeded far along Praed Street when he turned down a narrow thoroughfare and entered a dingy-looking house, the wire blinds of which bore the inscription, "Paddington Radical Club."

It was merely a private house, the interior arrangements of which had been slightly altered to make it serve the purpose of a club.

The two rooms on the ground floor had been thrown into one, and embellished with a bar. In this room a number of workmen were seated at tables, drinking beer, smoking, reading the evening papers, and discussing the latest political question or the prospects of the next racing season.

Somers glanced round at the occupants of the room, several of whom recognised him with a nod and a smile. Not seeing there the object of his visit, he advanced to the bar and asked the man who was standing behind it,

"Can you tell me if Mr. Blake is in the club?"

"Yes, I think he is upstairs in the reading room."

Somers proceeded upstairs, and in a room on the first floor, which was furnished with a number of chairs and a couple of tables, on which were strewn papers, books and pamphlets, mostly of a political character, he saw the object of his search.

Joe Blake, a carpenter by trade, was a short, thick-set man, of about thirty years of age. He had a swarthy face, which, though scarcely handsome, was attractive, by reason of the extraordinary power and intelligence it displayed. As Somers entered he looked up from the book he was reading.

"Hullo," said he, in a deep sonorous voice, "what brings you here at this time of night?"

"Oh, I've been out of town to-day, and have just returned, and thought I'd call, on my way from the station, and see if you were here. What are you busy reading up now?"

"Oh, I've just been reading what some parson has been writing about the housing of the poor. It's all very well, of course, but what's the good of it? We knew all about the evils before, and the only remedy he proposes is the old one of philanthropy at 5 per cent."

"Well, I wanted to know what you are going to do about the election."

"For my part I don't propose to do anything. I reckon I've got something else to do besides interesting myself about the doings of political dodgers."

"But doesn't the Federation[57] propose to do anything?"

"I don't know, but I should say not. We haven't got money for electioneering purposes for one thing, and then there is the question of candidates. I certainly think that the first Socialist member of Parliament should be a workman, and even if we could find the election expenses we are not in a position to maintain a workman should he be returned."

"Yet you have Jones running for Newcastle?"

"Well, Jones you see is quite an exceptional man. I should like to see him returned, though I scarcely think it possible. If he were returned I think we might get sufficient support among workmen themselves to keep him going, but that is not the case with others."

"Well, but, after all, is it so essential that your candidates should be workmen?"

"I think so."

"Well, I am inclined to think that if you sent a workman there alone he would make most terrible mistakes. Our friend Jones, for instance, excellent fellow though he be, would, with his impulsive character, be trapped by the party tricksters into the most egregious blunders. A man like that should have a middle-class man at his elbow to keep him right as to facts, figures and tactics."

"I don't agree with you at all; I think workmen have had altogether too much coddling by their so-called betters, and that has made them the abject creatures they are, but the workmen in this movement are quite exceptional men and are pretty well able to take care of themselves. But supposing I did agree with you, what middle-class man would you suggest? Rich, or Phillips or Barstow?"

"One of the reasons why I wanted to talk to you about this was because I feel sure that Rich will come forward if possible. Now he is a perfect ass, and would do more harm than good. Besides you'd never be able to control him."

"You don't suggest that he isn't straight, do you?"

"Oh, I think he's straight enough for that matter, but then he's so flighty and so uncontrollable, generally."

"Well, Phillips?"

"As to Phillips, of course he knows all about the economics of Socialism, and would be the very man, but his cursed egotism, his offensive and dictatorial manner would scare people away instead of inducing them to vote for him, and inside Parliament it would be the same with regard to any measure he might bring forward or support."

"You don't like him?"

"Don't I always oppose him whenever we meet? His personality is the weakness of the movement."

"Well, I fancy he has done as much or more for the movement than any other middle-class man."

"Perhaps so, but I don't like him."

"Why?"

"I don't know except that he is objectionable to me."

"What man do you like?"

"Oh! come, this is getting too personal. The question is, is it possible to run Socialist candidates at this election?"

"Well, as I've pointed out, to run workmen is out of the question, and the middle-class men I mentioned you object to."

"I don't admit that working-men candidates are out of the question, and there are other middle-class men. There's Barstow, for instance, or –"

"Or yourself," interrupted Blvake.

This was the point to which Somers wanted to bring his companion, so he smiled as he went on, "I believe there are people who would find the money for Socialist workmen candidatures if one or two middle-class candidates were run as well."

"I shouldn't object to taking their money, but I should object to doing their work, and I don't fancy that any of these politicians will part with any except to serve their own ends."

"But they might serve ours at the same time."

"I don't think so. We can only have working class politics with working class money. And, as I said before, I don't care a curse for this political dodgery, and I haven't given the election any consideration. I don't see what good we can do in it at present except to make use of the meetings for propaganda and to heckle the rival candidates. I am far more concerned about the unemployed agitation. I say, To Hell with politics and political trickery while a hundred thousand of my fellow-workmen are starving out of work."

"Yet you favoured those School Board candidatures?"

"Yes, because I think it of far more importance to get Socialists on administrative bodies than to get them into Parliament. Though less showy, the work that Socialists could do on the London School Board and similar bodies is more useful than anything they could yet do in Parliament."

"But about the unemployed. Surely Parliament could do more for them than any local bodies."

"Yes, but Parliament won't do anything until the local bodies move, and that is another reason why we should permeate these as much as possible with our views. The unemployed question is the most serious thing we have dealt with in my opinion. That meeting in the rain on the Thames Embankment last year did more good than any meeting we have yet held. And no other party seems prepared to deal with it."

"I am not so sure that they won't try, however," said Somers, "I don't quite see what you're going to do this winter."

"Well, that remains to be seen, but I don't think that anyone is likely to take the work out of our hands."

"The fair traders[58] are looking up, I hear."

"The fair traders! they're a discredited body, we've nothing to fear from them."

"But they've got the money."

"Money is a good deal, but it isn't everything in an agitation. We have managed to carry on ours with precious little, and I believe it is our poverty and the undoubted honesty of the men who are working in this movement that has won us the confidence of those whose cause we champion."

"Well, I'm off. I'll see you again about this Parliamentary business. I think the Federation ought seriously to consider it."

They shook hands outside the club, Blake going a few doors down the street to the house were he lived. Somers walked out into Praed Street, and, taking a cab, drove to Belgrave Square, where he occupied apartments with an old college chum.[59]

[27 October 1888]

Chapter XXI.

When Frank left his lodgings and entered the already busy street – it had hardly left off striking four o'clock – he paused. His look was that of distraction. He had tried all the engineers' shops he could find on the day before, and the same disheartening reply to his appeal for work awaited him everywhere.

On the edge of the kerb, his hands thrust deep into his empty trousers' pockets, his thoughts deep in reverie, his heart sunk within him, Frank stood motionless, pale and statue-like.

After standing thus for some minutes he turned in the direction of Black-friars. He crossed first one road, then another; up this street, across that square, till at last he found himself in the Blackfriars Road. Looking both ways, to see if any circumstance could determine him as to which way to go, for his limited knowledge of the geography of London could not settle it, he saw the lights on the bridge, and immediately started off in that direction.

On arriving on the bridge Frank experienced a momentary pleasure. It was the first ray of sunshine that he had felt since his escape. Although a practical engineer, and well able to work from models – although he possessed all the necessary knowledge for the execution of the various parts of the iron bridges that spanned the river – yet he had never witnessed such structures as the one he was standing on, or those over which the heavy trains, with their commerce and human burdens, were every moment crossing.

The vibration and oscillation astonished him, but convinced him of the perfection of the workmanship. Nothing he had seen or heard since his arrival in London had afforded him so much pleasure and gratification as the sight which now regaled him.

It was still quite dark but the quantity of traffic over the bridge, both vehicular and human was constant and incessant. It was a period of astounding sensation to Frank, and he completely lost himself in wonderment. The moments flew by, and nearly two hours passed, and Frank was still gazing around him. It was not until the objects on the river began to look black against the rising sun, and the stolid earnestness of the men who passed him showed that they were engaged in the desperate struggle for existence, that he awoke to a knowledge of his position.

He shook himself together and passed on.

At Ludgate Circus he again halted.

Looking up Fleet Street he noticed a deal of excitement and bustle, and hurried up this celebrated thoroughfare to ascertain the facts.

He needed not telling; the piles of papers, thousands of boys and hundreds of carts conveyed the necessary information. For a moment Frank began to ruminate on the wonders of the Press; but these pleasant thoughts soon gave place to much less joyous reflections.

"Every one of those sheets," murmured Frank, "proclaims me a murderer!"

The thought was too terrible; he turned rapidly on his heel, and strode off.

Turning again in the direction of the river – for Frank had sufficient knowledge to inform him that a commercial capital like London must have plenty of merchandise – he determined to try his luck at the dock gates. He tuned down Thames Street, and sauntered listlessly along till he reached Billingsgate.

Here a new excitement and another pang awaited him. Tons upon tons of fish – wet, dry and shell fish – were being carried on the heads and shoulders of the porters. It was a strange sight. Fine powerful men, with splendid physique, bending under the weight of trunks of fish. The lords of creation brought down to the level of beasts of burden.

Numbers of boats lay alongside the wharf, all laden heavily, even regardless of the Plimsoll water-line,[60] with what should form a staple food for the poor. But before any one of them started unloading there was an interchange of words between some half-dozen busy individuals who seemed to control the market. Frank noticed this, and concluded they were the men to whom he must apply for a job if he wanted one.

He was not allowed to remain in doubt very long, for a brief dialogue that took place between two of the porters explained the whole affair.

"It seems damned hard when a feller wants to earn a sprat or two he can't start till the blasted owners make up their minds to sell."

"It does so, Jim; and the buyers swear they can't get their money back. There's Charley West, him as come's down with that little black pony, you know; always stands up by the Monument –"

"Oh, yes, I know."

"Well, he swears he paid thirty hog[61] for a trunk of plaice last week and didn't get back three dollars."

"Well, he's rather particular; he won't fry small stuff."

"I know; but thirty bob's a long price for a trunk. Look how they're packed. Just about a dozen decent fish on the top, and the bottom is little bits of dabs that don't pay for cleaning."

"Well, there it is; these swines es got the monopoly, and no one else gets a look in."

"Hallo; there's old Cosh calling, Bill. They're going to start on that steamer."

There was no more time for talking. Everyone who wanted a job pushed and struggled to the front. Frank, who did not understand the *modus operandi*, soon found himself forced back to the rear, with no chance whatever of being taken on.

The dozen or so selected ones started at once, and the others came back, dispirited and quiet, to await the course of events.

A little while after the same process was repeated. There was another rush, another struggle, a few more taken on, and a lot more still disappointed.

This continued at intervals far into the day. Time after time Frank strained every muscle to get to the front, and time after time he was defeated. At last all the boats were unloaded; the fortunate men took their money and went home. Some of them, as they passed the little groups of unsuccessful applicants, seeming to smile with an air of superiority. Those who had failed to get taken on tried to console themselves with the hope of better luck tomorrow.[62]

One man, more agreeable-looking than the rest, attracted the attention of Frank. He ventured on an interrogation.

"Did you manage to capture, mate?" said Frank.

"Yes, old man; I got a couple of bob."

"I tried, but had no luck. Couldn't get near enough."

"You wouldn't have landed if you'd got ever so close."

"How's that?" said Frank.

"Why, you ain't got no badge."

"Well, what the deuce has that got to do with it?"

"Why, no one's allowed to go aboard any o' those boats without a licence."

"Is that so?"

"Yes, mate."

"Well, where to you get your license from?"

"Go into the office yonder, pay your dollar, and they gives you your badge and license."

"A dollar!" exclaimed Frank. "Then I don't stand a shadow of a chance, for I haven't got a cent."[63]

"No, well, that's it. It's the rule, you know; and you must go by it. So long. I wish you luck."

"Thanks," said Frank. "Good day," and they parted.

Not knowing exactly where to go or what to do, Frank strolled along Thames Street, mounted the steps and went on to London Bridge. Leaning on the parapet, watching the boats passing and repassing, his mind reverted to his past life.

A man alone with his thoughts at the best of times is an uncomfortable being. But in his position Frank was doubly so. He felt himself an outcast. He had committed no crime, yet he knew he was being hunted as a murderer. He had never shirked work yet he was denied the possibility of showing his willingness to do any. He had never wittingly offended any man, yet he felt he had not a friend in all the world. He had never been extravagant or wasteful, yet here he was, starving in the midst of plenty. He had had neither sup nor bite all day. The night was fast closing in, and he had no prospect of shelter. Where could he go? The excitement of the day, and the struggles for work had kept him warm hitherto, but now the dark, hopeless future, and the still more dreary and dismal present, sent a chill through his veins which made him shiver again.

The wind was perishing. A raw cold sleet was being driven along and froze on his scanty clothing. He was getting tired, too; and involuntarily he sat down in one of the recesses of the bridge.

The time passed wearily. Every hour the number of passengers crossing the bridge got less and less. The vehicular traffic had quietened down very much. The hoots of the steamboats were silenced. Cab drivers were changing places: they were taking home their first horses or bringing out their second. Now he hears big Ben strike eleven, and the traffic across the bridge seems to be momentarily augmented; but everybody is hurrying past.

They were, indeed, a mixed crowd that kept passing by. Some had evidently been imbibing something a degree stronger than tea and showed by their wobbling gait that they had surrendered their bipedal superiority to the influence of some bacchanalian liquid. Snatches of songs were rolling thickly and confusedly from their tongues, showing that they had evidently been to some place of amusement.

Occasionally a smart little dandy, swinging his cane in a careless nonchalant manner, puffing away at the stump of a cigar, would start back on discovering anyone in the recess.

Some of the passers-by were not of either of these descriptions. They seemed to Frank as though they were settled down to a certain style of walking – their hands in their pockets, their eyes turned more often to the ground than to the skies, their gait more of a resigned shuffle than an upright military step, their pace often less than three miles an hour – a style which, to Frank, revealed the secret of their being workmen of the twelve-hour-a-day class[64] – shop assistants, porter, messengers and such like.

Every now and then a poorly-clad man or woman came and sat down beside Frank, but none of them seemed disposed to stay. He wonders if he will survive the morning if he has to stay out in that bitter cold.

The greatest dread he has is the possibility of being interrogated by the police, but they don't seem to notice him.

At this juncture a very commonplace incident occurred which entirely diverted the current of his thoughts. A 'bus from London Bridge Railway Station was travelling homewards and northwards. Directly opposite to where Frank was sitting stood apparently a man and wife. Seeing them the conductor of the 'bus called out, "Angel, angel. Last 'bus for the Angel."

There was nothing very remarkable in this, but the one word "Angel" set Frank thinking. Was it possible that his angel could see his suffering? He pondered and thought till he fell asleep – and dreamed.

[3 November 1888]

Chapter XXII.

The surroundings of Frank were not of a nature to suggest very pleasant thoughts, yet strange to say he slept peacefully, the light of a happy and contented mind was easily traceable through the grimed face and hard outlines of his features.

He fancied himself back at Cranston's, with all the old familiar faces, standing at his lathe and singing over his work. He seemed to hear Crosbie's cheerful voice giving him instructions in his new sphere as under foreman.

Then it seemed as though his day's work was over, and he was at home by his own fireside. He could see the kettle on the hob giving forth its little jets of steam; he could hear the happy laugh of his wife as he complimented her on the nice cup of tea she had made.

Now the tea is over, the table is cleared, and they sit down, side by side, to talk over the happier prospects of the future.

Polly asked him whether he didn't think it possible to get a small piece of carpet for the parlour? And, accompanying her interrogation with something more than a mere show of affection, she threw herself on her knees, took his face between her hands, and kissed his forehead lovingly, if not rapturously.

"Frank," she said, in a calm, soothing tone, looking up into his eyes with an endearing glance, "Frank, do you know what I've been thinking? Well, I thought, now you're getting thirty shillings a week I might save up to get a feather pillow for poor mother, she does complain of her head aching so in the morning; and I thought perhaps a feather pillow would do her good. Now you are surely not jealous of your mother? But look here, I've bought a new pair of socks for you."

Then he seemed to be suddenly transported to another Elysium of bliss. Side by side with his true, affectionate little wife he was pulling weeds out of his little cottage garden. Running a little way from him she plucked an innocent wild-flower, and holding it up to him she exclaimed,

"Forget-me-not! Did you know we had any forget-me-nots in the garden? Do you know the language of flowers? What is the meaning of forget-me-not?"[65]

Then he felt as though he were trying to snatch the flower away from her, but could not seize it. Every time he tried, the flower seemed to change its shape. From a little blue forget-me-not it changed to a large water-lilly. She tauntingly threw it into a silent lake that was close by. Then springing away from him as he pursued her, she stepped on to one of the leaves. A fairy-like halo of enchantment seemed to surround her. The mystic swans came gliding towards her. She threw some light, flowery tendrils around their necks, and they gently, slowly, and gracefully drew her over the face of the placid lake. She beckoned to him to follow, but he felt himself riveted to the spot; he tried to speak, to beg her to stay; but the only words he could utter were "My angel."

The exertion awoke him. He heaved a deep sigh, and found that he had been dreaming.

Frank could not tell how long he had been asleep. The strange, unreal vision that had passed before him was a great trouble to him. He could hardly realise the truth of the situation.

He gazed around him; but a strange haze of astonishing density prevented him from seeing anything. It was a London fog, and of a thickness that might be felt.

Frank wondered what he should do. He stretched out his hands to determine whether his sense of feeling was left him, for he had almost persuaded himself that he had lost his sight and hearing. He had often seen the mist that floats silently over the fields in the early morning. He had seen the hoar frost rising from the earth when the sun's rays had begin to make their influence felt. But he had never seen a London fog before.

He was by no means convinced that his sense of touch was intact, for the cold had so benumbed his hands and feet that nothing short of a forcible concussion with a fixed substance gave him any satisfaction of the retention of those senses.

After straining his eyes to the utmost, and listening attentively to catch the slightest sound, and not being successful in seeing or hearing anything, he sank back on to the stone bench that had been his bed, and swooned.

On reviving he fancied he could see a glimmer of light in front of him. He sprang to his feet at once, joyous that he was not blind; but they were so frozen that they refused to support him, and he fell headlong across the pavement, with his head hanging over the edge of the kerb.

How long he lay in this position he could not say, and only recollected the circumstances when a kindly carman, in whose van he found himself lying, told him the story of his being found by him.

As Frank turned over, and showed signs of consciousness, the carman feelingly addressed him.

"Cheer up, old man; you're all right now. I'm blessed if ever I thought you was going to speak again, let alone sit up."

"Shove that sack on, and stand up here if you can."

Frank complied, and was delighted with the cheerful and friendly appearance of his new companion.

"Well," said the carman, "where are you going to?"

"Anywhere," replied Frank, "if I can only get a job."

"Oh, that's it; yes I know – out of work. Got no doss money and won't go to the 'Lump'; been sleeping on the bridge and got fruz."[66]

"That's it," said Frank, although the words "doss money" and "the Lump" were not familiar to him.

"Well, look here mate, I've only got couple of slices and a brown[67] for a cup of coffee. You can have half of that if you like. There's a coffee-stall just down here."

"Thanks," said Frank, the tears rushing to his eyes and his voice being stifled with emotion.

The carman pulled up at the coffee-stall, insisted upon Frank sharing with him, and then told him how he had found him lying.

"Walking along the kerb," said he, "for it was so blooming thick on the bridge I couldn't see the crock's head from my dickey,[68] I tumbled up agin something. Hallo, says I, what's up. Here, jump up, old bloke, or you'll get gulleytined, I says, 'cause your head was hanging over the kerb. I couldn't make you speak, so, some bloke coming along, I says, give us a hand, old man, and he helps you into my van, I'll take him to the hospital."

"Thank you," said Frank, "I'm better now."

"Yes. Well, where are you going to look for a job? What kind of graft do you want?"

"Anything," said Frank, "I thought of trying at the docks."

"Well, jump up then: I'm going down to the West India Docks for a load. Perhaps I can put a word in for you."

They journeyed on together, chatting about the condition of work, and the difficulty to get a job. Frank was by no means encouraged at the description his companion gave of the process of getting on at the docks, and feared that his present weak state would prevent him holding his own with those whom he would have to meet.

Arrived at the docks, he took a friendly leave of his new companion and expressed a hope that they would meet again.

Then the struggle commenced; at first Frank hesitated somewhat and seemed almost disposed to give it up; but the pangs of hunger made him try again.

Every time he pushed himself forward, he found that he would have to fight more fiercely if he meant getting on.

As the day wore on, and he was still unsuccessful, the pangs of hunger made him mad.

Just at that moment there was another call, and Frank set his teeth resolutely. Striking out right and left, with such fearful blows as often to lay the unfortunate man who received them prostrate on the earth, he rushed and pushed with a maddening desperation. He sprang on to the back of one man whom he could not move away, and tore his hair so savagely that the man yelled again.

For a moment all eyes were turned in the direction of the noise, but seeing Frank's determined frenzied look they recollected their own struggle.

Climbing over the shoulders of those he could not push away, tearing at the heads of anyone who dared to present an obstacle, he at last found himself at the ganger's box[69] just as the last one was taken on.

Frank appealed to him for help, saying he was starving; but the man was so used to such expressions and such scenes that he was perfectly callous and indifferent. He dismissed his pleas, prayers and entreaties with a wave of his hand.

Frank stood gazing with an air of absent mindedness that betokened abstraction, and when he did recover himself he found all the rest had gone.

By this time the day was well advanced, the sun had broken through and the fog had been dispersed.

After making enquires of some men who were helping to unload the cargo of an Indian tea merchant's boat, Frank found that there was not the remotest likelihood of anyone being taken on during the evening, as several of the vessels that ought to be in dock were fog-bound in the Channel.

Another day, was, therefore, destined to pass, and Frank was no nearer getting a job than when he came to London.

The oft-recurring problem, What he should do? was no nearer a solution now than ever.

He was too weary, too fatigued, and too disheartened to try any of the other docks.

He sauntered listlessly back to the bridge, making fruitless calls at several wharves and warehouses on his way back. For the first time since he arrived in London he felt a longing for a smoke. He put his hand in his pocket, found the pipe, and the remnants of a screw of tobacco. He lighted his pipe, strolled along slowly, and almost forgot his troubles. He arrived at the bridge, and sat down in the recess that had befriended him the night before.

He had thought of applying at some casual ward, but a natural diffidence to workhouses and unions made him prefer spending another night in the open rather than personally prove the accounts he had heard of their discomfort.

As he sat, lost in despair, he allowed his thoughts to travel back to Ben Green, and he recollected what he had said about knowing who the murderer was, and when the proper time arrived he would reveal the secret and save Frank's neck. This thought made Frank half resolve to give himself up, and trust to Ben to get him clear off. Then he thought, perhaps Ben had only said so much to cheer him up, and after all he did not know the real murderer, and to return to Benton as Frank Wilson, would be to surrender himself to the hangman.

He sighed. Anything was better than that. He would starve. He would die!

[10 November 1888]

Chapter XXIII.

When Frank awoke the next morning he felt more rested than he thought possible, but still more depressed. He seemed sorry, almost, that he had not died during the night, when he realised that he had again to enter into the contest against the world for his living.

He had arrived at that stage of despondency that makes a man say, Anything must be better than this. He had been in London since Saturday night. It was now Thursday morning, and there seemed to him no more chance of getting a job than if he were in the back woods of America or the Australasian bush region.

He wondered whether it would be possible for him to keep on like this much longer. Some men, so he had heard, were out of work for weeks and months at a stretch: How did they manage?

He rose to his feet, yawned, shuddered and sighed. He looked into the water, and called to mind one of Ben Green's favourite quotations from his favourite author –

> "Whether 'tis nobler in the mind to suffer
> The slings and arrows of outrageous fortune,
> Or to take arms against a sea of troubles,
> And by opposing end them?"[70]

Passing over the bridge, down Tooley Street, he strolled along in a dull, dreamy mood, scarcely caring whether he got work or not. Nothing interested him now, and a melancholy, callous demeanour was the only thing traceable in his appearance.

So absorbed was he that if he had not had to go out into the road he would not have taken any notice of a large number of men congregated outside a wharf gates.

It was a miserable looking group. Old men of sixty and youths of eighteen, all wearing the same look of stolid indifference nearly all smoking clay pipes. Here and there two or three were engaged in conversation, but the majority were silent, leaning against the wall and the gateposts on either side of the entrance; their ragged coats of cloth, fustian, or corduroy, buttoned close under their chins, their hands thrust into the pockets of their threadbare trousers, their gaze stolidly fixed on the pavement.

Frank walked backwards and forwards in front of the gateway several minutes before venturing to speak to any of the men. He naturally imagined they were waiting for a job, and presently, turning to a rough looking individual with a greasy cloth cap on his head and a short black pipe in his mouth, "Any chance of a job here?" he asked.

"Dunno," replied the other, without looking up or taking the pipe from his mouth.

Frank turned away and addressed himself to another lounger. "What do you wait here for?" he asked this one.

The young fellow addressed took his pipe out of his mouth, eyed his interrogator from head to foot, spat upon the pavement, and drawing the back of his hand across his mouth, replied shortly, "A call."

"There it goes," he added quickly, as a shrill whistle was heard, and dashing away his pipe he joined in the stampede up the yard.

Frank joined in the rush. Such a scramble it was! He could never have believed there were half as many men standing about as there were now rushing up the yard. Pipes were thrown away, except those which were coloured with usage; these were carefully emptied and concealed in waistcoat pockets. The yard, which but a few moments before was completely deserted, was now a scene of noisy confusion, in which some hundreds of men were pushing, shouting, fighting; all struggling to reach a comfortable looking, well-dressed individual, who, with a jaunty air, his felt hat stuck on the back of his head, was standing at a warehouse door, halfway up the yard, and was singling out of the crowd before him, whose hands were outstretched as if in supplication, a man here and there to whom he gave a ticket.

Frank had managed to force himself to the front. With that ferocity begotten of want and competition, he had used the physical strength which had made him the champion of the Benton football team, to force back men older and weaker than himself who were engaged with him in this fearful struggle for work. When he found himself the fortunate possessor of a metal ticket, and was following the others through the warehouse door, he could not forbear a pang as he glanced back on the crowd of those who, disappointed, were already turning dispiritedly away, and almost wished he had not succeeded, since it meant the disappointment of someone else.

He had little time for meditation, however. The men who had received tickets had been mustered in the warehouse and were now being told off[71] in gangs.

"Now you," said the foreman to Frank, "come here. What's your name?"

"Frank Watson, sir."

"Oh, a yokel, eh? Here Bilton, take him with your lot."

Frank was led off in company with about half-a-dozen others, under the guidance of the man the foreman had addressed as Bilton, to the quay by the side of the warehouse, alongside of which a small vessel was lying. A gang of men were already on board opening up the hold prior to discharging the cargo, which consisted of bags of sugar.

A chain was lowered down into the hold from a crane overhead, and the work of unloading began. A number of the bags were placed in slings and hauled up to the bank, where they were taken charge of by Bilton's gang, each of whom, placing a bag on a small hand-barrow, wheeled it into the warehouse, where it was weighed and checked, and where another gang was engaged stowing away.

Bilton was at the weighing machine, and was constantly shouting to the men bringing in the bags, "Now my lads, play up at 'em," "Let's have yer," and other such phrases calculated to keep his gang up to their work.

The other men in the gang appeared to be old hands, but to Frank the work came very hard. The cobblestones over which he had to wheel the truck shook it so as to make his hands tingle. In a short time, cold as it was, he was in a profuse perspiration. Once or twice the jolting of the stones caused his load to tumble off the truck, when the man behind him would sing out, "Now then, countryman, don't you come any of them tricks to get out of your turn."

He had to work hard to keep up. His feet were sore, walking over the uneven stones, his hands were blistered, and he was feeling faint with hunger; yet he was constantly urged to greater exertions by the ganger and the men who followed his turn. "Play up at 'em, yokel," shouted the ganger, "don't keep me waiting."

Frank knew that the men with him had shifted; he had been cheated into taking one or two extra turns. He was first but one in the gang now, though he started nearly last. By and bye the man in front accosted him with, "I heard them call you 'countryman' just now, what part do you come from?"

"—shire," replied Frank, naming the county.

"So do I," returned the other, "where abouts?"

"Oldbury."

"Oh, I know, about nine miles from Benton, where the murder was a few weeks ago. What's your name?"

"Watson."

"Hard up, I reckon. Never done any of this before?"

"No."

Frank was glad when they knocked off for dinner, though he had neither money nor food. He was glad of the rest, his arms and feet ached, and he felt that he could go on no longer.

"Got no grub, I s'pose?" said the man who had asked him about his native place, as they walked out of the yard together.

"No."

"I'll soon show you where to get some," said the other, leading the way to a public house, a couple of doors from the gateway.

"Here, missus," said he to the woman behind the bar, "Let's have two two's of bread and cheese and two halves of four – on this," tendering the metal ticket he had received in the morning.

The beer and bread and cheese were soon forthcoming, and Frank fancied he had never tasted anything so delicious before in his life. It was the first food he had had for thirty-six hours. His companion plied him with many questions about his native country, the recent murder, and the probability of Wilson's escape to all of which Frank replied as shortly as was consistent with civility.

The dinner hour was soon over. Frank felt stiff and tired as he got up to go back to the work, but the food and drink had refreshed him considerably. As they were walking back, one of the men in his gang said, "You be careful what you have to say to Nobby Wright; he'll be trying to convert you; he's a red-hot Socialist."

"Is he?" returned Frank, feeling very uncomfortable, though scarcely knowing why.

All the afternoon he avoided, as far as possible, his dinner-hour companion; yet he could not help eyeing him curiously. He did not seem to be very different from the others. He did not wear a heavy beard, nor a slouch hat, and so far as Frank could see there were neither pistols in his belt nor dynamite in his pockets.

Still, a Socialist! All that Frank had heard about these extraordinary people caused him to regard them with distrust, not unmixed with terror. He resolved, if possible, to find out more about Nobby Wright.

At six o'clock work ceased. They went in a gang to the office for their day's pay, which was handed to each in exchange for his metal ticket.

Frank noticed that the potman from the neighbouring public house was standing outside the office with a pocket book in his hand and a number of metal tickets, which he gave to the men to whom they belonged, standing close to the elbow of each as he took his money from the office widow, so as to receive what was due to him before they left the yard.

Frank received three and ninepence. He sought out Wright as soon as he was paid, and offering him threepence said, "Here is what I owe you for my dinner."

"Oh, you needn't trouble about that," returned the other; "you may do as much for me some day. Where are you going tonight?"

"Oh, I shall have to find a lodging somewhere."

"Well, in that case you'd better come home with me. We'll find you a doss tonight, anyway."

Frank could not refuse this kind offer, the more as he felt curious to find out what sort of a man his Socialist fellow-workman was, though he could not repress a feeling akin to aversion.

On the way home Frank found his companion very affable and talkative, and expressed his satisfaction at having met him.

He felt almost happy when he became thoroughly at home with Nobby Wright's honest, and sympathetic frankness.

[17 November 1888]

Chapter XXIV.

It was about twenty minutes' walk from the wharf to the place where Wright lived. A narrow thoroughfare, at one end of which was a flight of three stone steps leading down out of the main road, at the other end three posts were erected to prevent the ingress or egress of vehicles. The houses which stood on either side of the court had evidently been the residences of well-to-do people some century previous; they were now in a most dilapidated condition, and were let out in tenements.

Wright led his companion carefully down the steps and to the second house in the row. The court and house were in darkness. Frank had been accustomed to getting about in the dark in the country, but the darkness there had never seemed so dense as in this narrow court. He could not see a step before him. The front door was open and Frank gropingly followed his companion inside and upstairs. On the second landing Wright turned the handle of a door and motioned Frank to enter. It was a comparatively large room in which Frank now found himself, larger than generally compose working-class dwellings, but the ceiling was blackened and cracked, the cornice was broken, and the paper on the walls was so torn and dirty with age that its pattern was quite indiscernible. The only other occupants of the apartment beside Frank and Wright were the wife and daughter of the latter.

The room was poorly furnished. In the corner behind the door stood a bed; an oblong deal table stood in the centre; while three or four wooden chairs and a chest of drawers completed the furniture. A meagre coal fire was burning in the grate, by the side of which the mother and daughter sat sewing. The former, a woman of middle age; the latter a girl of about seventeen, whom care and work had aged beyond her years.

One thing noticeable amidst all this poverty was the thorough cleanliness of everything subject to the application of soap and water. The long deal table was almost white, and many a wealthier housewife would be proud of it.

The chairs had had all the varnish washed off them long enough ago, and it was only because they held together, and were prepared and willing to bear the weight of argument so often put on them, that they were retained.

The flooring, too! Everyone who saw this floor wondered whether there really was any other process of cleaning beside scrubbing.

The women themselves had everything as clean and nice as their circumstances would allow, and the orthodox cotton dress and apron were cherished a great deal more than the richest brochure silk or satin could ever be.

The comparison between the care and cleanliness of the occupants of this room and the utter neglect of everything which belonged to the landlord was most remarkable.

At the moment Frank and Wright entered the women were huddled up in the corner taking advantage of the light shed by the little bursts of gas from the coal.

Every hour that they could do without the lamp was so much oil saved, and they generally managed to struggle on in this way until father came home.

It was a matter of very common remark amongst the women that whenever they wanted to thread the needle the "blessed fire wouldn't blaze."

"Nobby" Wright was a firm, resolute man, of temperate habits. He was never known to take all his money to the "pub" to clear his accumulated score, neither did he stay there drinking and spending till it was all gone.

He spent a good deal of time there, however, because he was very fond of conversation and discussion. He was not a thirsty soul, and one half-pint has often lasted an hour or more when any important social question was on the board.

"You've been to work to-day, father, haven't you?" asked the girl.

"Yes, thank goodness. I managed to get a job to-day. Haven't you had any tea?" he asked, looking round at the bare table.

"No," answered the woman, "I couldn't get any money. Nelly took that work back to Mrs. Pearce's to-day, but she said she had no change, and we must send to-morrow for the money. It was only a shilling. I do think it hard, wanting the money as bad as we do, that we can't get it when we have earned it."

"Then, you have had nothing to eat to-day?"

"Not since you went out this morning."

"Well, Nelly had better go and get something now, then," said he, handing his wife the three and threepence that remained of his day's pay.

"Who's this – one of your Socialist friends?" she asked, glancing towards Frank, whom she had not hitherto noticed.

"No, not exactly, he's a countryman of ours; comes from Oldbury."

"Oh, indeed; won't you come a little nearer the fire, Mr. —?"

"Watson," said Frank, coming forward.

"I didn't know any Watsons at Oldbury. We lived not very far from there, but I suppose you wasn't there long?"

"But you have been in London some time, I suppose?" queried Frank, purposely evading an answer.

"Yes, about ten years. It was all right at first when Joe had plenty of work. He used to work in the tanyards, but work there is very slack, and he's been out for some time."

"What shall I get, mother?" asked the girl, who in the meantime had put on her bonnet and shawl.

"Well, you'd better bring some tea and sugar and some bread and butter. Mr. Watson'll have a cut of tea with us, I 'spose?"

"Mr. Watson is going to stop with us to-night, Susan," said Wright, "so you'd better bring in enough, Nelly."

"Last year," continued Mrs. Wright, when the girl had gone, "Joe took up with the Socialists. They was holding meetings about here about the unemployed. What they said was right enough, but I don't see as they done any good. There seems to be just as many out of work now as there was then."

"You're not a Socialist, Mrs. Wright?"

"No, I should be if I see as they done any good; but here you have all this agitation, as Joe calls it, and meetings and demonstrations, and it don't seem to do no good. As I says to Joe, it's all very well for them as has got nothing else to do and plenty to live upon, but a man with work to look after and a wife and family to support has no business to trouble his head about such things."

"That's how my wife always talks," said Wright, turning to Frank, "as if we who work oughtn't to consider why it is that we have to work so hard and receive so little. If all who have to work would but trouble a little more we should soon have an alteration."

"Yes, if they all would," returned the woman; "but you know very well they won't, so what's the use of talking."

"I suppose you don't know much about Socialism, Watson?"

"No. I read about some of those meetings last year, and, from what the papers said about it, it seems to me a lot of nonsense. As far as I can understand it, Socialists want to share out equally all the wealth that there is in the country. They want to seize all the property, take it away from those who have it, and share it out among those who have none. Now, I have got nothing, and such a doctrine might be supposed to appeal to me, but it seems to me to be the most monstrous thing possible and one which all honest men should oppose. Besides, if you were to share out to all equal to-day, some men would save, while others would not, the old inequality would ensue, and you would have to share out again the day after. Now, how often should this be repeated."

"Well, I may as well tell you that you are entirely wrong. But we won't argue the point till we've had a little snack of something to eat."

Nelly had just returned with her purchases, and her mother set about getting the tea.

"You'd better go and fetch a couple of haddocks, Nelly," said her father.

In a short time the haddocks were cooked and on the table, and the little party set to with a will.

The absence of forks did not prevent each one of them from enjoying the fish, and Frank thought the tea more delicious than any he had ever tasted. He could not repress a feeling of sadness, however, as he thought of his own happy home lost to him for ever.

He wondered how his mother was getting on in the workhouse; how they had buried his wife; how Ben Green was getting on, and whether they would re-capture him, or find the real murderer; and his mind wandered back to the commencement of all his troubles – the day he got the sack from Cranston's.

He was re-called to the present by his host remaking:–

"Well, now, we have somewhat satisfied the inner man, I'll tell you what I understand by Socialism. Of course, I don't pretend to known all about it, but I have learnt all I can, and the same means of learning are open to you if you care to know anything about it. There's some pamphlets on the drawers there that you can read. They put the question in the most simple manner. Then we have a weekly paper and meetings and lectures. There's no need for anyone remaining ignorant who wants to know. Would you like to go to our meetings, Mr. Watson?"

"I should very much, so long as there was no fear of being blown up."

"Well, you'd better come with me next Sunday. Now for a little explanation. You understand Socialism to mean a general dividing up. This is a very common impression, but an erroneous one. Our view is that there is altogether too much dividing up at present. For instance, you'll admit that the land is necessary to the existence of the community – that without the land men could not exist?"

"Yes."

"And yet this land is divided up among a number of individuals who can do just as they like with it, and, as a matter of fact, could practically depopulate the whole kingdom if they choose. The same with regard to what is commonly called capital. This is owned by a few individuals to do as they like with it. Well, we Socialists say that the individual ownership of these means and instruments of production is productive of most of the misery and all the poverty that afflicts the community, and that the remedy is to make these things national or municipal property, not to divide them up, but to use them for the benefit of all collectively."

"Well, that's all right, so far as the dividing up goes; but it seems to me you propose the universal confiscation of property, and I don't see how you are going to bring it about."

[24 November 1888]

Chapter XXV.

Frank was a little surprised at himself in thus combatting the views of the man who had so far befriended him as to afford him food and shelter. Wright himself was by no means put out by Frank's objection.

"That, of course, is what everyone says. 'Wholesale confiscation'! No, we have no desire to confiscate anyone's property, but to prevent the confiscation that is now going on. You are a workman, don't you recognise that everything you see around you is the result of the labour of your class? and yet how little they receive, and how large a share is taken by their masters. There is confiscation, if you like; the confiscation of at least three-fourths of your property."

"They can't confiscate any of my property," returned Frank, "for I've got none."

"You've got none, and why haven't you? You've been at work, I should say, some few years at any rate?"

Frank nodded.

"Well, you invested your capital, your physical strength embodied in your labour, that is; everybody tells us that the labour force of the workman is his capital. You've invested this capital for some years and yet you haven't got any property! When a capitalist invests his capital he not only expects to get it back, but something in addition, which he calls profit or interest. He'd never be satisfied to get back the equivalent of what he invested, unimpaired. Where would be the reward of his abstinence? But you haven't even got your capital back, you haven't maintained it unimpaired, that is. Every year you live your capital becomes less valuable as it approaches the time when it will cease to have any value at all. And yet you have no property, you have made no profit on it. Well, the reason you have made no profit on it is because the employing class has confiscated that profit; you have no property because they have robbed you of it."

"I don't quite follow you," said Frank. "It seems to me that my trouble is not having the opportunity to invest my capital. But anyhow I don't see what this has to do with confiscating the property of the capitalist and the landlord."

"And who wants to confiscate their property? The things of which we propose to deprive these gentry are not property in the sense that they are useful or enjoyable to them. A mill-owner doesn't own the engines, the buildings and the machinery which constitute his capital because he likes to hear their noise and rattle, or because he likes to breathe the heat and dust they create, but because they enable him to make a profit out of the human machinery he uses up with these; the railway shareholder doesn't own a railway share because he likes to look at a bit of scrip, or to have it framed and glazed and hung up in his drawing room, or because the rolling stock and the permanent way are excellent; all these things may be of the best, but what concerns him far more is that the railway should pay a good dividend; and his share represents to him a perpetual pension on the labour of the community. The same with the farmer, the landlord and the house-jobber;[72] all these people own their 'property,' as you call it, for the same reason as the burglar owns a crowbar and a dark lantern – simply as instruments of robbery."

"Oh, come, that's rather rough, comparing landlords and capitalists to burglars."

"Yes, it's rather unfair to the burglar, I'll admit; he only robs the rich, while the others rob the poor, and rob them because they are poor."

"Well, but surely you must admit that even if the profit of the capitalist is robbery, as you term it, his capital is used for beneficent purposes. As much cannot be said for the burglar, whose enterprises are purely destructive. I'll own that the landlord is a useless and even a mischievous individual, but it seems to me that the capitalist does at least perform a useful function."

"That's purely accidental. A capitalist may employ his capital for the production of bread or dynamite, food or poison, bosh butter or leaden bayonets, beef, biscuits, or machine guns; it is entirely immaterial to him. What he is concerned about producing is neither the food nor the poison, neither the butter nor the bayonets, but profit. The production of these commodities is but a means to that end. If in the production of that profit a few people are killed – poisoned in a chemical works, blown to pieces in a mine, or drowned in a coffin ship – this is merely incidental to the obtaining of his booty by the capitalist; just as a burglar in breaking into a house may or may not have to break a window or knock somebody on the head to secure his 'swag.'"

"Yes, but his action is, generally speaking, beneficial to the community. And then this profit, which you seem to regard as being taken from our class and which you talk of as robbery, could not be obtained from the workmen if they didn't care to work for the capitalists. They need not do so unless they choose, they are free to refuse; but as a matter of fact we are only too glad to be employed."

"Yes, and that is the measure of our freedom, that we are forced by necessity to work for those who take advantage of this necessity to make us produce wealth and luxury for them, while we get but a bare subsistence for ourselves. Free! yes, free to work when it answers their purpose to employ us, and free to starve when it don't. We can't employ ourselves. They own all the means with which we can work, the proceeds of former robbery; and then while they goad us with the fear of want and starvation – far more powerful than any slave-driver's whip – they mock us with a pretence of freedom."

"Well, I don't see how you're going to take their capital away from them, even admitting that it would be right to do so; and if it would be right in the case of the big millionaire capitalists you surely wouldn't think of confiscating the property of a man who had saved up a little capital by his own exertions."

"Why not? you wouldn't defend the right of the poor burglar to rob, or to retain his instruments of robbery, any more than you would that of a rich one, would you? What a man has saved from the results of his own exertions undoubtedly belongs to him, but not what he has screwed out of others, and whatever he may have made by his own labour does not give him the right, if it does the power, to exploit the labour of others. As for taking their capital away from them or from those bigger capitalists, for whom you appear to have less sympathy, there are several means by which this might be done, but it would be rendered useless and burdensome to them if the workers had the opportunity of working for themselves. Capitalists would be powerless without a foodless and workless proletariat, condemned by want to make profit for them."

"Well, you have given me some new ideas, I must admit, although I am not prepared to agree with all your conclusions."

"Oh, I don't expect to convert you all at once. If I did so, I shouldn't think much of your conversion. But you come to our meetings and read those pamphlets and you'll see whether our position isn't sound."

"Well, I must admit, you don't appear quite such a terrible set as I at first thought you."

Wright turned the conversation to Frank's own career, but on this the latter was naturally reticent; answering only in monosyllables, though ready enough to talk about the natural beauties of his native county.

They sat talking to a late hour, when, noticing that his companions were getting sleepy, Wright said, "I reckon we'd better turn in, old man; the missus'll make you up a bed in the other room."

With this he lighted a candle and led the way to an adjoining apartment, his wife and Frank following him. This room was much smaller than the other, being only large enough for the bed, which was lying to one side on the floor, and a chair. The walls and ceiling were as filthy as those of the other room, but the floor and the bed were clean.

"This is Nelly's room," said Wright, holding the candle while his wife was arranging the bed, "but she'll have to put up with a shakedown in the other room while you're with us."

"I'm sorry to disturb your arrangements in this way," said Frank.

"Don't mention it; we're far better off for house room than most of the people living in Beulah Place,[73] I can tell you. I never could stand it, to be stived[74] up in the way some of 'em are."

"Well, I'm sure you're very kind," said Frank. "I don't know how I shall be able to return it."

"Oh, don't trouble about that. You tuck into bed, and go to sleep. Good night."

"Good night," said Frank, as he shut the door.

He had become so immured to hardship this last two or three days that kindness, consideration, or sympathy was a new thing to him, and seemed strange.

He threw himself down on the bed and was soon asleep.

Beulah Place was not a Paradise, neither were all the residents angels, but they were mortals – mere flesh and blood – and sometimes some of them quarrelled.

It so happened that, whether through excessive drinking or bad tempers, two women, neighbours of Wright, were jangling rather loudly, and Frank, not being accustomed to it, woke up.

All the other sleepers in the house slept on, but Frank lay awake, listening. Curses, threats and invectives were hurled about as plentifully as the limited vocabulary of the combatants would allow. There was the usual washing of each others' dirty linen before every one present – and there were apparently about twelve or fifteen, judging from the various voices that Frank heard – the usual questioning as to each other's morality, the usual reference to antecedents, and so on.

It was the reference to the antecedents that brought the snarling to a fight.

"What was your father, I should like to know? A bully for a publican – that's a fine thing to boast of."

"Well, that's better than your bloomin' relations. All the blessed lot on 'em's been in quad for priggin'[75] – father, mother, sister – all a bloomin' lousy lot."

"Are they? Well, you take it out o' the old gal."

Then followed a few execrations, an appeal to the deity to deprive them of certain senses, to strike them blind, stiff and speechless, if they did not accomplish the threats they were making about knocking one another's eyes out, breaking jaws, or even killing one another.

Then came the murmurs of approval from the crowd as the two women prepared themselves for the encounter.

One expression that Frank heard told him that they were stripping.

"Take yer shift off, Loo; you'll only get it torn."

After this came sounds of a series of struggles. Yells, screeches, sounds of heavy substances falling; more curses, scuffling of feet, murmurs of approval and dissent.

This sort of thing continued till the form of the policeman in the distance made them seek refuge in flight.

Frank dropped off to sleep, and did not wake again till Wright called him.

[1 December 1888]

Chapter XXVI.

At seven o'clock Wright went and knocked at Frank's door. He was fast asleep and snoring, so he opened it gently and walked in.

"Watson," he said, "are you going to get up?"

Frank had soon dressed himself, and entered the other apartment, where breakfast was being prepared.

"Well," said Wright, "how did you pass the night?"

"Nicely, thank you. I heard one of your fanciful London rows, last night."

"Oh," chimed in the girl, "it was old mother Harris and Totsie Birkley. Did they swear?"

"Now, Nelly," said the mother, "just you finish getting breakfast, and don't trouble so about what don't concern you. Did you sleep all right, Mr. Watson? Was you cold? You're ready for your breakfast, I guess? Go down with Wright to the sink; he'll show you where to wash. Here you are, here's a clean towel; it's rather old, but it's clean."

Mrs. Wright was always very versatile first thing in the morning, but she was generally so confused and hurried – questions, answers, directions, scoldings, instruction and counsel all jumbled up together with a rapidity that would astonish an elocutionist – that few people understood her, and no one ever answered.

Wright and Frank went down to wash, while Nelly and her mother busied themselves clearing up the room and preparing the breakfast.

It was a very homely breakfast, and very little preparation was needed.

However, the two toilers finished dressing, and sat down to the meal prepared for them. The tea was made rather stronger, and by way of a change and as a relish the stale bread was toasted.

Breakfast over Wright and Frank prepared to go.

"Will you be home to dinner, Dad?" said Mrs. Wright.

"Yes, about one;" and away they went to the wharf gates once more to do battle for a living.

This time, however, Frank was not so fortunate as to get taken on when Wright did. He ascertained from some of the others who were standing about outside, that there was sometimes a "call" later on. He accordingly waited.

The hours passed slowly and he felt numbed with the cold, still he waited, and still there was no "call." By and bye the men came out to dinner. As soon as Frank saw Wright he made his way to him, and said.

"Come on, I'll stand Sam[76] this time, any way; I've got my pay from yesterday."

"I know you have; keep it, my boy; we may want to draw on it to-morrow; but I'm going home to dinner to-day. I didn't go yesterday because I didn't reckon there'd be any, but there'll be enough for us all to-day."

Frank accompanied him home, and after dinner spent the rest of the day in aimless wandering through the streets. The next day, Saturday, he was equally unfortunate, but Wright provided him with food and lodging. On Saturday, however, Frank insisted upon paying over to Mrs. Wright the three shillings and ninepence he had earned on Thursday.

At four o'clock Wright had finished all the work he would have that week, and having paid off all scores, or whatever money he had borrowed, he returned home. As he turned into Beulah Place he saw Frank, leaning against one of the posts.

"Hallo, mate; what are you standing out in the cold for? Why don't you go inside?"

"I didn't care about going in without you. That is, I don't want to take advantage of your kindness, or to make myself a nuisance."

"Ah, bosh! Look here, Watson. I tell you what it is. You'll have to take some of the starch out of your own collar. Conventionalities are all very well with the middle and upper class cads for the purpose of killing time. But working men – dock and wharf labourers especially – have no time to stand upon ceremony; neither have they the necessary stiff-necked training to be able to do it without being offensive. It's disgusting to me, and quite unnecessary to my shanty. Come in."

Frank felt rather abashed, and did not reply. However, Wright would not let him feel uneasy so he turned the conversation.

"After tea we'll have a look round the neighbourhood, while the missus and the girl do the shopping that is required. What do you say?"

Frank complied, and began talking a little more freely. Tea was soon served, and as soon disposed of. A clean face and boots, and all was ready.

Passing along the Boro',[77] where a number of stalls with their miscellaneous goods created a partial obstruction of the foot-path traffic, Frank suddenly stopped and pulled up.

Wright noticed this, and asked him what was the matter.

Frank merely muttered a reply and pushed on. But his face turned so deathly pale, his limbs trembled, and his whole manner was so changed that Wright felt quite alarmed.

"Come in and have a nip of brandy, old man. You are not well. You have not had enough food lately."

"No, thanks; it was only a momentary pain. I shall be all right directly."

"But a drop of brandy can't do you any harm, and it may do you good."[78]

Wright almost pushed Frank into the bar of the Crown, and called for two pennyworth of brandy.

Frank was not at all sorry to find himself thus forced inside – not so much for the sake of the brandy as to get out of the hustling crowd, and to escape the scrutiny of an individual who was walking the reverse way to them.

Wright, of course, did not notice any one in particular, but really did think that Frank had been taken suddenly ill.

This was not the case, however. The cause of Frank's spasm of alarm was his sudden recognition of features. A young man, with a high hat, a black cloth suit and a walking cane; a rosy complexion but a dull glaring eye. He swaggered along in a nonchalant manner, swinging his cane and holding his head up with an air of superiority and pride.

These peculiarities would not have been observed by the ordinary passer by, but Frank noticed them. He had often seen them before, and he knew them too well. Rage, fury, hate and revenge were all doing battle with each other in his mind. Memories of unpleasant contact with this man darted across his mind. He suspected him of no good intentions; in fact he thought he was watching him, and dogging his steps. He fancied he saw him on Friday, but was not sure. This time he knew he was right. It was George Cranston!

When Wright suggested that they had better go home, Frank readily complied.

It was the Sunday after Jack Somers' visit to Benton Park that Frank Watson, as Wilson now called himself, accompanied his friend Wright to the Socialists' meeting place. It was at the corner of a turning out of the main road, where on Sundays there was little or no traffic.[79]

Bidding Frank wait at the corner, Wright entered a neighbouring coffee shop and quickly reappeared, bearing a small portable platform. To the front of the platform, when he had deposited it in a convenient place, he attached a red oil-cloth banneret, bearing the motto, "Work for All, Overwork for None."

As soon as the platform had been pitched a number of men, who had been lounging at the street corners as though waiting for something, gathered round. Others of Wright's friends soon arrived, one with a bundle of papers under his arm, and another with a red-painted money-box. Frank was struck with the cordiality with which they greeted each other, and him also when they found he had come with Wright.

It was half-past eleven. They began to look round for the lecturer. Shortly after, Blake made his appearance.

"Now, Wright," said the man with the papers, "get up and open the meeting."

While Wright was briefly explaining the object of the meeting and introducing the lecturer, Frank had a look around on the crowd, which had increased considerably. It was of even more motley appearance than that with which he mingled at the wharf gates. There were some of the latter there; the poorest and most woebegone looking of the lot, wearing the same tattered garments, the same shapeless hats, and the same dilapidated boots as they adorned themselves with on a week-day; and smoking the inevitable short clay pipe. Besides these, there were a number of working men, rather better dressed, but still in their working clothes; and others again who had donned the cloth of respectability in honour of Sunday. The Socialists were mainly of the latter, though some of the number were among the waterside labourers.

When Blake began speaking there were between two and three hundred men standing round, but his sonorous voice attracted the passer by until his audience had increased to fully five hundred. He dwelt upon the immediate object of their meeting there that morning. It was not, he said, for the mere fun of the thing, just to hear each other talk, or to pass away an idle hour; they had not even met in the cold weather that then prevailed for their ordinary object of disseminating the principles of Social-Democracy; but to agitate for immediate steps to be taken on behalf of those unfortunate thousands who were unemployed.

The speaker went on to describe in pathetic language the horrors of being "out of work;" a description the realities of which many of his listeners had evidently experienced, and none more so than Frank. The lecturer wound up with an earnest appeal to all, especially those in work, to do everything in their power to assist in this agitation.

It was a dull cold day and the north-east wind caused many of those who were standing round to pull their threadbare coats closer round them as they shivered beneath its blast; yet they almost forgot the cold in their earnest attention to the speaker.

At the close of Blake's address the man with the box passed it round for a collection. Wright then got up, and having stated the amount collected to be 10s., asked if anyone had any objection to raise or any question to ask.

The audience had considerably diminished by this time, and neither questions nor opposition being forthcoming, Wright announced that there would be a lecture that evening in the neighbouring coffee-house at eight, and closed the proceedings.

It was one o'clock, and after taking back the platform, and bidding good day to Blake, Wright and Frank made their way back to Beulah Place.

"Well," said Wright, when they had gone a little way, "what do you think of it?"

"Oh, it was all right, so far; but I have not learnt very much more about Socialism than I knew before."

"No, perhaps not; Blake is more of an agitator than an agitatationist, but anyway you can't expect to learn all about Socialism in one lecture."

[8 December 1888]
Chapter XXVII.

Dinner was ready when they got home, and frugal as it was it was the best Frank had ate for many a day. After dinner Wright read the Sunday paper to his wife, while Frank busied himself with the socialist pamphlets his friend had shewn him.

In the evening, directly after tea, Wright announced his intention of going to the branch meeting. Frank accompanied him. The room in which the meeting was held was at the back of the coffee shop, through which they had to pass. It was capable of seating about a couple of hundred persons. There were about twenty present, who were busily discussing the weekly business of the branch, when Frank and his companion arrived. This was continued till half-past seven when Somers, who was the appointed lecturer that evening, arrived, and one of their number threw open the door leading from the shop and then took up his station outside the shop door to announce the lecture.

By eight o'clock the room was fairly filled, and, a chairman having been appointed, shortly after the hour Somers began his lecture.

His subject was Socialism and Economics. He contended that there was not so great an antagonism between orthodox political economy and Socialism as was generally understood; that a knowledge of economy was necessary to the proper understanding of Socialism; that no one, therefore, who had not had a good education was capable of teaching it; and proceeded to demonstrate the economic soundness of the palliative measures advocated by the Socialists.[80]

The majority of the members of the branch seemed to be highly pleased with the lecturer, and paid great attention to him; Wright, in fact, pushed himself to the front at the conclusion to congratulate him. But Frank was very uneasy. Once or twice he thought of retiring, and getting right away from all these people. There was something in the appearance of the speaker which reminded him very much of a most unpleasant circumstance. He could not dissociate him from one of the personal friends of the Cranstons, or, at any rate, he felt certain this man was present at the picnic at Cranston's Paddock on the occasion of his being charged with stealing watercresses.

Again and again Frank eyed him with suspicion, but did not feel positive about him until the time of questions.

While Frank was evincing great uneasiness at the person of the lecturer there were several members of the branch who were watching him. They wondered who he was. His behaviour was very strange to them. He looked glaringly all the time, either at the lecturer, or else round the room. Every now and then he would make a move as though about to retire, but would sit down again and appear consoled.

At the conclusion of the lecture, the chairman announced that anyone might ask questions, or speak in opposition to the lecturer.

There was silence for some time, as though the people were afraid to speak. Presently there was a little bustling, and some excitement, and up jumped a fair but respectably dressed young man.

"May I be allowed to ask one question Mr. Chairman?"

"Certainly."

"Does Mr. Somers propose that if a father dies and leaves an estate to his son, that estate is to become national property, and the son turned into the world to fight for his living?"

"The estate would undoubtedly become the property of the nation. But the son would hardly have to fight for his living as he does now, inasmuch as competition would be swept away."

"What would you do with poachers, burglars and thieves?"

"They would disappear in a very short time, as everyone would be so well satisfied with the remuneration for his labour that it would be easier and less risky to work than to steal."

The answers were deemed satisfactory, and everyone seemed pleased with the stranger for asking these questions.

Who was he? No one knew. Wright had never seen him before, and didn't even know his name.

The climax of Frank's discomfort was reached when the fair middle-class man rose to ask questions. He was certain now that he knew the lecturer; and he also knew the questioner.

Frank felt faint and giddy; the room became suddenly oppressive; he seemed to be losing his senses; he was becoming distracted; he must get up and go out, or he would lose his reason. He stepped as lightly down the room as he could, but everyone turned round and stared. Those who got a glance at his face remarked how pale it had become, and one man, more concerned than the rest, followed him to the door. When he reached the door this stranger touched him on the shoulder, and asked him how he was.

This sudden and unexpected concern on the part of a stranger so surprised Frank that he started and made use of some short sentence that set his would-be benefactor thinking and talking.

When the meeting was over, Wright wanted to introduce Frank as a new member, and to shake hands and congratulate the lecturer. But when he looked for Frank he had gone.

"Hallo, Cranston," said Somers, as he stepped off the platform, "what brings you up to London?"

"Business, my boy."

"Who told you to come here?"

"Nobody; but I heard you were going to lecture here, and I thought I would form one of your audience."

"You heard! How did you hear?"

"Oh, it's all right, Jack Somers. But you must allow for other people to be half as cute as you. Where is Alice Steggles?"

"God knows! What, is she missing, then?"

"Well, I thought you'd know something about it. But I'll meet you to-morrow. We can't talk here."

George Cranston and Jack Somers walked off in the direction of the West, while Wright began inquiring for Frank.

He looked all round the hall, and at last ascertained that he was waiting outside. On seeing him, he thought he looked strange and pale.

"Ain't you well, old man?"

"Yes, thanks. But the room was rather hot, and I felt very faint."

"Well, how did the lecture suit you?"

"The lecture was very good, but I did not like the lecturer so well as Blake. He's too supercilious for me."

"Well, he's a new comer amongst us, you see. I don't know much about him, but he seems all right. Of course we are glad to get all the active men we can, and as for his superciliousness, he hasn't got over the idea of the superiority of his own class yet."

At the Elephant George Cranston and Jack Somers parted, the former in the direction of the Boro' and the latter went back to Belgrave Square.

"So you've got over that confounded lecture of yours," said Jack Somers' friend when he arrived at his lodgings. "Why the devil can't you leave the whole thing alone. You are no Socialist, you know that. There are plenty of other things with which you can amuse yourself without taking up with that rubbish."

"That's just where you are wrong. There are not plenty of other amusements, they are all played out."

"Yes, but Socialism above everything else! It is the richest joke I ever heard of. Jack Somers, the egotist, the cynic, the man absolutely devoid of all human sympathy, taking up with the altruistic theories of Socialism! Now, confess it Jack; you have no sympathy with these fanatical idealists, now have you?"

"Sympathy, my dear fellow! Why I have no sympathy with any human being in the world. As for the workingmen, inside the Socialist movement or out of it, they are not worth a curse. You and I Gus and the fellows in our set would kick up a rumpus if we were in their position, but these workmen are like a set of curs and deserve to be treated as such. No, I have no sympathy with them. Damn them. But I've got a certain amount of ability – I never did hide my light under a bushel – and I fancy I should shine as a legislator."

"Well, why the devil, then, don't you come forward as a member of one or other of the respectable parties? Label yourself a Tory, or a Liberal, and nobody could say a word against it; but Socialist, phew!"

"Liberal and Tory are both played out, my boy. I must be original, or nothing. There is nothing original to be said on either one side or the other. Besides, heartless though I may be, I hate humbug and hypocrisy. I could not pose as a Liberal or a Tory when I know that the principles of both are absolutely rotten. I have no sympathy with Socialism or with Socialists, yet my detestation of humbug compels me to be a Socialist in spite of myself, because I know Socialism is true."

"You're a bit of a humbug for all that," muttered his companion, as he turned to his bedroom.

On the Monday George Cranston and Jack Somers met at Gatti's.[81] There was a strange indifference in tone and manner towards each other, George Cranston evincing a certain amount of caution verging on suspicion.

After the usual preliminaries of "How d'ye do?" and so forth, there was a long and perplexing silence. Each seemed afraid to broach the subject upon which they had met, and yet both wanted to know the other's opinion on the matter.

Somers was the first to speak.

"Well, what's this about the girl Steggles?"

"Why, she's disappeared from her home."

"But where has she gone? When did she disappear, and why did she leave?"

"They are questions which I thought you would be best able to answer."

"Me? Why me?"

"On calling in at the Red Lion two days after you and I went in together, I found the old man behind the bar, and in great grief. He told me that Alice had been out on an errand on the previous evening and had never returned, and as you appeared to be rather sweet on her I thought you had probably something to do with her disappearance. She has not been heard of or seen since."

"But, damn it, you don't meant to say that you think I should be fool enough to elope with a girl of that sort. She's a jolly nice girl, I'll admit, but not quite the pattern for Jack Somers."[82]

"Well, anyhow, I promised the old man I'd come up to London and see if I could glean anything from you."

"Cranston, your cool impudence annoys me. I detest it. Good day."

Jack Somers turned on his heel and strode up Pall Mall, while George Cranston went back into Gatti's and called for some further refreshment. He muttered something between his teeth which sounded very much like a curse. He could not altogether persuade himself that Jack Somers was entirely ignorant of the whereabouts of Alice Steggles. He, however, resolved that he would not rest satisfied until he had learned a great deal more of Jack's ways. Preaching Socialism was almost too empty an excuse for living in London.

[15 December 1888]

Chapter XXVIII.

Ever since the night Alice parted with Frank – the night of his wife's death and the discovery of his hiding place by the doctor – she had been very much concerned about his safety. It was little more than a week, but it seemed a month to her. She actually read the weekly paper through, from first to last, to see if there was any mention of his whereabouts. Not once only did she pore over the columns of the paper, but a dozen times at least.

It was during one of these searchings of these hitherto untraversed fields of information that she happened on an advertisement that decided her course of action.

She was certain Frank was in London, but what part she could not imagine. Her idea of London was a very limited one, and her knowledge was entirely wanting. But she felt that if she could only get there she would be sure to see Frank.

Her longing to see him again, to ascertain whether he was alive or dead, whether he was in prison or free, whether he was working or starving, made her undertake this romantic, wild goose chase.

The advertisement was for a barmaid, and she determined to go to London to try for the place. She laid her plans accordingly, and on the Thursday evening she got clear away before anyone missed her. The night got very advanced, old

Steggles had dozed off and awoke again two or three times before he got concerned. At last he consulted the clock. It was past four.

"What," he muttered to himself, "has that gipsy allowed me to sleep on here sooner than wake me to let me know the time she came trapsing[83] in? I'll let her know."

Jumping up from his chair he shouted out vigorously, "Alice! Alice!" No answer. "Alice!" he shouted again. Still no reply, "Alice!" He literally screamed with rage. "Come down to me at once! You must hear me, and if you don't come it'll be all the worse for you."

He continued shouting and talking for some time, but finding it was of no avail he at last went up to her bedroom.

The door was open, the bed untouched, and principal clothing gone. That she had not returned home he was now perfectly certain. He went off to the county police station and gave information, but it was "too late and too early" as the functionary on duty put it, "to go waking people up to ask questions."

He returned home a broken-hearted man. He had not been a bad father, and he could not understand her behaviour.

In the morning everybody's mouth was full of the disappearance of the girl.

"Oh," said the prima donna of the town gossips. "Well, I'm not surprised. No good'll ever come of her. She was too fast, too flighty. She used to think too much of chaffing the toffs, and talking to the men. I always did say she would turn out wrong."

"But think of her poor old father," said another. "Anything that happens to her'll serve her right, but it's a pity the old gentleman takes on so."

"He couldn't have been much of a father," suggested a third, "or else she wouldn't have left home."

The whole of the morning was thus spent in speculating as to what had become of her.

Meanwhile Alice had arrived at Paddington quite safe, and had succeeded in getting her new place.

Time passed on and still she had not met Frank.

One day, however, while waiting to cross the Strand by the Law Courts who should come along but Frank Wilson.

Alice did not at first recognise him. But when Frank approached her more closely – for he identified her at once, although almost dumbfounded at meeting her – she saw who it was.

It took Frank some time before he could recover himself from the surprise it occasioned him at meeting Alice. When at last he recovered himself sufficiently to talk he proceeded to pour so many interrogations into her ear that she was unable to answer them.

By repeating his questions one at a time, however, he succeeded in learning all the news of Benton.

She then asked Frank to call and see her at the Flint and Steel – the sign of the house where she was employed. It was a small house, just off the Euston Road on the Hampstead Road.

At first Frank felt afraid to leave the neighbourhood where he had been staying, and told Alice so; but when she told him that she had come all the way from Benton on purpose that she might see him, he waived his objection and promised to come on the Sunday.

As soon as they had returned from the Sunday morning meeting at which Frank was now a regular attendant, and dinner was over, he asked Wright the straightest and nearest way to Euston Road.

"What, are you going out this afternoon, Mr. Watson?" queried the wife. "It will seem a funny Sunday afternoon without you."

"Well, it will be strange to me also; but I fancy I have a friend living somewhere near there, and I want to try and find them."

"That's almost like asking for Mrs. Brown, London isn't it?"

"Not quite so bad as that. I know the sign of the house and the name of the road where they are supposed to be staying, although I didn't say so before."

"Beware of pretty barmaids, Mr. Watson," laughed Mrs. Wright.

"Thank you," said Frank, "Good bye."

He arrived at the Flint and Steel just before the three o'clock closing time.

Alice whispered across the bar that she would meet him outside at half-past three, but kept him talking there until time was called; Frank then walked up and down outside till she came.

"Now, look here, Mr. Wilson – or shall I say Frank?"

"Frank, if you please, Alice."

"Very well. Now, you don't really know do you, who shot Gripper?"

"No; I wish I did."

"Well, don't you think we ought to be able to find out? There are not many people in Benton that I do not know, and I think I ought to be able to tell who it was."

"So do I, for the matter of that. But I shall certainly have to get something more definite than a mere guess before I could venture back to Benton."

"I don't propose to trust entirely to guessing. But I thought now that you are away, that if I went back and worked myself into the confidence of the suspected party I might be able to draw from him some kind of confession."

"Who do you mean by the suspected party?" said Frank, his eyes sparkling with the thought of being proved innocent.

"Well, I don't know, exactly. But there were only two persons besides yourself who were known to have gone in that direction with a gun."

"Ben Green and George Cranston," Frank hinted.

"And do you think they are both innocent, as well as yourself?"

"It's hard to say."

"Ben Green: –"

"Oh, it's not Ben Green I feel certain. In fact, he told me that when it came to a serious issue he would reveal the murderer and save me."

There was a terrible pause. Frank could say no more, and Alice was afraid to reply. It was very evident that a corroborative conviction possessed both their minds. It must have been George –

No more was said at this time, and presently Alice wished Frank good evening, and arranged to meet him again on the following Sunday.

Frank retraced his steps to Beulah Place. All the way home his mind was full of thoughts, misgivings and unpleasant forebodings. He would have been in time for the evening meeting at the hall, but he was so distracted that he preferred going home, hoping to have a few quiet moments to himself for thinking.

He was sadly disappointed, for Mrs. Wright kept him going all the time answering her interrogations respecting the neighbourhood he had been in.

She was very anxious to know why Frank had been in the direction of Euston Road, and kept hinting and chaffing him for a long while about being in love, and sweet on a barmaid.

Frank took no interest in this kind of chaff, and paid very little attention to what she was saying, merely answering yes or no where she was so importunate as to compel him to say something. Once he answered so sharply that she rebuked him, telling him he might answer civilly.

In his excitement while with Alice he had forgotten to tell her, before parting with her, where he lived, but he knew her address, and therefore decided to write. He was a long while making up his mind what he should say, and even then seemed afraid to post it.

The epistle he sent contained little else than a wail over his unhappy position. When Alice read it, she seemed thoroughly upset, on his behalf, and resolved to use her energies forwards securing his freedom by a conviction of the real murderer.

How to go about it she knew not. The time for bed arrived, and Alice turned in. She could not sleep but kept turning from one side to another, trying hard to arrange some plan whereby she might discover who was responsible for the crime with which Frank was charged.

Hour after hour passed but still she could not sleep. Frank was ever uppermost in her thoughts.

The London train had scarcely pulled up at Paddington on Thursday evening when an elderly passenger, with a third-class ticket, stepped out on to the platform.

He was of middle age and middle height; his complexion and hair, too, were medium; he was between the extremes of fat and lean, but just sufficiently developed in the corporation to entitle him to be classed as a pot-bellied publican; this development, however, was not enough to hinder him in his usual little sprintings across every road he went over; between one crossing and another he trotted along quite quickly, looking at everything and everybody, and seeing nothing and nobody; arrived at the edge of the kerb, he looked around him, all ways, north, south, east, west, up in the air, and finally down on the ground; having persuaded himself that he would not impede the vehicular traffic by crossing at such a time, he would dart over.

It was after one of these little moments of anxiety – when he attempted to dodge in front of a hansom and behind an omnibus, without counting on the immovable nature of the policemen on point-duty at the end of Hampstead Road – that he felt somewhat agitated and nervous, and called into the Flint and Steel to have a toothful of brandy to calm his nerves.

There was a female behind the bar, and old Steggles – for he it was who had just escaped being run over – almost fainted in recognising in the barmaid who was about to serve him his runaway daughter Alice.

Quite an exciting scene ensued. Alice, with the convictions of a guilty conscience and the remorse of a prodigal, cried bitterly; while her father alternately cursed and blessed, wept and scolded, censured and sympathised.

[22 December 1888]

Chapter XXIX.

Frank passed some weeks in this way, going with Wright every morning to the wharf, and sleeping every night in the back room in Beulah Place. Some days he would be successful at the wharf, at other times, when he was not taken on, he would wander around to the different factories, trying to get a job in his own trade, without success. Christmas came, and Beulah Place put on a festive appearance. The inhabitants got their Sunday clothes out of pawn – those who had any – the chimney sweep who lived opposite Wright's dwelling got more than usually drunk on Christmas Eve, and, with loud volubility, declared his willingness to fight any adjective Socialist in the court for a "pot." No one evincing any desire to contend with him for this valuable stake, he practised his pugilistic powers on his unfortunate better half, who appeared the next day with a couple of black eyes. The smoked haddock vendor at the corner did an exceptionally brisk trade on the Christmas Eve and made things noisy with a concertina on the following day. The Beulah Place people had few holidays, and of these Christmas was the principal one; they had fewer pleasures, of which beer was the chief. Much beer was consumed in Beulah Place that Christmas time and there was much beery jollity in consequence. In this Frank and Wright had little participation. They had not been particularly fortunate during the preceding week and they had little to be jolly with. To Frank the time was particularly cheerless; he could not help contrasting the present time with the Christmas of a twelvemonths earlier. Then, as always, he was wondering what was taking place at Benton. He had not written to anyone, nor had he heard anything since seeing Alice Steggles. He was afraid of his letters being intercepted and Alice had only written to him once since. Was Ben Green still in work, or had he again taken to poaching? What had become of his mother? How was she getting on in the workhouse? Were the police on his track? Had the real murderer been discovered?

He was so frequently preoccupied inconsequence of this mental trouble that Wright and his wife had frequently noticed it, and had both come to the conclusion that Watson had "something on his mind."

Frank had become a constant attendant at the Socialist meetings, but no persuasion on the part of Wright could induce him to join the organisation.

"But you agree with our objects and you accept our principles," said Wright to him one day after he had been vainly urging him to join the branch.

"Yes; I am convinced you are in the right," was his reply, "and I am prepared to do all I can for the cause; but I won't join. I don't know how soon I may have to go away altogether."

One morning they had gone down to the wharf as usual, and with a number of other men outside the gates were discussing the topics of the day.

"Well, I do think it's a blasted shame," said one, "this here dodge of taking ye on for half an hour. They'll keep on and keep on till there's a blooming row, I reckon. We put up with almost anything but they'll drive us too far one of these days if they go on."

"Who'll kick up the row?" asked another, "Why, you know you're all jolly well afraid to speak. You don't seem to have the pluck of a mouse or you'd have kicked long ago. And look at the lot of us, and look at all them as is out of work; here we go, marndering[84] on day arter day, with just enough to keep body and soul together, when if we made up our minds to go for it we might get what belongs to us."

"Yes, that's very well for you, Bill Smart," said Joe Wright; "but what are you doing yourself? If you believe in what you say, you'd come and join us."

"What's the good of one? If you could get the whole lot of us together it might be some good, but for just one or two to try is only wasting time. I agree with your views to some extent, only you don't go far enough for me. All your talk is about organising, organising, organising. We don't want so much organising, we want ructions."

"Well, Wright," said another, "I see your friends, the fair traders, have taken up with this unemployed question, which you have been talking about."

"Oh, you mean Isaacs and Molley,[85] and that lot."

"Yes, I see they are going to have a meeting in Trafalgar Square next Monday."[86]

"Yes, I see they have called a meeting for next Monday, but they can't get a meeting. Their game's played out, people know what they are, and are not likely to place any confidence in them."

"Well, but it's a good thing to take up this unemployed business, ain't it? You Socialists have sneered at other people for not taking the matter up, and now you don't seem to like it because they have done so."

"It 'ud be all right if they were straight," said Wright, "but we know that these fellows are mere tricksters. They don't represent any section of the working classes, and they are doing this because they are paid to do it. You see the Liberals are in and the Tories are out; and these gentry are in the pay of the Tories, who would be glad to embarrass their political opponents, besides the pleasure of dishing us and deceiving the workers into the bargain."

"Yes, I know them to be a lot of scamps," said Bill Smart; "look what Molley did with the Waterside Labourers' Association.[87] It's that kind of thing that disgusts workingmen with all organisation."

"Well, I reckon it's about six of one and half-a-dozen of the other," said the first speaker; "I don't suppose Wright would take so much interest in it if he didn't make a good thing out of it."

"Do you dare to say that I make anything by the part I take in agitating on behalf of my class?" demanded Wright, hotly.

"Well, I reckon you do, or else you wouldn't do it."

"It's a lie," shouted Wright, angrily clenching his fists.

"More fool you, then; that's all I can say. If you don't make anything by it you've no business to waste your time and wear out shoe leather in tramping about after Socialist agitators. If you don't make something out of them they make something out of you."

Frank was about to take up the cudgels on behalf of his friend, when the whistle sounded and there was the usual stampede up the yard.

Frank and Wright were in the front of the rush, and were among the first to be taken on. It was a cold, frosty morning, and all were glad to get work.

Barges were bringing chests of tea to the wharf, and Frank with Wright and several others, was sent on board one of these barges to get the cargo out. The fog was thick over the river, and they could scarcely see the men on the bank. The man at the crane was quite out of sight. The sheets and decks of the barge were covered with frosty rime, which numbed their fingers as they hauled the sheet off the tea chests. They worked away with a will, however, until near midday. The fog was still dense. Every minute could be heard the loud and lugubrious detonations of the fog signals on the neighbouring railway; varied at intervals by the weird wailing shriek of the fog siren of some big vessel slowly steaming up the river. It was dark and cheerless, none but the objects nearest them could be seen. All were longing for dinner time. A load of chests had just been fastened in the slings, and the ganger had shouted the word "set up" when Wright noticed that the chain had failed to slip down taut. He rushed forward and caught hold of the slip chain to force it down. As he did so he stumbled, and the chain, slipping down that instant, caught his thumb between the chain and a chest. Before anyone had noticed what had happened he was lifted high up in the air. He shrieked; the ganger shouted, "Lower away?" Almost before the words were out of his mouth, Wright's thumb was wrenched off, and he fell in a heap on the deck, from which, rolling backwards, he was precipitated into the hold. There was a rush to the spot. Blood was flowing from his mouth and ears. They picked him up. He was dead. His neck was broken.

[29 December 1888]

Chapter XXX.

At Christmas-time at Benton Park, Colonel Ashville's residence, everything was life and activity. Even the servants, although it meant a deal of extra work for them, seemed perfectly contented and happy.

The young mistress, Miss Eva, was so kind, so good, so considerate. No one could dislike her. She was like a ray of sunshine. Ever sparkling, ever cheering; ever lighting up the gloom of the place.

Benton, in the winter, was rather dull for the women folk. When there was sufficient frost Eva Ashville and Louisa Cranston would take a turn or two on the skates; but they were generally accompanied by the gentlemen, and in that case the servants used to stay at home. Now and then, however, Eva would take her maids with her.

One day she chaffingly asked Jane – a young but plump and rosy girl, who was the cook of the establishment – whether she would like to have a spin?

"Yes, Miss, please."

"Really? But can you skate?"

"Oh, yes, Miss."

"Well, now; how strange I should never have thought of asking you before! My skates are too small, I expect; but I will borrow you a pair."

The skates were procured, Jane put them on, and went skating away with wonderful ease, grace, and rapidity.

"Well, there now, Mary, doesn't she skate beautifully? By-the-bye, can you skate, Mary?"

"I don't know, Miss, whether I could manage on the ice, but I used to be considered good on the wheels."

"Really? You must have a try then. Jane and I will look after you till you feel comfortable on them. What sized boots do you wear?"

"Threes, Miss."

"All right; I'll get you some skates."

This cheery little maid, who seemed most happy when she was adding to the pleasure of others, soon returned with a pair of skates for Mary. Jane was called, and away all three went, merrily skimming o'er the frozen surface, and making the surrounding country ring with their youthful laugher, and the clashing of their steel blades on the hard ice.

Only those who knew the distinctive relationships of the three lasses would have imagined that they were mistress and servants.

It was always the same with Eva, and she would have made the girls still more her friends but that experience had taught her that the surroundings of the girls, in some things, had not fitted them for all the advances and favours she would like to bestow on them.

Now, however, she and her dependents were engaged, not in idle pleasure, but in the, to them, serious, if agreeable, task of preparing for the Christmas festival.

Attached to the Colonel's mansion was a large hall, occasionally used to drill the local volunteers, for concerts, balls, and the like, and here Eva would often take the girls and let them have half an hour or so at waltzing while she played the piano to them.

It was in this room that they were decorating for the Christmas festivities. Evergreens and coloured-paper festoons hung in serried rows all round; from the walls to the chandelier in the centre stretched long chains of holly leaves, threaded with great care and dexterity on thin invisible wire; relieved at regular intervals by clusters of the bright berries; immediately beneath the chandelier was suspended a large bunch of mistletoe.

"There now," said Eva, as she jumped off a pair of steps, after having fastened the last rosette on the gas-jet over the piano, "the floor only needs to be waxed, and all will be ready."

The dining-room and drawing-room were decorated in much the same style, and even the kitchen had a few sprays of holly and mistletoe hung up here and there.

This was the first Christmas that Eva Ashville had been at home to act as the head of her father's household, and a number of guests, including the Cranstons and the rector, had been invited to do honour to the occasion.

Christmas broke in a very cheerful manner at the Park; every arrangement was as complete as it was possible to make it. The dining room was, perhaps, the most attractive picture for a hungry man. The table was bending beneath the weight of poultry, venison, and good old English roast beef. In the centre stood a large Christmas pudding, the making of which had been personally superintended by Eva. Brandy and other sauces were floating in the tureens, while every vegetable that could be procured was distributed all round the table.

The colonel objected very much to ceremony at the dinner table, notwithstanding his Tory leanings in other matters; but he was fastidious to a nicety. He would not look at venison unless it had been hung twice as long as necessary, and no fowl would be allowed to remain on his table that had not been trussed in the orthodox fashion; to east roast pork without apple sauce was impossible, and he always said the best part of roast beef was the horse-radish; boiled leg of mutton must have its accompaniment of caper sauce; and he even insisted upon pease-pudding with boiled pork.[88]

When, however, one had mastered these peculiarities one always found him an agreeable host. He did not want his visitors to interfere with him in these peculiarities, but to let him enjoy himself in his own way, and they could do the same themselves.

Dinner over, the ladies retired to dress, while the gentlemen devoted themselves to cigars and politics, occasionally pledging each other's health in some real old crusted port – the colonel said it was dated 1836.

In the course of conversation the Colonel incidentally remarked that he and Eva would be shortly going to London for the season.

"Ah, by the way, Vernon," said George Cranston, "I saw your friend Somers a week or two ago when I was in town."

"Oh, indeed; I suppose you called on him."

"No, I happened to be there one Sunday and I came across an announcement that a Mr. Somers was to lecture on 'Socialism and Economics,' at a hall near the Borough, and having nothing particular to do, I was prompted by curiosity to go and see if it was the Somers I knew. I was considerably surprised to find it was the same man."

"Mr. Somers lecturing on Socialism, and on a Sunday, too," ejaculated the Rector. "How shocking!"

"Most extraordinary," said the Colonel. "Do you remember how unmercifully he chaffed Eva about her Red Republican ideas, as he called them, when he was here?"

"You mustn't take too seriously anything Jack Somers does," said Vernon. "He's a queer fellow, and is always taking up with something or the other which he drops as quickly. I believe he has a genuine hatred of ordinary conventional life, and that drives him to eccentric courses, but he's not by any means a bad sort of fellow."

"And Socialism is his latest protest against conventionality, then, I presume?" said the Colonel.

"That's about it," replied Vernon.

"Well, I hope we shall have an opportunity of seeing him in his new character when we are in town," said the Colonel.

A little later and the whole party were in the ballroom, where the very atmosphere had been tempered and scented to make it pleasant.

Eva was the queen of the galaxy of country beauty that gave life and colour to the scene. Her dress was pale pink satin, prettily beaded, flounced and laced, and set off by the gold and diamond ornaments she wore around her neck and in her hair.

She chose George Cranston as her partner, for he was an excellent dancer.

The dancing continued till three o'clock, when the colonel escorted Mrs. Cranston to her carriage, while Mr. Cranston took charge of Louisa. As the Colonel turned from the carriage, George Cranston, grasping his arm, said, "May I have the pleasure of an interview with you to-morrow, Colonel, on important business?"

"Certainly, my boy; come to lunch."

[6 January 1889]
Chapter XXXI.

Benton High Street on Christmas Eve was not particularly brilliant. The shop-keepers made the best possible display of their wares; butcher, baker, grocer and draper did their best with gas, holly and evergreens to make an attractive show, but the effect was not striking. Even the influx of a large number of visitors from the outlying districts did little to mitigate the eternal dullness of the place.

It was about seven o'clock, and the High Street was at its busiest, when Ben Green passed through it on his way home. Paradise Row seemed more dark and dismal than usual; partly by contrast with the extra brilliancy of the High Street, and partly in consequence of the fact that most of its inhabitants were down town buying their Christmas provisions, or getting drunk. As Ben opened the door of his abode he found the apartment he entered in semi-darkness being lighted only by the glow of the wood fire which glowed on the hearth, and over which his wife was stooping, busily engaged in sewing. On the opposite side of the fire the two children were seated on a low stool.

As Ben entered, the younger child, with a cry of joy, ran to meet him.

"Here's daddy;" she cried, "I be so glad we shall have a light now."

"Don't like to be in the dark, do you, Sally?" said he, kissing the pale, elfish face peering, with half-frightened look into the cold darkness without.

"No, daddy," said the child, burying her face between his knees.

"I hope you've brought home something for to-morrow, Ben," said his wife, rising and lighting the lamp, "I s'pse old Ailer paid you to-night?"

"No, he didn't, the old rat. He said he'd want me there to-morrow morning and the morning after, and if he paid me before Saturday I should be boozing about all Christmas, and wouldn't be fit for work."

"What did you say to that?"

"Well, I felt like telling the old swine to go to hell; I can tell you, but that don't do. You have to knock under. I asked him to let me have a bob or two, but he said I ought to be ashamed of myself to want it, and turned on his heel and walked off."

"Well, I don't know what we're going to do; we've only got enough tea and sugar for to-night and to-morrow morning and there aint enough bread to last till Saturday. It's sickening; here's Sally wants a new frock – it's dreadful to see her shivering about in this cold weather – and they both want boots; and here we can't hardly get vittles for 'em, to say nothing about anything for myself."

"Yes, it gives me the sick, I can tell you; working hard all day and every day, and hardly able to get grub; and they talk about the 'advantages of industry,' 'honourable toil,' 'honesty is the best policy,' and all that rot! However, I've picked up something that'll get us a trifle for Christmas."

So saying he unbuttoned his slop[89] and drew from underneath a hare and a brace of pheasants.

"Aint she a beauty?" said he, stroking the fur of the dead animal. "We could do with this pussy ourselves, couldn't us old girl? but she'll be worth more to sell."

After tea, Ben put the game into a rush basket and set off to the Red Lion. It was the first time he had gone there with any game since he had been in employment, but he had no doubt of being able to sell it there. There were few people in the High Street, and he passed along comparatively unnoticed. He entered the private bar next the parlour. Only Alice Steggles was behind the bar. He beckoned her.

"I've got something her for the governor, can I see him?"

"He's lying down just now, but he'll be here directly."

"All right, you can take it over, and I'll go into the taproom and wait."

He handed her the basket, and turned towards the taproom, when he whispered, "Have you heard anything from Frank Wilson since he's been gone?"

"No; how should I?"

"Oh, I didn't know. I knew you were friends, and thought perhaps he might have written to you."

"No; I've heard nothing from him. I reckon he's afraid to write for fear his letters should get in to someone else's hands. And you've heard nothing of him then?"

"No, not since I was in London. I saw him then."

"Yes, I heard something about your going to London; it was the talk of the place for a day or two; but of course I didn't know you saw Wilson."

"No, it wasn't likely I should say anything about that."

Ben turned into the taproom, which was just getting lively. It being Christmas Eve a larger number than usual of the ironworkers had gathered there. As Ben entered, one of them hailed him.

"Hullo, Ben; why you are a stranger; how are you getting on?"

"Oh, roughish."

"Well, have a drink; Christmas only comes once a year, and we're going to have a bit o' harmony. You'll join in, of course. Joe here's going to sing the "Village Blacksmith."[90]

The burly smith gave off the well-known ballad, always a favourite with ironworkers, in fine style; after which Ben Green favoured the company with the famous old poaching song, "It's my Delight on a Shiny Night."[91] While the singing was progressing Sam Crosbie entered the taproom, and seeing Ben Green, sat down by him on the form. When another one of the company had taken up the harmony Crosbie asked Ben if he had heard anything of Frank Wilson.

"No. What should I know about him?"

"I suppose you didn't know he was at your place when his wife was dying there?"

"You know he told Dr. Smart that I didn't know he was there."

"Yes, but I reckoned he said that to screen you. Anyway, you are safe in telling me anything. Frank'll always find a friend in me."

"Well, I haven't heard from him since he went away; but if he took my advice he's gone to London."

"I thought that he would be most likely to have gone there, and that perhaps you'd be able to tell me his whereabouts. I'm going to London in a few weeks with our young boss, and I might perhaps drop across him."

"You might – such things do happen – but you might as well look for a needle in a bundle of hay as look for a man in London; and I don't know whereabouts he is."

Just then Mr. Steggles entered.

"Didn't you want to speak to me?" he asked Ben.

Ben nodded, and rising, followed him into the parlour. When they were alone, Mr. Steggles said, "Now, look here, I didn't expect these things, and so I don't very much want them; but I'll give you a bob for the hare, and Mrs. Treasure, at the bank would be very glad of the pheasants, I know; and she'd give you more'n I could afford to give for 'em."

Ben took the shilling and the basket with the pheasants, and departed.

He was just turning into the High Street when he felt some one tap him on the shoulder. He turned. It was Sergeant Warren.

"What have you got in that basket?" he asked.

"What's that to do with you?" returned Ben.

"We'll soon see about that."

"Well, it's my Christmas dinner, if you must know."

"Let me see," said the Sergeant, seizing the basket.

Ben snatched it away, and would have made off, but the Sergeant grasped him by the collar.

They struggled for a minute. Ben was getting free, when his antagonist shouted for assistance. A well-dressed young man, who was passing, rushed forward and helped him to secure his prisoner. It was young Treasure, the bank manager's son.

Ben was marched off to the lock-up.

[12 January 1889]

Chapter XXXII.

There was a cessation of work while the men carried the dead body of their comrade out of the barge into the warehouse. A doctor was sent for, and the men went back to their work, which was resumed as though nothing had happened. They were all silent and moody, however, and were glad when it was time to knock off for dinner.

Frank was debating in his mind whether he should go home (as he had come to call Beulah Place) to dinner or not. He did not know how he should face the dead man's wife and daughter. Eventually he resolved to go. "Bad news travels fast," he said to himself, "and they may as well know the whole truth at once."

Nelly was getting dinner and singing at her work as Frank entered the room.

"Why, Mr. Watson," said she, "where's father?" Then looking up, and seeing the grave expression of his face, she exclaimed in a tone of alarm, "Has anything happened? has he met with an accident? Can we go and see him?"

Frank scarcely knew what to say. The terrible event of the morning had shocked and upset him, and now the evident distress of mother and daughter completely unmanned him. He felt a sob rising in his throat as he sank into the chair and covered his eyes with his hand. Controlling his emotion with an effort, he said, "Do not be frightened. An accident has happened; but he is not in any pain now; you can do no good by going to him." He could get no further; the little speech he had prepared on his homeward walk, to break the sad news was all forgotten; "He is dead," he cried as he bowed his head on the table and wept audibly.

The women were overwhelmed with sorrow. The younger, clasping her hands over her breast, sank into a chair, her eyes glistening, her lips slightly parted, her face drawn as if in pain: the picture of silent grief; while her mother gave way to loud and bitter lamentations.

The sound of her cries roused Frank to a sense of duty. Stifling down his own sobs, he endeavoured to assuage the grief of the elder woman. The girl sat mute and still in her chair.

No one thought of eating. It was time for Frank to return to work. "For men must work and women must weep,"[92] he thought, as he left the two poor grief-stricken creatures and turned to the door. The girl leapt to her feet, put on her hat and shawl, and prepared to accompany him.

"Let me go back with you, Mr. Watson," said she; "I would like to see him."

She walked by his side to the wharf, both silent, both busy with their own sad thoughts.

They had taken the dead body of her father to a neighbouring public house, there to await the inquest they told her, when she presented herself at the gate. She turned in the direction indicated, and Frank went back to his work.

The next day Frank was equally fortunate in getting a job. He had come to regard himself as almost a regular hand now, but he sadly missed his dead comrade.

In the evening Bill Smart and several of the others called him into the beer-house where they had been in the habit of having their beer. While discussing a couple of pots of "four-half"[93] they broached the subject upon which they wished to consult him.

"It's like this here, d'ye see, we've known Wright a goodish bit," said Bill Smart, "and it 'ud be only right if we was to get him up a bit of a lead.[94] I dessay the landlord here would be agreeable, and this house would do firstrate. I could fix it up all right, if you don't mind writing the ticket. We could get 'em printed cheap, and sell 'em a tanner a time."

"I don't understand anything about it," said Frank.

"Oh, you'll understand it right enough. You just get out a ticket after this style," said another, producing a black bordered ticket, on which was printed:–

A Friendly Meeting

Will be held at the "Jolly Stevedores"[95]

To assist the bereaved Wife and Family of Joe Smith who died on Saturday, after six weeks' illness, leaving a Wife and Six Children totally unprovided for.

Chairman, Bill Hackett;

Vice, Punch Brown,

With a host of Waterside talent.

> Death to the grave poor Smith has borne,
> And wife and child are left to mourn,
> At such a time 'tis most they need,
> A friend should be a friend indeed.

Frank took the card and eyed it curiously. After some further discussion, another pot of four-half, and an interview with the landlord, it was decided that the friendly lead for Joe Wright should take place on the following Saturday evening at the house where they found themselves.

Saturday came, and Frank, about nine o'clock in the evening, made his way to the Horse and Groom, the house where the friendly lead was to be held. Nelly accompanied him. He had rather protested against this at first, but she assured him that it would be regarded as an affront by those who had taken the matter up if she did not put in an appearance.

Frank and his companion proceeded to a room, which was capable of accommodating about a hundred and fifty persons, was furnished with a number of deal forms and tables, at which were seated about sixty or seventy men, youths, women and girls, the youths and girls predominating. The latter were conspicuous in consequence of the enormous feathers they wore in their hats, and the brilliantly coloured shawls which adorned their shoulders.

Bill Smart occupied the chair at the farther end of the room. On a table in front of him were a couple of plates. Each person, on entering the room, walked up to the chairman and deposited a sum of money, varying from a penny to shilling, in the upper one of the two plates, the money was immediately shot off into the low plate, and thus the top one always remained empty. On Frank taking his seat beside the chairman, there was a slight interruption to the singing which was going on, and which was shortly after renewed.

About half past ten Nelly and Frank left. Everybody was then wanting to sing, and the harmony was at its height. The clouds of the tobacco smoke were denser than ever, and the landlord was doing a good trade in four-half.

The result of the friendly lead was the sum of three pounds, which Bill Smart handed over to Frank for Mrs. Wright.

In the meantime she had been to see the wharf manager with reference to compensation for the death of her husband. After several interviews he told her that the proprietors were not prepared to admit their liability in any way, but that if she would undertake not to involve them in any useless litigation they would be willing to bear the expense of the funeral. She concluded that it would be best to accept this offer.[96]

The funeral took place the day after the friendly lead.

It was a cold, dull, cheerless day, and Frank felt chilled to the bone as he stood there looking down on the "useless coffin"[97] that enclosed the mortal remains of one whom he felt to have been his truest friend. He was glad when it was over then they turned to go.

He had walked there, but Nelly came to him and asked him to ride back with them.[98] However, he preferred to walk.

On the way home a man whom he believed to be a member of the branch, and whom he had often seen at the meetings, said "I suppose you're going up to the Square[99] tomorrow."

"Well, I don't know; I shan't go to sympathise with those who have called the meeting, nor with their objects, but if I don't get a job I shall most likely go."

"Do you know if any of the Federation are going?"

"I don't think they'll take any part in it, but Blake and any of those who are out of work are sure to go."

"Well, it'll be a bad job for them; I reckon they'll get chucked in the water if they do."

"More likely the other fellows."

"Well, you'll see."

[19 January 1889]

Chapter XXXIII.

After leaving the park, George walked quietly home by himself, thinking of the morrow. Fully half-an-hour before the time at which the Colonel usually took his luncheon George Cranston could be seen walking up the gravel path to the Colonel's residence. The park had lately been very much frequented by George, and could the pebbles and shrubs reveal the secrets of men's hearts many thoughts might be made public which now remain buried in secrecy for ever.

The occasion of the present visit was, to George a very serious one, and he felt it as such. He was walking briskly before he reached the park gates, but now his eyes were fixed on the ground, and his walking-cane was incessantly knocking on either side every little pebble that his wandering eye lighted upon.

Outwardly he showed unmistakeable signs of agitation, and hardly knew how he would calm himself sufficiently to speak to the Colonel.

Arrived at the door, however, the sound of the knocker vibrating through the hall gave him fresh hope.

He was immediately ushered into the studio, where the Colonel was intently poring over some ancient documents, which, to George, looked like deeds of mortgage or transfer.

"Good morning, sir," said George, as he entered.

"Good morning," said the Colonel. "A little before your time, eh? Couldn't rest, I suppose? Sleepless night, I wager."

George hesitated to reply. He dare not contradict the Colonel right away, and yet his pride and conceit would not allow him to admit the Colonel to be right.

"Hardly so; but I presume you guess the purport of our conference, this morning?"

"Oh, yes, yes! But unfortunately, I am very short of available cash. Besides, I hardly think you ought to come to me for monetary help."

George was annoyed.

"My dear Colonel," he said, "I have not come to ask you for money. I am happy to say I have plenty of that. What I wanted to speak to you this morning about was –"

"Shooting," suggested the Colonel, with a triumphant twinkle in his eye.

"No, sir; not shooting either. I wasn't to know if you will accept –"

"An invitation to a return party? Certainly, my boy. Should be delighted."

"Well, that may come later on. But at present I want to know if you will accept me as your son-in-law? Or, in other words, may I congratulate myself on having won the hand and heart of Eva, the unhesitating consent of her father, and the sweetest little wife that Benton ever saw?"

"That sentence is too long, George; badly constructed, and unpoetical."

"Well, sir," said George, rather pettishly, "it is sufficient to explain why I wanted to see you to-day; and I hope my journey will not be fruitless."

"Come now, George," said the Colonel, "don't be upset; it was only a little friendly chaff on my part. I have no objection to raise to your suit, except that I had no idea of losing Eva so soon as your offer leads me to fear will now be the case. I have only one stipulation to make, and that is that you do not urge her to settle down in too great haste. You can both afford to wait a year or two."

George was soon calmed down, and explained that he was going abroad in a short time, and would be away for some months. He was, of course, anxious to know whether he could solace himself, while away, with the knowledge that when he returned he would be able to make Eva his wife.

After this explanation the Colonel consented, and then asked George for further particulars respecting his business abroad, adding the usual fatherly caution and wishes of success.

George then proceeded to explain that he was going to Natal[100] to open up a branch of the business there.

"How will you manage two concerns? You cannot be personally present at both places, and I never think a business left to the care of a second party worth much?"

"That's perfectly true. But there isn't a chance of extending the business in this country that I can see. There are too many in the field, and consequently competition is too keen."

"In addition to that," said the Colonel, "you must recollect that it establishes our prestige, and extends our commercial power."

George was about to reply to this observation, but it was no good. The Colonel, when once started on the foreign policy of the Government, showed all his Tory ideas[101] and proclivities at once, and monopolised the talking for a long while.

Just then the Colonel observed Eva come tripping along the gravel path, a large basket on one arm, and a thick woollen shawl wrapped around the other.

"You're a lucky man, Master Cranston. That girl is the treasure of my life, and her happy and missionary-like manner makes me think."

There was silence for some while. The Colonel couldn't speak. His heart was full. George couldn't speak – he didn't know what to say. It is impossible to say how long they would have sat vaguely staring at one another and saying nothing if Eva had not come in. But just as the silence began to get tedious she knocked at the door of the Colonel's room.

"Come in," said he.

"Oh papa, you know that man who was –"

She had begun talking directly she opened the door, but when she caught sight of George she drew back, and would have retired.

"Nonsense, my girl," said her father. "You must tell us at once what it is you have experienced that makes you so excited."

After she had spoken to George, she went on: "Well, if you must know I have been visiting this morning in the town, and some of the sights I have seen really surprise me. There's that poor Mrs. Green without any food; neither had she any dinner for Christmas Day. If it is their poverty and hardship that makes Mr. Green do what he is reported to do, I don't know that I can blame him."

"Eva," said George, "pardon me, but would that not be condoning crime?"

"Well, perhaps it might. But is it not just as much a crime to prevent these people from getting the necessaries of life?"

"Perhaps so; but two blacks cannot make a white."

"Nor three," said Eva, so sympathetically that George could not reply for a time. At last he said:–

"Why three?"

"Well, you see, we offend first by preventing these people from working when they are willing. We drive them to robbery and theft by our conduct, and punish them for doing what we have driven them to. There are two blacks that won't make a white – both of our forcing. Then the third is that we deliberately punish the innocent with the guilty. It doesn't matter how bad a man is, there is no justification for punishing the wife. When you lock a man up, you really inflict a greater punishment on the innocent wife and family than on your so-called criminal. Now will those three blacks make a white?" And she tossed her little head in proud defiance.

"How would you obviate this?" said George, off-handedly.

"Obviate it! Why I would pay the wife or mother, or whoever were dependent on the efforts of the offender his full wages, so that they should not be the victims of anyone's folly, as they are now."

"Your present prison accommodation would not then be nearly large enough to contain the number of men who would commit some minor trifling crime to get locked up so that his wife might get the money."

"Do you think so?" queried Eva, in such a tone that George thought he was beginning to score.

"I am perfectly sure of it," he said.

"Then all hail, say I, to the men who would go to prison sooner than let their families suffer hardship and privation through their want of work."

So triumphantly did Eva toss her head; so loudly did the Colonel laugh; so crestfallen did George look, that Eva decided to turn the subject.

"What a horrid condition those houses are in in Paradise Row."

"Well, you see the rents are very low."

"I don't think so. I consider them very high for the miserable accommodation afforded."

"But if you were to put these people into mansions and let them live there rent free, they would soon let them go to rack and ruin."

"Has anyone ever tried it?"

"Not that I'm aware of."

"Is it true, Mr. Cranston, that Mr. Green has been locked up again?"

"I believe it is."

"Who sentenced him? And on what evidence was he convicted?"

"He was caught red-handed, with the game in a basket. His case came before my father, and he sentenced him."

"Who is the owner of those miserable, neglected hovels in Paradise Row?"

"My father," said George, and he felt the hot flush of a guilty conscience smiting him.

It was then that they were told luncheon was ready, and George was very pleased to get away from the cross-examination started by Eva.

[26 January 1889]

Chapter XXXIV.

"Nothing up this morning, mate," were the words with which Frank was greeted by one of the group of men who stood round the wharf gate on the Monday morning after Wright's funeral.

"No chance of a job, then?"

"No; things seem getting rougher than ever."

"Not much good waiting here, then?"

"No; and not much good going anywhere else, and if you go home people say you're lazy and don't try; and if you walk about you only wear the shoes off your feet and do no good, but get hungrier all the time. I'm going to wait here till one o'clock and see if there's a call, then I shall go up to the Square[102] to this meeting."

Frank waited with the others. It was a dull, cold, cheerless day, and the hours passed slowly. Nine o'clock came, then ten, eleven, twelve, one. No call. They were all cold, hungry and weary with waiting. The majority decided to go home.

The man who had first spoken to Frank said, "It's no good my going home, they can eat what bit they've got there without me."

Frank's thoughts had taken the same shape; he nodded in sympathy, and they both walked off in the direction of Trafalgar Square.

There were only a few loungers in the Square when they arrived, mostly weary, hungry, unemployed workers like themselves, with here and there an unmistakable specimen of the genus loafer, but their number was being added to every minute by groups of men strolling in from all parts of the metropolis. In the course of an hour the crowd had considerably augmented, and now numbered several thousands. There was a commotion near the Nelson Column, the base of which the police were endeavouring to clear. A short, dark, well-built man,[103] whom Frank had seen several times among his Socialist friends, pushed his way through the crowd, and, after speaking to the officer in charge of the police, mounted the pedestal of the column and began to address the crowd. There were loud shouts from the audience as the speaker urged them to keep order and not to damage their cause by rowdyism or by supporting the played-out nostrum of the fair traders. He had scarcely finished his harangue and descended from the pedestal when the original conveners of the meeting put in an appearance, with a van carrying a couple of carpenters' benches to serve as platforms. When these were placed in position, the proceedings began. The majority of the crowd appeared to be hostile to the speakers, and Frank, cold and hungry though he was, could not help feeling amused at some of the shouts, more pungent than polite, with which they were occasionally greeted.

While he was standing thus looking on, a tall, well-built man, dressed in corduroys and coarse pea jacket, looking like a navvy[104] out of work, said to him, "It's all very well for these 'ere chaps to talk, but these 'ere meetin's aint no good. A little dynamite would do more good than all their spoutin'." Just then Frank felt his coat pulled, and looking round he saw his friend, who motioned him to come away. When they had moved away a few paces, he asked, "What was Dangford saying to you?"

"Who? Do you mean that navvy?"

"Navvy! He's no navvy, he's a 'tec,' and a precious artful one too."[105]

Frank narrated what the pretended navvy had said, and they turned from the spot. By this time the Square was beginning to get crowded. Speaking was going on from the balustrade facing the National Gallery, as well as from the platforms of the Fair Traders,[106] against whom signs of hostility were manifesting themselves. A riot appeared imminent. Suddenly there was a rush for the platforms, the speakers were swept off them, and the platforms were thrown into the fountains, their late occupants narrowly escaping the same fate. There were loud cries of "To Hyde Park," and Frank saw the short dark man, who had spoken from the base of the column, taken off the balustrade from which he was speaking, and raised on the shoulders of some half-dozen stalwart labourers. Waving a red flag he was borne off in the crowd, which swept round Cockspur Street into Pall Mall like an inrushing tide. On a corner of the balustrade, pointing with his umbrella in the direction the crowd was taking, like a pedestrian edition of the Wellington statue, stood a pale-faced individual, wearing the tall hat and waterproof coat of the middle-class.[107] His appearance attracted Frank's notice as presenting a marked contrast to the tatterdemalion crowd around him. Frank followed the crowd.

As they passed the clubs in Pall Mall[108] windows were thrown open, and they were greeted with jeers and laughter by the occupants. Outside one club they came to a halt, and the man with the red flag, standing on a pillar, commenced to address them. This was the signal for derisive shouts from several young fellows who were leaning out of one of the upper windows. As Frank turned to see whence the unseemly laughter was proceeding, he felt something strike him smartly on the cheek; as it rebounded it hit a soldierly-looking fellow who was standing by the speaker. As it fell to the ground Frank saw it was a small milk can. He put his hand to his face and found it was bleeding freely.

"Well, I'm hanged if I'm going to stand that!" said the other man who was struck. "Come on, lads, we'll very soon chuck the beggars out themselves, and that'll teach 'em better manners."

He was turning towards the door of the club when the man who was speaking jumped down, and seizing him by the collar, said, "Hold hard, old fellow; it's no use doing anything rash. Let's go on to the Park."[109]

The cry "To the Park," was taken up on all sides, and the crowd pressed on. Several others in the crowd, however, had been hit with missiles from the clubs, and had begun to retaliate by pelting the windows with such small pebbles as they could pick up in the street. The few Socialists who were in the crowd endeavoured to suppress this as far as possible, and Frank assisted them in doing so. He saw a man with his back towards him energetically kicking a stone up out of the roadway. As he seized him by the collar he faced round – "Crosbie!" he exclaimed, involuntarily.

"Yes, my name's Crosbie," said the other; "but who the devil are you?"

Frank was so taken by surprise that he could not answer. He bitterly regretted having been surprised into recognising Crosbie who stood staring at him in wonder.

"We want to stop this stone-throwing," said Frank, when he regained his speech.

"That's right enough. I was a fool to think about pelting those young cads, of course, but I felt rather riled at being pelted, and lost my temper. But what I want to know is how you know my name?"

"You don't know me?"

"No, at least, no. You're not – no, surely not – Frank Wilson?"

"Yes."

"Well, you have altered."

"Yes, I suppose I have. I didn't want to be known, so I'm glad of it. I can trust you, however; you don't believe I'm a murderer; you won't betray me."

"No fear, my boy. I believe you're innocent, and I shouldn't care to betray you in any case."

By this time the crowd had got some distance ahead. "We may as well go on to the Park," suggested Frank.

"Yes, I'd like to see the end of this. I have never been in a London mob before."

"Where are the police, I wonder. You don't often have a go in like this, do you?"

"No; I've never seen anything like this before. The leaders appear to have drawn the crowd away from the Square to avoid a row, and it looks as if they had led them into worse mischief."

Frank scarcely knew what to do. In spite of his companion's protestations of friendship he thought that he would not trust him too far, but would escape from him at the first opportunity.

[2 February 1889]

Chapter XXXV.

Frank and Crosbie walked slowly on towards the Park.

"You haven't told me yet what you are doing up in the smoke," said Frank.

"Oh, I'm up here with young George. We've got a big contract for some railway work out in Egypt. Young George is going out there to boss it, and I'm going with him. He has come up here to see some of the officials, and he thought it best to bring me along with him. I'm having a bit of a look round to-day. Curious I should have dropped across you. How've you been getting on?"

"Rough. Can't get anything to do except casual waterside work. What are you going to do about hands for this foreign job?"

"Well, some are going from the works; they'll meet us at Portsmouth; and I've got to engage one or two here. I wish I could take you on."

"I wish you could, too; but it's no use talking about it, one or the other would be sure to find me out."

They had reached the Park. The crowd had gathered round the Achilles statue, from the base of which speeches were being delivered by several of the Socialists.

Standing there in the gathering twilight of that chill winter's day, listening to the speeches which told of a better future for the workless, so soon as they had energy and intelligence enough to combine, Frank cursed the mischance that precluded him from taking an active part in the movement. Even now he felt that his meeting with Crosbie was a peril from which he must escape as speedily as possible. He turned to look at his companion. He was intently listening to the speaker. Frank quietly walked away.

As he was rapidly proceeding up the broad gravel path towards the Marble Arch, he thought he heard a scream behind him to his left. He stopped to listen; there was another scream; and then the sound of breaking glass. He ran across the grass in the direction from whence the sounds proceeded. As he neared the carriage drive, he saw, in the growing dusk, some three or four rough looking fellows gathered round a girl, while two others were engaged in rifling the pockets of a well-dressed elderly man, who lay stretched on the ground. A carriage, the windows and lamps of which were broken, was standing near.[110]

Another man was standing by the horses' heads, evidently on the look-out. The girl had ceased to scream, and was struggling vigorously to defend herself against the men, one of whom was trying to force her to the ground in order to facilitate his confederates' attempt at robbery.

"Come on lads," shouted Frank as he ran up, hoping to disconcert the ruffians, one or two of whom he thought he recognised as having taken a prominent part in defending the Fair Traders' platform.[111] In this he was partly successful. The two who had been robbing the man ran off, having doubtless accomplished their purpose. One of the others, however, aimed a blow at Frank as he dashed into their midst. Frank was too quick for him, and, as he parried the blow with his right arm, he got one in with his left on the fellow's jaw that sent him reeling almost under the horses' heads. The rest seeing him fall, and not being able to discern how many there might be following Frank, were seized with a sudden panic, and scampered off. As they did so, the girl, exhausted, would have fallen to the ground had not Frank caught her in his arms.

"Well, this is a pretty go," he muttered; "and a pretty girl, too," he added, mentally, as he cast a glance at his fair burden. "I wish the old swell would come to, or the girl; this is precious awkward."

As if in response to his wish the "old swell," as he had designated the prostrate man, began to show signs or returning consciousness, raised himself on his elbow, gave a look round, and sprang to his feet.

"My poor girl!" he exclaimed, as he caught sight of Eva, "they have killed her."

"No; not so bad as that, sir," said Frank. "The young lady'll be all right directly. Is this your carriage, sir?"

"Yes, though where the coachman is I'm sure I don't know. The fellow bolted as soon as those scoundrels attacked us."

"Well, we'd better put the young lady in the carriage, anyway," suggested Frank.

"Here am I, sir," said a voice from behind the carriage.

"Oh, you are, are you! Well, just jump up and drive us back to the Langham[112] as quickly as you ran away just now."

Frank, with the other's assistance, had placed the young lady on one of the seats of the carriage, where she speedily recovered consciousness.

"You've been of some little service to us, my man," said the stranger to Frank, "but I can't reward you in any way now, for those scamps have about cleaned me out. But if you will call at the Langham Hotel to-morrow I may be able to do something for you."

Frank nodded, and was turning away when the other added,

"Stay; you will be doing me a favour if you will accompany us out of the park. The roughs appear to be having it all their own way just now, and we may be subjected to another such outrage."

Frank assented, and was about to take his place by the side of the coachman, when the fair occupant of the carriage intervened.

"You might ask the poor man to ride inside, papa," she suggested, "he looks cold and ill-clad."

Her father silently assented, and held the carriage door open while Frank got in. He sat with his back to the horses, the girl and her father sitting opposite.

"I should imagine this adventure will cure you of your predilection for Socialists and Socialism, Eva," said her father. "I understand that they are responsible for the meeting which led to this."

"Not at all, dear papa. Those men were certainly not Socialists, and Socialism would abolish the condition of things which drives men to such outrages in order to get a small portion of the wealth which exists in such profusion around us."

"Well, you appear to be incurable. But you are not a Socialist, I hope?" he asked, turning to Frank.

In spite of the cold, Frank was feeling hot and uncomfortable, and this direct question rather disconcerted him.

"Yes, sir; I am a Socialist," he answered, "by conviction."

"Umph. My opinion of them has improved; they have some decent fellows among them, then, after all."

"There are none among them, I hope, sir, so cowardly as to commit an assault upon women and defenceless men."

"You don't think the fellows who attacked us were Socialist, then?"

"Certainly not. Socialists make war upon the system of society, not upon individual members of it. Not that I'm going to condemn those men. Your class, sir, is more responsible for what they do than they are themselves. I stand by my order – the workers. If any are driven to crime it is because crime is more profit-able than honest work. Who is responsible for that?"

"Bravo!' ejaculated the girl.

Frank had cast many furtive glances in the direction of the girl, and now that they had gained the streets he was able to observe her more closely by the light of the lamps. He was pleasurably impressed by the gentleness of her manner as well as by her exceeding beauty, the excitement through which she had just passed having rather heightened than diminished her attractions.

"Are you out of work?" she asked Frank.

"Yes, Miss. That is, except for what odd jobs I can get."

"Well," said her father, "if you will call at the Langham to-morrow, I can per-haps do something for you in the way of getting you work. Here is my card. I'll put you down at the Circus.[113] I don't feel fit for anything to-night, but if you'll call about ten in the morning I'll see you. Good evening."

The young girl shook hands with him as he left the carriage, but her father only bowed. The remembrance of that handshake lived long in Frank's memory.

At the nearest lamp he looked at the card he still held in his hand; he read – Colonel Ashville, The Park, Benton.

"Colonel Ashville!" he gasped. "Good Heavens! If he had only known! Well, he won't see me to-morrow, that's certain."

[9 February 1889]

Chapter XXXVI.

Frank did not go to the Langham the next day. He had lain awake nearly all night thinking over the extraordinary events of the preceding day. The break up of the Fair Traders' meeting, his strange adventure in the Park, made a sufficiently exciting day's experience to keep his thoughts busy during the night. Though his meeting with Crosbie and the Ashvilles seemed to bring the fear of detection and arrest nearer to him, yet were Frank's thoughts tinged with a sensation of pleasure.

The gentle voice of the young girl to whom he had been able to render such timely assistance was ever in his ears, her fair face and graceful form ever before his eyes. This, then, was Eva Ashville, the girl whom he had only once seen before, and then did not know her – but whose name was a household word among the poor folks of Benton. He had always felt grateful towards her for the kindness she had shown to his wife and mother when he was out of work at Benton. And yet how she would have loathed him if she had only known! Clearly he could not go to see her or her father. They might not – it was impossible that they should – recognise him. He smiled sadly as he glanced in the little looking glass that hung on his bedroom wall, and compared the picture he saw there with the one of the police notice he drew from his pocket. No, they would not recognise him.

Crosbie did not know him; certainly these people would not, who had scarcely ever seen him before. But he would not go. What could he say without betraying himself? No, he would not go, though he would have risked much only to have once more seen the beautiful girl who showed so much good feeling and strength of character allied with so charming a gentleness of manner and who, somehow, seemed to bring him nearer to his dead wife. He went to the wharf as usual, however and managed to get a day's work.

It was a dull, foggy day, and they knocked off early. All through that day and the next rumours of rioting were rife;[114] none but known men were taken on, and a number of police were quartered in the wharf warehouse.

He was still lodging with the widow of his late comrade and her daughter. He had nowhere else to go. He still felt a stranger in a strange land, and though the place seemed wonderfully silent now that Wright's cheery voice on longer sounded in it, yet memories of him still clung to it, and made the miserable apartments in Beulah Place hallowed ground to Frank. Besides, he felt that he owed something to the widow, and if his work was but casual, and what he was able to earn but small, it enabled mother and daughter to live better than they would have done if they had had to depend on their own exertions.

Frank was somewhat surprised, therefore, when about a fortnight after the burial of her husband, Mrs. Wright suggested that he should find other lodgings.

"Well, I don't know exactly where to go," said Frank. "You see it isn't easy for one like me, doing casual work, to get a regular, decent lodging. I should have to go to a common lodging house, I suppose; and even if I didn't, it wouldn't be like living with country people like you as I've got to know. Besides, I thought it would be to the advantage of all of us if I stayed with you."

"So it might have been, but you see people will talk. They are beginning to say all sorts of things about me already. And then there's Nelly. She's getting quite a woman now, and they'll be trying to blacken her character if you stop with us."

"Oh, blow what people say. While they are talking about us they are leaving everybody else alone. I don't see why you should drive me away, and make your own position worse just because of people's idle talk."

"Ah, it's all very well for you, Mr. Watson, but you're a man. You don't understand a woman's feelings in the matter. Look what a thing it would be if they took my poor girl's character away. We shouldn't be able to get any work or anything then."

They were seated by the fire in the larger of the two rooms comprising their apartments. Nelly was silently engaged in needlework by the table.

Frank was silent for a minute or two after the woman had spoken. He filled his pipe, which had become his constant companion now that he spent so many weary hours looking for work, lit it, and walked towards the window. As he did so he noticed the girl brush away a tear that was slowly coursing down her cheek.

"What's the matter, Nelly?" he asked kindly.

"Why," she said, "I do think it's a shame for mother to want to drive you away now. With father dead, you are the only friend we've got, and I do hope you won't go. What does it matter to us what people say? I don't care what they say. They can talk as they like about me, it won't make any difference as long as I know I'm honest."

"Yes, you can talk like that, but you don't think; you are just like a simple fool. If their talk takes your character away, what shall we do then? Who's going to give us work, then? It 'ud be different if we was well-to-do folks, or if we had a house and kept a girl and took in a lot of lodgers, but living here in two rooms it don't look well."

"Character – I don't see as character is much good. It don't get us a living, anyhow. We should be starving now for all we can do if it wasn't for what Mr. Watson brings home."

"But how will you get on when you are alone? How will you live, I mean?" asked Frank.

"Well, we shall have to manage somehow, I suppose. We shall be able to do with one room, then, so it won't cost us so much for rent. I shall be able to get a little work to do, needlework and charing, or something, and Nelly can get work at a factory or go to service, or help me. No fear; we shall be able to manage all right. Besides, we've no right to be beholden to you. You've paid for all you've ever had here and more. I don't want to drive you away, but I ain't going to have people say that I am your kept woman, and that I want you for a husband for may daughter."

"Well, whether you want to drive me away or whether you don't, Mrs Wright, I shan't go. Joe Wright behaved like a brother to me when I hadn't got a friend in the world, and was as low down almost as a man can go, and for me to desert his wife and child now he's dead and gone, poor fellow, would be to act like an ungrateful cur. I mayn't be always down on my luck. If I could get a job at my own trade we'd take a little house. You should be housekeeper, and could have a little girl to help, just for propriety's sake, and Nelly could go to school, or be apprenticed, or something. Never mind what folks say, we'll rub along together until something better turns up."

So he settled that he would stay, and no more was said then. But about a week later, on going home after a stiff day's work at the wharf, he found the room in darkness. On expressing his surprise to Mrs. Murphy, the woman who rented the house, she looked at him in surprise, and said, "What, didn't you know they was going?"

"No."

"Oh, yes; Mrs. Wright gave me notice a week ago. She said you didn't care about leaving 'em but she wasn't going to stay after what folks had been saying against 'em."

"Well, how am I going on? I suppose I can stop here to-night?"

"Oh, yes; she left your bed in the little room, just as usual, and as long as you pay the rent for the room you can have it, unless I want it for whoever takes the big room."

Frank felt too weary to talk longer. He was aching in every limb, and soon turned into bed.

In the morning Mrs. Murphy, not hearing him go out, went to call him. She found him so ill as to be unable to get up, and she went for the parish doctor.

"Rheumatics, cold, and low fever," said that functionary, as soon as he had seen his patient, "the result of exposure, bad living and worry. Keep him warm, and I will send an order on the relieving officer for some nourishment."

[16 February 1889]

Chapter XXXVII.

It was a bright day early in March. Colonel Ashville was looking over the morning paper, and Eva was reading her letters, when a waiter announced Mr. Somers.

"I have called," said their visitor, after the formal greetings, "to ask If Eva and you would go with a party I have made up for a slumming expedition?"[115]

"A what?" asked Eva, in a tone of perplexity.

"A slumming expedition, don't you know. It is quite the thing now. 'How the poor live,' is quite the newest idea. You go around and visit the slums, as they are called. Those delightfully dirty places in which the lower orders live, you know."

"And what good does it do?" asked Eva.

"Well, I think it makes one feel thankful that one doesn't belong to the lower orders."

"But what good do the poor derive from it?"

"Oh, I don't know that it does them much good except that you give them a shilling occasionally. A shilling goes a very long way in a slum. It is quite astonishing what the interesting inhabitants are willing to do for a shilling."

"You have had some experience in this direction, then."

"Oh, yes; you know I used to take a great interest in the improvement of the social condition of the working classes."

"Used to!" said the Colonel. "Why, it was only last Christmas your friend Vernon was telling us that you had developed into a full-blown Socialist."

"Ah, you heard that, did you? Well, I've given that up now."

"And taken to slumming instead, eh?"

"Well, you see those fellow don't seem to have much go in them. Of course, their economic theories are all right, you know; but I thought that after that flare up on the 8th of last month[116] they would have gone in for a big fight. What's the use of agitating, agitating, unless you are going to bring the thing to a head?"

"Yes, but surely you don't think that the Socialists should have already attempted to gain their ends by physical force?" asked Eva.

"They should either do so, or leave talking about it."

"Well, it seems to me that no one would resort to physical force to gain an end that might be gained by other means. It by no means follows, however, that one should never allude to physical force as a possible means, as it is quite possible that the fear of such force may accomplish as much as could be achieved by its application. Anyway, this is no time for it."

"It may be so, but I do not believe in threatening until I'm prepared to strike. By the way, did you ever hear any more of that fellow who came to your assistance in the Park on the occasion of the riots?"

"No; he never called."

"Got locked up, perhaps."

"Where do you propose to go this morning?"

"Well, they say there are some beautiful slums down by the south side of the river, and I propose to explore them."

"Shall we go papa?"

"If you like, my love."

"How do you get to this land of slums?"

"Oh, we will drive, if you like, to London Bridge, where we shall meet the others, and then walk."

Eva was soon dressed for walking, and they set out.

"Don't the people resent this kind of thing as an intrusion?" asked the Colonel, as they were being driven in the carriage towards London Bridge.

"Sometimes, but not often. They are too poor-spirited to resent any insult that is put upon them by their betters. If it were their equals they'd fire up quickly enough."

"Insult! You regard it as an impertinence, then, this slumming expedition, as you call it?"

"Certainly; or rather I should so regard it if I were one of the people visited. But these people are different, and what to us would appear an insult is to them kindness and condescension."

"Ah, you don't believe that."

"They do, though, and that's the main thing."

"But wouldn't it be a good thing to teach them to be more self-reliant and self-respecting?"

"You can't do it, my dear sir; the conditions under which they live are altogether against it, they are condemned by these conditions to slavery, and slaves they are in body and soul."

"You as a Socialist claim to be working for their emancipation from this mental and bodily slavery, I imagine?"

"Well, no. I have come to regard that as hopeless. Besides, I don't think that very much matters. These people are happy enough in their way, and you couldn't do anything with them. I've never had any deep sympathy with them. Of course, that doesn't make any difference to the soundness of Socialism. No one can dispute that wealth is the result of labour, and that, in strict justice no one ought to enjoy the wealth who doesn't assist in its production. That is all right in theory, but in practice we find it much more conducive to our comfort to get others to do all our dirty work for us. Especially when those others rather enjoy the doing of it."

"We don't know that they enjoy it."

"Well, they appear to do so, and they have neither the spirit to resent it nor the pluck to fight their way out of it, so why commiserate them?"

They had reached London Bridge, and, dismissing the carriage, they were joined by some half-dozen other young people. Laughing and talking, as on pleasure bent, they walked down Tooley Street and into the rookeries of Horsleydown.[117]

"These places are not nearly so delightfully dirty as those we visited in the East End," said one dainty young creature, turning to Somers with a pretty frown.

"Oh, we'll soon find some dirtier," said he, leading the way to Beulah Place. "I understand that the houses here are in a terribly tumble-down state. The landlord never comes near them, but the rents are rigorously collected by an agent."

"The people about here look too poor to pay any rent," suggested Eva.

"They have to pay though, or go. They are not allowed to get into arrears here, if they are in Ireland."[118]

"Can't we go into one of the houses?" asked the girl who had complained that the places were not dirty enough.

"Yes, rather," said Somers, knocking at the door of the most dilapidated-looking house.

The door was answered by a big brawny woman of about forty, her sleeves turned up to her elbows, displaying arms like a blacksmith's.

"What the devil do you want?" she asked, eyeing her visitors suspiciously.

"We thought you wouldn't mind our looking over the house," suggested Somers.

"You go to hell!" replied the virago. "This aint a show place, and we aint wild beastesses to be looked at by a set of stuck up toffs like you with a pane of glass in your eye.[119] Be off with yer!" So saying she shut the door in their face with a bang.

Somers turned to his companions with a smile and a shrug of his shoulders.

"What a terrible creature," said the fastidious damsel.

"Let's try again," said he, knocking at the next door.

Mrs. Murphy answered the door, and to the request proffered by Somers to be allowed to see the house, she invited them inside.

"It is fortunate that you should have come now as I've got some of my rooms empty," said she, as she led them along the dark and dirty passage, and up the broken dirty stairs. "In that room," she said, pointing to a door on the first landing, "is a poor fellow who's been laid up for some time. He owes me rent, which I reckon he'll never pay, for I'm afraid he'll never work again."

"There is no danger, I hope?" said Somers, in a tone of alarm.

"Oh no; but the doctor says he won't get no better unless he could go away out o' this. He wants rest, good food, and proper attention. I do what I can for him, but I has my own family to look arter, and I can't do everything, o' course. You can come in and see him, if you like," said Mrs. Murphy, opening the door.

They followed her in. Much to the surprise of Eva, there, lying on a bed on the floor in a corner of the room, much changed by illness, was the man who had come to her rescue in Hyde Park. She uttered a slight scream of alarm, and tried to get him to speak, but he seemed too weak to talk, and they quickly withdrew.

When she got back to the hotel with her father she commented on the strange coincidence, and suggested that something should be done for Frank. He agreed with her suggestion, with the result that Frank was sent away to a convalescent home at Folkstone.

[23 February 1889]

Chapter XXXVIII.

For some time after Frank arrived at the convalescent home he remained so extremely prostrate that he was not able to leave his bed. He received several notes from Miss Ashville, and even the Colonel penned a few lines of encouragement to him. With the exception of these letters, and the small amount of enjoyment he could obtain from reading the local papers, very little variation from the routine of the home was afforded him.

One morning, early in May, he was looking anxiously for the postman to bring the letters, when he saw a carriage driving along the road in the direction of the home. It came straight up to the gates, and was then lost to sight. The walls surrounding the building obscured it. There was nothing peculiar in the incident, so he strolled away to the other side of the room. He sat down to the table and began to read.

He had hardly made himself comfortable when the matron announced that a lady wished to see him.

"To see me?" said Frank, with an emphatic declaration of astonishment.

"Yes, sir; to see you. Will you follow me, if you please?"

"Certainly," said Frank.

On reaching the room where his visitor awaited his arrival he was much surprised to see Eva Ashville.

"Good morning, Mr. Watson," she said. You are looking better. Are you getting stronger?"

"Yes, thank you, Miss. I hope to be home again in a day or two. But where to look for a job, I really don't know. I am not strong enough to take on with wharf work."

"Have you any trade of your own?"

"Yes, Miss. I am an engineer by trade, but I can turn my hand to almost anything."

"Papa and I have been talking about you, and trying to think what would be the best thing we could arrange for you. We leave London to-morrow for Benton, and papa thinks he can find you something to do at the Park."

This was said in an interrogatory manner, but Frank didn't answer it. He was too much occupied with his own thoughts concerning his connection with Benton to make any reply. A long silence ensued, during which Eva eyed him curiously.

Frank – in his thoughts – had wandered back to the home of his childhood. He wondered whether his mother was all right; whether Ben Green was still about there; whether any of his shopmates would know him; in fact, whether it would be safe for him to return there.

Eva thought he was cogitating as to whether he should accept the responsibility, so she essayed to relieve him from his supposed embarrassment.

"It will not be anything very difficult. But it may be a permanent situation for you if you like it."

"Where do you say it is?"

"Benton, near Oldbury."

"Oh, yes; I know. Wasn't there some tragic occurrence there some time ago?"

"Yes; a police sergeant was shot by some poachers, and the circumstantial evidence went to prove a man named Wilson to be the guilty party. But I have my own opinion about it."

"Did you know him?"

"Well, no. But I visited his poor wife and mother, and never witnessed such frightful distress before or since. He escaped from custody, and was thought to be drowned, but unexpectedly discovered at the death-bed of his wife."

"His wife died of a broken heart, I suppose?"

"Accelerated by extreme privation. His mother went to the union, where she died – poor thing. If anything, she was more cut up than his wife."

Frank hardly knew how to hide his emotion. He wanted to reply, but he could not utter a word. He fidgeted about with his collar – he felt choked. After an extreme effort he succeeded in observing:

"It was a most lamentable affair, indeed. But I fear I am taking too great a liberty with your time, and not getting near the business you have come about."

"Oh, don't trouble," said Eva. "I must confess I did not come to Folkestone on that matter alone. Papa had some business here, and as I am his constant companion I came with him. Then I thought I would like to see you – I owe you a great deal, you know, and I don't know how to pay you."

"Don't mention it," said Frank, "I only did what any man would do."

"Well, papa will be tired of waiting. Do you think, now, that you are likely to consent to my proposition?"

"When did you say you return?"

"We leave for London immediately, and to-morrow we leave London for Benton. But if you would like a little time to consider, which perhaps would be best, you can address your reply to Benton."

"Would Miss Ashville, Benton, find you?"

"Oh, I beg your pardon. I daresay it would, but here's my card."

"Thank you."

"Good bye, Mr. Watson. Now think it over. Good bye."

Frank stood for some time gazing at the doorway through which she had passed, as though he expected her to return. He had never felt so strange before. He involuntarily put his hand to his head. This brought the matron to his side, who reminded him that he could either lie down or take a stroll; there was fully an hour between now and dinner time.

"Thank you," said Frank, "perhaps a walk would be best."

"Very well; you know the regulations. You must not go into a public-house, neither may you go down the proscribed streets."

"Oh, no," said he; "the cliffs are my destination."

Frank passed through the gates and on to the cliffs in the direction of Dover. Presently he came to a beautiful grass plateau, at an elevation of some hundreds of feet above the level of the sea. He threw himself on the grass and began to reflect. The various scenes of his life during the last two or three months had been bitter enough, but now there seemed dawning, on the horizon of his near future, a bright prosperous day. It was to him a complete romance, heightened by a feeling he could not suppress of intense love for the sweet creature who had become his guardian angel. He felt very dubious about returning to Benton, amongst all his old acquaintances, for fear he might be recognised. Yet the sweet face and tender manners of Miss Ashville were irresistible. Yes, he would go. He felt he could not help it. Crosbie had not recognised him; George Cranston had not recognised him; Alice Steggles; yes, she did. But he had not heard from her for some time. Besides, she would not say anything.

He sprang to his feet joyously. For the first time for some months he felt an irresistible desire to whistle or sing.

With a jaunty air and a springy step he strolled back to the home. It was din-ner time, and the fumes of roasted meats gave him a most contented expression.

The matron met him on the threshold, and congratulated him on his punctuality.

"Did I tell you before you went out that it would be your turn to act as captain, to-day?"

"No madam," said Frank. "And I hope you don't mean it now."

"Oh, but I do. And I shall not listen to any excuse or apology."

"But I don't thoroughly understand the duties."

"Perhaps not. But once doing it will impress you more than twenty oral lessons. Let me just tell you, however, what you are expected to do. You will preside at the table, carve the joints, and see to the requirements and demands of all the others; you must check waste and gluttony, excessive drinking and unpleasant remarks; don't be domineering, but give the table a cheerful, happy, and contented tone."

Frank smiled as he bowed concurrence, and replied that he wanted to have a short conversation with her after dinner. She promised him that she would make an opportunity.

The matron was a homely, motherly little woman, generally chatty, but sufficiently discreet and discerning to prevent any possibility of scandal. She had a great partiality for Frank, and nothing but an heroic devotion for the calling she had espoused could have prevented her from making it known to him. When however, during the conversation she had with Frank after dinner, she learned that he was going to leave almost at once, she gave way – but only for a moment – to a feeling of jealousy.

"Oh, indeed," she said. "That's what the lady wanted, was it?" Then recollecting her position, she said, "Very well, Mr. Watson, I will make out your order."

A few minutes later, and Frank was arranging for his departure from Folkestone. He wrote to Miss Ashville accepting the appointment, and stating that he would be down there by the following Friday.

[2 March 1889]

Chapter XXXIX.

It was with very mingled feelings that Frank Wilson or Watson, as he still called himself, stepped on to the platform of Benton Station a few days after the visit of Miss Ashville to Folkestone. That lady had sent him sufficient money to pay his fare to Benton, and to buy him a new outfit, and it would have required a very keen observer to have detected in this well-dressed clean-shaven, pale, rather stern-faced individual the miserable-looking wretch who had left the station in charge of the police some six months ago, or the cheery dark-bearded Frank Wilson of a month or two earlier.

Colonel Ashville had sent a man to meet him at the station, and together they set out to walk to the park. To Frank everything seemed so familiar and yet so strange. Great as had been the contrast which the huge metropolis had presented in his mind to Benton it was as nothing to the contrast which his native place seemed to present to its former self. The railway station and the surrounding buildings seemed but miniatures of the places he had been familiar with. The railway bridge, which he had frequently admired as a model of engineering skill, appeared only a toy-shop model after all. Everything appeared to have diminished in size. When he reached the High Street, and looked at the Corn Exchange he was astounded. Was this the stupendous monument of local architectural genius upon which he had so often, in his boyhood's days, gazed with awe and wonder, and, compared with which the most magnificent buildings in London looked mean and dwarfish. He could scarcely believe his eyes. This was Benton sure enough, every house, every stone almost, was familiar to him, yet it all seemed so changed. The street itself, which had always impressed him with its wideness looked narrow and mean, while the shops on either side, always so magnificent, seemed to have shrunk to a quarter of their former dimensions. And then the silence. The still quiet of that almost empty street, for which he had often sighed in the noise and rush of London life, oppressed him strangely, and he almost wished himself back in the stir and bustle of the Tooley Street wharf. Then, for the first time, he realised the colossal vastness of the huge human hive called London.

In spite of the disappointment which he felt with regard to the appearance of his native place, it was with something like a pang that he turned from the familiar street in the direction of the park.

It was with difficulty he kept the tears from his eyes as he gazed upon these scenes of his youth, from which he seemed to have been long absent and as he thought of the loved ones he had lost for ever.

What troubled him most, however, was the loquacity of his companion. He would have given anything almost to have been alone with his own thoughts. As a stranger, however, he could not dispense with the company of the man who walked beside him, who was an intelligent young fellow, and whose companionship he would have enjoyed under almost any other conditions, who tattled on unmercifully, plying him with questions, and giving him information about Benton of the most valuable and varied character. Frank allowed his companion to carry on almost the whole of the conversation, only here and there interjecting a monosyllable, with the result that the latter voted him as "Rum a sort of cove for a cockney, as I ever did come across."

Frank was glad when they reached the park and he escaped from this infliction. He was soon ushered into Colonel Ashville's study, where that gentleman received him cordially, and complimented him upon his improved appearance.

"I am glad you have come," said he. "My daughter has taken a deep interest in you, and is most anxious that I should find you some employment about the place. Fortunately, I can offer you a situation here if you like to accept it, or I might be able to get you something else, if you do not care to accept what I offer you. You are an engineer, I understand?"

"Yes, sir."

"Well, we have some ironworks in Benton, of which a friend of mine, Mr. Cranston, is the proprietor; if you would prefer to work at your trade, I daresay my influence would get you employment there. I suppose you have never been accustomed to anything else?

Frank was frightened at the prospect of going back to the old shop. "Well, sir," he hastened to explain, "of course, I am entirely in your hands, and whatever you may do for me I shall be equally grateful; but I can turn my hand to almost anything, and I understood from Miss Ashville that what you would have to offer me would be a permanency; whereas work in my own like is always precarious."

"Just so; only what I could offer you just now would not pay you as well as work in your own line, you know, and you would be more tied. At the same time it would mainly depend on yourself as to whether it became a permanency. You see we are almost total strangers to each other. I do not know your capabilities for the work you would have to do. I am taking you on trust, so to speak."

Frank looked rather disappointed.

"I am not saying this to discourage you, only I want to avoid disappointing you by raising your hopes too high. My daughter is an enthusiast, and sees only the good side of humanity, and is therefore apt to colour matters too brightly. You don't know anything of country life, I presume?"

"Oh, yes, sir; I am a countryman."

"Ah, indeed! I should scarcely have imagined it by your speech."

"No, sir! I think I have the faculty of adapting my language to those with whom I am conversing."

There was an unconscious significance about this remark, at which the Colonel smiled.

"Yes, sir," Frank went on, "my father was a gamekeeper."

"Ah, yes, then you will, perhaps, be more at home in your new duties than I imagined. What I want is some one to act as assistant to Markham, my steward. He is getting old, and though he fancies he can perform his duties as well as ever, that is not so. He has no son, but I want a younger man to assist him now, and to take his place when he goes. It would break the old man's heart to dismiss him from his post, even with a pension, and I should never dream of doing so. Of course, you would not have much salary; but you would have a place to live in with firing, and the prospect of stepping into the old man's shoes if you proved yourself worthy.[120]

Frank gratefully closed with the Colonel's offer. In fact, he was completely taken by surprise. He had never anticipated anything half so advantageous. To be steward of Benton Park exceeded his wildest dreams. He could have wept for joy. And then once more he felt the aching void near his heart as he reflected how little he had to make this tempting order worth accepting, to make life worth living at all, since those who might have shared his newly found happiness were lying cold and still in Benton Churchyard.

"You may as well have lunch with us," said the Colonel, as Frank was standing, hat in hand, irresolute, not knowing where to go, "and then you can stay here till Markham calls this afternoon."

"You needn't be frightened," he continued, as Frank began to make excuses. "We shall be quite alone, and my daughter said I was to make you stay. Ah, here she is," he added, as the sound of hoofs was heard on the carriage drive. "She has just returned from her morning's canter, and will be expecting to see you."

He led the way into the dining room, where they were shortly after joined by Eva. Her presence seemed to give light and sweetness to the rather dull apartment. Yet, though Frank felt an inexpressible pleasure at being near her and hearing her voice, he was ill at ease and uncomfortable, and was glad when the meal was over.

[9 March 1889]

Chapter XL.

Frank found his new duties neither difficult nor unpleasant. The whole place seemed so familiar to him that it was with difficulty he avoided occasionally betraying himself. Old Markham at first regarded him with the suspicion which always characterises the manner of old country folks towards strangers. This young man was a cockney, with a cockney's ignorance and conceit, and what on earth the Colonel wanted to bring him here for he couldn't imagine; a fellow doubtless who couldn't tell a mangel-wurzel from a pheasant.[121] But there, he didn't suppose it would last long. This chap would soon get tired of pottering about the woods and the fields and would be glad to return to the dirt and smoke and din of London. So the old man reasoned to himself, when he first introduced Frank to his wife – a little old woman, somewhat more aged than himself – and his new quarters. As time wore on, however, his opinion changed, and his feeling warmed towards the young man who had come there as a stranger, but whose intelligent interest in every detail of his work had gradually relieved him of every care and anxiety incidental to his position.

The estate consisted mainly of arable land, the whole of which, with the exception of a couple of hundred acres – which was called the Home farm – was let. The management of this farm, under Markham's direction and the superintending of the well-stocked coverts, constituted Frank's duties during the first six months of his stay at Benton Park. He would often smile to himself while supervising the farming operations, or while strolling, gun in hand, through the copse, as he thought of his patron's naïve suggestion that he would probably be better off as a workman in Cranston's factory. It was a revelation to him of the complete ignorance of even intelligent members of the well-to-do classes of the real condition of the workers. Here was he, though a dependent, living in solid comfort – no care, no anxiety, well-housed, well-fed, and plenty of leisure, and yet many doubtless, like his employer, imagined that the overworked slave of the factory-bell was better off than he.

Frank found that Eva Ashville took a lively interest in everything connected with the estate.

Often would he see her in the habit which displayed her graceful figure to the best advantage, mounted on her stout bay pony, flitting along the roads and lanes around the Park, or, in the bright June days, halting her pony awhile to listen to the rhythmic "swish" of the scythe as the men cut the succulent grass in the few acres of water-meadow near Benton Mill. And later on, when the corn was ripe and the fields echoed with the voices of the reapers, with the laughter of little children, whom their mothers had brought with them to the harvest field, and with the ringing of the whetstone on the sickle; Eva Ashville's bonny face was frequently to be seen among the harvesters, shedding mirth and joy around her.

Frank, with the instinct of the mechanic alive within him, was desirous of applying machinery wherever possible in the farming operation. To this Markham, as well as the Colonel, was strongly opposed, and it was only in one or two small details that Frank had succeeded in introducing machinery, and for this he had gained no goodwill among the farm hands. "Wants to get rid o' we;" "Trying to take the bread out of our mouths," that was their verdict, though up to the present no one had suffered in any way in consequence of Frank's innovations.

It was eleven o'clock one sultry day in August. He was standing in the cornfield watching a group of reapers who had ceased work while they partook of the beer, which a lad from the house was handing round from a brown pitcher, when Miss Ashville rode up, radiant as usual, but looking anything but a Belgravian belle.

"Good morning, Mr. Watson," she said, "You are not opposed to beer in the harvest field, then, evidently, in spite of your new fangled notions," she added, playfully.

"No, Miss," he replied quietly, "people working in the harvest-field require something to drink, and there's nothing more wholesome than mild ale, whatever teetotallers may say.[122] All this talk about beer in the harvest field is simply so much cant. The real object is to reduce the cost of labour."

"This looks better, at all events, than your ideal of cutting it by machinery, one man driving round the field perched on a hideous thing of cranks and cog-wheels, at the imminent risk of his life," said she, pointing with her riding whip to the scene before and around them. "This looks quite happy and idyllic."

"Yes, it looks pretty enough, Miss; but you cannot possibly imagine the absolute torture involved in work in a harvest field. I tried it once, and I can assure you that I would prefer working in the hottest foundry. It seems to me criminal to compel people to do such work when it could just as well be done by machinery. Look at that girl there," he added, pointing at a young woman who had assumed an upright position to ease her aching back, "she is about your age. In a few years time she will be a withered hag, while you will be still a beautiful woman," said Frank, touching his hat and turning to go.

"I am going back to the Park, if you are going in that direction," said Eva, walking her pony beside him.

The girl to whom he had directed her attention eyed them curiously as they left the field together. "He's a hard nail, he is," she soliloquised; "it'll be a bad job for the poor folks about here when old Markham dies if that chap bides here, I'll be bound. If I was the Colonel, I should keep a sharp eye on 'un, too, for if he ain't making sheeps' eyes at Miss Eva, it's a rum 'un to me."

This girl was a daughter of an old fellow-workman of Frank's, but she, with the rest of the harvesters, had not the slightest suspicion that the pale, clean-shaven, taciturn under-steward, was the jolly Frank Wilson they had most of them known so well.

In the meantime Eva renewed her conversation with Frank.

"But what would you do to obviate the torture of which you spoke?"

"Use machinery."

"But to what good? These poor people look forward to the harvest, and if they had nothing extra to do then, look what a hardship it would be for them."

"Yes, I know. They would probably curse me for my pains. In fact, I believe they do now, a good many of them because I put a limit on the work they shall do, and will not allow them to work the children, if I can help it. I've got a bad name among them, I know; and yet Heaven knows I think more of their interest than of my employer's. Because, after all, Miss, though Colonel Ashville has been a benefactor to me, and I am, and always shall be, deeply grateful to him, there is not a man among those harvesters who hasn't as much right to this estate as Colonel Ashville."

"Yes, and Colonel Ashville has as much right as any of those men. You are too good a Socialist to imagine that anything would be changed if the Colonel divested himself of his property and set to as a labourer."

"Yes, I know nothing would be changed except that there might be a far worse man in his place. Consequently, it is useless for the individual to do anything except help on the economic development and spread the Socialist propaganda. Therefore, I say, apply machinery here and subscribe to the Socialist funds."

"I'm afraid it will be a long time before you will induce the Colonel to do the latter. As to the former, I think his opposition is due rather to a regard for 'his people,' as he calls all who ever work here, than to any dislike to innovations. I think, however, you will have considerable difficulty in overcoming Markham's prejudices. For myself, now you tell me that harvesting is so exhaustive I would willingly use my influence on your side, if I could see how machinery could possibly be applied without inflicting greater hardship on the poor people."

"Well, Miss, something will soon have to be done. The home farm pays, of course, because a good deal of the produce is for home use, and the rest we can find a good market for in Benton, but with the other farms it is not so. Jackson and Curtis are both giving up their farms, and we shall have the both on our hands. They couldn't make them pay – I believe they could be made to pay very well, but they'd have to be worked differently. The Colonel won't discuss it with me. 'Talk it over with Markham,' says he, and Markham is wedded to the old ideas."

"Don't you think you could let them out in allotments?"[123]

Frank shook his head.

"No," said he, "allotments wouldn't pay. You'd have to charge the labourer a higher rent than the farmer, because of the increased risk. This is manifestly unfair, but it is unavoidable. Then, again, the labourer has less means of cultivation than is possessed by the farmer, so it stands to reason that if the farmer can't make it pay the labourer could not possibly do so, unless he put into it an altogether disproportionate amount of labour."

"What do you think of associated farms?"[124] asked Eva, after a thoughtful pause.

"That was my idea," said Frank. "I think we might try it, if I could only bring Markham round to my view."

About a couple of months later the death of Markham gave Frank the position of steward and enabled him to put his idea into execution.

[16 March 1889]

Chapter XLI.

Previous to the demise of Markham, and while Frank Wilson was acting simply as his assistant, Frank had very little occasion to go much into the town. His duties were almost entirely confined to the preserves and the home farm. Now and then he would have to transact a little business with the local tradesmen, but he rarely did more than ride over to the shop, pay the bill, or give the order, and ride back.

His interest was concentrated on his responsibility. Although, at times, a slight hankering after the old familiar places and faces made him long to call in at the Red Lion, he never gave way. His disposition altogether seemed changed. He no longer desired the excitement of company, but preferred the solitude and isolation of the Park.

One day, when he had gone on a flying visit to the grocer, and was just about to throw himself into the saddle and return, he saw a woman coming towards him. In a moment he recognised her. It was Alice Steggles. Bridle in hand, and one foot in the stirrup he awaited her approach. "Would she recognise him?" he queried, "or should he make himself known?"

He was not long allowed to remain undecided, for with a hurried glance round Alice made straight to him.

She grasped his proffered hand firmly and would have kissed it, but for the fear of being seen.

Frank looked steadfastly into her eyes, which were full of tears, and whispered:

"You know me, then?"

"Yes," she replied; "I shall never forget you, and no amount of disguise will ever destroy my remembrance of your original self."

"I cannot stop now," said Frank, "but meet me on the bridge when it grows dusk; I want to talk to you."

After he had finished his daily routine, Frank shouldered his gun, whistled up his dogs, and started on his nightly rounds. Instead, however, of going all through the coverts he simply fastened the dogs to the fence and turned his steps to the bridge.

Alice was already there waiting for hm. She was dressed in deep black, a thick black fall[125] hiding her face and giving her the appearance of a recluse or a nun. When she saw Frank approaching she went to meet him, and glanced anxiously round to see if they were alone.

There was a peculiar sensation and excitement in the whole affair, but when she felt the warm impress of Frank's lips on her cheek – for he kissed her – she was thoroughly overcome.

"I hope you are not offended, Alice," he said. "Perhaps it was a liberty; but after all, we are cousins, you know, and you are the only one of my friends that I dare recognise now."

No doubt was left in Frank's mind, although Alice never answered, for she affectionately returned the kiss. He then felt that he had done wrong, and was encouraging her in a manner that he had no intention of continuing. Alice, of course, felt pleased, and seized this opportunity of speaking her mind – an opportunity which she had long waited for.

"Frank," said she; "I mean, Mr. Watson –"

"I like Frank best, Alice, from you."

"Well, Frank; I want to say something to you. I am –"

She stopped, she pressed his arm (she had taken hold of it), she looked into his eyes, but she could not say a word.

"Well, Alice, what were you going to say?"

"Oh, nothing."

"Why you just this moment said you did want to say something."

"Did I? Well, I've forgotten, I suppose?"

"You suppose you've forgotten. Well, suppose you try and think."

Frank was getting curious now. Alice had played her cards just sufficiently well to make him persistent.

"I tell you what it is, Alice," he said, after a pause, "I shall not explain how I came to get down here to work, or what I am doing, unless you do tell me."

Then she began chaffing him about his being in love. She chided him with neglecting to answer the epistles she had sent to him in London. She kept up a long run of conversation, applying all the wiles and arts of a woman's character to create in him a desire for her company. She tried to rouse his jealous nature by telling him how many lovers she had had while staying in London; she enumerated the young "toffs" of Burton[126] who were incessantly popping into the Red Lion, and who extended their stay according to the encouragement she gave them in her conversation. She grasped his arm firmly, and every now and then cast glances into his eyes which would have entirely subdued a less preoccupied man.

Then she became severe, and accused him of being unkind and thoughtless.

After walking about for a little while without speaking, they parted. Frank went back to the Park. Alice retraced her steps towards the Red Lion.

When Frank arrived at the Park he found his dogs growling most ominously. He spoke to them and tried to quiet them, but it was of no avail.

Presently they stopped, and began to sniff earnestly at the ground.

Frank knew by their conduct that there was someone hiding in the copse, and he called out to his visitor, whoever he might be, to come from his hiding place. He listened a moment, but there was no answer. He tried again, threatening that if they did not come out he would let the dogs loose, and would fire upon the first man he saw.

It was an anxious time for all parties. Evidently the poachers, if they were such, were not disposed to surrender without a struggle. Some seconds passed in silence. Frank stood motionless and irresolute.

He pulled the dogs up and began to undo the collars when a large rabbit rushed close to his feet, being followed by a smart little terrier – a "little pocket companion," as he thought.

"Come back, damn you," growled a voice immediately behind Frank.

Without uttering a word or hesitating a second Frank turned suddenly round and dashed into the dark mass of foliage from whence the sound came.

"Now, keep back, young 'un," said this same stern voice, "I'm not a man to be trifled with."

Frank made no reply, but seized the man by the collar.

He had made a mistake, however. His antagonist drew himself back sharply, thus breaking away from Frank, and then struck out such a fearful blow that had it met his face uninterrupted it must have completely smashed his nose. Frank baulked the blow and looked out for another, in which he was not disappointed; for with wonderful rapidity his opponent struck out left and right, flinging his arms about in windmill fashion.

Frank tried to close with his opponent. His arms were already beginning to give way under the fearful blows they were stopping from his face, and he felt sure that if he did not close with him speedily his chance would be gone. With both arms folded over his face he rushed forward.

"You're a game 'un, young 'un," said the poacher, "but I'm not going to give way to you without a struggle."

Frank strained every nerve to throw his antagonist, his antagonist tried every trick to throw Frank. Ejaculations, oaths and curses were blurted out each time the demand for fresh wind compelled them temporarily to desist.

Frank was trying the cross buttock,[127] and had nearly brought his opponent to ground when by a terrific strain and a Herculean effort the poacher turned the odds and threw him instead.

"Now, my smart man," said the poacher, drawing from his breast a long knife, "you're my prisoner. Lie still, get your own wind and let me get mine. If you call or move, here's six inches of cold steel ready to reply. I don't want to do anything desperate as you're a new 'un; but I'm not goin' to be collared alive again, that's straight."

"Put your knife away, Ben Green, and let me get up."

"What! Frank Wilson!"

A few moments sufficed to explain everything: Frank related every incident from his meeting with "Nobby" Wright in London down to his appointment as under-steward at the Park. Ben Green told of his wife's death, and the disappearance of his eldest girl; how he had tried to obtain work, but without avail; how he was hounded from place to place, and compelled to poach or starve. They sat and talked for some time, until Frank thought he ought to be getting back. They then parted, arranging to meet again soon, Frank slipping into Ben's hand some substantial assistance.

[23 March 1889]

Chapter XLII.

Frank's experiment proved even more successful than he had anticipated. The farms which had become vacant had been let to an association of labourers which he had organised; and the cultivation was carried on to the greatest possible extent by machinery. Fences were levelled, the drainage and manuring were improved, steam ploughs tore up the fallow, and steam harrows broke up the clods, while the sowing was performed by the most improved drills. The money necessary for the purchase and hire of these implements had been advanced by Colonel Ashville, as well as the funds necessary for the maintenance of the labourers until they secured a return, and Frank was glad to find at the end of the first year the concern returned sufficient to enable them to pay the same rent as had been paid by the gentlemen farmers, and to pay off what had been advanced for sustenance, while retaining a balance with which to start next year.

The farmhouses had been demolished, and in their stead there had arisen a number of roomy, beautiful cottages, to each of which was attached a large garden, where the labourers grew fruit and vegetables and flowers. The cottages, each surrounded by its garden, formed a hollow square, in the centre of which was a large grassy plateau, surrounded by trees, on which the rustics would disport themselves in the summer evenings.[128] Beyond the cottages were the farm buildings, with a smithy, an engineer's and a wheelwright's shop; and beyond these again the wide, open fields, the meadows, and the woods.

The Colonel took a platonic interest in all these improvements. His new steward suited him very well. He showed a good return on the Home Farm, kept the coverts well stocked, while poaching seemed to have become a thing of the past. His employer, therefore, was willing to gratify his mania for improvements. The more so, as it was difficult to know what to do with the unoccupied farms other than this, while by allowing his steward to carry out this scheme, the Colonel afforded extreme gratification to his own daughter.

Colonel Ashville was by no means a hard man. Though an ardent sportsman,[129] he generally dealt so leniently with such poachers as were brought before him, as to excite the derision of his fellow magistrates. Still he was very pleased with this diminution of poaching, which, to tell truth, was as much due to Watson's disinclination to arrest poachers as anything else. But, in addition to this, the Colonel was interested in the well-being of his dependents, and when he saw that Watson's new scheme really resulted in their benefit he was pleased, though he did not share in the enthusiasm of his steward.

As for Miss Ashville, she was delighted. The success of the associated farm had become her object in life. Scarcely a day passed in which she did not ride over the scene of operations with Frank, proposing, planning, advising. The cottages had been built according to her ideas, and the plateau, with its fountain and trees, was of her suggesting.

To the good people of Benton, Frank's associated farm was at once a wonder and a scandal. To be sure, it had almost depleted Paradise Row of its worst characters – Frank had made a point of enrolling the most notorious poachers in his association, for he knew by experience that they were often the best workmen, and Ben Green was one of the most useful men on the farm – but it would come to no good in the end. It was the talk of the town, and numbers of the shopkeepers visited the little colony, but the wiseacres shook their heads. "Yes, it might succeed for a time, but it wouldn't last. What did this Cockney fellow know about farming? And then to go and set labouring folks up to be as good as their betters! It was downright sinful – a regular flying in the face of Providence."

The Rev. Theodore Gray was particularly bitter about it, and actually took the trouble to get up an original sermon on the duty of men to be content in the position in life in which it had pleased God to place them.

"Why, sir," said the reverend gentleman to Mr. Cranston one day, "the fellow is a downright atheist. He never comes to church, and I hear he is trying to establish a reading room on this precious farm. Going to encourage working men to read newspapers as well as drink beer. It's downright monstrous. The less they read, the better."

The ironmaster only smiled and shook his head. Frank's mania for mechanical improvements had secured Cranston and Son one or two good orders, and although the repairs were now done at the engineer's shop on the farm, still he was not going to fall foul of the new steward while his star was in the ascendant.

What scandalised the townsfolk of Benton most of all, however, was the familiarity that appeared to exist between the new steward and Miss Ashville. It was really scandalous, they agreed, and the Colonel ought to be remonstrated with on the fact that his daughter and his steward were so constantly together. No one, however, undertook to remonstrate with him, and if anybody had, they would have had their labour for their pains. He had implicit confidence in both his daughter and his steward, and if he had ever condescended to trouble himself to reason the matter, he would have argued that as a steward is only a servant, there was no more significance in his daughter being constantly in Frank's company than there would be in her being followed by a groom.

To Frank, however, Eva's companionship was by no means a matter of such indifference. Her deep sympathy with the poor, and the similarity of their views had caused an intimacy to grow up between them which had gradually ripened into a sentiment warmer than mere friendship on his part. It was rather more than a twelve month after the idea of associated farms had first been discussed by them, and Frank and Eva were returning from some rural sports that had been held on the Green to celebrate a successful harvesting.

"How delightful," said Eva, as they rode side by side, "it is to witness the pleasure of these poor people, and all the more when one feels to some extent to have been the dispenser of it."

"Yes," said Frank, "but it is not so pleasant to reflect that in a short time all this may be changed. These people have no security and a new owner of Benton Park may have very different views to those held even by Colonel Ashville."

"Well, Colonel Ashville is the present owner, and will be for years to come, and, in any case, I am his heiress."

"Has it ever occurred to you, then, how much depends upon your choice of a husband?"

The tone in which this question was asked sounded so significant that Eva felt the hot blush rise to her cheeks as she turned away her face.

"Pardon me, Miss Ashville – Eva," said Frank, clasping the hand with which she held the bridle, "I must speak now. I have tried to conquer myself, but in vain. I know it is presumption, madness, but I cannot help it – I love you. Dear Miss Ashville, dear Eva, dare I hope that it is not in vain?"

He felt the hand he held tighten on the rein. Finding she did not answer, he went on: "I probably should not have dared to make this confession, to ask you to bid me hope, but that I know that you are as far superior to your class in sentiment, as you are to me in position. I know that you despise conventionality, and that to you the barriers of rank have no existence. Do not despise me so far as to imagine that this confession is due to the fact that you are Colonel Ashville's heiress. Oh, my darling, it is the love of my whole heart I offer you, the heart of an honest, if poor, man; do not lightly reject it. Think before you speak of all that depends upon your answer. Think of the happiness of those poor people whom we have just left. Reflect that their future is to a large extent in your hands at this moment. Think that in all your class you may not find one who shares the views we hold in common. Think of this, and oh, my darling, think how I love you."

For a moment Eva's patrician pride struggled for the mastery, and words of scornful rebuke were rising to her lips.[130] But her finer feeling conquered, and she said gently, but calmly and coldly, "Mr. Watson, you pain me exceedingly. I had no idea, I never dreamed that you entertained such sentiments towards me, and though I am willing to remain your friend you must never again give utterance to such ideas, but dismiss them from your mind absolutely. I think I will ride on alone," she added, and suiting the action to the word, she put her pony into a canter, and was soon out of sight.

Frank allowed the reins to fall loose on the neck of his steady-going cob, as he rode on like a man in a dream. He had staked his hope of happiness and had lost. He felt no resentment towards Eva; she was too good, too pure, to be actuated by any unworthy motive in rejecting him. But he cursed his folly for having dared to hope. Now he scarcely knew what to do. He felt that he ought to resign, and at one moment made up his mind to do so. Then he reflected that he owed something to the people, the current of whose lives he had changed, and decided to stay. All that night he roamed the woods in a state of feverish unrest. In the morning he felt a great dread as he approached the house to have the usual business interview with the Colonel, and was immensely relieved at not seeing Eva.

They never rode out together again, but in a fortnight's time he knew why he had been rejected, for George Cranston had returned home, and everybody was busy preparing for the wedding festivities, which took place a week later. Among the numerous guests at the Park were Lieutenant Vernon and Jack Somers, Tory M.P. for a London constituency.

[30 March 1889]

Chapter XLIII.

It was to Frank a period of unmitigated misery. He had no one in whom he could repose confidence. His secret was unknown to all save one, and how bitterly he regretted that he had ever made it known to her. The fact that George Cranston was his successful rival made his disappointment additionally bitter. It seemed as if the Cranstons were his fate. "Curse him!" he muttered to himself, as he strode backwards and forwards in the parlour of the little house where he still lived with Markham's widow. "It is to him and his that I owe all my misfortunes. They murdered my wife and my mother, and now he comes between me and my love. Curse him."

Frank was in attendance at the house on the day of the wedding, and was introduced to the husband of his young mistress just before they took their departure for Weymouth on their way to the Continent. The dislike, which he could scarcely conceal when Cranston and he shook hands, was instinctively felt by the other. As Frank looked into his hard cold face, a feeling of pity for the fair young creature who had preferred this grasping, money-loving capitalist to himself, mingled with the bitter hatred at his heart. "It is ever thus," he thought, as he noted the fond trustfulness with which Eva regarded her husband. "The best women generally bestow their affection upon the most worthless objects. Will she always love him as she does now, I wonder." He was glad when they had gone, and things assumed their normal aspect.

The newly married pair were to be gone a couple of months. During the first part of the time affairs went on in the usual course, Frank attending to the daily routine of his duties as if nothing had happened to break the monotony of his life. His temperament had undergone a change, however. He had become so dull and abstracted that his changed manner attracted the attention of those around him. Mrs. Markham occasionally rallied him on his apparent melancholy.

It was late one afternoon, about a moth after the wedding. Frank, who had been out all day, was sitting by the parlour fire reading, a big dog, half mastiff, half greyhound, dozing at his feet. Mrs. Markham was sitting at the opposite side of the fire, knitting. The ticking of the Dutch clock in the corner alone broke the silence until Mrs. Markham spoke:

"I can't make out what's come over you, lately. Ever since Miss Eva has been married you've been as quiet and as dull as a country churchyard; anybody would think as you were in love yourself."

Frank shook his head and smiled.

"Well, I don't see as you shouldn't be. You're a young man, and there's many a decent young woman about Benton who'd be proud to be the wife of the Park steward. But I suppose you lost your heart to some smart miss in London."

"No," said Frank, "I haven't got a sweetheart. And I don't see that I want one. I'm comfortable enough here with you, and if I brought another woman here we probably should not be so comfortable."

"Oh, I don't know. I think I should be happier with a young woman to keep me company while you are out. And I am sure that you would be more comfortable. I think you ought to get married."

Frank was about to give some off-hand reply when there came a knock at the door, and their little maid-of-all-work complied with his short "Come in," by entering the parlour.

"If you please, sir," said she, "here's Joe come from the House, and he wants to see you very particular."

"Tell him to come in."

Frank was startled by the scared appearance of the stable hand, who was ushered into the parlour.

"Why, whatever is the matter, Joe?" he asked.

"Why, sir, the Colonel was out with the hounds to-day, as I s'pose you know. The fox, it appears, led 'em across the Ten-acre bottom, and just at that nasty bit by the gravel-pit, the Colonel's horse – the chestnut, you know, sir – leaped short in clearing the fence, and toppled over into the pit. The Colonel was well in front, and when the others came up they found him and his horse lying at the bottom of the pit. The chestnut, I believe, is dead, but one of the party rode on to the House to tell the housekeeper to get a bed ready, and then rode off for the doctor. He said that they were bringing the Colonel along, and so the housekeeper sent me on to tell you."

Frank lost no time in making his way to the house, where he found the injured man had been borne, and that the doctor was already in attendance. He waited in the breakfast room until the housekeeper and the doctor came down. The medical man looked grave. When Frank asked him what was the matter, he shook his head.

"There is no hope," he said, "he had received terrible injuries, and will probably not live through the night. He is quite unconscious now, and doubtless will remain so. I can do nothing, but will wait."

Frank did not speak. He felt stunned by this fresh blow. He walked out of the house and round to the stables, called Joe to saddle his horse and rode off to the

Benton post office, where he wired to Eva at Nice, asking her to hasten her return as her father had been taken seriously ill. He then rode back to the Park, and all that night he sat by the bedside of his dying patron.

He was overwhelmed with grief, but his face wore a hard stern expression that displayed no trace of the tumult that was going on in his mind. He thought of the terrible blow the loss of her father would be to the sweet girl he still dearly loved, and to shield whom from harm he would willingly give his life. Then he thought of his new master; the idea of being under the domination of George Cranston was gall and wormwood to him. What should he do? Then there was the farm, which he had organised and in which Eva had taken so much delight. What would George Cranston do about that? Eva positively worshipped her husband, of that Frank felt assured, all unworthy as he knew him to be, and his word would be law to her.[131] Frank felt that his associated farm was doomed, and cursed himself for the innovations he had made, which he saw now would only work harm to the people he had endeavoured to benefit.

Towards the morning the Colonel became conscious; he motioned Frank towards him. Frank touched the bell pull; the injured man shook his head, and his lips moved as though he was speaking. Frank bent over him.

"It's no use calling anyone," said the dying man, in a whisper, "I know I'm going. I wish I could see Eva before I die, but I shan't. Good bye, Watson. You've served me faithfully. I wish I could reward you, but it is too late now. Tell Eva it was my wish to do the right thing for you – and the others. Turn up the light – How dark it is – Give my love to my darling Eva – I hope Cranston will be a good husband to her – Tell her I died with her name in my heart and on my lips. Good bye – Eva."

He was dead.

* * *

When Eva returned with her husband, the second day after the accident, she was almost inconsolable in her grief. Frank, in the presence of Cranston, who scowled grimly, delivered to her her father's dying message. His new master mentally resolved that the steward at any rate should benefit little by the Colonel's death.

Frank was not mistaken in his anticipation as to the misfortune that would befall in consequence of the change of masters at the Park. It was scarcely a week after the funeral of Colonel Ashville, when, on calling to see Cranston as to business arrangements, that gentleman said to him: "I have to inform you, Mr. Watson, that it is my intention to manage the estate myself. That being so, I shall have no need of your service as steward. I may be able to offer you a situation in a humbler capacity, if you choose to accept it. If not, we shall have to part. Meantime, Mrs. Cranston is desirous of carrying out to the full the wish of her father as conveyed to her by you, and she therefore presents you with the sum of a hundred pounds. Should you decide to leave my service you will, of course, have no further claim on me, and you can consider your engagement at an end from to-day. I shall require you to give me an account of your stewardship up till to-day, and an account of receipts and expenditure in connection with that associated farm affair, which folly I intend to knock on the head at once, I cannot imagine how Colonel Ashville could have allowed himself to be drawn into any such absurdly Quixotic experiment. Anyway, I intend to farm the land myself, and shall get rid of those precious tenants of yours as quickly as possible. I intend to go in for larger game preserves than have hitherto been kept up, and if you like to take a gamekeeper's place, you can. Think it over, and let me know to-morrow."

[6 April 1889]

Chapter XLIV.

Frank was not at all surprised at the determination of his new employer. He went back home and told Mrs. Markham what had happened. The old lady was indignant and horrified. "Then you'll be going away," she said, "and I shall have to leave here, and where shall I go?"

"You need not trouble, mother" – Frank had got to calling her mother – "I shan't go away; I shall accept his offer, that'll suit me very well, and we can continue to stay here, even if we have to pay rent for the place."

This conversation, and the events which had preceded it, brought forcibly to Frank's mind the occasion when, in London, death had robbed him of his best friend, and the misfortune had been accentuated by the disappearance of that friend's relatives. Then, however, he had been tormented with the fear of being arrested for murder. Now so much time had elapsed that he felt perfectly safe. He reproached himself for not having kept up communication with those he had become acquainted with in London. As it was, he felt in want of a friend to confide in and to consult with. As he threw himself into a chair in the little parlour he caught sight of the London morning paper lying on the table, and began carelessly looking over it. Almost the first thing that caught his eye was a paragraph headed: 'Sad Suicide,' and which ran as follows: "Yesterday an inquest was held on the body of a young woman, which was found the day before in the river just below Waterloo Bridge. From the evidence of several witnesses it transpired that the name of the deceased was Nelly Wright; that she had for sometime past been living with her mother in a lodging-house near the Waterloo Road; both women maintaining themselves by needlework. Recently, the mother was taken ill and died, and since then the girl had been unable to get work. In consequence she had to undergo the greatest privation, and had been turned out of the lodging-house. The jury returned a verdict of suicide while in a state of temporary insanity induced by privation."

Frank was inexpressibly shocked by this narrative. He had no doubt that it was the daughter of his old friend who had come to this untimely end. It seemed a reproach to him for not having tried to seek out his old friends during his brief period of prosperity. It was another illustration of the fact which experience had so forcibly brought home to him; that human beings are the creatures of circumstances.

George Cranston kept his word. The tenants of the associated farm all received notice to quit except a barely sufficient number to carry on the work. They were given to understand that their interest in the concern was to cease forthwith, and that they would be paid the ordinary wages and charged a rent for their cottages. Frank found his position very considerably changed. He had to pay rent for his house; had to find his own firing and light; while his salary was reduced by half.

He often wondered what Cranston's wife thought of the changes that were being effected, whether she approved of them or not. As a matter of fact, she knew nothing of what was going on. Her husband was all the world to her. He told her that she had made mistakes; that she was lowering her dignity to take so active an interest in business matters as she had hitherto done, and she trusted him implicitly. She did not now have the leisure for rustic pursuits she had hitherto had. What with paying visits and receiving company she found her time fully occupied.[132]

The whole tenour[133] of her life seemed changed. The House where, during Colonel Ashville's lifetime, peace and quiet had reigned supreme, was now the scene of constant boisterous revelry. Instead of having, as in the Colonel's time, an occasional visit from one or two staid county families, the Cranstons were constantly entertaining whole parties of George's London friends.

The result of the changes on the estate was to cause considerable distress in Benton. The men who had been turned out of the cottages of course had no claim on Cranston. They had had to betake themselves to the hovels in Paradise Row, and were most of them out of work. They had had a pretty good time on the farm, and that made their present misery all the harder to bear. The little money each one had received as his share-out after the second harvest was soon all gone, and as the winter advanced they found themselves in a pitiable condition.

Ben Green, and a few of the more determined men amongst them, had again taken to poaching rather than starve. The preserves at the Park were the most frequently visited. The men were animated by a strong spirit of revenge as well as a desire for game, and the "Cranston coverts" afforded both. Every time they went there they prepared for desperate work. Vengeance was their password and the insults and hardships they had to endure goaded them on.

Frank pitied them, but was powerless to help them. His new master was quite as much enamoured of machine agriculture as he was himself, the only difference was that whereas Frank was anxious to use the machinery in order to relieve the labourer of grinding drudgery, Cranston used it to displace the labourer and increase his own profits.[134] The worst of the matter to Frank was that, in the minds of the labourers, a very considerable odium attached to himself. Instead of blaming Cranston they blamed him for having introduced the machines. Whenever he went to Benton, which he did more frequently of late, he found himself confronted by the black looks of a number of these unemployed men. He used to drop in at the Red Lion of an evening now. He had got over the fear of detection, and felt more desirous of company.

They had had a busy day at the Park. Cranston and a party of friends had been battue shooting,[135] and Frank had been directing the beaters and felt tired. The game had been left on the ground to be gathered up in the morning. At the last moment, however, it was decided to do this that night as soon as the moon had risen. This gave Frank an hour or two to spare, so he took a walk down to the Lion. It was a clear frosty night, the air was exhilarating, but Frank's spirits were not in harmony with the outer atmosphere. He felt depressed and moody, and desired companionship. He thought he would like to have a talk over his own affairs with someone. What should he do? Should he make a confidant of Alice Steggles? Undecided, he walked into the bar. There were few customers there, and after standing for a few moments over a glass of ale he said to Alice, speaking almost involuntarily: "Won't you come out for a walk for a little while, I'd like to talk to you."

"Yes, I can get out directly, if you'll wait for me on the bridge."

Frank walked out, and stood pondering for a while as to what he should say. He had not long to wait before Alice joined him. They walked along the road for some time in silence. At last he spoke.

"Do you know, Alice," said he, "I feel very miserable?"

"Miserable! Why? I suppose, though, it is because of the changes that have taken place at the Park."

"No, it is not exactly that. Suppose I told you I was in love?"

"Well, I should say that ought not to make you miserable."

"Not if my love was hopeless?"

"I don't see why it should be."

"Ah, Alice the dear creature I love is so far above me. I knew her when I was Frank Wilson. I learnt to love her in a far-off reverential sort of way for her kindness to my poor wife, and during the last year or so my love has grown too strong for me to keep silent. And yet what right could I, a suspected murderer, have to talk of love. But she was one of the very few who believed me innocent of the crime that was laid to my charge. But this could be no justification for my audacity; she so pure, so good."

"She could not be too good for you," answered his companion in a low tone.

"But should I be justified, do you think, I, a mere servant, in confessing my love, and asking her hand? Should I not merit a contemptuous rejection?"

"Dearest Frank, can you ask?" she returned, as she grasped his hand, and looked up into his face with tear-dimmed eyes.

Frank realised the mistake he had made. Alice had fondly taken his half-confidences for a proposal!

They had left the road, and were walking along a path which ran for some little way by the side of the hedge, and then branched off in the direction of the Park. Engrossed in conversation they had not heard the footsteps of a man walking in the opposite direction on the other side of the hedge, who, hearing them talking, stopped to listen.

[13 April 1889]

Chapter XLV.

The listener was George Cranston, who, leaving his guests at the house, was taking a walk round to see that his keepers were at their posts.

What he heard changed his plans.

"Good Heavens!" he muttered, "that fellow, our late steward, Wilson the murderer! Whoever would have thought it! Well, I never did like the fellow. This is a discovery, to be sure. I'll go and let the police know about this. We shall know where to find him, that's one thing."

In the meantime Frank and Alice walked on, oblivious of the fact that Frank's identity had been discovered.

For a while Frank was silent. He scarcely knew what to do. Alice had accepted his unintended proposal, that was clear. "How should he undeceive her?" Then again he asked himself if it were worth his while to do so at all?

He himself had felt the "pangs of despised love,"[136] should he inflict the same suffering on her? True, he did not love her. But he liked her; she loved him. He could make her a good husband, they would be comfortable together, and she need never know the truth. He bent down and kissed her lips, and she felt supremely happy.

They were turning back towards Benton when they were startled by a shot fired in the vicinity of the Park.

"Good God!" exclaimed Frank, "what's that? Pardon me, my dear girl, but I shall have to ask you to go home alone. I fear there is trouble going on over yonder."

So saying he dashed off in the direction from whence the sound proceeded.

Alice did not go towards home, however, but with a dread of impending evil in her heart, walked slowly along the path towards the Park.

Frank was not long in reaching the spot where the gun had been fired. There was quite a party of men there, most of whom he recognised as having been workers on the associated farm. They were filling bags with the birds which had been killed in the day's battue.

"You must ha' bin a dam fool, Ben, to shoot that rabbit," said one of the gang, as Frank pushed his way through the bushes. "You'll have all the blasted keepers down on us now. I reckon we'd better cut."

"What the devil do I care about yer keepers?" exclaimed Ben Green, with a hoarse laugh. "I'll give them something if they try to tackle me; and their master as well if he likes to come."

He didn't have long to wait to make good his words, for the keepers, who were on their way to the spot, came rushing in on them from several directions.

Ben and his companions discharged their guns at the keepers as they approached, and then, grasping the pieces by the barrel, began using them in club fashion with terrible effect. Frank was one of the first to fall by a stunning blow which stretched him insensible for a minute or two. In a few minutes the keepers were all either senseless on the ground or flying for their lives.

Ben Green was laying about him like a demon. Intoxicated with his success, he exclaimed just as Frank was regaining consciousness, "Come on lads, leave the bags here, we'll make a proper finish to this night's work."

Frank saw them make off with a yell of triumph in the direction of the house.

He staggered to his feet, and slowly followed after them. He could not travel fast, his head ached, and he felt dazed with the blow. He was still some distance from the house when he saw a bright flame shoot up towards the sky. "Good God!" he exclaimed, "they have fired the house." He hurried on as well as the pain would permit him.

When he reached the scene he found that the back of the house was one mass of flame. The guests, most of them in a half-drunken state, had rushed out of the front door, and now stood in a little group at a safe distance helplessly watching the progress of the flames, while Ben Green and his companions stood loading their guns on the opposite side.

"Wait till Cranston comes out, we'll pay him for robbing us of house and home," shouted the poacher, almost beside himself with the ferocious joy with which the sight of the flames seemed to inspire him.

Frank looked around for the women; the servants, it appeared, had fled, but the safety of one alone concerned his thoughts. He went from one to the other of the half-drunken guests asking them if they had seen Mrs. Cranston. At length one, a little more sober than the others, informed him that Mrs. Cranston had retired to rest before the fire broke out. Without a moment's hesitation Frank dashed up the stone steps and in at the front door. Up the broad staircase, which gleamed in the bright light of the flames that were rapidly coming nearer, he flew.

As he reached the first landing he heard a yell, and then the discharge of firearms. Some keepers, attracted by the flames had arrived, and they were fighting down below. But he hesitated not. Up, up, he went, on to the second landing and along the wide corridor, which was scorching beneath his feet. Which was the room? Should he ever find it? He heard a faint shriek in a room to his right. He tried the door; it was locked. Placing his shoulder against it, with the strength of despair he forced it open. The room was bright with the light of the flames which were flickering in at the window. Mrs. Cranston was sitting up in bed, staring wildly round her.

"My husband! where is my dear husband?" she cried, as she fell back fainting.

Frank took her in his arms, wrapped the blanket tightly round her, and rushed towards the window. No hope that way. All the framework of the window and the balcony were in flames. The only escape was by the door. He rushed to it, and found the corridor full of smoke. On he went, while the crimson flames, as if in play, darted out at him from the doors of every room, scorching his clothing and blistering his face and hands as he rushed towards the staircase. But he never felt the heat nor the smoke. He only knew that for one precious moment he held his beloved in his arms. What mattered the scorching flames or the blinding choking smoke as long as she was safe?

Again and again as he sped along he rapturously kissed her pale unconscious face. Down the stairs he leaped, each burning step giving way beneath his weight as he reached it. Breathless, almost blinded, he reached the ground and deposited his burden on the lawn. As he glanced around he saw that the keepers had regained the mastery. Several of the poachers were lying on the sward, among them being Ben Green, who had been shot in the groin and appeared to be fast sinking, while others were in the custody of the keepers, who were idly watching the flames.

It had all been so sudden. Only a few minutes before he had been walking peacefully along the road with Alice, and now he was surrounded by these horrors! It was a striking picture: the fiery ruins, lit up with a lurid light; the neighbouring woods; the green sward; and the recumbent figures of the wounded poachers. But where was his employer? He had not seen him since the afternoon. Had he perished it he flames? Deep down in his heart Frank almost hoped that he had. He went towards Ben Green, who appeared to be bleeding profusely, and was about to speak to him, when he saw George Cranston, accompanied by a couple of policemen, come up with a run.

For a moment George Cranston gazed around him with a look of horror. He could scarcely grasp the situation. Suddenly his eye fell upon Frank. Immediately he connected him with the outrage that had been perpetuated.

"That's him! That's the scoundrel! That's Frank Wilson, the murderer!" he cried, turning to the policemen, and pointing to Frank.

"You're a liar, Cranston!" hoarsely growled Ben Green, raising himself on the elbow of the hand with which he still grasped his gun. "I shot Gripper – I'm not sorry for it. And, by God! for a good last shot I'll shoot you!" and suiting the action to the word the dying poacher placed the gun to his shoulder and pulled the trigger.

Quick as he was, however, he failed in his object. As he spoke, the words "Where is my dear husband?" accompanied by the thought that, after all, Eva loved Cranston, flashed through Frank's brain like lightning, and as Green fired, he threw himself in front of him, and seized the muzzle of his gun. He received the charge full in the temple, and fell prostrate at the feet of his old friend.

As he fell there was a shriek, and Alice Steggles burst through the crowd of keepers and sportsmen who were gathered round.

"Murderer! He is no murderer!" she cried, rushing forward and throwing herself on the body of her lover in a paroxysm of grief, "But you have murdered him! Frank, Frank! My darling, speak to me! Kiss me again! No, no," she wailed, "You have killed him – He is dead!"

LABOUR ELECTOR

Anon., 'A New "Labour" Paper', *Labour Elector*, 22 February 1890, pp. 116–18.

The *Labour Elector* (1888–94) was edited by Henry Hyde Champion, published by his company, Modern Press, and followed his first independently produced penny periodical, *Common Sense* (1887–8). The *Labour Elector* was priced at one penny and published monthly between the first issue in June 1888 and October of the same year. Between 1 November and 1 December 1888 the periodical was published fortnightly, and from 5 January 1889 to 19 April 1890 it was published weekly. Publication was suspended after 19 April 1890, when Champion moved to Australia to organize a strike of dock workers. Champion had been instrumental in the 1889 London dock strike, and the *Labour Elector* had been an important publication supporting the strikers and the cause. During the strike the periodical sold up to 20,000 copies a week, and according to Champion's biographer, it was probably edited by Michael Maltman Barry (1842–1909) while Champion was organizing the strike along with Tom Mann and John Burns.[1]

The *Labour Elector* published very little fiction and only the occasional poem; it focused more on investigative journalism and the promotion of independent parliamentary representation and the eight-hour workday. Given that Champion wrote a great deal of the content for the *Labour Elector*, it is possible that he is the author of this anonymous dialogue story. Champion was related to the old Scottish family the Urquharts through his mother's side, and he was educated at Marlborough College. He was commissioned in the Royal Artillery after graduating from the Royal Military Academy and served in the Second Anglo–Afghan War. He read Karl Marx (1818–83) during a period of illness, resigned his commission and joined the Democratic Federation (later the Social Democratic Federation) in 1883. His working relationship with Maltman Barry, who was involved with both the socialists and the Conservative Party, brought accusations of Tory intrigue, particularly after the 'Tory Gold' scandal, when Champion accepted money from Barry to fund two SDF candidates in the 1885 general election. The accusation reared again when he was involved in Keir Hardie's (1856–1915) election campaign for Mid-Lanark in 1888. Champion withdrew from the SDF (or, according to Hyndman's autobiography, was ejected) in 1888 after having published the short-lived *Common Sense*, and he began the *Labour Elector* in June of that year. He briefly returned to Britain in 1893 after working on the Australian dock strike, only to suffer financial difficulties and further accusations of dealings with the Conservative Party. He emigrated to Australia in 1894 and lived there for the remainder of his life.

Notes

1.   J. Barnes, *Socialist Champion: Portrait of the Gentleman as Crusader* (Melbourne: Australian Scholarly Publishing, 2006), p. 124.

Anon., 'A New "Labour" Paper' (1890)

Scene:
    The garret of a Grey-haired Agitator.

Persons:
    A Grey-haired Agitator.
    A Youthful Enthusiast.

Y. E. – Mr. X., I think?

G. A. – Yes.

Y. E. – I am the Secretary of the Western Extremity of the Metropolis Liberal and Radical Association.[1] You remember I wrote to you a little while ago.

G. A. – (*Who received hundreds of such letters, has no recollection of the circumstance, and no notion of his visitor's name.*) Oh, yes.

Y. E. – I am also a member of the Fabian Society.

G. A. – I notice that often happens with members of Liberal and Radical Associations.

Y. E. – I daresay you may have heard that the Fabian Society is thinking of starting a paper of its own?

G. A. – Indeed?

Y. E. – With the support of the Lightning Conductor Makers' and Steeple Jacks' Trade Union. Their general secretary is with us, and they are very anxious to have an organ of their own.

G. A. – Oh, is it to be their organ as well as the Fabians'? Won't it be a little awkward to keep you organ grinding with a divided control of the handle?

Y. E. – Oh, but the Fabian fully intends it to be a distinctly Trade Union paper. And the Executive of the Street-Sweepers' and Lamplighters' Union will support us, too. *They* want to have a paper of their own.

G. A. – But does the public want to have their papers? That, I take it, is where the difficulty comes in.

Y. E. – Well, you see, we have a most exceptional opportunity. We have the opportunity of acquiring the *North London Press* – an established paper, with a circulation and advertisements. It would not be like the risk of starting fresh.

G. A. – And your motto, I suppose would be *Absit omen*.[2]

Y. E. – Oh, no, a new name.

G. A. – And run it on the same lines?

Y. E. – Well, no, not exactly.

G. A. – And you expect, with a new name, new management and new policy, to keep the same readers and the same advertisers?

Y. E. (*fervently*) – We expect greatly to increase them. We think there is a great opening for a Labour paper, and we hope that you will help us by writing on your own special subject.

G. A. – You are very kind. But I should like to be quite clear about this. Of course, a paper run by the Fabian Society will be a Liberal paper?

Y. E. – Oh, dear, no! A Labour paper, absolutely independent.

G. A. – I am afraid you will find some difficulty in persuading the public of that; for as, no doubt, you know, most people – and I, I must own, among them – regard the Fabian Society as a mere adjunct of the Liberal party. I presume that the staff of the new *North London Press* will be, like the staff of the old, composed of gentlemen who also write for the *Star*?

Y. E. – I assure you it is quite a mistake to suppose that most of the Fabians write for the *Star*. It is quite a small minority who ever contribute to it.

G. A. – But is there a minority, even of one, which ever contributes to a Conservative paper? Will an organ of the Fabian be ready to praise a Conservative for any service in the cause of Labour?

Y. E. – Oh, yes, if any Conservative ever does any.

G. A. – It will be ready, for instance, to own that Lord DUNRAVEN, in spite of his being a Peer, a Conservative and an Irish landlord, has done more by his "Sweating System Committee" to push forward Labour questions than any single Liberal?

Y. E. – Oh, I don't know that I would go so far as that. But I would certainly give him great credit for it.

G. A. – But will the Editor of the Fabian Society's paper do so?

Y. E. (*with dignity*) – I, I believe, am likely to be the Editor; and if I have anything to do with it, it will certainly be an absolutely independent Labour paper.

G. A. – Although you are an official of a Liberal and Radical Association? However, let that pass. If you mean to stand apart from both parties, it must be your intention to run a rival paper to the LABOUR ELECTOR, and try to draw away Mr. CHAMPION'S readers.

Y. E. (*with some embarrassment*). – Oh, no; I have no feeling against Mr. CHAMPION personally. No doubt, he has done a great deal for the workers.

G. A. – But you mean to do your best to injure him if you can, by drawing away the readers of his paper?

Y. E. – Oh, well, you know, really – his paper! It has disgusted everybody. You can't expect working men to read it.

G. A. – I never expect anything of anybody. I got beyond that a great many years ago. But I own I thought – speaking as an outside observer – that a good many working men did buy the LABOUR ELECTOR. Perhaps they don't read it. I can't say. But you – who are still young enough to expect – you expect working men to read a paper of yours, run on the same lines as the LABOUR ELECTOR?

Y. E. – On the same lines – Good Heavens, no! Not at all on the same lines.

G. A. – Oh, I beg your pardon. I thought you said so. I am at sea again. What are to be your lines?

Y. E. – On the same lines as the LABOUR ELECTOR! After Mr. MALT-MAN BARRY[3] has been allowed to write these articles in it?

G. A. – Er – which articles?

Y. E. – About the PARKE case.[4]

G. A. – Oh – you mean "that paragraph!" And what reason have you for thinking that Mr. MALTMAN BARRY wrote that paragraph?

Y. E. – A man connected with the paper told me so.

G. A. – Ah! Should you think he desires to be connected with your paper, too? But let us assume that Mr. BARRY wrote it. *I* don't know. Men connected with papers don't come and tell me things, as a rule – you are a shining exception. Well, then. We will say that Mr. BARRY wrote it. Whether he did or not, Mr. CHAMPION, and nobody else, is responsible for its appearance in his paper.

Y. E. – Exactly; that is the point. He is responsible for his paper, and he allows Mr. BARRY, out of sheer Party spite, to write that infamous article.

G. A. – Excuse me – paragraph. But, assuming that Mr. BARRY wrote it, what ground have you for supposing that he did so out of sheer party spite?

Y. E. – Why, he is a Conservative agent.

G. A. – And Mr. PARKE is a Liberal editor, which is just as valid a ground for saying that he brought terrible charges against the son of a Conservative Duke, out of sheer party spite. Mind, *I* don't say so. I am not in a position to give any opinion upon the merits – or rather, the demerits – of the case, for the simple reason that I have not read it. It does, however, seem to me conceivable that Lord EUSTON was not guilty, but that Mr. PARKE honestly believed him guilty and wrote his accusation in good faith, that the judge summed up honestly, and the jury gave an honest verdict, and Mr. BARRY (on the previous assumption of his authorship) commented honestly, and that Mr. CHAMPION published the paragraph honestly. Or, again, it seems to me conceivable – though, I am happy to say, less conceivable – that every one of these men acted flagitiously throughout; that Lord EUSTON committed these crimes, that Mr. PARKE did not believe him guilty, but denounced him, nevertheless, out of sheer Party spite, that the judge summed up and the jury gave their verdict because they loved a Lord and hated a Liberal, and that Mr. BARRY wrote the paragraph and Mr. CHAMPION printed in the same spirit as the judge and jury. But let us have it one way or the other. Don't let us have all the virtue on one side of the Liberal editor and none on the side of the Conservative agent – let alone the Labour editor.

Y. E. – You may say what you like; he had no right to publish those articles – well, I mean paragraphs. And then, he repeated them. Why did he repeat them?

G. A. – When you edit your paper and put into it paragraphs which you believe in, and when you are attacked for doing so, shall you withdraw them or stand by them?

Y. E. – Stand by them, of course. Well, yes, I do own that, as an editor, he could not do otherwise than stand by it.

G. A. – And I do own that if I were he I would never have put it in at all; not because it was or was not a fair comment (I don't know whether it was or was not) but because it was off the line of sheer Labour questions. I should say the same if Mr. PARKE had been the editor of the *Evening News*. I wonder whether you would?

Y. E. – The whole bias of the paper is Conservative. Of course Mr. CHAMPION has a perfect right to be a Conservative if he likes. But if he pretends not to be, why did he help the Conservative to get in at Deptford?

G. A. – He did not do so.

Y. E. – Oh, the people down there say he did.

G. A. – Did you watch the facts of the election? Did you know any of the people? Did you attend any of the meetings?

Y. E. (*who was evidently at school two years ago*) – No; not myself. I only know what people down there say.

G. A. – Well, I did watch the events, and I know something of the people, and was present at more than one of the meetings held – very lively meetings they were, too. I don't know that I have enjoyed anything quite so well, since. The facts are these: The Deptford Liberal and Radical Association drew up a pretty advanced programme, and agreed to accept no candidate who would not go for it. But Mr. WILFRED BLUNT[5] being then in prison in Ireland, the Liberal section of the Association (without consulting their Radical brethren) chose him, though he had not accepted, and could not and would not accept, the programme, because, when all is said, he *was* a Tory. Some of the Radicals seceded and looked around for another candidate. I believe they applied to Mr. T. R. THRELFALL,[6] who had talked a good deal at a Trade Union Congress about forming a separate Labour Party. But Mr. THRELFALL does not seem to have felt like running. Then they tried Mr. CHAMPION, who consented to stand if they brought him a request from a reasonable number of electors – a hundred or a hundred and fifty, I think. They did, and he agreed to stand, and not to withdraw unless they gained certain promises – quite mild ones – from Mr. BLUNT, and certain other promises as to future fair dealing from the Liberal Association; and he continued his candidature until they did gain these points, and then he withdrew, offering publicly to help Mr. BLUNT'S supporters in any way he could, by speaking or canvassing. Then the *Star* said Mr. CHAMPION was "a man of honour;" for which certificate of character from such an authority, he was, of course, very much obliged. Do you see anything to object to in that course?

Y. E. – No; I admit that all that was quite legitimate. But there have been other occasions. There was the Holborn election, now. Where would you find a better Liberal candidate than LORD COMPTON?[7]

G. A. – Where, indeed? I quite agree that he is as good a candidate as the Liberals can put forward. That is why I say, remembering LORD COMPTON'S position when he stood for my own constituency, that Liberal candidates are not good enough.

Y. E. – Well, if *he* is not good enough, what about GAINSFORD BRUCE – the highest and driest of Tories? How could any man who cared for the workers oppose LORD COMPTON and support GAINSFORD BRUCE?[8]

G. A. – Who supported GAINSFORD BRUCE?

Y. E. – Mr. CHAMPION did.

G. A. – That is absolutely false.

Y. E. – Well, people in the constituency say he did. He issued a circular against LORD COMPTON.

G. A. – As I was living in the constituency at the time – though without a vote, thanks to the provision of the Act facetiously called "Representation of the People Act,"[9] – and as I happen to be the person who distributed those bills (which, by the way, were not issued by Mr CHAMPION, but by a committee mainly composed of working men), I may be allowed to be some authority on that subject. The committee decided that no candidate deserved the support of working men who would not pledge himself to vote for an Eight Hour Day[10] in Government works and chartered monopolies. That was not very extreme, was it?

Y. E. – (*Not without scorn*) No, indeed!

G. A. – The question was duly put to Mr. GAINSFORD BRUCE, who refused point blank, which was clear and honest. He, having refused, was not for us. Then the question was put to LORD COMPTON, and there was a considerable difficulty in getting an equally straightforward answer from him or his agents. At last he said that he would vote for it if the Labour representatives introduced it (I suppose he meant Mr. BROADHURST[11] and others who had been workmen, though they represent Liberal majorities, just like other people), and if he were convinced that the working men of the constituency wanted it.

Then Mr. CHAMPION went to an open-air meeting of LORD COMPTON'S at Cambridge Circus, in the dinner hour on a very chilly November day. I was there, so I know what happened. Mr. CHAMPION spoke and said, as you or I do, what an excellent person LORD COMPTON was, and what a high opinion he had of him personally; then he went on to this point about the Eight Hours, and how LORD COMPTON did not think the working men of the district wanted it, and before anyone could stop him he asked them if they did want it to hold up their hands. It was a big meeting – nearly all working men – and only one man held up his hand the other way. But still, LORD COMPTON, when again pressed, would not promise unconditionally even to vote for the measure. Then a handbill was issued, saying that neither candidate would give this promise and that, therefore, working men should oppose both. Do you call this supporting GAINSFORD BRUCE?

Y. E. – No, perhaps not; but he did oppose LORD COMPTON.

G. A. – Could he help it? And besides, don't we all know that in Holborn, as in Deptford, the Liberals had not a chance from the beginning?

Y. E. – Still, there are other things. I myself saw a paragraph quite lately in the LABOUR ELECTOR that seemed to advocate Protection.[12]

G. A. – You could not speak with more horror if it had seemed to advocate assassination. Would you never, under any circumstances, advocate any form of import duty?

Y. E. – Never, never! The whole principle is wrong.

G. A. – Not even in trades (and there *are* some) in which foreign foods can be produced cheaper, not because of any natural advantage, but solely because the foreign workman is harder worked or worse paid than the Englishman? Would you not make an exception in those cases?

Y. E. – In no case.

G. A. – Supposing (the example and the figures are quite imaginary) that a pair of English scissors made by men working at Union rates cannot be made for less than a shilling retail, while the same thing can be made in Germany for ninepence – the materials costing the same – solely because the German works longer hours for less pay – do you think that an English buyer does right to buy the German scissors at the cheaper price?

Y. E. – Certainly not.

G. A. – Do you think that the law would be justified in preventing him from getting it at the cheaper price?

Y. E. – We must look for action on the part of the Germans to shorten their hours and raise their wages.

G. A. – And in the meantime you would do nothing? You would not take any steps for the improvement of the Englishman's condition till the other nations took similar steps?

Y. E. – Oh, in a lot of trades you might.

G. A. – But not in these particular trades. You would not impose a tax in the meantime?

Y. E. – Certainly not. It is altogether wrong in principle. It would enable manufacturers to make a "corner" and raise the prices.

G. A. – They can do that now. If they did it to any greater degree then the German manufacturer could undersell them, and that underselling would not be at Labour's expense. The tax, you remember, is to be exactly equivalent to the difference in wages.

Y. E. – It could not be done. It would be impossible to fix it.

G. A. – But if it could be done, would you be in favour of it as an intermediate thing till other countries came up to our standard?

Y. E. – No, the principle of Free Trade must be maintained. And besides, if you gave protection to one class you would have to give it to another. The agricultural labourers are just as poorly paid. They would make an outcry for a tax on corn. Cheap foreign corn is the cause of their poverty.

G. A. – Is foreign corn so cheap because the men who plough and reap it are underpaid?

Y. E. – I don't know. I don't suppose so.

G. A. – *I* don't suppose so. If foreign corn were cheap because the men who work to produce it were underpaid, and if their underpay caused our men to be underpaid, I, for my part, would support a duty that allowed our men to be well paid, but I would be for the abolition of that duty the moment the foreign workman got the same; and I venture to say the foreign underpaid workman would have good cause to thank us for such a tax. But, as foreign corn is cheap for other reasons – naturally and honestly cheap – I should oppose any duty on it.

Y. E. – Still, you could not make a duty on the other things and not on corn. The agricultural interest would make a terrible outcry.

G. A. – Perhaps a terrible outcry does not seem quite so alarming to me. I have seen a good many terrible outcries in my time. For my part, if I were a judge or a divider in Israel, I hope I should not be debarred from giving TOM his due by the knowledge that if I did, DICK would cry out for more than his due. I am quite with you as to the ultimate desirability of Free Trade, but I want to see Labour free first, and I am not inclined to let the English labourer go in heavier and heavier chains until such time as all the other galley slaves rise up to knock off theirs. I would rather see Trade go in temporary shackles than Labour. I own that I think the trades in which duties might be needed would be few. Still, few or many, we have to face this problem in regard to them; the Englishman must fare as ill as the foreigner; or the foreigner must possess the English market; or the foreigner must be prevented from competing on unfair terms. I would choose the third way; you, apparently, would choose the first. But, I doubt whether the working man would thank you, or whether the advocacy of Protection, in that sense and to that degree, is likely to diminish the sale – among working men – of the LABOUR ELECTOR.

Y. E. – I am sure Protection is wrong, in principle and altogether.

G. A. – When you can show me a fourth way which will retain the market without starving the worker, I shall be delighted to agree with you. But are you going to start a paper to cut out the LABOUR ELECTOR with only that one point of difference – oh, and, I forgot, the PARKE case – between you?

Y. E. – It is not the only point of difference. The real thing is that Mr. CHAMPION is a Conservative. Why does he always attack Liberal employers and never Conservative ones?

G. A. – I am afraid you neglect the first rule of the prudent politician, which is, to read up the papers on the other side. I am sure you cannot have studied the LABOUR ELECTOR from the beginning, with care.

Y. E. (*Scornfully*) – Indeed, I haven't.

G. A. – If you had you would be aware that several Conservative employers have been denounced in it, though not, I grant you, nearly so many Conservatives as Liberals. But there's a sadly sufficient reason for that. I, as you know, have rather a special knowledge of the conditions of a good many trades; and I assure you I can only point to two bad employers, within my own knowledge, who are Conservatives. I know of many good employers who are Liberals; at the same time it is a fact, as far as my experience goes, that the bad employer is, in nine cases out of ten, a Liberal – ay, and a Radical at that. Still, Mr. CHAMPION has found some Conservatives to attack – as Mr. MAPLE[13] could testify.

Y. E. – Oh, MAPLE! But then all the other partners in MAPLE'S are Liberals.

G. A. – Alas! I hoped you might confute my statement, and you confirm it. I did hope that, as the Secretary of a Liberal and Radical Association in a shop-keeping district, you would have brought forward some wicked Conservative whom I might have noted as an example for future use. Why are not the Directors of BRYANT, MAY & CO.,[14] leading lights among the Conservatives? Why doesn't Mr. WHITELEY[15] cut down all his *employées* wages and go into Parliament as a high and dry Tory on the savings? I don't know why these things don't come to pass, but I know they don't. You must really not blame the Editor of the LABOUR ELECTOR for not denouncing more bad employers on the Conservative side. I don't suppose he can find them. I know I can't.

Y. E. – You are a Conservative, too, then?

G. A. – I? Heaven forbid!

Y. E. – You can't be a Liberal.

G. E. – What, because I own that many Liberals are bad employers? Still, it is true; I should say "Heaven forbid!" to that too, although I should always have called myself a Liberal until the days when I began to think. I can't remember the time when I did not believe that land ought to be nationalised; and I wanted Home Rule for Ireland long before any official Liberal saw anything but treason in it. I desire both those things still; but not nearly so much as I desire to see Labour in every way better off. I don't care a bit from which side the advantage comes to us; and, honestly, I think it is just as likely to come from one side as the other. That, as I understand it, is pretty much the position of the LABOUR ELECTOR, too. Is it going to be the position of your paper?

Y. E. – Well – if there were any chance of its coming from the Conservatives, we would take if from them, of course.

G. A. – And meanwhile, will you say in plain words: "We are not Liberals?" How can you, when you label yourself a Liberal?

TO-DAY

Ivan Tourgeneff, 'Only a Dog', *To-Day*, September 1883, pp. 502–22.

'Bauer und Dichter', 'Eros or Erin. A Tale of an Irish Conspiracy' *To-Day*, [Chapter I], December 1886, pp. 191–9; Chapter II, January 1887, pp. 4–13; Chapter III, February 1887, pp. 34–4.

Fabian Bland, 'Blood', *To-Day*, October 1886, pp. 126–34.

R. G. B., 'Birds of a Feather', *To-Day*, July 1886, pp. 3–7.

John Broadhouse, 'How He Lost his "Strad"', *To-Day*, November 1886, pp. 160–3.

A. Gilbert Katte, 'The Whip Hand. A Political Story – in Three Parts', *To-Day*, [Part I], February 1888, pp. 31–8; Part II, March 1888, pp. 63–7; Part III, April 1888, pp. 94–102.

John Law, 'The Gospel of Getting On. (To Olive Schreiner.)', *To-Day*, March 1888, pp. 83–4.

H. Bellingham, 'Chips', *To-Day*, September 1888, pp. 81–3.

To-Day: A Monthly Gathering of Bold Thoughts (1883–9), later subtitled *The Monthly Magazine of Scientific Socialism*, was published between 14 April 1883 and June 1889. It was printed first by Henry Hyde Champion's Modern Press, then by William Reeves, and was originally edited by SDF chairman Henry Mayers Hyndman, until he was accused of being autocratic. He passed editorial control to Ernest Belfort Bax and James Leigh Joynes (1853–93), who worked on the periodical from January 1884 until 1887, when Hubert Bland (1855–1914) took over the editorial role. Bland was editor until June 1889, when Hyndman again resumed control and changed the name to the *International Review*.

To-Day carried lengthy articles on issues such as socialism, economics and the gender question, the latter being famously debated in a series of articles between the editor, Bax, and Annie Besant (see Bax, 'Some Heterodox Notes on the Woman Question', July 1887; Besant, 'Misogyny in Excelsis', August 1887; Bax, 'No Misogyny but True Equality', October 1887). Hyndman, under the pseudonym 'John Broadhouse', serialized a translation of Marx's *Das Kapital* between January 1886 and April 1889. *To-Day* also had a high literary content, including literary criticism, and each issue would carry a poem – poets included E. (Edith) Nesbit (1858–1924), Ferdinand Freiligrath (1810–76), Tom Maguire (1866–95) and others. The periodical serialized Henrik Ibsen's (1828–1906) play *Ghosts* between January and March 1885, six years before its first performance in English at the Independent Theatre, London, in March 1891. George Bernard Shaw's first two novels were also serialized: *An Unsocial Socialist* between March and December 1884 and *Cashel Byron's Profession* between April 1885 and March 1886.

In the selection of fiction presented in this volume, three authors publish under their own full name: the unidentified authors H. Bellingham and A. Gilbert Katte, and Ivan Tourgeneff (or Turgenev). Ivan Sergeevich Turgenev (1818–83) was a Russian author descended from minor Russian royalty whose stories were popular during the mid-century and whose novels were translated into French, German and English as well as many other European languages. Turgenev and his family moved to London in 1870 to escape the Paris Commune and returned soon after its fall. This story was written in 1852 and was originally published under the title 'Mumu'. The events and the character of the mistress of the house are based on Turgenev's mother and her attitude to her servants. In this translation the ending has been changed; while the original ending has Gerasim [*sic*] return to his mistress and continue serving her faithfully,[1] such an ending would sit uncomfortably in a periodical promoting the freedom of the workers, and therefore it was changed to accommodate hope for the future.

The author who published under the initials R. G. B. has not been identified during the research carried out for this project, nor has the identity of the pseudonymous author, 'Bauer und Dichter'. The pseudonym, translated from the original German, means 'peasant and poet' and is presumably a reference to the opera *Dichter und Bauer* (1846) by Franz von Suppé (1819–95). John Law is the pseudonym of Margaret Elise Harkness (see the headnote for the *Labour Elector*, Volume 2, pp. 69–70, for Harkness's full biographical details); and Fabian Bland is the pseudonym used by E. Nesbit – best known for her children's books, including *Five Children and It* (1902) and *The Railway Children* (1906) – and her husband, Fabian treasurer Hubert Bland, when co-authoring work.

Notes
1.   See L. B. Schapiro, *Turgenev: His Life and Times* (New York: Random House, 1978), p. 16.

Ivan Tourgeneff, 'Only a Dog' (1883)

In one of the streets of Moscow, occupying a great house with white columns and a balcony grown crooked with age, once lived an elderly lady, a widow, surrounded by her numerous domestics. She rarely went out, passing in solitude the closing years of her lengthened and monotonous existence. Her day, which had never been gay or bright, was now drawing near its end, but her evening was darker than night itself.

The most remarkable of her servants was her porter Gerassim, a tall, strong man, two arshines and twelve vershoks[1] in height, built like a giant, but deaf and dumb since his birth. His mistress had brought him from the village where he lived alone, apart from his brothers, and where he was considered one of the most honest and punctual of taxpayers. Being endowed with extraordinary strength, he could do with ease tasks which it took at least four other men to perform. He did his work rapidly and well, and it was really pleasant to see him in the fields when, urging the plough forward with his mighty hand, he seemed to cut through the hard ground without any help from his miserable horse – when, at hay-time he used his scythe with such execution as to fell even young trees, or when, raining down quick and unceasing blows with his flail, three arshines long, the firm and strong muscles of his shoulders seemed to move up and down like so many levers. His constant silence, added to his unwearying toil, gave him an air of solemn gravity. Gerassim was a good-looking fellow, and had it not been for his misfortune there was no peasant girl in Russia who would not be married to him willingly.

On Gerassim's arrival at Moscow he was supplied with boots, a coat for the summer, a sheepskin, a besom[2] and a shovel. At first his new life strangely displeased him. He had been accustomed to field work from his childhood up. Cut off from society by his misfortune, he had grown dumb yet mighty in his silence, like a tree springing up from fertile ground. At last domiciled in a town, he felt uneasy and in suspense, like a young bull suddenly taken from the field where the grass had reached to his breast, placed on the wagon of a railway train, and then nearly suffocated by smoke, sparks, or steam, suddenly whirled away in the midst of the noise of the wheels, of the shrieks of the locomotive. But whither – heaven only knew.

After the hard life he had led as a peasant, Gerassim could not help regarding his new duties as a good joke. It took only half an hour to do the whole of the work required of him; and when it was accomplished, he would either stand in the middle of the yard to gaze with open mouth at the passers-by, as if he looked to them for a solution of the problem that perplexed him, or he would hurry to some secluded corner, push away his shovel and besom, throw himself on the ground, and lie there for hours without moving, and with his face turned towards the earth. But in the end people get accustomed to everything; and so Gerassim got accustomed to his life in Moscow. He had not a great deal to do. It was his duty to keep the yard clean, to bring water twice a-day, to split and carry wood to the house, and to guard the building from strangers by day and from thieves at night. And it must be confessed that he did his duty conscientiously. You never saw any chips or dirt in the yard, so scrupulously clean was it kept; and if it happened that the sorry animal given to assist him with the water-barrels stopped at any time – in dirty weather for instance – Gerassim had but to put his shoulder to the wheel, when not only the cart but the horse itself, were compelled again to go forward. When Gerassim cut wood you could hear his hatchet ringing like bell-metal, while the chips could be seen flying in all directions. As for strangers, there was little danger from that quarter, for Gerassim had caught thieves, and had knocked them against each other so violently that all the neighbourhood had come to be afraid of him and to respect his prowess. To the rest of the domestics he was neither a friend, for all held him in awe, nor an enemy. He simply regarded them as belonging to the house. They explained to him what they wanted by means of signs; he understood them, fulfilled all commands, but at the same time stood up for his rights, nobody, for instance daring to occupy his seat at dinner. In a word Gerassim was of a very serious turn of mind, and was fond of order in everything. Even the cocks were not permitted to fight in his presence, else he would seize them by the legs, turn them round several times, and then throw them away from him in various directions. Geese were also bred in the yard, and being known to be self-important and judicious birds Gerassim esteemed and took care of them. He almost looked like a sedate goose himself.

Gerassim's room was above the kitchen. He had arranged it to suit his own taste. His bedstead, standing on four legs, and provided with oak boards, would have sustained the weight of a hundred pouds[3] if necessary, without giving way. There was a trunk under the bed, and in one of the corners of the room a small table with a chair before it on three legs. Gerassim secured his room by means of a black lock, the key of which he always wore attached to his girdle.

A year passed, and then something happened to Gerassim. The old lady in whose house he acted as porter, adhered to the customs of her forefathers, and had therefore a large retinue of domestics. There were not only washerwomen, seamstresses, tailors, and dressmakers, but there were joiners, even a harness-maker (who was also a veterinary surgeon), and a physician to prescribe for herself and her servants. Most important of all, however, the lady had her own shoemaker – Capiton Klymov, and a terrible drunkard into the bargain. Klymov considered himself a very ill-used person. He was in the habit of saying that Moscow, where he had to live unknown, without occupation and without honour, was no place for a cultivated man like himself. As for his intemperate habits, he drank merely to drown his grief. In saying this he spoke deliberately and beat his breast at intervals. One day the lady spoke concerning him to her head steward Gavrilo, a man whom, judging by his small yellow eyes and duck-like nose, fate seemed to have destined for a superior position in life. She regretted Capiton's vicious habits, remarking that only on the previous day he had been found lying in the street quite tipsy.

"What do you say, Gavrilo?" she queried suddenly. "Had we not better get him a wife? What do you think of it? We should, perhaps, have him steadier then."

"Why not?" replied Gavrilo.

"But who would have him for a husband?"

"I don't know who will. However, if you desire it, we must do something. He is of some use at the worst, and then he must be reckoned among your serfs. He cannot be banished from the village."

"I think Tatiana suits him."

Gavrilo would have liked to have replied in the negative, but compressing his lips he said nothing.

"Yes, let him pay court to Tatiana," remarked the lady, taking a pinch of snuff. "Do you hear me?"

"I hear, and shall act in accordance," replied Gavrilo, at once departing to give effect to the desires of his mistress.

Having reached his room he reflected awhile – the lady's decision having visibly affected him – but in the end he sent for Capiton.

And while Capiton is on the way, it may not be superfluous to say a few words about Tatiana, and to explain why the steward had been so perplexed by his mistress's injunction.

Tatiana was a washerwoman, yet withal a woman of parts – so skillful and learned in her avocation, in fact, that nothing but the thinnest and finest linen was ever entrusted to her. Twenty-eight years of age, neither tall nor stout, she was fair-haired and had moles upon her left cheek – a sure presage of a wretched life. From her earliest childhood she had been ill-treated. Not only was she over-worked; her mistress clothed her badly, and her wages were altogether insignificant. She either had no relations, or could not remember them. An old man in the village said he was her uncle, and several other peasants made a similar claim. Beyond these, she was altogether without relative. For years she had enjoyed some reputation as a beauty, but that was all gone now. Her nature was shy rather than quiet; you could never offend her, perhaps because she had such a constant fear of offending others. Her chief anxiety was to get her work done in time. She therefore spoke to people very rarely; of her mistress she was so much afraid that the mere sound of her name would often plunge her into a terrible fright.

When Gerassim came from the village, Tatiana almost died from fear at the sight of him, so huge he was and strong. She had, therefore, avoided him as much as possible, almost closing her eyes when she had to cross the yard in his presence, running meanwhile as quickly as she could to the wash-house, and trying to pass by unperceived. At first Gerassim paid her little attention. Gradually, however, he got into a habit of smiling as she approached, then of looking at her with a kind expression in his face. At last of refusing to turn his eyes away from her. Heaven knows what it was attracted him! Was it her features alone, or was it the shyness and timidity that betrayed themselves in all her movements?

One day while crossing the yard, holding high over her head her mistress' starched jacket, she felt herself grasped all at once by the elbow from behind. Tatiana screamed, looked back, and almost fainted. Gerassim stood behind her with a silly smile on his face, he was offering her a gingerbread cock with golden tail and wings. Her first impulse was to refuse the gift, but he pushed it into her hand, and went away, making an unintelligible sound as he did so. From that day Gerassim gave her no peace. No matter where she went, he was sure to be in her way. He greeted her with unintelligible noises, smiles, and other manifestation of his affection. Sometimes he would pull a new ribbon out of his bosom and offer it to her, at other times he would insist on sweeping the dust from the pathway over which she had to go. The poor girl hardly knew what to do with herself. The gallantry of the dumb porter soon became known to the whole house, and all sorts of sarcasms and caustic allusion were showered down on Tatiana. As for Gerassim, no one ventured to ridicule him, he did not like jokes; and in his presence, even Tatiana was left in peace. So that, voluntarily or involuntarily, she had the advantage of his protection. Gerassim, as is usually the case with the deaf and dumb, was very sharp-witted, and could always tell when he or she was being made a subject for ridicule. One day at dinner the castellan's wife, Tatiana's superior, jeered at the poor woman until she was on the point of bursting into tears with anger and shame. Gerassim thereupon suddenly rose, stretched out his enormous arm, and laying his hand on the head of the castellan's wife looked at her so fiercely, that she involuntarily bowed her head to the table in fear. Having given this warning, Gerassim resumed his seat, took up his spoon, and went on eating his cabbage soup. On another occasion, noticing Capiton in rather too familiar conversation with Tatiana, Gerassim beckoned him away, led him to the coach-house, and there, taking up a beam from the corner, quietly but significantly threatened him with it. Thenceforward nobody cared to carry on a prolonged conversation with Tatiana. And Gerassim's conduct did not bring any punishment in its wake. It is true that the castellan's wife fainted as soon as she got to her room, and otherwise played her part so well that Gerassim's rudeness was brought to the knowledge of his mistress that very day. The whimsical old lady, however, only laughed at the episode, making the castellan's wife repeat it to her several times; and the next day she sent the hero of the story a silver rouble.[4] She had a certain affection for him, for he was faithful as well as strong. Gerassim feared her somewhat, as did the other servants, but he relied upon her favour and was going to ask her permission to marry Tatiana. He was only waiting until he had received a new coat promised him by the steward. It was while he was meditating how to present himself to his mistress in a suitable condition, that it entered into that lady's head to marry Tatiana to Capiton.

It will now be easy for the reader to understand why Gavrilo felt perplexed after the interview with his mistress.

"How," he asked himself, "can I tell my mistress that Gerassim wishes to court Tatiana? The lady would never approve of such a marriage, and what sort of a husband would a deaf mute make? And then, on the other hand, were this were-wolf (God forgive me!) to hear that Tatiana was going to be compelled to marry Capiton, he would pull the house down. Impossible to reason with a diabolical personage of his stamp! Impossible!"

The arrival of Capiton here interrupted the course of Gavrilo's reflections. The shoemaker, on entering the room, placed his hands behind his back, leaned against the wall near the door, thrust his right foot before his left, and shook the hair from his eyes as much as to say, "Now, here I am. What do you want with me?"

Gavrilo looked hard at Capiton and began tapping the window-frame with his finger. Capiton's eyes twinkled a little but were not lowered; a slight smile flitted over the face of the shoemaker. As he stroked his greyish, disheveled hair, he seemed to be saying, "Yes; it's I and nobody else! What are you staring at?"

"Very handsome you are – in a fine condition, too," ejaculated Gavrilo.

Capiton merely shrugged his shoulders by way of protest, wondering to himself. "And you – are you any better?"

"Now just look at yourself," continued Gavrilo. "What are you like?"

Capiton cast a placid glance upon his ragged coat, and patched trousers; attentively examined his boots, full of holes though they were, paying special regard to the one on the toe of which he was balancing his right foot; and finally raising his head again to stare at his questioner, ejaculated, "Why do you ask?"

"Why?" repeated Gavrilo. "Why? Why, you are more like the devil than anyone else; and may God forgive me for saying so. That's whom you are like!"

Capiton began to wink in a knowing manner.

"You've been drunk again," went on Gavrilo. "Have you not? Answer!"

"I admit I have been drunk, but it was on account of my bad state of health."

"Your bad state of health, eh? Ah! You have not been punished enough – that's clear. Were you not, by the way, sent to St. Petersburg to be educated? And what did you learn there pray? Why, you don't deserve the bread you eat!"

"If that's the case Gavrilo Andreich, then I have but one judge and that is God, my Lord, and no one else! He alone knows what sort of a man I am in this world, and whether or not I deserve the bread I eat. As for my excessive drinking, the fault is not mine, but that of my companions, who having persuaded me against my will, left me in the lurch."

"Left you like a goose in the street! Oh, you dissolute fellow. But enough of that. I've something else to say to you. Our mistress (a pause) our mistress wishes to see you married. Do you hear? She believes matrimony will improve you. Do you understand?"

"Of course – how could I help understanding?"

"Well then. If it were my case, I should be inclined to be severe with you. But as she chooses to be indulgent, that is her business, not mine. What do say? Do you give your consent?"

Capiton smiled contentedly, observing, "Marriage is always a good thing for a man, Gavrilo Andreich, and I agree to it with the greatest pleasure."

"Of course you do," ejaculated Gavrilo, thinking to himself, "the fellow talks like a book." "But listen," he added aloud, "I fear the bride will not suit you."

"And who may she be? if I dare ask the question."

"It is Tatiana!"

"Tatiana?" demanded Capiton, opening his eyes wide, and taking a step from the wall.

"Now, then! what is it frightens you? Will she not suit you? Are you not pleased?"

"Who talks of not being pleased, Gavrilo Andreich? The girl is both gentle and industrious. But don't you know that the great werewolf – the phantom of the desert – is himself on the point of –"

"I know all, friend," said the house-steward, testily, "but if –"

"For heaven's sake, Gavrilo Andreich, take pity on me! He is certain to kill me; he'll squeeze me between his fingers like a fly, for he has a hand – you yourself must have noticed what a hand he has. Why it is as mighty as that of either Minin or Pozharsky.[5] And how heavy are his blows! That's because he's deaf – because, being deaf, he does not hear the sound of his own blows. And oh! when he begins to brandish his enormous fist! You can't get him to stop. Why, you yourself know, Gavrilo Andreich! It is because he is deaf and dumb, and, above all, as stupid as a block of wood. He is an animal, Gavrilo Andreich – an idol – nay, worse than an idol![6] Then why am I to suffer at his hands? I feel myself a lost man – a wretched being inured to suffering of all kinds, improved by use like an old pot! Still I am a man!"

"You needn't tell me, my dear fellow, I know all about it."

"Oh, heaven! then – what is my unfortunate avowal to end in? wretch that I am! Is there no end to my misery? What an unhappy fate is mine! When a child I was beaten by my former master; later in life I was thrashed by my companions; and now in my mature years what is there for me to look forward to?"

"Enough! leave me!" exclaimed Gavrilo, impatiently.

Capiton at once retired.

"In Gerassim's absence would you consent then?" Gavrilo shouted after him.

"I vow I would," replied Capiton.

The house-steward took several turns round the room. At last he sent for Tatiana.

In a few moments Tatiana noiselessly entered the room, pausing, however, for a moment on the threshold.

"Have you any orders for me, Gavrilo Andreich?" she asked in a very soft voice.

The house-steward stared hard at her. "Well, Tanusha,"[7] he began, "have you a mind to be married? Our mistress has found you a husband."

"'Tis well, Gavrilo Andreich. But who is it that is destined to become my husband?"

"Capiton, the shoemaker."

"Very well, sir, I shall obey."

"He is a thoughtless fellow, it is true, but our mistress relies on you to improve him."

"Very well, sir!"

"The only inconvenience about the matter – Let me see, is not Garaska (Gerassim) courting you? However did you manage to tame such a bear as he? He may kill you yet."

"He will certainly kill me, Gavrilo Andreich – he is sure to kill me."

"Kill? Let him kill if he dare! We shall see. Kill! How can you suggest such a thing? What right has he to kill?"

"I don't know, Gavrilo Andreich, whether he has any right or not."

"What a strange girl you are! I suppose you have made him no promise of any kind?"

"What do you mean, sir?"

Gavrilo remained silent a moment, thinking to himself, "How resigned the good creature is!" "Very well," he went on, "we'll talk the matter over again. You may go now. I am beginning to see, Tanusha, what a weak woman you are."

Tatiana turned, leaned for an instant against the door post, and then went out.

"Perhaps madame will forget all about this wedding to-morrow," thought the house-steward. "In any case why should I allow it to bother my head? If necessary we can easily hand the saucy fellow over to the police. Ustinia!" he called in a loud voice to his wife, "put coals into the *samo-var*,[8] dearest."

Tatiana did not leave the wash-house the whole day. She wept a little, but wiped her tears away, and was soon going about her work again as usual. Capiton remained till late in the evening in a wine cellar, telling a rather monotonous companion the story of his sojourn in St. Petersburgh, and of his employment by a gentleman who only had one defect – an excessive love of order. His hearer listened attentively, but, on Capiton declaring that something had happened which might tempt him to put an end to his life on the morrow, broke silence with the observation that it was time to go home.

Gavrilo's anticipations were not realised. The notion of marrying Capiton interested the lady so much that she spent the whole night in talking about it to her *femme de chamber*.[9] Gavrilo was in the habit of visiting his mistress every morning for the purpose of submitting his daily report, and now the first thing she asked him was, "What about the marriage?" His reply was, "Swimmingly! Capiton is coming to express his thanks to you in person."

The matter was, however, too important to pass unheeded by the domestics and officials of the household. The steward summoned a large number of them to his own room for purposes of deliberation. Tatiana displayed her usual modesty, and was silent. But Capiton protested that he had only one head to lose, and not two or three. Gerassim frowned through the apprehensions that were plainly depicted on his countenance. The first business of his "council of war" had been to shut up Capiton in a small pantry. Violence was at first suggested, but as somebody pointed out that madame might get to hear of it, more peaceful inclinations were allowed to assert themselves. It was well-known that Gerassim detested the vice of insobriety, and could not bear even the sight of drunkards. When a tipsy man passed, Gerassim always turned his eyes in another direction. It was decided, therefore, that Tatiana should pretend to be drunk, and present herself to Gerassim in an apparently advanced state of intoxication. The poor girl, much against her will, had at last to bend to the wishes of the assembly. She herself, indeed, saw no other way of getting rid of her troublesome lover.

Tatiana departed to do what was required of her. At this moment Gerassim was sitting on a stone near the gate, apparently absorbed in thought, and unaware that he was being watched by scores of eyes from behind the blinds of adjacent windows. The artifice met with the most complete success. As soon as Gerassim perceived Tatiana he began to make the usual signs of welcome. But a moment afterwards he rose, seized her by the hand, and half dragged her, half ran with her into the room where the domestics had assembled, and there rudely pushed her into the arms of Capiton, who by this time had been set at liberty.

Then, after steadily gazing in her face for a few moments, Gerassim – a disdainful smile playing about his lips – turned on his heel and tramped heavily from the room, immediately returning to his own cabin. He shut himself up there for twenty-four hours. The stable-boy afterwards narrated how, peering through a chink in the door, he had seen Gerassim sitting on his bed, swaying his body to and fro, his head meanwhile resting upon his hand. Yet on the following day nobody could detect any change in Gerassim. He went to the river for water as usual, but this time came back without bringing any – he had broken the barrel on the road. And at night he groomed his horse as usual, but did it with such vigour that the animal was scarcely able to keep its legs.

What is narrated happened in spring. At the end of the succeeding twelve months Capiton had so incapacitated himself for work by inebriety that he was sent to a distant village with a transport of carts as an idle and useless person. Tatiana, as his wife, accompanied him. At first he tried to appear contented, even gay, but he ended by looking more gloomy than ever. On the morning of his departure, everything being ready for the valedictory "God with you," Gerassim issued gravely from his cabin, went up to Tatiana, and gave her as a keepsake a red cotton handkerchief. Until this moment Tatiana had bourne all the vicissitudes and trials of her life with the most exemplary fortitude, but now she could no longer restrain her emotions. She burst into tears, and kissed Gerassim on both cheeks three times. He had intended to accompany her to the environs, but went no farther than the Crimea Ford, there waving his hand and making a sign of renunciation.

It was already evening but not night. In his return walk along the river Gerassim saw something moving in the mud of the bank. He approached the object and saw that it was a small black-spotted dog struggling to regain dry land, but every moment slipping and falling back into the river. One look at the unfortunate creature was enough to enlist sympathy. Gerassim picked it up, thrust it into the bosom of his coat, and strode forward again. On reaching his cabin he placed the rescued dog on his bed, covered it with his heavy smock frock, and then went for straw and milk. The poor animal was not more than three weeks old. Its eyes had only just opened, and one of them still seemed bigger than the other. Taking its head between his fingers, Gerssim pushed its nose into the milk. The dog drank eagerly, sniffing, trembling, and almost choking itself. Gerassim looked at the creature for a while, and all at once burst into a loud laugh.

He watched the animal the whole night. Never did mother care more for her child than Gerassim for this miserable dog which he had rescued from drowning. Yet, fatigued by his cares, he ended by falling asleep at its side, and his sleep was a calm and happy one. Weak at first, and not over handsome, the animal, under his fostering attention, soon grew stouter, and in eight months was transformed into a pretty dog with long ears and large expressive eyes. It was soon passionately attached to Gerassim. It never quitted its master for a moment, and was always at his heels, contentedly wagging its tail. Gerassim gave it the name of "Miti," which was extended by those who like the animal to "Mitinia" – a diminutive of affection. Miti however loved only Gerassim, and Gerassim returned its affection with interest. So fond was he of it that he did not like others to caress his favourite. It awoke him every morning by tugging at his blanket, it led his horse by the reins, followed him to the river, mounted guard over his besoms and shovels, and allowed no one to approach his cabin without the permission of its master. For the special convenience of the dog, Gerassim cut an aperture in the door of the cabin through which it could go out and in. Miti scarcely slept a wink at night, but never barked without cause, as is the fashion of crazy old watch-dogs. True there was another dog in the yard in addition to Miti. Its name was Volchok. But it was kept chained and was not released from its kennel even at night. It was too old and demented to sigh much after liberty – only from time to time did it emit a hoarse sound, somewhere between a bark and a growl, desisting however immediately, under the consciousness, no doubt, that its protestations and warnings were without the slightest avail. Miti never entered the house, and when Gerassim carried wood thither, it always remained at the door, awaiting his return with impatience, listening attentively and turning its head to right and left at the least noise.

When another year had passed in this manner, Gerassim was still to be found at his duty, and seemed, on the whole, to be quite satisfied with his lot. All at once, however, something occurred to disturb the peaceful current of events. One day the lady took a stroll with several of her guests. She was in a very good humour, though her companions did not relish her gaiety over much, simply because it never lasted long, and was always followed by a period of gloom and bad temper. To-day she was particularly pleased, for the cards – which she was in the habit of consulting every morning – had disclosed four knaves in sequence – a sign that all her desires were to be accomplished. She liked the tea, and to the servant who had prepared it she tendered, not only complimentary observations, but a coin of the value of ten copeks.[10] With a smile playing about her withered lips, the lady passed through her parlour to the open window. It was summer, the air was fresh, and right in front of the house there was a blossoming flower-garden. But beneath a rose bush in the finest of beds, the lady's eye caught a strange object. It was Miti, busy with a bone.

"Heavens!" she screamed all at once, "whose dog is that?"

The domestic addressed hardly knew what to reply, feeling the hesitation always seen in menials when they do not know what action or remark will best suit their superiors.

"I really cannot say," the woman at last replied. "I believe it is Gerassim's dog."

"Dear me! It seems a pretty little thing; let it be brought in. Has he had it long? Why have I never seen it before?"

To Stepan, an active fellow, employed in various duties about the house, was delegated the task of bringing in the dog. But when he was on the point of seizing it, Miti adroitly evaded his grasp and ran to Gerassim, who was at the moment cleaning a barrel, which he turned about with as much facility as if it had been a toy drum. Stepan pursued, but all his activity was no match for the agility of the fugitive. At last he had to explain to Gerassim by signs that the dog was wanted in the house by madame herself. Gerassim, though visibly surprised, called his dog, took it in his arms, and then handed it to the servant. Miti trembled much in the presence of the lady, and would have escaped by the door of the apartment had not some one been stationed there to prevent its exit.

"Miti Miti, come to your mistress. Don't be afraid, you silly little creature?"

But Miti did not move an inch except to look anxiously all round for a means of escape.

Stepan brought in a dish of milk, but this temptation was insufficient – Miti would not so much as smell the food.

"Why, you silly creature!" ejaculated madame, approaching the dog, and bending as if to caress it. At this moment the dog emitted a low growl.

Frightened, the lady drew away her hand. Miti gave utterance to a low cry, as if appealing for mercy. But the lady frowned, and leaving the room, returned to her cabinet. This she was followed by several women. "Dear me, has it bitten you?" "My goodness! Whoever heard of such a thing?"

"Take it away!" commanded madame, her voice completely changed, and all her good humour gone.

Stepan seized the animal and threw it out of doors, where it fell at the feet of Gerassim.

Half-an-hour after this event, there was a deep silence throughout the building. The old lady sat on her sofa, gloom and anger depicted in her countenance. The whole day she spoke to no one, refused to have her usual game of cards, and spent an unusually bad night. The next day Gavrilo was summoned into her presence a full hour earlier than usual.

"Tell me," she demanded, "what dog that is in the yard – the animal that barks all night and prevents me from sleeping a wink."

"Dog! what dog? let me see – perhaps it's Gerassim's dog her ladyship means," gently suggested Gavrilo.

"I don't know whose dog it is, but I know that it deprives me of rest. And what do we need with so many curs here? Have we not a yard-dog of our own?"

"Of course – there is Volchok."

"Well then, of what use is a second? It merely makes work and creates disorder. And all because there is no master to look after these things! Besides, why should Gerassim have a dog? Who gave him permission to keep one in my yard? It must be sent away – do you hear?"

"Very well, your ladyship – your orders shall be obeyed."

"There must be no delay, remember. And now you may go."

Gavrilo dutifully transmitted the order to Stepan. Five minutes later Gerassim came up, carrying an immense bundle of wood, and closely followed by his inseparable Miti. While Gerassim entered, the dog, as was its habit, remained behind. As it stood at the door listening, Stepan pounced upon it, and this time the dog did not escape him. Mounting the first cart which passed by, he took Miti to the market and there sold it for fifty copeks on consideration of the dog being kept fastened up for a full week. Stepan did not return through the gate: he got into the yard by jumping a hedge, for he feared to meet Gerassim. But he was fearful without cause, for Gerassim was not in the yard at all. The moment he emerged from the house he missed his dog. He looked for it in all directions. He sought it in the cabin, in the hay-loft, and in the street, but found it nowhere. Lost! Then, overwhelmed with despair, he addressed himself to the domestics, telling them by means and signs that he had lost something half an arshin high – he held his hand at the distance from the ground, and then drew in the air with his finger the shape of the missing animal. Some of them answered with perfect truth that they knew nothing whatever of the dog – others knew what had happened and treated him with derision. The steward was too much occupied in looking after the coachmen to pay any attention to Gerassim's voiceless complaints. At last Gerassim left the yard. When he came back the night had grown cold. His weary countenance, unsteady gait, and dusty clothes, all showed that he had traversed half the streets of Moscow. The next morning the inquisitive stable-boy could assure his companions that Gerassim had spent the night in sighing and groaning. The whole of the next day Gerassim kept indoors, and the coachman had to take his place as water-carrier. The morning after Gerassim was again at his work. He also presented himself at dinner, but ate in silence, and did not make the slightest bow to anyone. His face, although it had always worn an inanimate expression, now seemed turned to stone. At night, the sky being serene, and the moon shining brightly, Gerassim might have been seen lying in the hay-loft. From time to time he fetched a deep sigh, and every now and then turned from side to side. All at once he felt something tugging at his coat. A fit of trembling seized him, and for some moments he dared neither to raise his head nor to open his eyes. But when the pull came a second time, and now with two-fold vigour, he sprang up and saw – Miti, with the fragment of a rope still clinging to its neck. Gerassim uttered a low moan of pleasure. He hastily clutched his dog, covering it with kisses, and the dumb creature replied by licking its master's nose, eyes, whiskers, and beard.

Gerassim having been informed by the domestics that the animal had bitten their mistress, he resolved to keep Miti in the cabin during the day, to visit it there from time to time, and only to allow it out at night. The aperture in the door he stopped up with his old coat, and at day-break presented himself in the yard as if nothing had occurred. Poor Gerassim never imagined the dog was capable of betraying itself. Yet sooner than he had bargained for, everybody knew of the animal's return.

Gerassim, nevertheless, laboured lustily the whole of the day. He cleaned out the yard, weeded the flower beds, and renewed the hedge stakes – did so much work in fact, that he drew upon himself the notice, if not the praise of his mistress.

It was midnight when he sallied forth for a walk with Miti. As they were passing a hut on the road a rustling sound became audible. Miti, pricking up his ears, barked vigorously for some seconds.

Gerassim's mistress, who had not long before fallen asleep after a nervous attack, was aroused by the barking of the dog.

"Help, help!" she screamed, stretching out her arms in distress. "That horrid dog again! Call the doctor! I see they are bent on my death." As she uttered this last exclamation her head fell back and she appeared to faint.

The physician was quickly in attendance. His knowledge of surgery did not go much farther than the feeling of the pulse, but he wore boots with India-rubber soles,[11] and prescribed for his perpetual patient nothing stronger or more bitter than cherry drops. On this occasion he made her sniff the odour of burnt feathers,[12] and on the lady opening her eyes offered her the inevitable sweet-meats. The lady swallowed them, and thus fortified began to complain of the dog, of Gavrilo, of her ill-luck, in a word, of everybody and everything.

Miti, meanwhile, had begun to bark again, Gerassim vainly endeavouring to bring it to silence.

"There again!" screamed the lady.

The physician whispered something to a domestic, the domestic ran to awaken Gavrilo, and Gavrilo, losing his head on the spot, quickly aroused the whole house.

Looking back, Gerassim saw lights moving at the windows. His heart told him there was something wrong. Hastily seizing Miti, he ran to the cabin and there shut himself in, locking the door.

A few moments later five men were knocking loudly for admittance. The bolt of the lock, however, kept them on the outside of the cabin, and when Gavrilo came up, quite breathless, he ordered the men to remain there till morning. This command given, Gavrilo went to the head housewife, Lubov Lubinovna – the domestic who was in the habit of helping him to certain perquisites of tea and sugar – with instructions to her to report to the lady that although the dog had broken loose and returned, it should be put away for good on the morrow. All this was duly done yet the tranquilising effect which followed was due, not to the head housewife, but to the doctor. He, unhappy man, instead of pouring out only twelve drops of a sedative, administered at least forty, the result being that his patient fell soundly and almost immediately asleep.

Gerassim meanwhile lay on his bed pale and agitated. The next morning the lady awoke earlier than usual. Gavrilo, who had come to ask her to assent to forcible measures for the recovery of the dog, stood awaiting a severe reprimand. But the storm had blown over.

"Lubov Lubinovna," she called, "you see what a frightful condition I am in. Go and speak with Gavrilo Andreich. Can it be possible that a nasty dog is of more value than the peace of mind, even the life of his mistress?"

Lubov Lubinovna went into Gavrilo's room. What passed there is unknown, but it is certain that soon afterwards quite a crowd of people were seen moving in the direction of Gerassim's cabin. In front of them marched Gavrilo, hat in hand, though there was not the slightest breeze stirring. At his side walked the domestics, and the rear was brought up by boys. The party found the cabin guarded by three men, two of whom were armed with sticks.

"Open the door!" commanded Gavrilo, advancing and striking the wooden structure with his fist. A suppressed barking was the only answer.

"Open, I say!" he repeated.

"You forget," remonstrated Stepan from below, "that he is deaf and cannot hear."

A loud burst of laughter followed this speech.

"What's to be done then?" asked Gavrilo.

"Don't you see – there is a hole in the door – try to do something there."

Gavrilo bent down.

"But it's stopped up with something – a coat."

"Push it in, then!"

Another half-suppressed bark.

"There! it's betraying itself again."

"No, friends," observed Gavrilo, scratching his head, "if you want the coat pushed in, why, come and do it yourself."

"Why not? make room!" Here Stepan climbed up, pushed the coat inside, and moving his stick about through the hole, called, "Come out – come out!"

As he was thus engaged, the door suddenly opened. Everybody flew down the staircase – Gavrilo first.

"Softly! Look out! Take care of yourselves!" shouted the leader of the retreat.

Gerassim meanwhile stood stock still on the threshold. The crowd ventured to draw a little nearer. Gerassim looked down upon it. He held his arms akimbo. In his red shirt he seemed a giant compared with the rest.

Gavrilo made a step forward.

"Mind what you're doing, and don't be vicious." Gavrilo then explained by signs that the dog was wanted, and must be given up.

Gerassim pointed at the animal, and drawing his hand round his own neck, looked at Gavrilo enquiringly.

"Yes!" nodded Gavrilo, "and without delay."

Gerassim then made the assembly understand that he would handle Miti himself.

"But you will probably deceive us?"

Gerassim replied to this suggestion by a scornful smile, immediately afterwards entering his cabin and slamming the door to.

"What's the meaning of that?" asked Gavrilo. "He's locked the door again."

"Let him alone, Gavrilo Andreich," enjoined Stepan. "He has promised, and he will do what he promises. I know him well."

"Yes, he is right," affirmed the assembly. "Gerassim will do what he has promised."

"We shall see," observed Gavrilo. "But we must not remove the guards. Here, Tegoshka, take a stick, sit here, and tell me when anything happens."

Tegoshka did as he was instructed, taking up his place at the lowest step of the staircase. The crowd thereupon dispersed. Gavrilo went home and sent Lubov Lubinovna to inform her ladyship of the state of affairs. On hearing the news his mistress poured some *eau de Cologne* on her handkerchief, placed the latter to her nose, drank some tea, and immediately thereupon went to sleep again.

An hour after the subsidence of the tumult the door of the cabin opened wide. Gerassim was ready. He had his Sunday coat on, and was holding Miti in a leash. He slowly descended to the steps, and made his way to the gate. He only once looked back, and did not put on his hat until he had reached the street. A little distance along the road Gerassim turned into a tavern. He was well known there, and his signs were understood by everybody. He first ordered cabbage soup, and then, leaning his head on his hand, began to ponder over the undertaking he had given. Miti stood near his chair, quietly watching him with its large, intelligent eyes. The hair on the dog's coat fairly shone, having just been combed. The soup was brought. Gerassim crumbled some bread into it, added meat cut into small pieces, and then placed the bowl on the floor. Miti, nice as usual, at first hardly touched the soup even with its nose. Gerassim meanwhile gazed long and steadily at his favourite. All at once two great tears started from his eyelids. One of them fell on Miti's forehead, the other dropped into the bowl of soup!

Gerassim buried his face in his hands. Miti ate half of the food, then withdrew from the bowl, licking its nose and mouth. Thereupon Gerassim started from his seat, paid the tavern keeper, and went out. He was followed at a distance by Tegoshka, who observed all his movements. After pausing for a while at the corner of the street, as if in hesitation, Gerassim set out with tremendous strides for the Crimean Ford. Only once did he slacken his pace. It was when he entered a yard where house-building was in progress to bring thence two bricks, with which he resumed his journey. Having reached the Crimean Ford, we went some distance along the river bank to a spot where two boats had been moored. Into one of them he jumped, accompanied by Miti. At this moment an aged peasant came out of an adjacent cabin to make gesticulations and utter incoherent noises. But Gerassim merely shook his head, and began to row away from the shore with such vigour that, in spite of the tide, which was running in the opposite direction, he was soon at a distance from the bank of three or four hundred yards.

The old peasant, to whom the boats belonged, stood for a few moments scratching his back first with his right then with his left hand, but finally limped back to his cabin.

Gerassim, meanwhile, rowed on and on. Already he had left Moscow far behind. Fields, kitchen-gardens, meadows with a hut in them here and there, began to appear. At last, fully in the country, Gerassim threw down his oar; then, bending towards Miti, who sat on one of the crosspieces (the bottom of the boat being full of water), he took the animal in his hands and kissed it. The current, meanwhile, was slowly drifting the boat back in the direction of the town. At length Gerassim raised his head erect. With a hasty, nervous movement he fastened the bricks to a piece of rope, at the other end of which he made a running noose, and attached the whole to the neck of Miti. Then, with an expression of pain and anger on his countenance, he slowly raised the animal over the side of the boat. He was gazing upon it for the last time, and he devoured it with his looks. The dog regarded its master with the most perfect confidence – so far was it from feeling afraid that it wagged its tail in token of joy.

Gerassim turned his face away, closed his eyes, relaxed the grasp of his fingers on the rope, and –

He heard nothing – neither Miti's sudden scream nor the loud splash of water. The noisiest day was as calm and quiet for him as the stillest night is to us. And when he again opened his eyes there was nothing to be seen save the tiny wavelets that chased each other as far as the shore, or broke against the sides of the boat with a gentle splash.

Tegoshka, having lost sight of Gerassim, had hurried back to relate what he had seen.

"He'll drown it," said Stepan. "You may depend upon that – once he promises anything –"

Gerassim did not come to dinner, and when supper-time came he was again absent.

"What a strange fellow Gerassim is," ejaculated a stout washer-woman. "How can he absent himself so long, and all for the sake of a dog?"

"But Gerassim has been here," suddenly observed Stepan, taking a spoonful of gruel.

"How? When?"

"Two hours ago. I met him at the gate, as he was going out again. He came in from the yard. I intended to ask him about the dog, but he was in a bad humour, for he gave me a rude push. Perhaps he merely wanted more room to get past – perhaps he took that way of showing that he wanted to be left alone. At any rate the push was so violent that –" Here Stepan smiled, rubbing the nape of his neck. "Yes," he added, "Gerassim has a heavy hand, a mighty hand, it must be confessed."

While the domestics were laughing at Stepan there might have been seen striding along the highway a giant-like figure with a bag at its back and a stick in its hand. The figure was that of Gerassim. He had hurried home, and hav-ing hastily packed in an old horse-cloth the miserable chattels that belonged to him, he at once set out for his native village, the place of his birth. He was acquainted with the road, for it was along this road he had come to Moscow. The village was twenty-five versts[13] from the highway. It was easy to find. Therefore he marched boldly forward with a resolution in which there was mingled both despair and joy. On he walked, just as eagerly and hurriedly as if he could hear his aged mother calling for her son – looking for him and awaiting him after long sojourn in foreign lands and amongst strangers. The summer night had just fallen – warm and mild. The sun had left colour in the west – to the east the sky was involved in a bluish darkness. It was from the east that night came. Hun-dreds of quails flew above and around him, and the voices of many night-birds rose on the air. But Gerassim could not hear them, nor could he hear the soft evening whispering of the trees. He was only conscious of the scent of the ripen-ing rye – he felt, too, the caresses of the welcoming breeze – the breeze that blew from his home – as it touched his face and played with his hair and beard. Far on before him ran the white road, straight as an arrow, to his native village; above him innumerable stars shone, casting light on his path. So he strode bravely and steadily and unweariedly forward, and when the red and moist rays of the rising sun fell upon him Gerassim had gone thirty-five versts from Moscow.

Two days afterwards he was at home. His first act was to offer up a prayer before the holy images. Then he set off to see the bailiff, who, though at first greatly surprised at his return, was pleased to have so powerful and industrious a worker again in his service, and all the more so because the harvest was just beginning.

Gerassim, scythe in hand, at once began working as in former days – that is to say – with such execution as gave great displeasure and offence to his more idle fellow-workers.

In Moscow a great tumult followed the discovery of Gerassim's flight. His cabin was rummaged, Gavrilo questioned, the police communicated with, but all to no purpose. Gavrilo merely shrugged his shoulders, being of opinion that the fellow had either run away or got drowned with his stupid dog. The lady fell into a passion, had a fit of weeping, and finally ordered Gerassim to be found at all costs, declaring that she had never given any orders about the killing of the dog.

News was ultimately brought to the effect that Gerassim had gone back to his native village. This reassured and tranquilised the lady somewhat. At first she desired them to bring Gerassim back to Moscow, but after consideration, intimated that she did not desire to have anything more to do with such an ungrateful fellow.

Her decision was not interfered with, for she died soon afterwards, and her heirs had too much else to think about to trouble their heads with Gerassim. In this way the dumb giant was left to himself – to his wretched life and his solitary hut. He seems as healthy and as robust as before, still does as much work as four other men, and preserves his old steadiness and gravity. But his neighbours have discovered a peculiar aversion to women – with whom he refuses all intercourse – and dogs, with which he rejects all companionship.

"Happy fellow!" reason the peasants, "not to trouble himself about women. As for a dog – of what good could one be to him? *His* yard is sure to be safe from thieves, whatever attractions it may offer!"

And this is what the peasants say about the deaf and dumb giant Gerassim!

'Bauer und Dichter', 'Eros or Erin. A Tale of an Irish Conspiracy' (1886–7)

[December 1886]

"Oh, shut up, Luttrell. We shall have a Coercion Act[1] for England presently, I hope, and if you go on in that sort of way, you'll leave these 'garish lights' for the gloomier atmosphere of Newgate or Portland."[2]

So spoke the "junior" in the office of Messrs. Atkin and Aubury, merchants, East India Avenue, to his second in command.

The "garish lights" were the green-shaded gas-burners, which threw their glow on what was just then an extremely untidy-looking office. Blotting paper and pens lay scattered about the desks, just as they had been left by the rest of the staff in the hasty exodus which always followed the departure for the day of the junior partner.

"That sort of way" bore reference to an outburst of eloquence denunciatory of the English government and all its works, which had followed Lawrence Luttrell's glance into an evening paper. It was an autumn evening, just after the passing of the Peace Preservation Act,[3] and almost every telegram from Ireland brought news of fresh arrests and acts of stringency on the part of the Irish Executive.

"Newgate or Portland," repeated Luttrell. "Well they've held many a better man than I, and will again, I dare say."

"Well, never mind politics. Let's be off. We can catch the 7.30, if you're sharp. You'd better come home with me, and forget Erin's[4] woes to the tune of Chopin's waltzes. Alice plays them awfully well."

"She does everything awfully well, I think," said the other; "but I can't possibly come to-night, though, of course, I should like to. I've got to meet a fellow."

"Not that beggar, O'Hara, I hope?" Fred Oakhill put the question with a little frown, but Luttrell made no reply – simply threw down his paper, and walked into the principal's room.

Oakhill put on his hat and coat without another word. "It *is* O'Hara," he said to himself, and presently left the office, calling out as he went, "Shall I tell them you'll be down to-morrow?"

"Thanks, yes," said Luttrell; and the office door closed with a bang behind the junior clerk.

Luttrell had been in the city four years. He had taken a clerk's place less for the salary than to learn the routine of business, for his father had died leaving him money enough to live on. He had had a University education, but had wisely determined to turn his mediocre talents in the direction of commerce, rather than add another voice to the bitter cry of the outcast Bar; to undertake the salvation of bodies under the sanction of a diploma, or of souls under that of an M.A. degree. For the Army and Navy his Nationalist principles shut him out.[5]

He had got on very well with his clerical duties, but not quite so well with his fellow-clerks. The only one of them with whom he was in the least intimate was Fred Oakhill. The difference in their age was balanced by the similarity of their tastes, and the friendship was strengthened by Luttrell's visits to Sydenham, and by an attraction which he soon found was strong enough to draw him to Lawn Villas about three times a week. Alice Oakhill was pleasantly conscious of her own magnetism, and was not displeased at its effects on her brother's friend. Indeed, on one or two occasions, when for three successive nights Fred had come home alone, her brown eyes had been clouded by a transient shadow of disappointment.

It was at Lawn Villas that Luttrell had first met Mr. O'Hara, whose growing intimacy with him was looked on with disapproval by the Oakhills in general, and Fred in particular.

There was nothing to be said against Mr. O'Hara, except that no one knew where he got his money. Mrs. Oakhill was his second cousin, and knew that he had only about £90 a year of his own. This income he managed so judiciously as to belong to some of the best clubs, to drive habitually in hansoms, to dress in the pink of fashion, and to smoke cigars at three figures the box. Skill at whist, an inspired knowledge of coming sporting events, a steady hand with a cue, and a keen eye for pigeons – Mr. O'Hara had quite enough charitable acquaintances for all these suggestions to have been hazarded over and over again; but no one really knew any more of the man than he chose to let them know.

This well-dressed social enigma was waiting for Luttrell at Purcell's. He rose and shook hands warmly, and the two sat down at one of the little square marble tables.

"Well, have you settled the morality of the question yet?" he asked.

"Yes, I think I have," said Luttrell. "I had pretty well made my mind up this morning, and if I had not, this evening's news would have done it for me. Anything is justifiable against a brigand Government like this."

"Then you'll not stop at sympathy – you'll join us?" said the other, watching him like a mesmerist, and stroking his close-cut light beard.

"I should like to know a little more about your society. Our aims are the same, and I believe your method the best and bravest in the end – but who am I going among, and what can I do? Do the parliamentary leaders recognise you?"

"They will when they are asked. The trusted politicians may be still further trusted to recognise accomplished facts, especially when those facts are convenient ones. I have trusted you pretty well for an outsider. You know enough already to send me to the 'stone jug,'[6] if you felt so disposed. If I told you more just now I should be breaking my word, and putting others besides myself in your power – not that I wouldn't trust you, for I would. I can read men as well as cipher dispatches," he added, with a laugh. And so he could.

There was a moment's silence, and then he spoke again.

"Well, do you feel disposed to come to the 'Commissioner to Administer Oaths, &c.'[7] to-night? 'This is my name and handwriting' – it's not a very solemn affair."

"Yes; I'll come now and get it done," said Luttrell rising, "but I don't know what use I shall be to you. It's simply nonsense to talk about fighting yet."

"Quite so," said O'Hara, "and I haven't talked about it, and the less we talk about anything the better. Our little *affaire* means to act, not talk. But we had better cab it; it's too far to walk."

They were in front of the Bank[8] by this time, and as they stopped to hail a passing hansom a wretched-looking outcast, all rags and misery, came shivering up, and begged a copper. Luttrell gave him a coin. With an impatient gesture O'Hara said, "Oh keep your money for your own countrymen, Mr. Luttrell! There are thousands like that on the hill-sides of Connemara. By the way," he added, when they were in the cab, "you were asking what you could do to help. Since you have loose coin to give away I can tell you of plenty of channels for it. We must feed men before they can fight. We have many rich men in our ranks, though."

"Well, of course I shall do all I can."

"Yes, I know you will. And when you know as much as I of our cause and our plans you will feel as I do, that you can never do too much. To further them is the one thing left to live for – ay, and to die for."

There was a thrill of feeling in his voice, and a flash of enthusiasm in his eyes, which were not lost upon Luttrell, who, looking at him, recalled all the harsh judgments he had heard pronounced on him, and thought how different the inner self of the man was to that outer crust which had earned O'Hara the world's unfriendly comments.

His frank eyes must have betrayed the thought, for the other said,

"Ah! our friends at Sydenham haven't a magic mirror, fortunately, so are driven to guessing as to how I spend my time. The worst of it all is that a few of us cannot work as we would like to do, but have to idle half our time away so as to be able to use the other half at all. One must keep touch with the world, high and low, and the 'high' don't care to rub shoulders with frayed coats or acknowledge bows from last season's hats."

Luttrell felt relieved, somehow, by this very natural explanation. It is an old saying, that if you throw mud enough some of it is sure to stick, and, in spite of his strong liking for O'Hara, he had not been able to shake off the remembrance of hints that he had heard.

Presently the cab stopped in a dark street leading out of the City Road. O'Hara dismissed the cabman, and walked with Luttrell some few hundred yards, in the course of which they turned several corners. At last they stopped before a house, on whose shabby door-post was a zinc plate, "J. Prawle, engraver, first floor."

On the first-floor landing O'Hara stopped, and flicked half-a-dozen times on a door with his forefinger nail. After a moment's waiting the door was opened, and someone said, "All right, O'Hara."

It wasn't J. Prawle, engraver, however, but an open-faced youth of about twenty-two, with a good deal of polished boot and new broadcloth about him. He was in evening dress, and had an expensive little spray of stephanotis[9] in his button-hole.

"I managed to come, you see," he said, when the door was closed. "Old Waring's inside, as busy as ever. I can't get a word out of him."

"Mr. Luttrell, this is one of our warmest friends, Mr. Arthur Lowrie."

The two shook hands.

The room in which they stood was littered about with dusty engraver's tools. A few half-finished plates were on the dusty mantelpiece, a large deal table fitted close against the wall under the window. The place was small and dirty and ill-cared for, and looked as if Mr. J. Prawle was not in a very thriving way of business. The inner room, to which Mr. Lowrie led the way, was smaller but cleaner, and bore no trade marks about it. It was evidently used as a counting house, if Mr. J. Prawle ever had anything to count. Its only furniture was a chair or two and a large desk, at which sat, writing busily, a man with iron grey hair and moustache, and a certain military air which was very noticeable in spite of his shabby light jacket. He finished the sentence he was writing before he looked up.

"Our secretary, Mr. Waring," said O'Hara, then – "Waring, this gentleman, Mr. Luttrell," with an introductory wave of the hand, "wants to join us. I introduce him on my own responsibility, and am ready to answer for his fidelity."

Waring rose, and extended a courteous, welcoming hand. "I am always glad to meet with a friend," he said. "We ought really all to know each other at a time like this. There must be thousands of men whom we know nothing of who would be glad to join us. Union is what we want."

Luttrell muttered a few indistinct words of assent.

"Well, to business," said O'Hara, lightly. "Where's the roll of honour?"

Waring opened a drawer, and drew out a rather large black book with a brass lock, and "J. Prawle, Diary," on it in gilt letters.

"Mr. Luttrell understands of course," he said, selecting a little key from the small bunch at the end of his watch-chain, "the nature of the promises which we expect."

"I have asked Mr. Luttrell for no promises," said O'Hara.

"Then I must ask for them. Mr. Luttrell will give us his word of honour, which we esteem more binding than an oath, that he will repeat to no one outside our circle anything that he may know now or come to know hereafter of our plans. That he will keep secret the names of members of our association and our place of meeting, and that he will do his utmost in all ways to forward our designs."

"I shall give you my word without hesitation," Luttrell bowed.

"At the same time," said Waring, "we don't want to force anyone to do anything. Every service in our cause is voluntary. Intimidation has been the curse of all previous efforts."

By this time he had unlocked the book, and Luttrell saw as he turned the pages, that a good many of them were filled with names.

"This is our London register. Our Dublin one is, of course, much fuller."

Luttrell thought this one seemed pretty full, but said nothing.

> Lawrence Luttrell.
> Arthur W. L. Lowrie.

When those names, with the date, were written on a clean page of the diary, Lawrence felt a certain sense of exultation. Now, surely, he was on the way to helping his country and her noblest sons. He felt likewise no little relief at that announcement of Waring's that he would have to do nothing he did not wish to do, for, though enthusiastic enough in the cause of Ireland, he felt no leaning towards dynamite and the knife.[10]

"That's over," said Arthur Lowrie. "Are you going my way, Mr. Luttrell? We might go together."

Their ways were the same, and they did go together, leaving Mr. Waring to resume his secretarial work. O'Hara went with them as far as the City Road, and there left them. He was going to St. Pancras, he said, *en route* for Manchester.[11]

The two young men walked towards the City; Lowrie's conversation was simply a panegyric upon the cause, the society and its members, especially O'Hara.

"He's so devoted, so hard-working, so self-sacrificing and so run down by a parcel of fools, who think they can judge of a man by knowing his tailor."

"You talk of self-sacrifice!" said Luttrell at last; "but what can one sacrifice?" He looked at his companion, and it certainly occurred to him that he, at least, seemed to have dropped self-denial before it grew inconvenient. There was a self-sacrifice, apparently, which is not incompatible with dress clothes and stephanotis.

"Your pocket," said Arthur. "Mine's pretty empty just now, but when I have money I don't spend it all on Gaiety stalls.[12] It isn't to be expected that we should all have brains like Mr. Waring Prawle; but we all have something, and if it isn't brains, it's time or money."

"But they don't seem to ask for money. I suppose one doesn't hand O'Hara odd sovereigns promiscuously."

"Oh, no, no! No money goes through O'Hara's hands but his own. The treasurer is Mr. O'Brien, and money is paid into his account at the National Bank, Dublin. None but money from members is paid into that account. You're supposed to send your name in, but I don't always," he added ingenuously, with a little blush, for which Lawrence rather liked him.

So it happened that next day £50 was paid into the Bishopsgate-street Branch of the National Bank of Ireland to the credit of Mr. James F. O'Brien, Dublin. The young man who paid it in gave no name.

While Luttrell was taking such steps for helping his country as could be taken in the limited area of Mr. J. Prawle's rooms, his friends at Sydenham were talking of him in a way that should have made his ears burn – if there be any truth in the old adage.

When Fred Oakhill's latch-key grated in the lock of the front door that evening, there was a little flutter of expectancy in the drawing-room. Mrs. Oakhill laid down her work in readiness to welcome her son, and Alice looked up from the Shelley she was reading, in her low chair by the fire.

As she leaned back carelessly, the graceful lines of her throat and head thrown into relief by the white chair back, her pretty figure in its china blue dress, her bright brown hair and mobile mouth, made the sort of picture men love to look upon.

Fred stood in the doorway, – "Well mother."

"At last!" said Alice, but her eyes seemed to be searching beyond him, in the semi-shadow.

"There's no one else, Alice," he laughed. "Luttrell could not or would not come to-night."

"How was that?" said Mrs. Oakhill.

"Well, the only excuse he vouchsafed was that he had to 'meet a fellow'; and I'm rather afraid it's O'Hara."

"Why afraid?" asked his sister, tapping with one little foot on the floor. "Do you feel yourself responsible for Mr. Luttrell's friends?"

Her mocking tone annoyed her brother a little.

"Yes I do," he said, shortly, "when the friends are met at our house, and are, moreover, relations of ours."

"Well, for my part, I can't see any harm in Mr. O'Hara."

She seemed to be taking up the cudgels out of pure contrariety.

"There's harm in spending more money than you have."

"As a matter of fact, you can't do that. You can only run into debt. Have you heard that that is among Mr. O'Hara's vices?"

"No," said Fred, "I believe he pays his way. But how does he get his money?"

"I fail to see that that is your concern, my dear boy," remarked his sister, with a little amused smile. "But if you must speculate, why not put down his means of livelihood as scribbling of anonymous magazine articles, newspaper writing, secretaryship of mission societies, or anything else respectable, instead of giving him credit for the darkest crimes because he doesn't go about labeled 'solicitor,' 'author,' 'clerk'?"

"Why, my dear Alice." Mrs. Oakhill looked over her spectacles in mild remonstrance, "it was only the other day you were saying –"

"I must have been in a bad temper," Alice interrupted. "We all say uncharitable things sometimes; but it's a terrible thing to have a domestic recording angel to make notes of them. The fact is, Fred," she went on, "you don't like Mr. O'Hara, because you are jealous if your Mr. Luttrell speaks to anyone else. You had much better get ready for dinner, and you will find that after it you will be able to feel much more kindly to your inexplicable fellow-creatures than you do now, dear."

"Confound it!" Fred said to himself in his impetuous boy's fashion; "it's all my fault. I wish they'd never met here. Old Luttrell is such an enthusiastic, hot-headed, up-in-the-cloud sort of fellow. He always believes in everyone, and there's no knowing what bad ways that brute O'Hara may get him into. And yet I don't believe Lawrence would do anything wrong."

Still, he could not get rid of that uneasy feeling that no good could come to Luttrell of this new acquaintance. He said as much at breakfast to his fair-faced sister.

"I should have thought your school training would have taught you at least one lesson, Fred," she answered – "to leave your elders to manage their own affairs. Seriously, I believe you're troubling yourself about nothing."

Though she spoke so lightly, she had been thinking about O'Hara a good deal since Fred's home-coming on the foregoing evening and had thought of Luttrell too without getting at any satisfactory explanation of the friendship which seemed to be growing up between them. She scented a secret, and felt the growth of a curiosity. She would find out all about it, somehow, she was determined. It was this resolution, perhaps, that caused her to be so bewilderingly charming when Laurence Luttrell redeemed his promise to Fred, and spent that evening at Lawn Villas. Through all the intoxication which Luttrell felt at this new, strange, graciousness of hers, he was yet able, with his national[13] adroitness, to avoid answering directly any of her half-veiled questions, and was really successful in leaving in her mind the impression that he, like so many others, had only been caught by O'Hara's knowledge of men and things, and by his conversational powers, and that there was no other bond between them.

The influence of music, of her singing, and of this new softness in her manner, combined to hurry Lawrence Luttrell over the precipice to the edge of which Alice's beauty had long since drawn him. For the first time he was sure that he loved her. When Lawrence at last said "Good-bye," and their hands met, there was a look in her eyes which was a revelation to him – a revelation of hope. She might care for him.

Full of his deep delight, he passed through the still night air, and in the crowded train he saw nothing of the Crystal Palace excursionists[14] with whom his compartment was filled. His mind was filled with those delicious rosy visions – those lovely dissolving views which love's new magic lantern can cast upon the white sheet of our consciousness. Alice, and life's possibilities in relation to her, completely occupied his mind to the exclusion of everything else. It was with the feeling of a man waking from dreams of Oriental indolence to the cold realities of the morning tub that he remembered, as he entered his room and took up John Mitchell's "History of Ireland"[15] from his table, that he was bound to-day by a tie from which he had been free the day before yesterday. He had made a solemn engagement last night, and it came upon him in a flash, that he had no right to bind himself by other obligations till he could see whither the path he had entered on would lead him.

The decision which had taken him to Mr. Prawle's, though in itself quickly made, was really only the last link of a long chain of thought which, unknown to himself, had been leading him through the past three or four years to this conclusion. All the principles of his life converged towards this point. The best parts of his character actuated him in this decision of his, and, for all his light-heartedness, enthusiasm, and spirit, he was not one to turn back from the plough when once his hand had been laid to it. He must wait.

[January 1887]

Chapter II. 'A Catastrophe.'

To wait was not easy. Nor was Luttrell a man to whom it came naturally to possess his soul in patience. But if sometimes in the months that followed he found it hard to adhere to his resolution of advancing no further on the lines which might be followed by Alice's lover, his renunciation had its compensations. Occasional visits to Mr. Prawle's, chance talks with Mr. O'Hara or with young Lowrie kept him informed of the progress of the "movement." The roll of members in all large towns was lengthening. Many old soldiers who had helped to fight England's battles abroad were now named among the ranks of her enemies at home. O'Hara's boast about the rich members had not been an idle one evidently, for a subscription-list was sent round when any money was wanted, and Luttrell was almost ashamed to add his modest mite to the list of big sums which it contained. He fretted, at first, at simple inaction, but presently began to discern a little of what the future might hold for him.

"Have you ever been in the army?" asked Waring one evening, when Luttrell had been delivering himself of a little impatient speech.

"Well, no, not in the army," said Lawrence; "but I was a Volunteer for four years. I had a commission in my university corps."

"Ah, then you'll have a chance of using your knowledge before long, perhaps, Mr. Luttrell. We shall want leaders, and we don't want to choose them all from the other side of the herring pond."[16]

He did not visit the engraver's often enough for Fred Oakhill to notice any change in his manner of life, and he continued his visits to Sydenham pretty regularly. He had determined to return as early as might be to those relations which had existed between him and Alice before that evening when her gracious hand had seemed to hold before his eyes the hope of a life's happiness. To this end he went not less often to her mother's house; and while his changed manner roused in her, first pique, then annoyance, then curiosity, then a deeper feeling, he contrived to carry out his intention. She sometimes wondered whether it had been her fancy. Had there really been anything unusual about that special evening?

While Lawrence was congratulating himself on his success, and feeling that he might rely on his own powers of self-control, an event occurred which led to their being taxed to the uttermost.

There had been an important conference at Mr. Prawle's. The small room had been quite crowded – there had been six or eight men there. Mr. Waring had announced that the police were getting particularly active, and a little extra intelligent. This meeting was called to decide whether they should change their quarters. After some confused talking, a man, in the clothes of an artisan, and with the straight-forwardness characteristic of his class, advocated a policy of boldness – said that to change their meeting place would only be to invite further suspicion, and in short enforced his views with so much vigour and persistence that he carried the meeting with him to a man.

Business being over, they dispersed one by one. Luttrell was the first to go. He was getting rather tired of this hole-and-corner, dark-lantern sort of business.

As he walked up the City Road he presently became aware of a little crowd hard by the Eagle. There was generally more than one crowd to be passed as he went home from Mr. Prawle's, and as a rule he passed them indifferently, but to-night he felt inclined to seek excitement, even in witnessing a street row. He elbowed his way through a knot of half-grown youths and street-corner loafers, and saw this:

Crouching against the wall on one knee, with his arm raised as a guard, was a boy whose white face showed not only terror but delicate health and the lines drawn by constant physical pain. From a cut in his forehead a thin stream of blood was flowing. Lawrence noticed with a thrill of added indignation the ill-formed shoulders and the crutch that lay on the pavement at the boy's feet. His eyes were fixed on the huge form of a more than half-drunken navvy,[17] whose attitude quite justified the boy's terrified expression. His brawny chest was visible through his open red shirt, his eyes were flaming with ungovernable passion, and raised in his hands was the heavy stone hammer with which he had been mending the road near by. A few cries of "Shame!" and "Bully!" seemed to be all that the crowd intended to offer in the way of expostulation or interference. They appeared to look upon the whole affair as a sort of rough joke, and upon the upraised hammer as a mere threat that was meant to be feared, not fulfilled. Luttrell, however, saw what the crowd did not see, that this giant in corduroy was either too infuriated or too drunk to care whether he stopped short of murder or not.

He saw that the time had passed by for such appeals to the navvy's humanity and shame, as were favoured by the on-lookers. He saw that there was only one thing to be done, and he did it. He dashed two men aside and went straight for the road mender; but before he could close with him the hammer had fallen, not to beat life out of the brain of the crippled boy, but to maim and mangle how own right hand, which caught to the full the descending force of it, and fell helpless and shattered to his side.

Perhaps the pain of that broken right hand added a little force and vigour to the well-planted left which landed home right under Goliath's jaw. Luttrell's Irish blood was up, and he rushed in to follow up the attack. Science and skill with one arm would probably not have proved equal to madness and strength with two arms and a hammer, but the issue was never tried. The brief, sharp action had roused the crowd from its apathy, and a score of hands were ready to drag the boy to a safer position, and to pin down his late assailant.

Then a couple of policemen, who had been busily moving on an inoffensive applewoman a half-dozen yards off, appeared on the scene, and in a few seconds order reigned temporarily in the City Road.

Luttrell turned to where the lame boy was standing, pale and trembling, leaning on his crutch and on a stick which he held in his right hand.

"Well, my young friend," said Luttrell, "you've been getting into nice company. I should advise you to choose a man of your own size next time you want a row."

"I was looking at him because he seemed so big and strong. He told me to be off, and I wouldn't, because father said he'd meet me just here, and then he knocked me down. I wish father would come. He'd thank you better than I can. The saints in heaven bless you, sorr!"

The accent was unmistakable.

"I'm Irish too," said Luttrell instantly, "and we Irishmen always stand by each other. Where do you live?"

"In Lambeth-marsh."

"Must you wait for your father? You'd better go home in a cab, I think. You look rather dazed."

"No sir, I must wait; father won't be long. But your arm, sir?"

"I'm off to have it seen to," said Luttrell, with his left hand in his pocket. "I'm awfully glad I came along. Good-bye! Get a cab if you feel worse." He put a couple of half-crowns into the boy's thin, white hand, and turning quickly, left him before he could utter a word either of thanks or of refusal, had he been so minded.

That was the explanation, then, of the arm in splints, which excited the comments and questions of his fellow-clerks at Atkin and Aubrey's next morning. He made some attempt to do just the rougher part of his work with his left hand, but the attempt was such a failure that he was fain to carry an apologetic account of it to his principals. Of course they were not to be put off with the nonchalant chaff with which his juniors had had to be contented. He gave them, however, a very modest and unembroidered version of the affair. The end of their inquiry was to send him back to the outer office with a week's holiday before him. The prospect was not a pleasant one, he thought, as he lay on the hard horsehair sofa in his lonely lodgings all through that day. In the evening, however, things were brightened considerably by the advent of Fred Oakhill.

"Poor old wounded Don Quixote,"[18] he said, seating himself by the half-hearted little fire that burned as if unwillingly in the grate. "I've come to carry you off to hospital. My mother will insist on looking after that arm of yours, and my sister thinks you must look quite interesting."

The chance of escape from a week's lonely suffering in those suburban lodgings of his was too seductive to be resisted. Luttrell and Oakhill caught the next train to Sydenham.

Perhaps Luttrell did look rather interesting as he entered Mrs. Oakhill's drawing-room, with his arm in a sling, and his face paler than usual. With his chestnut hair, his frank blue eyes, his tall, straight figure, he was certainly as good-looking a young fellow as one need wish to see.

He was a favourite of Mrs. Oakhill's, and she did her best to make this week of rest pleasant to him. It would have been delightful had it not been for the difficulty which he soon found in baffling Alice's gentle but determined curiosity about his relations to O'Hara. In sheer self-defence, he used to rush off into disquisitions on the most remote topics, and led Miss Oakhill, rather to her own amazement, into the discussion of Buddhism, or Patent Medicines, or the Sea

Serpent, not caring how far he was carried off his feet in his speculations if he could only get away from the uncertain shallows of personal matters into the deep water of generalisations.

"There have been broken heads in Ireland again, I see!" she said, one morning, looking up from the paper. "What a pity that interesting little wound of yours was not gained in a nice Land League row!" she added, a little maliciously.

"Well, it was got in an Irish row. The navvy, I hear, was a countryman of mine, and so was the other gentleman."

"How these Irish love each other!" she quoted, musingly. "I wonder how it is that Irishmen are always in every disturbance, and are generally found performing the lowest duties? They are nearly always either general servants or hodmen."[19]

"They are thought worthy to fight England's battles, and often to lead her armies[20] any way, but as for what you say, if you treat people like slaves for a few centuries, you will find that a good many of them will only be fit to do slaves' work."

"If that is so," said Alice, "is it safe to trust slaves with freedom? Granting that their condition has been brought about by oppression had we not better recognise it as an accomplished fact, and govern them accordingly?"

"If you let your sense of justice guide you, instead of your daily paper, you would not say that sort of thing."

Luttrell spoke very gravely. He had rather avoided this subject before in talking to her, though he had not found it easy to seal his lips; but now he could keep silence no longer, and in five minutes Miss Oakhill knew more Irish history than all her school books had taught her. He told her of the gallant struggle his countrymen had so often made against overwhelming numbers; of the cruel persecution to which they had been subjected because they remained true to an old faith while their conquerors adopted a new one; how, when Ireland was in the bitterest pangs of famine, and women and children were dying of starvation by the roadside, butter, eggs, milk, and other supports of life were being exported to England to pay the rent of absentee landlords. Then he told her of the cruel evictions which were going on at that very moment, and how sick women were being driven from their homes by the bayonets of police. Told by Irish lips, from an Irish standpoint, the case of Ireland was a revelation to an English girl, brought up in an atmosphere of middle-class Conservatism.[21]

Her eyes flashed with a reflected enthusiasm while he was speaking, but she had a fine Philistine contempt for easy conversions, and it was perhaps a reaction from the sympathetic interest with which she had listened that made her say rather lightly, "Well, I daresay there are two sides to the question. Of course it's very absurd; but, do you know, I should like Ireland much better if your friend, Mr. O'Hara, were not an Irishman."

This sudden and unexpected thrust caught Luttrell off his guard.

"O'Hara!" he cried; "he's one of the best fellows going. If all Irishmen were like him, your morning paper would be rather different reading."

"So," said Miss Oakhill, with treacherous quiet, and the feeling of having distinctly scored, "Mr. O'Hara is one of your 'patriots,' is he?"

Luttrell could have bitten his tongue out for that phrase of indiscreet laudation.

"Don't you think he is?" he said.

"He does not pose in that character, you know," said Miss Oakhill demurely. "He probably has a better reason than I can guess at for keeping that side of himself out of view."

"Since he has reasons I can't guess at for keeping his political views in the shade, I am too much his friend to wish to speak of them. If I had known that he kept his opinions secret I would not have spoken of them – even in his defence and to you."

This Alice rightly interpreted as an implied request that O'Hara's sympathies, and what she had just learned of them, should go no further than herself, and, though she was annoyed at this sudden check, she could not help admiring the adroitness with which Luttrell protected his heedless admission from being turned to greater advantage, and himself from the fire of further questionings.

"Let us dismiss Mr. O'Hara, then, since he is too mysterious to be even talked about," she said; and, as a relief to the awkward little pause which ensued, she rang for afternoon tea.

But Mr. O'Hara was not so easily dismissed, for the tea was hardly in train before he was announced *in propria persona*.[22]

His arrival put an end to their *tête-à-tête*, one of the many which were so pleasant to Luttrell, and so dangerous to his resolution.

"I have been making some duty calls at Forest Hill," he said, "and could not resist the temptation of coming to beg for a cup of tea."

"Mamma is out," said Kate,[23] more amiably than she usually spoke to him, – perhaps because she had been criticising him rather adversely; "you'll stay and have dinner with us, won't you? I'm sure mamma will be please to see you."

Mr. O'Hara did not accept this invitation – he had to return to town almost at once, he said; but, as he sat there talking small nothings and sipping his tea, he did not seem to be quite as much at ease as his friends were wont to consider him. There was an indefinable something in his manner which made Luttrell uneasy – though Kate did not seem to notice it – and his uneasiness led him to say, when after half-an-hour's purposeless talk O'Hara rose to go, "I had forgotten. I want to send off an important telegram this afternoon, Miss Oakhill; so I will take this opportunity of making my journey to the station in good company."

"How fortunate you remembered your telegram at all! These very important things are always being forgotten."

O'Hara treated her to a rather pretty compliment, whose only effect was to make her wish to box his ears, and to make Luttrell wish he had been quick-witted enough to say it himself.

When they had turned out of the garden gate, O'Hara said, taking the other's arm, "I'm glad you offered to come with me, Luttrell. If you had not I should have had to ask you right out to do so. I came down purposely to see you, and on devilish unpleasant business. My 'duty call' was at your diggings, and your landlady told me where you were. There's the deuce and all to pay up at Prawle's."

"What's wrong?" asked Luttrell, with a sudden tightening at the heart, and feeling that something was very wrong indeed.

"This time to-morrow we may all be in Newgate.[24] We are having a council of the few members who can be got together at a moment's notice. You must come up to town with me."

After a little consideration Luttrell dispatched the porter with a humbly apologetic note to Mrs. Oakhill, and as the next up train whirled them along O'Hara gave him the details of a catastrophe which had never been contem-plated by anyone, and the seriousness of whose consequences could not well be over-estimated.

It seemed that Waring had, contrary to his custom, left the diary of J. Prawle's which contained the rules of the society and names of members, together with subscription lists and other important papers, in the "engraver's" office for an hour or two while he went West on unexpected business; that in his absence the room had been opened with a skeleton key; and this damnatory evidence had fallen into the hands of one who was high up in the detective force.

"At present," said O'Hara significantly, "he alone knows what that book con-tains; and he alone will know it up to twelve o'clock to-morrow. It is for us to decide what we are to do."

"Where are we going now?" asked Lawrence.

"To Lambeth – to John Delaney's. He's a thoroughly trustworthy man, and has done us splendid service among the working-classes in London. Of course, we mustn't go near Prawle's."

Not another word was said, but the seriousness of the situation came home to Luttrell with terrible force. Brought face to face with the darker realities of intrigue, he felt inclined to curse that first step of his, which had risked so much to win what seemed about to turn out so little.

When they reached Lambeth, Luttrell recognised in John Delaney the artisan whose speech and manner had impressed him at a former meeting. He received them at the door, and led them into a room in which sat Lowrie and Waring.

A few terse words from Waring put the whole situation before them. There was little more to tell than Luttrell already knew, save this, that the detective had named his price, and that price was a high one – £5,000, for which sum, paid down before twelve to-morrow, he would give back the book and papers; unpaid, every prominent member would be imprisoned.

"The position is a desperate one," ended Waring, "and yet not so bad as it looks. If the money is paid we shall have a clever detective in our power, and that is worth £5,000. As I myself am most to blame in this matter, I am willing to give all I have, which is £500. Mr. O'Hara and Mr. Lowrie will make up £1,500 – but still £3,000 remains."

"I will do my share," said Luttrell; "but considering the number of members, Mr. Lowrie and Mr. O'Hara appear to be rather heavily taxed. The treasurer ought to be able to meet this without dropping down so heavily on so very few of our London members."

"When you know as much of this sort of thing as I do, Mr. Luttrell, you'll see that treasuries like ours are always empty. Hungry friends and powerful foes, are not compatible with large balances. However, we want to divide the burden as much as possible, and that is really what we want you to help us in. There are three rich members to whom you must go to-night. Tell them all this, and ask them for help. We had rather you went, because you are not known to anyone much in connection with Prawle's, as you have not been one of us very long. You must bring back their answers to us here to-night. It is certainly serious, but we can see daylight still."

"There is another way we might take," said John Delaney. "We might bolt. But, then, though that would save us, the few who can be warned in time, 'twould ruin 'the cause,' and sacrifice the rest of us, and it's not that we'd be doing, eh?"

There was an assenting murmur as he looked round for approval. When Luttrell had received the addresses of the members, he started at once on his errand. Lowrie, as he had often done before, went a little way with him. As they passed a lamp, Luttrell was struck with the hopeless expression on the young man's face.

"It's devilish hard," Lowrie said suddenly. "I've done all I can, and I've had to borrow to do that. I'm cleaned out, and upon my soul I don't believe I care a hang whether I go to prison or not. There's nothing before me now that's much brighter to look forward to."

"Oh, come," said Luttrell, cheerily, "matters aren't so bad. These fellows may do the handsome, and then you'll come off easier; besides, we're bound to help each other."

He shook hands heartily with Lowrie, and started on his quest. The first member was very ill – no one could see or speak to him. With a sigh of vexation, Luttrell gave the cabman the second address.

"Mr. Brightside was out of town; would not be back for several days. Address not known."

The last address was in Curzon-street – Mr. Graytern? Why, did he not know? Mr. Graytern was dead – had been run over two days ago.

Sick at heart, Lawrence Luttrell considered. It was twelve o'clock – too late to go to any other members, if any were available. It was not only the terrible calamity which threatened the organisation which was maddening him – he was not too heroic to feel his own personal danger very acutely. There was still the resource of flight. True. But flight seemed nearly as hateful as prison – quite as disgraceful – and would probably be as fatal to his chances of happiness.

He walked to the little house in Lambeth, and told the men who waited for him how his mission had failed.

"Yes," answered Waring; "of course, want of time is the difficulty. In a week we could raise twice the sum, but it must be raised at once. Mr. Luttrell, some day your country will thank you for this. I feel assured we shall not need to accept more than a few hundred as a gift either from you or Mr. Lowrie."

Next morning Luttrell paid a visit to his broker, and the result was an advance from him of £3,000, which was handed over to Waring in the presence of Lowrie, O'Hara, and John Delaney.

This was the second sacrifice which Lawrence Luttrell made, and which was rendered inevitable to him by the web of conspiracy into which he had been drawn.

He had given various sums before from his capital, and he had now no income but his salary from Atkin and Aubury.

Parting with a large sum of money, and seeing it disappear as if by magic, is always attended by an extremely unpleasant sensation. The woman who spends half a year's income in one morning's shopping, and has her purchases sent home at once, has the satisfaction of realising her capital in a form which appeals to her senses: but the old lady who has just invested her whole in Consols[25] goes home rather uneasy, rather desolate, feeling that the strip of paper, some seven inches square, is a poor substitute for the crisp bank-notes and glittering gold which appealed so tellingly to the eye and hand. A strong distaste for this empty feeling, is the secret which lies at the bottom of every miser's heart, and to men thus constituted the difference between money in hand and money at the bank is the difference between a Greuze[26] in their back drawing-room and a Greuze at the National Gallery.

Lawrence Luttrell was not a man of this type, but he experienced, to a certain extent, the uneasy feeling I have mentioned, and it was with some relief that he opened a letter in Waring's handwriting, a few days after that operation of his on the Stock Exchange. It was very short and business-like. It told him that there would be no more meetings at present; that, though matters were all right in a certain quarter, there were other directions from which interference was to be feared, therefore they had better not be seen more together than was absolutely necessary; and that the matter of the £3,000 would be settled as soon as it was safe to call a meeting again. All this was very craftily worded, and would have conveyed no idea of the real state of things to any third person.

[February 1887]

Chapter III. 'Confessions.'

It was meant to be a reassuring letter, but it somehow failed in its effect. Lawrence Luttrell began to feel grave doubts as to whether he would not be called upon to bear more than his share of his country's burdens. He knew O'Hara and Waring would stop short at no sacrifice themselves, and it was not unnatural to suppose that they would credit him with the same sort of whole-souled devotion, and would not make any very strenuous efforts to restore to him what he had advanced. And yet Waring had spoken with certainty about the repayment when he borrowed it. And now he seemed to think less of repayment than he had done, whereas Luttrell thought more of it than when the money had been lent. He had now had time to realise what it would mean to him to lose his capital. It was not so much the reduction of his income by something like £200 a year: but the postponement – almost indefinitely – of his chances of being his own master. Without this £3,000 of his he would be simply on a level with any of the thousand clerks who jostled elbows with him daily in the City – his chances of success about equal to theirs.

It was said of the soldiers in Napoleon's army that each one carried a marchal's bâton[27] in his knapsack, and we have been informed *ad nauseam* as to the grand possibilities which lie before young men who come over London Bridge with a half-crown in their pockets. But Luttrell recognised as well as you or I would the fallacy that underlies the saying that "any man" one should read "some few men." He knew that the chances of success for any one man were about as ten thousand to one, and he had a desponding conviction that he was exceedingly unlikely to be anything more than one of the unsuccessful ten thousand.

He took an afternoon train to town, therefore, and after a search, which for some time was fruitless, through some half-dozen of O'Hara's favourite haunts, he came upon him at last at a comfortable little club in St. James's Street. The patriot was "helping the nation's cause" by defeating the hated Saxon at pool. A very faint shade of annoyance crossed his face when Luttrell entered.

"It was rather unwise of you to come here, Luttrell," he said, in a low voice. "I suppose Prawle wrote to you as he did to me?"

"Yes," said Lawrence; "but I want to speak to you very particularly."

"All right. We'd best not be seen much about together. Say your say here; no one will hear you with this devil of a row," answered O'Hara, with his eye on the balls, and chalking his cue.

"I don't want to say much, O'Hara, but have *you* any idea what my chances are of seeing that three thousand again? I know these sort of things don't affect you much, but it's serious for me – more serious than it would have been a short time ago."

"I've no doubt you'll soon have it again all right; but even if it should not be found possible to repay you, surely you don't think the price too long to pay for your liberty?"

Something in the tone of this speech displeased Lawrence, and confirmed that latent suspicion of his that now the emergency had been met, and the danger warded off, the society, as represented by its executive, would not exert itself overmuch to repay what had been borrowed.

"For *our* liberty," said Lawrence; "but there were a few names in that book beside yours and mine, O'Hara. By the way, I saw in the *Morning Post* that Mr. Brightside is in town again."

"Indeed!" said O'Hara, making a rather neat stroke which took one of his opponents' lives, and put another in danger.

"Well!" said Luttrell, a little bit exasperated by his *sang-froid*. "I think I'm sufficiently in it to take upon myself to try again to carry out the mission on which you and Waring sent me last Tuesday."

"I think you'd better do nothing of the sort!" said O'Hara, with a little more hurry than was usually in his voice. "If he's back in town, of course, Waring will see to it in a day or two. It would come better from him than from you, under the circumstances."

"I'm not quite so sure of that. The reasons which existed last week for my going are just as strong now, I imagine."

"Well, please yourself!" said O'Hara, calmly; "only I think you ought to give Waring notice. It would mix things if you and he both applied."

"I'll write," said Lawrence. "I suppose this address will find him," and he drew out Waring's epistle.

"My dear fellow, don't carry letters about with you in that reckless way. What a fine conspirator you would make! Suppose you were run over? Yes, that address will find him after to-morrow. He returns from Manchester then. By the way, how's the fair Kate?" he added, with a careless turning of the subject, which irritated Luttrell to such a degree that he promptly remembered an appointment, and left the club, without answering that "by-the-way" question.

The game of pool being ended to Mr. O'Hara's entire satisfaction, he strolled a little way down St. James's Street, and presently, hailing a passing hansom, was driven swiftly to Lambeth.

* * *

Luncheon was just over at Lawn Villa the next day, Mrs. Oakhill was settling down with her knitting for an afternoon of half industry, half siesta. Kate had arranged her drawing materials and was beginning to wash in the first tints of a study of snowdrops and ivy leaves, and Lawrence Luttrell was reading aloud one of the "Songs before Sunrise."[28] He had written to Waring, and having done one thing, and decided to do more, he felt less restless and more disposed to give himself up to the quiet pleasure of the moment.

Suddenly his voice faltered, he lost his place, and recovered himself with difficulty, for a chance glance out of the window had shown him John Delaney coming up the path to the house.

In another minute or two a servant, who looked respectfully puzzled announced that a man had called to see Mr. Luttrell.

"He's in the hall, sir," she added, dubiously.

"May I see him in the morning-room?" asked Luttrell of his hostess; and in the morning-room he did see him.

"Well, Delaney," he said, when the door was shut; "what's wrong? Another book lost? It's no use coming to me."

"No," said Delaney, looking straight before him; "it ain't another book. It's something as concerns yourself sir."

"Well, out with it! What is it?"

"It's just this: there'll be a warrant out against you to-morrow, or even to-night, maybe."

"A warrant? Then all that money's gone for nothing."

"Not exactly. It is that man that this warning comes from. One of our new men has peached.[29] He only knew about half-a-dozen members – amongst them yourself and Mr. O'Hara, and all he has named are wanted."

"Well, if none of us turn Queen's evidence I suppose it's all right. He can prove nothing."

"That's as may be," said Delaney, quietly. "Mr. O'Hara doesn't agree with ye. He's off to-night. And I've been sent here to warn you and to help you off, if you want to follow his example. They know where you are, that's very certain. If you choose you can come with me. You'll be out of their way at my little place – for to-night, at least."

Luttrell thought hard for what seemed a long time to John Delaney. Suppose he faced it out. There did not seem to be a very strong case in their favour, since O'Hara himself – the hopeful, confident O'Hara – saw no resource but flight. Would Kate ever speak again to a man who had been in prison? Kate with her English ideas, her English pride. In another country he might win a fair position yet; and some day, when this affair had blown over, might return, and –. In any case, he could not now ask for Kate's love, and it would not seem further off if he were earning an honest living in America than if he were eating his heart out in

Portland. Not so far – not nearly so far. There must be something deadly serious, he kept saying to himself, or O'Hara would never have gone.

"Well, Delaney, I'll accept your offer," he said, with one of his quick decisions. "Shall I come with you now?"

"Not for worlds, sir," answered his countryman. "I want to help you all I can, but I don't want to get myself into the same boat, thank you. Come any time you like after dark. If you take my advice, you'll not go back to your own lodgings first. You can write your friends to see after your things."

When Luttrell had shewn out his unwelcome visitor, he went to Mrs. Oakhill and told her that he was called away on business, and must leave immediately after dinner. His apologies and regrets were so evidently sincere that Mrs. Oakhill said nothing to add to the vexation which her guest seemed to feel, and it was left for Kate to question him point-blank as to the reason of his departure.

She came into the drawing-room half-an-hour before dinner. Mrs. Oakhill was, presumably, dressing for it, and there was no one in the room but Lawrence. He rose as she came in. She crossed the room and stood beside the fire, leaning one arm on the mantelpiece, without speaking. Her rounded cheeks looked pale against her dark, soft, evening dress.

Suddenly she raised her eyes to his and said, "Shall you be long away?"

"I am never coming back," he answered curtly.

Some of the feathers from the screen[30] she was holding in her nervous fingers fell on the rug at her feet.

"I don't understand," she said slowly.

"I hardly understand it myself. I have lost all my money and risked my liberty, but I have done nothing disgraceful. You'll believe that, whatever you may hear, won't you, Kate?"

He could not have called her Miss Oakhill at that moment to save his life. She did not seem to notice this use of her name.

"It's Mr. O'Hara's fault," she answered: "I'm certain of it. I always knew no good could come to you from him, but I never thought –"

"It's not O'Hara's fault at all," said Luttrell. "It's as hard for him as it is for me. Not quite as hard," he added, in a lower tone.

She looked up inquiringly. That look settled it. Luttrell's self-control, which had borne so many strains, broke down.

"O'Hara doesn't love you," he said, abruptly, "and I do – with all my miserable soul."

Kate's screen dropped to the ground.

"But you don't trust me?"

"I can't tell you more. I have told you too much already. I never meant to trouble you at all with my worries. Please forget what I have said, Miss Oakhill, and forgive me for having been so wanting to myself. In my position I have no right …"

Approaching steps stopped the sentence, and Kate had only time to say, "Write to me," when Fred entered, full of inquiries and suggestions, and no other word was possible between them than the merest commonplace, from which Luttrell felt even the dreaded good-bye to be a relief.

At the gate he turned to take one more look at the house and it seemed to him that the lighted hall, with those three faces framed in the door looking out to see him depart, was the last glimpse he would have of the old world of light and life and hope from which he was drifting away so quickly.

The new world into which he was passing seemed dark and cheerless enough as he knocked at the door of John Delaney's little house in Lambeth-marsh. The street was very dark, and the night was rainy and wretched.

"Come in," said a voice, as the door was opened – a voice which was not Delaney's, which yet seemed somehow familiar to Lawrence Luttrell.

He followed the voice to a little room, very neat and very comfortable. A bright fire burned in the grate, and warm curtains were drawn across the window. A parrot in a cage croaked a greeting as he came in. There was a lamp on the red-covered table, on one end of which a white cloth was laid. He had hardly taken in these details before his familiarity with the voice that had welcomed him was explained. His left hand was caught and held fast, in an ecstasy of grateful recognition, by the lame boy for whose sake he had incurred the injury which still kept his right hand in splints.

"O, my friend!" he said; "we've met again, then. Do you belong here?"

"John Delaney's me father, sir. He's often wished to thank him as saved me life but he or I little thought it was you, as was a friend of his already, as had gone out of your way to do me a good turn."

"Ah well," said Lawrence, "it's your father's time now to do me a good turn. By the way where is he?"

"He told me to tell you he may not be back till the morning, but that it's all right, and will you make yourself comfortable, and consider you're a hearty welcome here, and so say I, sir," ended Delaney, junior, at last relinquishing his hand; "so please sit down, and I'll get you some tea."

From his comfortable arm-chair Lawrence watched the mis-shapen figure moving about, deftly preparing the meal. When it was ready Lawrence drank three or four cups of tea, the boy waiting on him assiduously.

"Father said you'd better get as much sleep as possible, sir," he said at last; "you may have to be up early in the morning."

Lawrence was glad of the opportunity of being alone, so he obeyed orders, and flung himself upon the bed to which Brian Delaney led him – though not with any idea that he should sleep. In this, however, he was mistaken, and when Brian peeped in at the door an hour later he found his father's guest sleeping heavily.

When Delaney came home about three o'clock Brian was sitting up for him, full of excitement at the fact that they had under their roof no less a person than the hero of that City Road adventure. Delaney said little, listened patiently to his boy's raptures, and after half an hour of them dismissed him to bed, with a good-night whose tenderness was more like that of a mother than an ordinary father. Then he sat long staring gloomily into the dying fire.

Lawrence did not know how long he had been sleeping when he was roused by a hand laid on his shoulder. He shook the hand off and struggled into a sitting position, to find John Delaney standing by his bedside,

"Get up, Mr. Luttrell," he was saying. "I have something to tell you that won't keep no longer."

"What the devil's up now?" said poor Luttrell, sleepily. "Another surprise?"

"Yes. This will be the last though. What I have to say concerns more than us two, and before I say it I want you to swear that you'll not use what I am going to tell you against any of the people concerned."

"Curse all these mysteries! I've made promises enough already."

"The others have been in the interest of other people. This promise is in your own, sir; that's all."

"I suppose it doesn't matter much now – so fire away! I'll promise."

Prepared as Luttrell was for surprises, he was utterly unprepared for the disclosure which followed.

It was so strange that he hardly knew whether he was dreaming or waking, as he sat there in the light of the one tallow candle. Could all this be really true? He was told that from the night he had joined O'Hara's "society" to that moment he had been the victim of a well-organised swindle; that there was no monster society – only a few sharp adventurers and a few dozen dupes. That Delaney himself, though now sharing the profits of this villainy, had in the first instance been trapped in much the same way as his hearer. That the £3,000 they had got from him was the supreme achievement of the "Long Firm," and that the story which he had heard yesterday at Mrs. Oakhill's was a fabrication based merely on the fears of the conspirators that the game would soon be up, and their determination to get him out of the country forthwith. That Delaney himself had been made use of as a tool to work on the humbler victims, while Mr. Lowrie, besides being a dupe himself, had been skillfully used as a decoy for a nobler game.

"You're a double traitor, then," said Luttrell contemptuously,

"Perhaps I am, sir," said the man; "but I should have been worse than that if I had gone on any longer with this thing, after what I heard last night.

"When you saved my boy's life you saved the only thing that makes my life worth having, and for that I owe you a good deal more than this secret – more than I shall ever pay. I only got £500 as my share; but that you shall have back, sir. You see he's all I have, sir. His mother died years ago, and, him being weak and crooked, I've got to making a deal of him: and after I'd lost my little savings and my good place through these clever ones, there seemed to be nothing left but to take up with their ways, and so keep the lad in comfort. I've fell into it a bit at a time, but it was for his sake mainly."

"But if this is all true, how about those men I went to see? Are they swindlers, too?"

Delaney laughed a short mirthless laugh.

"Lord bless you!" he said, "that was Mr. O'Hara's little bit. He is an artful one; he knows his way about. Why, they knew before ever they sent you that you'd not see these men, and they knew the reasons. They're no more members than my poll parrot. It was your saying you'd go to Mr. Brightside that frightened them and sent Mr. O'Hara to me and me to you at Sydenham."

"And you expect me to let these fellows off – to meet O'Hara as though I knew nothing about it! What do you think I'm made of?"

"You won't have to meet Mr. O'Hara nor Mr. Waring either, I'm thinking. I shall go to them this morning, and tell them that you know. If they like to stop, and face you afterwards, I'm not to blame; but if I know the men, they won't."

"And I must tell Lowrie if, as you say, he's innocent of all this."

"You can tell Mr. Lowrie if you like, but on the same conditions, that you give these men time to get away."

"Are you going with them?"

"No," said Delaney, "I shall stay on here, and try to get back into work again; but I dare say I sha'n't get on. Rogues don't often turn into honest men."

"Oh, well, you don't seem to be all rogue, Delaney. And you've done me a kinder turn than you think. Perhaps I may be able to help you to keep in straighter paths, and I hope you will, for the sake of the lad."

Luttrell did help him, being a man of his word, and Delaney's good resolutions bore more fruit than such plants usually do.

Before the family at Sydenham had sat down to breakfast, they were electrified by the entrance of Lawrence with a brighter face than he had worn for the last four months. The change of business plans was easily explained to Mrs. Oakhill, but to Kate the story wanted a little more telling, and the effect of that tale was to bring about a state of things which leaves little doubt in the mind of any of his friends as to the ultimate fulfillment of Lawrence's dreams – only that fulfillment is a little further off than it would have been had Lawrence never been introduced to Mr. J. Prawle, engraver.

Does anyone feel an interest in the fortunes of Ocatvius O'Hara? Wherever he may be, such talents as his are not likely to be hidden in a napkin.

Fabian Bland, 'Blood' (1886)

Roland Ker and I had been friends all our lives. We were together at the Shepherds Bush Young Gentlemen's Preparatory School, together at Rossall, together at Guy's.[1] It was no small grief to me when he started for Leipzig, while I was obliged to go the weary rounds of an assistant in a large and poor practice. At Leipzig he met an American doctor, who persuaded him to cross the herring-pond in search of money and experience, and so it was that we completely lost sight of each other, though we continued to correspond with regularity. Young men do not write to each other detailed accounts of their smaller adventures, and I knew very little of my friend's life, save that he had been fairly successful and had married soon after he had reached the United States. This did not surprise me. Ker was always an inflammable young dog, just the man one would expect to see married in a hurry. But what did rather astonish me was that he should, on his marriage, have given up medicine, and have retired with his bride to a remote village "down East." Medicine and pleasure had been the twin deities of Ker's devotion, and in leaving the beaten tracks of life he necessarily gave up his chances of much practice of the one, or much pursuit of the other. I could only conclude that his love for his wife must be of a more lasting nature than his passions had usually been, and that he felt her society to be a compensation for all that he had foregone.

I had not seen Ker for seven years, when a certain uncle of mine died. He had made an immense fortune by a patent pill warranted to cure gout, and on the strength of this lived so well that in his fiftieth year he succumbed to an attack of that malady. I don't know if he ever tried his own patent; it is more than probable that he did not. I had always expressed the warmest belief in the pill, and had always returned him at least a tithe of his tips in cigar-cases, fusee[2] boxes, and the like, so he naturally looked upon me as a young man with sound ideas of the subject of expenditure, and left me a very comfortable little fortune – nothing Rothschildian[3] certainly, but enough to free me from my bondage to Dr. Bolus, and to enable me to travel about and visit my friends and relations. This was not so great an advantage as it may appear, for my relations were few and uncongenial, and my only friend was in New Hampshire. Seven years' separation does a great deal in the way of cooling down friendship, especially between men, and perhaps Ker and I should never have met again, if the sweetest girl in the world had not been going to New York just about that time. Her name was, as well I can remember, Almira Finch. She had been at school in Canterbury for three years, and now her parents had come to take her home. Had this happened at any other time, it would have plunged me in despair, of course; but in my moneyed position a trip across the Atlantic was a trifle, and I took my passage to New York in the "Albatross."

I need not enlarge on the opportunities which the voyage offered to young lovers, especially as I did not avail myself of them as much as might have been expected. There was another man – but there, that's ancient history to me now. However, by the time we reached New York life had ceased to have any attractions for me. I bade a stern farewell to Almira and plunged into the wild dissipation of a journey to New Hampshire. I telegraphed Ker and received an enthusiastic reply.

He met me at the station with a conveyance which he called a buggy. In spite of his beard, he seemed at first very little altered, but before I had been driving alongside him for five minutes I was conscious of a change in him, and that not merely the change which seven years might have been expected to produce. In the first excitement of our meeting he was the old merry "medical," who had boxed, played billiards, done anything and everything but read and attended classes, in our old days at Guy's. But as we went along, and our first incoherent greetings gave place to something like sustained conversation, I noticed in his face a worn, anxious look – and observed this look and tone in men who live from hand to mouth, and are wearing their lives out in a struggle against poverty. But this I knew was not his case. And I have noticed them in men who have made unhappy marriages.

"I hope my sudden arrival will not inconvenience Mrs. Ker," I said, and pricked my ears for his answer. There is a special tone which you can recognise – if you are sharp enough – which always accompanies, even in the most guarded natures, an allusion to the "unloved wife".

But it was not in this tone that he answered. On the contrary, there was a new tenderness and softness in his voice as he said:

"No, she doesn't care much about strangers, but you're not *that*. Whatever pleases me always pleases her too."

No, that was not the trouble.

"Have we much further to go?" I asked presently.

"Miles," he said. "Quite the other end of nowhere."

"What made you come here?" I asked. "Are you near your wife's friends?"

"No," he answered, whipping up his large-boned grey mare. "We're near no one, and we like it."

After that there was no more to be said on that point. We fell to talking of old time, and, under the influence of reminiscence, the cloud lifted more than once, and Roland seemed almost himself again.

"Do you remember all our absurd experiments in Torrington Square?" I asked presently. "I've often wondered if you kept them up. I soon left off those sort of games, and kept rigidly to the orthodox lines. But you really did do some rather big things in Germany, so I heard. Have you done much since?"

"Yes," he said, and there was a feverish uneasiness in his manner. "Oh, yes. I've done a good deal since I came to America. I've done enough to last me all my life. I do nothing but study now."

"Ah, I see," I said. I did see. I saw that somehow or other this love of experiments was connected with the change in my friend's manner. Perhaps he had murdered someone in the interests of science, and had a tenderer conscience than most experimentalists. The evening shadows were deepening; the wind was driving light patches of cloud across the face of the pale, just visible moon. The country was singularly uninteresting, and the road went up and down, up and down, over a succession of rolling hills, only one of which could be seen at a time. The farmhouses grew scarcer and scarcer, the woods less thick and less frequent. I was rather tired with my journey, and I was really, I think, half asleep, when Ker drew rein in front of his house. It was a very English-looking house – as far as I could see, for the trees that surrounded it were thick and many. It lay in a little hollow – caught, as it were, on the arm of a hill – and was built in the solid, lasting fashion of the early Georgian era. It had a wide, straight front, with a good many windows, through which tasteful draperies of muslin could be seen. The whole place looked comfortable, well-kept, and refined, but in spite of all it looked very lonely, and I couldn't help thinking I should not care to live there.

As an old serving-man took the reins I remarked on the lonely situation of the house. "But I suppose you keep a revolver and half-a-dozen house-dogs," I added.

"I have a whole armoury of firearms," he answered, as he got out of the trap, "but no dogs. My wife doesn't like them; in fact, her dislike amounts to antipathy. She hates even to hear them mentioned. But come this way. Hiram will take your traps to your room."

The corridors through which we passed were softly carpeted, and throughout the house I noticed a luxury so studied and so at variance with Ker's former happy-go-lucky tastes and meagre exchequer that I at once laid the credit of it to Mrs. Ker's taste and Mrs. Ker's money. My room was comfortable and carefully arranged, and there were little touches about it which spoke of the hand of a cultivated woman. I made haste with my toilet, for I was quite anxious to make the acquaintance of Roland's wife. I felt a conviction that she would be charming. She was.

Roland Ker was waiting for me at the foot of the stairs, and led me into a large, low, somewhat old-fashioned drawing room. A fire burned on the open hearth, though it was July, and on the soft fur hearthrug before it stood my hostess. She was not actually tall, but was lithe and slender, and had a suggestion about her of being much taller than she actually was. She had a grace of movement which few women have, and which modern poets describe as "panther-like." She had eyes which the same school would term "unfathomable – beautiful changing eyes – the 'greenest of things blue – the bluest of things grey.'"[4] She wore a dress of some white clinging woollen material, trimmed with soft white fur, and setting off to advantage the perfect curves of her figure. Her hair was of the rarely seen colour which we call *blond cendré*.[5] She was nervous, as I judged from the little start she gave as we entered the room. A shy look came into her eyes, but passed almost at once as she came forward, and, without waiting for an introduction, held out two deliciously soft white hands, and said in a very low and sweet voice –

"You are Ernest Wicksteed. Of course I have heard all about you. I hope you will stay a long time and be happy with us."

She spoke in a curiously childish, hesitating way, with an air of having learned her little speech by heart. But I found that was her habitual manner.

The dinner was very good. Among the courses were several kinds of fish prepared with great skill. I concluded that the Kers paid some attention to their table, as in that out-of-the-way place fish must have been difficult to get. The wine was good, but Mrs. Ker drank only milk.

"Wine is not good for her," said Ker, when I offered her Burgundy, and I fancied his tone had some hidden meaning. Good heavens! Was it possible that wine had any temptations for this lovely creature? I could not think it. And yet that would certainly account for Roland's harassed and worried look, and for his choosing to live in this remote part of the world.

The evening passed delightfully. Neither Ker nor his wife seemed to have grown rusty in their retirement, and our conversation was lively and interesting. As we talked and she grew animated, I was struck by a subtle change in her, whose cause of nature I was for some time unable to determine. After a while I found that the mystery lay in her eyes, which changed with every change of voice and gesture. They dilated and contracted in a most bewildering and fascinating fashion, which would have been perilous for the modern "singer" who might come within their range.

"Let us have some music, Pussy," said her husband, and she smiled at him and went obediently to the piano.

Her voice was a *contralto*, bull and *vibrante*.[6] I don't know what she sang, but it was something slumberous and passionate, that was like her eyes – like herself. As she played and sang her whole body swayed and moved in unison with the music. It was evident that music was a part of her nature. Never, before or since, have I heard anything at all like her singing. When she ended I thanked her again and again, and begged for another one. She would have granted it, I think, but to my amazement, Ker crossed to her side and closed the piano abruptly.

"Not to-night," he said, laying a caressing hand on her head. "You will tire yourself, Pussy."

She acquiesced at once, and came back to the fire, but talking did not seem easy after that music, and she soon bade us Good-night. The day's journey and long ride had tired me, and after a social pipe in Roland's den I prepared to turn in.

"Sleep well," said Ker, as we parted.

But that was exactly what I could *not* do. From a shelf of books in my room I took down a volume of Poe's tales and read for hours – getting wider and wider awake. Tired out though I was, I could not sleep. At last I thought I would try smoking as a sedative, but not in this dainty dormitory. I opened my door; the house was very still. I crept down slipperless to the little room where Roland and I had had our pipes. The door was partly open, and to my surprise I saw that the fire still burnt there. There was no other light, but I gave a start that almost betrayed me as I saw him sitting in a chair, his elbows on its arms, his fingers buried in his short brown curls, and in his eyes a mixture of hopelessness and anxiety indescribably painful. What was this secret sorrow? It was evidently not a moment to thrust my presence on him, and I was about to turn to creep back as silently as I had come when he made a movement that for a moment made me think he had heard me. He leant forward to something on the hearthrug. My eyes followed his hand. It rested on the head of his wife, who lay curled up in an almost indistinguishable heap at his feet. Some dark, heavy mantle seemed to be thrown over her white dress.

I turned away instantly and regained my room, with a heart-ache for my friend's sake. What a terrible and unmistakable confirmation of my suspicions! My journey downstairs had certainly failed to supply a narcotic, and I did not close my eyes till dawn.

When I went down to breakfast the next morning I was almost able to persuade myself that I had dreamed this strange *tableau vivant*. My hostess was in the lightest of spirits and fresh as the June morning itself, and Ker had not about him even such marked traces of anxiety as I had noticed on the previous day.

He and I spent the day in the saddle, riding thirty miles to visit some acquaintances of his. We got home to dinner at seven, and the evening passed as had the previous one, save that we had no music. I felt baffled again. In spite of what I had seen I could not believe that my friend's wife was the slave of any horrible propensity such as I had imagined. It was quite evident that this was a singularly happy match. The two were more like lovers than the ordinary Darby and Joan.[7] Of course I don't mean that they made love to each other in that offensively obtrusive way which always suggests secret wrangling. Only they seemed to suit each other, and to a close observer (I flatter myself I am one), it was evident that they had few, if any interests apart from each other.

We parted early. Ker looked worn out, and I did not wonder, remembering the vigil in which his last night had been spent. I myself was in not much better case, and fell asleep almost before my head touched the pillow.

I awoke with a start in the grey of the morning. The loud and vigorous barking of a dog came sharp through the chill air. Someone breaking in was my first thought, and then I remembered that my friend did not keep a dog. I sprang up, and put my head out of my open window. Almost immediately below it, his four thick legs planted uncompromisingly far apart, stood a big lurcher-looking brute of a dog, his white teeth and red tongue plainly visible, and his hair bristling from crest to tail. His barks were so vigorous that with each one he lifted all his four feet off the ground at once. What on earth was the matter with him? I followed the direction of his eyes, and saw – good heavens! – was I dreaming, or was it really my friend's wife who was clinging fast with feet and fingers to the sheer side of the woodstack over against the house, the hanging train of her furred white dress draggled and muddy just above the reach of the dog's angry teeth? No, not the woman I had seen before, but a horrible mad likeness of her; all the softness and beauty gone, her lips drawn back from her teeth in what seemed an agony of rage or terror, her wonderful hair actually seeming to be *on end*, her whole frame trembling with excitement, and her great glowing green eyes fixed on her assailant. This was not a time for close observation or prolonged reflection. The revolver I had brought from England was in an instant in my hand. I fired. Missed. Fired again, and saw the brute of a dog leap up and roll over. I flung on some clothes and rushed downstairs. As I passed Ker's door I dashed it open and called his name without stopping. Guided by the freshness of the air I found the back door, and in a moment was in the yard. She was not there. At least I did not see her at first.

"Mrs. Ker!" I cried. "It's all right. The dog's dead."

A fierce shriek answered me, and those eyes looked at me a moment from the top of the woodstack. Madness was in every line of her face; her whole appearance was more that of some wild creature of the cat tribe than of a woman. Her hands were stretched out like claws, and her body drawn back like a tiger's before the spring. The heavy fur cloak and dress that in her frenzy she had wound tightly about her added to the illusion. Was she really a woman? I moved towards the woodstack, still shouting my soothing commonplaces. This takes some time to tell; it did not take a minute to act. And before that minute was over Ker was beside me. They fixed their eyes on each other.

"Come to me," he cried, in a voice of passionate tenderness and appeal. "Come to me my darling, my Pussy."

The horrible appropriateness of this last epithet struck me even at that moment.

There was no answering tenderness in her eyes. With unabated fury gleaming in them, she sprang cat-like from the woodstack, and leaped at him. As he clasped her in his arms she fastened her teeth in his shoulder, with a horrible inarticulate sound, half hiss, half howl. I saw the blood spurt out, staining his white shirt. He winced and set his lips hard, but gave no other sign, only stroked her hair with his hand. He was deadly pale, but he held her fast, and murmured to her the tenderest words of endearment and love. In a few seconds she sighed, her whole frame seemed to relax, to give way; she flung her arms round his neck, and broke into slow, heavy, heart-rending sobs – distinctly human, these.

He lifted her and carried her into the house, laid her on the sofa, and knelt beside her, stroking her head with the gentle touch that I was growing accustomed to see in him. Her sobs grew fainter and fainter. Presently they ceased altogether, and her breathing grew steady and regular.

"She is asleep," he said, turning to me, and then he hid his face in the folds of her dress and gave one hard, broken sob.

I laid my hand on his shoulder.

"What is it, old friend?" I asked. "What does it all mean?"

"I suppose I must tell you?" he asked wearily.

"Tell me nothing," I interposed. "Let it all be as though it had never been."

"I *will* tell you," he said impatiently, "I have never told any one yet, and I feel as if telling it might keep *me* from going mad too."

So, sitting by his wife, with his hand never intermitting its slow, soothing movement over her blond hair, he told me her story. She was the daughter of the American gentleman who had persuaded him to leave Leipzig. He had fallen in love with her at first sight, and she with him. The only drawback to their happiness had been the extreme delicacy of her health. She showed symptoms of pulmonary disease, and her father and Ker had both feared that she would not live another year, her decline was so rapid and so complete. Passionate love and his old fondness for experiments had combined to inspire him with an idea. He became convinced that transfusion of blood would be the only thing to save her life. He would gladly have given his own blood, but to that she would not consent. And then came the strangest part of the story. She had always been fond of cats, and now she herself suggested that animal. She had insisted on this, and he had supported her in it, believing that it would save her life. The operation was successfully performed, and her life was saved. She was almost restored to fully bodily vigour. But her mind! Almost immediately after the operation, a change took place in her. Was it really the effect of the cat blood, or had the bare thought of it affected her brain? Her old tastes were mixed and modified by an ever-increasing love for warmth, softness, and all the things that cats love, and a corresponding antipathy to all the things that cats hate. She had seemed to be half cat, half woman. Her father would have broken off the engagement, but Ker's deep and ever-increasing love put that out of the question. He had married her, and had given up his life to the task of trying to strengthen the woman, and weaken the cat nature. But, in spite of all, these paroxysms came upon her at intervals with ever-increasing force. She had never had so severe an attack as this. He had thought the attack had spent itself on the previous night, and so had been off guard. She must have got up while he was asleep, and this chance tramp's dog had turned the current of her blood. The story was a long one as he told it, a story told out of the very heart of the man.

"She was so sweet, so lovable, so perfect," he said at last, "and this is all my fault, all my fault! – And yet, as she is, she is my whole world. If I lost her – Oh! heaven, I cannot bear to think of it; my whole life's light would go out. She will be all right now; she is always all right after a sleep. My darling; my only love, my wife." He spoke to her, forgetful of my presence, leaning over her to look in her sleeping face. Then he sprang erect with a cry that I shall never forget.

She was asleep. She was "all right," and Roland Ker's whole life's light had gone out.

R. G. B., 'Birds of a Feather' (1886)

I was a governess in a private family; not a resident governess, but something rather freer than that, a daily governess.

It happened early in the year 18—, I was then twenty-four, that my employers took a house in Leicestershire for the hunting season. I, as part of the general luggage, went with them. It was uncomfortable for me; but I tried to smile and look cheerful, and I said (may I be forgiven the lie) that I was delighted at the idea, and that I was prepared to be happy under any circumstances.

When we arrived at our destination the house was found to be smaller than had been expected, and a bed-room was accordingly found for me in a cottage close by. In my bed-room I was very happy, there was always a cheerful fire, a table with ink and writing paper, and, in fact, everything that could make me comfortable.

My employers were most kind and considerate, they were unusually generous, and tried to make me feel at home; my pupils were clever, and it was no trouble to teach them; but yet, in spite of all these things, I felt miserable. I was not home-sick, yet I could not make myself happy. I hardly ever opened my lips to speak except when alone with the children; I felt weighed down with the feeling that nobody wanted to speak to me, that everybody was anxious to be kind to the governess but that I, personally, was nothing at all to them. They were kind to me, yes, but then they were kind to their dogs. One evening I went to my lodging about 9.30, feeling unusually depressed. According to my custom I undressed, got into my dressing-gown and slippers, and sat down in my arm-chair over by the fire. I sat thinking over my life, and wondering why I felt so lonely. I finally came to the conclusion that the reason of my loneliness was the total difference of character and of tastes between myself and my employer. The mother of my pupils was a gay, lively, worldly woman; I, on the contrary, was serious, and the position in which I was placed, made me seem heavier than I really was. I felt that however much Mrs. Webster pressed me to stay and sit with them after dinner, she would probably say as soon as my back was turned, "Little fool! How old maids do worry me! I cannot stand their cackle."

It would never occur to her that perhaps the cackle of a married woman of nearly forty, might also be trying to an old maid of twenty-four.

I remembered as I sat in my chair by the fire, many of the remarks which, on previous occasions, Mrs. Webster had made to me, and I involuntarily shuddered. I remembered how she had said to me with raised voice, and with extended hands, "I tell you, Miss Beetle, it is a woman's first duty to look out for a husband: when she has found a husband, then the highest aim of her life is realized; every woman should hold a baby on one arm, and make its food with the other." I smiled, remembering that she had two nurses to hold her baby, and two more to make its food.

Thinking in this strain, I felt how impossible it would be for me to be at all happy in such uncongenial society; and I found myself wishing to be well out of it, and imagining at the same time, an handsome young woman with a great desire for a husband taking my place, setting her cap at the step-son of five-and-twenty, surreptitiously flirting with the husband and father of the household, and, in other, and equally stirring ways, upsetting the equanimity of the establishment. How Mrs. Webster would rejoice in the presence of a governess who was evidently trying to attain to a high standard of propriety.

How Myra, the eldest daughter, would profit by such a brilliant example of clever worldliness! and how happy should I be, having left an uncongenial atmosphere to work with people of my own way of thinking, in fact with birds of my own feather; people to whom I could talk on equal terms, and who would really be friends to me! How often I had longed for birds of my own feather as companions.

I determined to tell Mrs. Webster, on the next day, that I would leave at the end of the term, and gaining happiness in my new resolve, I gave up thinking of myself and my troubles, leaned back in my chair and went to sleep.

While asleep I dreamed that I died and went to hell. I lost all sense of my own identity, and all remembrance of my past life. I seemed to become someone else – with other loves, sorrows, and memories. I thought I had been a freethinker when on earth, had disregarded convention and the world's word, and had lived unmarried by form – but married by fidelity and love – to one who shared my a-religious opinions, and on these accounts had been sent to the lower regions. As I came out of the station, hell appeared to be a gloomy place, the streets empty, and a perfect stillness reigned, but as it was about half-past-one in the afternoon I concluded that everybody was lunching.

Nothing looked green and flourishing; the trees were covered with brown and drooping leaves, the grass was brown, and the only flower I saw in blossom, was the deadly-night-shade. I walked into a dark and dingy street, with large houses on each side, each enclosed in high walls, and surrounded by the brown trees above mentioned. Over the entrance-gate of every house was a sign-post, which enabled the new comer to find easily the home most suited to his tastes and requirements. I went on, led by some mysterious force, till I came to a house, with a sign-post stuck out bearing the inscription "Freethinker's Hall." I entered, feeling that this was to be my future abode. I was curious rather than despondent, and went into the first room I came to, where, standing by the table, I saw a man whose face I knew. It was the face that had been all the world to me when on earth, the face of the man with whom I have lived in open defiance of the world's opinion, though no marriage vows had been exchanged by us. I had loved him, truly and faithfully – and now, overjoyed I went up to him, when, to my astonishment, he waved me back with his hand.

"Leave me," said he, "leave me, oh woman! We were friends on earth, but the order of the day here is, that "birds of a feather flock together;" it was your creed on earth that women were not undeveloped, abortive men, but that they were a totally different species, perfect in their own way; go then to your own species, the birds of *your* feather live at the opposite side of the house."

"Oh hear me," I cried. "Do you not know me? I am your love, your help-meet, your wife."

"Leave me, fond woman; can you not leave people of a different species alone? Go and herd with your own kind!"

I left the room sorrowful, but still curious, and I saw facing me a door, with the words "Women's apartments," printed upon it.

I entered, and seeing no one I walked to the book-shelves. There were many books which I had read with pleasure when on earth; the works of John Stuart Mill, Philosophy by Kant and Comte, "Esoteric Buddhism," by Sinnett[1] and many books of the "Science of Ethics" etc. etc.

As I stood looking round me George Eliot and Mary Wollstonecraft[2] entered. They appeared melancholy, but at the same time a little pleased to see a new face, however they thought it would be a breach of good manners to show their feelings too much.

"How do you do? How do you like the idea of living here for the future?" said Mary Wollstonecraft, wishing to be friendly.

"It seems a little sombre," said I, "but I think things might be worse than they are; I, at least, look forward to the pleasure of the society of people of my own stamp, and I see here books which will give me pleasure for years."

"Those books," said George Eliot, "don't mention them. We would give all our possession for a change of literature; I thought of asking you if you had such a thing as a novel with you, you might perhaps have bought one to amuse you on your journey down here. I would not have deigned to read a book with a yellow cover when I was on earth; a *Punch*[3] I should have called "Philistine," but now I wish, I wish I had a *Family Herald*!"[4] Here the good lady struggled to keep back a rising sob. "You did not happen to bring 'Much Darker Days'[5] in your pocket did you?"

"I have read it," I said, "but I have not been able to bring anything with me; I was told that I should find everything I wanted here, and that those things I liked best on earth would be put within reach of my hand below. But anyhow, I do not think I should have brought 'Much Darker Days,' it is a most vulgar skit."

"Vulgar! Did you say it was vulgar? I can't tell you how I long for something vulgar as a change. A good piece of vulgarity would do me good, would do us all good; oh! how I wish someone would send me a vulgar valentine!"

I stared in astonishment, thinking perhaps the lady was losing her reason, and then said, to change the subject, "I have been travelling for a long time, and am hungry, do you think I could have some lunch without putting the kitchen to much inconvenience?"

"Certainly," said Mary Wollstonecraft, and rang the bell, at the same time I observed her exchange a glance and half smile with George Eliot.

"I don't think you will care about it much," said the latter; "perhaps at first however you may like it; but I may as well tell you at once that everything here is devilled;[6] one occasionally gets tired of devilled food, but that is part of our life. We never see 'the devil walking about as a roaring lion,'[7] but oh! if only he would devour us instead of making us devour devilled food!"

The luncheon was served, and I partook of it gladly; and, as it was my first meal, I enjoyed it, but I thought it just possible that I, like Mary Wollstonecraft and George Eliot, might, in time, get a little tired of devilled food; it also occurred to me that after a little I might get weary of the companionship of such celebrated people as George Eliot. However, I did not communicate my thoughts to those about me, who seemed delighted at the sight of a new face, and anxious to make me feel at home.

After luncheon George Eliot offered to take me out and show me about a little. I heartily agreed, and we started. Presently we came to a large house surrounded by a garden; on the sign-post, overhanging the gate, was a picture of the "Scarlet Woman." In the garden women were walking, gaudily-dressed women with painted faces; ladies belonging to widely differing historical periods, but with very much the same stamp of countenance.

I saw Potiphar's wife, Messalina, and Madame de Pompadour.[8] I turned to my companion, and said: "At least we have been dealt with justly; you and I have both broken the earthly laws concerning marriage, but our conscientiousness in the matter has been taken into consideration, and we are not classed with the harlot and adultress."

"So we find to our disgust," was the reply. "'The Scarlet woman' now is an object of interest to me, what a pleasant change it would be to talk to her! And how delighted she would be to speak to us, although she would have laughed such people as ourselves to scorn when on earth. But let us pass on."

We next came to the home for mesmerists.

"This is really a most painful sight," said my guide. "Look at these men, do you see how they continually try to mesmerize each other? Formerly they were never able to manage it; but the other day a weaker man came amongst them, whom, to their joy, they found they *could* mesmerize. He, poor wretch, cannot help himself at all; he is seized and operated upon by all in turn, without even being asked if he objects. Look! He is over there now, talking to himself; let us go nearer and hear what he is saying."

We advanced, I heard the poor man speaking thus:

"What *shall* I do? I am absolutely helpless her in the hands of all these men; if only I could go I would mesmerize the Pompadour lot for a change! But I am forced to stay with these men. If only that Mr. Smith, whom I used to mesmerize so satisfactorily on earth, would come down here, I should then have my turn; but they say that he probably will be long-lived; and then they have hinted that he has joined the Salvation Army,[9] and has turned from the error of his ways, and is mesmerizing no more. No; I am afraid there is nothing for it but to live on with these men for ever – what a wretched, hopeless existence!"

My companion, with a sudden movement of disgust, accidentally brought her elbow sharply against my chest, and I woke with a start.

If morals were not so old-fashioned, and if this particular moral were not so evident, I would add one to this story. As it is I will only say that I did not do on the morrow as I had intended, but remained where I was until my pupils had grown too old for the schoolroom.

John Broadhouse, 'How He Lost his "Strad"' (1886)

He did not look more than forty, and yet his hair was quite white – almost as white as snow, though it did not exactly equal that superlative whiteness. We were the only occupants of the snug commercial room at the "White Hart," the best inn of the little town of Broadley, and had travelled together by the train from Eversdean, getting to Broadley just in time for one of those substantial dinners for which mine host of the "White Hart" is famous.

We had never met before, but I knew in a moment that he was a musician. His appearance struck me at once. His moustache and beard were jet black, but his hair, as I have said, was almost as white as snow. He was tall, broad-shouldered, well-built, and altogether a good-looking man. We sat waiting for dinner, and enjoying a preliminary cigarette and glass of sherry by way of *hors d'œuvres*. The waiter came in with the soup, and we fell to work in real earnest. By-and-bye he looked at me enquiringly.

"You want to know what turned my hair white? Everybody does," and he shuddered.

"Well," I said, "I am curious, I must admit, but if it is a painful subject –"

"It is ten years ago to-night." And although we had only just got fairly under weigh with our dinner, he pushed his chair away, went to the window, pulled back the blind, and looked out. "Come here!" And he beckoned with his finger mysteriously. I went, of course. "You know Broadley Common?"

I nodded assent.

"Did you ever walk across the Common to Enderby on just such a night as this?"

"I have walked there in broad daylight," I said.

"Ah, that's a different thing," and he again shuddered. "Let us go on with our dinner, and I'll tell you all about it over a quiet pipe afterwards."

We ate in silence, for he seemed under a spell. I tried him with one or two casual remarks, but it was all to no purpose, for he did not even seem to hear me. The waiter moved in and out of the room in solemn silence, and at length took away the cloth, set our chairs one on each side of the fire, opened another bottle of Burgundy (at a sign from me), and left us. When we were comfortably seated he began his story: –

"It was a terrible night," he said. "I had come from Eversdean with only one companion, just as I have to-night. He wanted to get me into conversation, but I felt moody and reserved, and only replied with a 'yes' or 'no,' as the case required. He got out at Broadley, and we rode together in the 'bus to the 'White Hart.'

"I had come there to play first fiddle at a grand concert next day at the Hall, and had with me my old 'Strad,' which had been in the family for nearly 150 years, and was worth five-hundred guineas. The talk hung fire a good deal at dinner-time, and I went to bed at ten, wishing my companion good-night with hearty good-will, for I was glad to be rid of him. With my usual caution I locked and bolted my room door, and saw to the window-fastenings. Shortly after I had done so I heard the door of the next room closed and locked, and concluded that my companion had followed my example, and gone to bed in good time.

"My fiddle was too big to put under my pillow, so I put it on a chair close to the side of the bed, taking the precaution to tie a piece of string round the handle and round my wrist. I did this from habit, and not from any fear of being robbed on that particular night. As to my companion in the next room, I hardly gave him a second thought.

"I must have been asleep some time, when I heard a noise as of someone leaping from a height to the ground. I started up in a moment and felt instinctively for my fiddle. The string had been cut, and it was gone! I rushed to the window. The night was as black as ink, and I could only just manage to discern a figure making off at a good rate. I shouted for help, unlocked my door, and tried the door of the next room. It was unfastened, the window was open, and the bed was empty!

"As quick as thought I rushed back, slipped on my clothes, got my boots from outside the door (where I had put them before getting into bed), dropped from the window to the ground and set off in pursuit. I was guided by the retreating footsteps of the run-away, who had made for the Common. As I ran I fired my revolver (I never travel without one), but the thief had got too much start of me, and beside it was so dark that I could only hear him – seeing him was out of the question.

"Suddenly I thought of the old stone quarries, and my heart almost stood still when I thought of the awful danger I was running. One false step, and I should inevitably be dashed to atoms at the bottom of one of those ghastly pits. The quarries had not been used for years, and by day, or even on a moderately dark night, it was easy to pick one's way without danger. I remembered that the path lay between two of these holes, and that there was plenty of room and no danger if I only kept to the path. These two pits were of an awful depth – nearly a hundred and fifty feet, and the sides were mostly as straight down as the wall of a house.

"Suddenly a shriek rent the death-like stillness of the night – a cry of horror and despair such as I have heard once – and *only* once, thank God! – from drowning men struggling at dead of night with the merciless waves. I was close behind him – I had seen him but two seconds ago, and was just reckoning how soon I should be up with him, when that awful cry of despair broke the silence. Great God – he had gone headlong into the abyss! And I was close at his heels! Though my stumble broke the force of my fall. A mist came over my eyes; my knees gave way; I stumbled, fell headlong, rolled over, and clutched wildly with my outstretched hands in the vain hope of saving myself. But I was too late. Another couple of yards would have saved me, but I was on the very edge of the precipice and I rolled over the side of the pit with a shriek as full of horror as that which had just rent the air!

"When I felt myself going I dug my nails into the turf, though I had no hope of saving my life. But the grass had grown right to the edge, and I held on for dear life. The thin soil yielded to the pressure, and my hands grasped the bare rock, to which I clung with a fearful grip. The wall in front of me was as smooth as glass, and I hung in the very jaws of the grave, with nothing but the strength of my wrists between me and a horrible death! That the quarry would be my tomb I felt sure.

"How long could I hold out? It could not be much past midnight. Would they be guided by the sound of the firing and follow us, or should I hang for a few minutes, a quarter of an hour, half-an-hour, and then – ! To die in the bloom of manhood, and such a death – it was horrible. As I hung there, with the heavens as black as ink above me, and the pit still more black and awful beneath me, the picture of the thief, as he lay below, a mangled and bleeding corpse, presented itself with awful vividness to my mind. My imagination brought every ghastly detail of his death before me with tenfold force. I saw his bloodless face turned up to the pitiless sky, his eyeballs fixed on me, as though he was waiting for that moment, which I knew would surely come, when my last remnant of strength would give way, and I should follow him down, down, until my life too was dashed out on the rocky bottom of the quarry. I shouted as loud as I could, but the only response was the mocking echo of my own voice, which came back from the depths below as if to torture me with the thought that no help was near. I was a mile or more from any house, and could not hope to make myself heard. Besides, the effort of shouting weakened me, and I wanted to save all my strength for my grip in the rock, which was my only hope. And what a hope! Every moment I felt my strength ebbing, and at last I knew that it was a question of minutes, and perhaps seconds. My wrists were swollen, my shoulders burned as though molten lead were being poured into the joints, and the physical agonies I suffered were rapidly becoming intolerable. My pain reeled, and though I kept my eyes wide open I could see nothing – not even the black wall in front of my face.

"Gradually I felt my fingers relaxing their hold. I was slipping slowly down – only my finger-tips rested on the ledge now, and in one second more I felt the rock had gone away from me. Oh God – can I ever forget that moment? I was falling into the horrible abyss when Providence mercifully cast over me the veil of forgetfulness, and I knew no more.

"When I came to myself," he went on, "I was in my bedroom, and the fragments of my priceless 'Strad,' on the chair close by. The doctor stood beside me, his finger on my wrist and his watch in his other hand. When he saw me open my eyes he put the watch in his pocket, and placed his finger on my lips. 'Not a word yet,' he said 'you shall know all about it when you are a little better able to bear it. At present you must be quiet.' I closed my eyes again, and slept till the afternoon, when the landlord came in and sat with me. I asked him how they got the violin, but I dared not ask him anything about my companion. I told him how I had held on till I could hold no longer. 'You need not have held on at all, sir,' he said. 'Need not – I do not understand you?' 'I daresay not, sir,' he said; 'but there was a ledge about twelve feet wide not above a yard below you, and there we found you at daylight this mornin', lyin' in a dead swound.[1] *He* must have gone clean over, for we found him at the bottom, as dead as a door nail, and the fiddle, smashed to a thousand pieces not far off.' I turned away, for the awful remembrance came back upon me with terrible force. 'Perhaps I'm talkin' a little bit too much for you, sir,' he said, and left me.

"The next morning I felt much better, and got up and dressed myself. When I went to the glass I started back with affright; I looked ten years older, *and my hair was perfectly white*, just as you see it to-night."

A. Gilbert Katte, 'The Whip Hand. A Political Story – in Three Parts' (1888)

[February 1888]

The Minister had been cordial but cautious. He had not actually committed himself to anything, it was not his way; but he had given Sir Reginald to understand that if the present Chancellor of the Exchequer[1] and leader of the House succumbed to the dangerous illness from which he was suffering – his, Sir Reginald's, claim to the vacant seat in the Cabinet should have due consideration. And he had gone further, he had hinted that even if the bronchitis, aided by the bitter east wind, failed to get the better of the struggle with the eminent physicians and carry poor old Mr. Smeeth over to the permanent majority, it was still possible that the same change would be made. For Mr. Smeeth was old, both in years and views, and was hardly the man to lead the very shaky and insubordinate majority against an eager and unscrupulous opposition in the stormy times which were coming upon the Government.

Sir Reginald Hastie stood a moment or two on the steps of Lord Branstock's chocolate-coloured little house in Curzon Street,[2] twisting the ends of his long light moustache, and turning rapidly over in his mind the main points of the Prime Minister's conversation.

Yes, there could be no doubt about it, the wily old peer had made up his mind though his language had been diplomatically vague; and in a few weeks, possibly in a few days, the country, and especially the business part of it, would be startled by the news that Sir Reginald Hastie – the rebellious school boy of *Punch*[3] – had made one step from below the gangway to the Ministerial Bench, and that the finances of the Empire were entrusted to a man who had never had the previous drilling even of an under secretaryship.[4]

He tucked up the collar of his overcoat, stepped down on to the pavement, looked up the street, down which the bitter March wind was cutting like a million invisible razors, and then crossed over towards South Audley Street.[5]

"I think I'll call again;" he said half aloud, "poor old boy, I hope he'll get better and go up to the Peers,[6] he'll be all right there, and there'll have to be a little shuffling of the pack anyway. For I know one thing, if I go in, Dodder and Dawdle will have to go out, or wake up considerably."

"Dodder and Dawdle," were the nick names by which he always thought, and very often spoke, of two members of the Government, one a new Yorkshire Baronet, and the other a rich Banker, whom Lord Branstock had put into the Cabinet in order to give it that solid and middle-class air which a commercial nation demands.

As he approached Grosvenor Square several carriages passed in succession, to some of whose occupants he raised his hat.

"Glad they didn't catch me in Curzon Street," he thought, "they might have guessed what was up."

Within a few dozen yards of the corner a man turned it whom he knew. It was Lord Nimrod, a Liberal peer, who was rapidly gravitating towards Conservatism, and of whom an evening paper had spoken as a "future premier." He had lately taken an active part in politics; that is to say, he had attended several public meetings, and spoken with ease and intelligence. Hitherto he had been known to fame only as a mighty hunter of big game.

The two men caught sight of each other at the same moment and saluted with umbrellas. They stopped –

"You are going to call at 28," said Lord Nimrod, "don't go, it's no use now."

"What do you mean?" asked the other, "You don't mean to say –"

"About half an hour ago, he went quite suddenly at last; it's this accursed east wind. Are you going down to the House to-night, I suppose they'll adjourn."

"Of course they will; no I don't think I shall go to-night – poor Smeeth, I'm awfully sorry."

"Yes, he was a useful sort of man. What will Branstock do, do you suppose?"

"Haven't the remotest idea. How frightfully cold it is. Good-bye."

At the corner of the square Sir Reginald stopped and looked towards number 28. A carriage was just starting from the door, and two men, members of the House, were raising their hats to someone inside. He took his cigar case from his pocket and then, remembering that he could not light a match at that corner in that wind, put it back again. Just then the carriage passed him, and he recognised in it the leader of the opposition, looking very old and rather pale and ill.

"By Jove!" he said half aloud, "he looks bad. If he comes out on days like this he'll be following poor old Smeeth, and then there'll be nobody left worth fighting. It's impossible to score off booky prigs like Rawley or glib cads like Courtier; what a lot they'll be!" At this moment a hansom driveled slowly towards him from across the square, driver and horse vying with each other as to which should look the most downcast, cold and miserable. It suggested something to his mind. "I'll go and see Kate and have a cup to tea with her," he said. "She had the best right to know what's coming, and she'll be much more pleased than Ethel – Ethel can wait."

He hailed the cab. "118A, Maida Vale,"[7] he said, jumping in.

While he is on his way we will give the reader a few of the facts which had led up to the present position of affairs.

Sir Reginald Hastie was what is called in political life "a *very* young man," that is he was just in the forties. He had entered Parliament for a pocket borough[8] eight years before through the influence of his uncle, the Marquis of Lawder. In those eight years he had spoken more often and moved more amendments and adjournments than any other man in the House, not excepting the followers of the Irish leader himself.[9] He had had the good fortune to take his seat at a time when the leader of his own party had just gone up to the Peers, and when the party itself was a dejected and disorganized opposition. He at once began a series of virulent, though often pertinent, attacks upon the leader of the House and all the occupants of the Ministerial bench. He constantly challenged divisions, and led many a forlorn hope into the lobby; but once or twice he managed, by sheer skill in passing resolutions, to reduce the Government's majority. He had a faculty for finding out his opponents' sore places and he always hit on the raw. Over and over again the House had been amused and a little scandalized by the spectacle of the gray haired premier lashed into a fury by the attacks of this young free lance below the gangway. He had practically no personal following, but the few who did stand by him were young, physically strong, and rhetorically smart, and, although only about half a dozen in number, were a party which had to be reckoned with in every big debate. When the general election came which sent his party back to power, Sir Reginald, with his usual pluck, threw up his little borough and stood for a great democratic constituency in the North of England. At first his chances looked desperate and the Liberal press, with its accustomed foresight, made much fun of them. But, Sir Reginald had the true democratic style about him and he addressed the great, sweating, crowded audiences "as though he loved them." His advanced policy, his flashy and often brilliant rhetoric, his ready repartee, went down with the well-to-do artizans who made up the majority of the constituency, and, backed by the whole of the Commercial class, when polling day came he defeated the "steady and stolidly" Liberal who opposed him by a substantial majority. He was helped in his canvass by his rich and pretty wife.

When the new government was formed all the world expected that he and one or two of his friends would receive at least some minor official posts; but somehow or other they were passed over; Lord Branstock did nothing original this time. Then Sir Reginald changed his tactics. He posed as "the candid friend" of the new administration – and his criticisms were so very candid that he soon became a thorn in the side of Mr. Smeeth, on whom Lord Branstock's mantle had fallen, and for whom it was much too large and heavy. As the opposition became better organised and more active, it became more and more impossible for the Government to have this powerful and ready debater continually harassing its flanks. Lord Branstock, one of whose chief merits was his frank recognition of facts, "climbed down," and hence his private conversation with Sir Reginald on the very day that Mr. Smeeth succumbed to the east wind and acute bronchitis.

As Sir Reginald sprang out of the cab at 118A Maida Vale, he recognised about fifty yards further along towards Kilburn the back of a fellow M.P., and old school fellow. The sight seemed to cause him some displeasure. "I suppose he's just left," he said to himself as he watched the retreating figure for a second or two, "what the devil does he want here?"

Almost as soon as his hand touched the knocker the door was opened.

"Mistress in?" he asked of the neat little maidservant, and taking the affirmation in her face for an answer made straight for the drawing room.

The lamp had not yet been lighted, but the whole room was aglow with the flames of a brightly burning fire. Gazing fixedly into it, and leaning with one elbow upon the mantle-shelf was a woman of about five and twenty; but who looked some five or six years older at the present moment owing to the troubled and puzzled expression on her face. Her perfect mouth was drawn down a little at the corners, making the short upper lip just the sixteenth of an inch longer than usual. Her rather high, broad forehead, fully displayed by the way in which she wore her dark golden wavy hair, was furrowed by two lines of perplexity. One white hand held a large scarlet Japanese fan tightly against the folds of a brown coloured dress, made of what the advertisements call "art fabric."[10] Her figure, small and slight, was at the moment too tightly braced and rigid to be entirely graceful.

Sir Reginald had time to close the door behind him, and the displeased expression had left his face and given way to one of real pleasure, before the noise of his entrance reached her ear. She turned towards him, tossed her fan into an armchair, and came swiftly forward holding out both hands –.

"Oh, Rege, whatever's the matter? I never expected you to-day. You've only just missed Camelot. I'm so glad he's gone."

He caught her by both elbows, bent forward and kissed her, then turning her towards the fire led her, with one hand on her shoulder, on to the hearthrug.

"I saw him just up the road," he said, in a not very pleasant tone of voice, "It seems to me he spends a good deal of his time here, Katie. I should think you had better ask him when *I* am coming if you want him at all."

"Oh don't be silly," she answered, catching him by the lappet[11] of his overcoat and giving it a little shake. "I don't want him at all, but I certainly don't want him when you *are* here. Why are you always so stupid about Camelot, Rege? Do you know I do believe he's the best friend you have in the world."

"Oh, very likely," with a half sarcastic laugh, "and therefore I don't want to have him for an enemy. But bother Camelot, I was only joking, of course I know it's all right little woman," he added hastily, seeing a troubled look come into her face. He put his arm round her waist, drew her to him, and raising her chin with his left hand went on. "I have brought you great news to-day, Katie. I have come straight from Branstock."

"From Branstock!" freeing herself from his arm, "Did you see him? Did he send for you?"

"Yes, he's caved in."

"Oh, Reginald! I knew it would come. What are you to have?"

"Guess!"

"Ireland?"

"No thanks. The Exchequer."

"*What!* And Smeeth?"

"Dead – to-day; but it would have been all the same anyhow."

"O-o-h! but who will lead now!"

He struck a senatorial attitude.

"*You! you!* Oh, that's too impossible! My dear boy, you must be dreaming."

"It does seem like it, doesn't it?" he said, taking off his overcoat, "but really, Kate, it isn't for you to say so, it's only what you've been prophesying all along."

"Oh, but not so soon! What *will* people say? Oh, for to-morrow's papers – poor, dear old *Standard*."[12]

"There'll be nothing about it in to-morrow's papers – they'll be deliciously wrong. Branstock, you and I, are the only people in London in the secret at present. Can't you let me have some tea?"

"Of course," she said, going to a little table and coming back with a cup, "but you'll stay for dinner, do not go away to-night, Reginald; we must have a long, long talk, and settle the business of the nation for the next five years."

"I am afraid I can't, my pet," he said, taking the cup and looking away from her a little awkwardly. "I must dine at ho— at Cathcart Place to-night, I've promised."

"Of course, it's always the way." There was something in the tone and manner in which the words were spoken that caused him to look up with a shade of annoyance on his face. It grated on his ear. Slight as it was, it marked the speaker off as belonging to a different order from the women whom he was accustomed to meet in his friends' drawing-rooms. Had any of these women heard it, even from the other side of a screen, "she's not one of us," they would have thought, and they would have been right, as they always are in these matters. There was an absence of "fine shades" only, but still the "fine shades" were not there.

He put down his cup, and drew her on to his knee. "Now don't be an unreasonable girl," he said, "you know I can't help it. She told me this morning she wanted to talk to me about something. I wouldn't stop then so I put her off till to-night. I must go. I don't know what it is she wants to say; the old subject I expect – money."

She got off his knee, though he tried to detain her, and, turning her back to him, put up one foot on the fender and looking into the fire asked in a low voice –

"Do you think you could do without the 'married woman' altogether now Rege?"

"It would be devilish awkward, Egypt,"[13] he answered with a harsh laugh.

"You'll get £5,000 a year, won't you?" Not changing her attitude.

"Yes, but the situation's not permanent, Katie."

"What would you do if you *had* to give her up, or if she gave you up?" she questioned, turning and looking full at him.

"God knows! a colonial governorship I suppose, but why discuss it? The question can't very well arise. I must tell her of the new move to-night. It will put her in a good temper possibly; she'll see she's getting value for her money."

There was a sudden *frou-frou* of drapery and she was kneeling at his side. "Reginald," she said. "*Don't* tell her to-night. *Don't, don't*, I *can't* bear it."

There was so much pleading and pathos in her voice that he leaned forward and drew her head tight against his breast. "Why my dear little girl what on earth's the matter? Of course I won't if you don't wish it. But what does it matter? She must know soon."

"But not to-night," she whispered, "let me have the secret all to myself to-night."

"All right, then, you shall," he said, "I'll leave it until to-morrow."

They sat in silence while the blaze of the fire burnt itself away to a mere red glow. When the room was almost dark she spoke again.

"Exactly how much do you care for the 'married woman' Reginald?"

"Well, upon my soul I don't know: about as much as she cares for me I fancy. But why bother about her?"

"She helps you a good deal," she said, not noticing the question. "They all say she won the seat for you; even Camelot thinks so."

"Camelot knows nothing about it," he answered testily, "I won the seat with my own brain and my own tongue. Ethel got the votes of half-a-dozen snobby trades-men, but my majority was 800. This 'influence of woman' business is absurdly overdone. A pretty woman loses as many votes as she gains by offending the women – merely by being pretty – and then they put pressure on their husbands."

"That looks as though women *had* some influence doesn't it?" she asked with a mischievous smile.

"Well yes, you rather had me there Katie," he answered laughing, "but to return to the subject, if Ethel does help me, it's not because she cares for me but because she likes meddling. Help – it's *you* who help me, my sweetheart," catching her face between his hands, and speaking with passionate enthusiasm. "It was your letters that won Ralston – your confidence and encouragement, your hope. Why, one dear little note from you put more devil into me than any number of 'promises of support' that Ethel brought in with her to dinner. *She* never believed that I should win."

"But I *knew* it," she said springing up. "There, go now Rege, I'm not jealous, not a bit. Now put your coat on. Goodbye – Come to-morrow" ... "Rege" she called as he was closing the door. "You may tell the 'married woman' to-night if you like, I don't care, I knew first."

He came back, caught her in his arms again, kissed her and then left the house. When she heard the front door slam behind him she sank down into the chair in which he had been sitting, and in a few minutes her face again assumed the puzzled, troubled expression it wore when he had entered. "What ought I to do?" she asked of herself. "He shall be Prime Minister and he must have the money. Well, anyhow, I hold the whip and that's almost as good as using it. No, there shan't be a scandal if I can help it." Then she started up with a sudden thought. "By heaven," she said, "I've a good mind to write and warn her. That *would* be a sacrifice for him." Further self converse was cut short by the entrance of a servant to clear away the tea-cups.

Meanwhile, Sir Reginald Hastie was saying to himself as he walked rapidly down the Edgware Road, "I'm glad Katie was sensible about my telling Ethel, she's a dear little brick not to be jealous. By God, how some women would worry me. I'm afraid I should have had to have told Ethel anyway. It'll put her in such a good temper. She's been awfully queer lately and I *cannot* stand home worries just now. I must keep a clear head. By Jove I never asked what Camelot had had to say. I wish he wouldn't go there quite so often."

[March 1888]

Part II.

When Sir Reginald Hastie entered his drawing-room, half-an-hour before the usual dinner time, his first glance at his wife's face told him that the sooner he made known his good news the better. Lady Hastie was a beautiful woman, but never did a beautiful woman look less like being a pleasant *vis-à-vis* at a dinner table than did she at that moment. She was sitting in a rather stagey attitude with one arm thrown over the back of a sofa, and in her other hand she held on her lap a monthly magazine. Two or three novels lay on the sofa beside her. She had evidently found it difficult to read. She looked up at her husband as he entered, and then turned her dark eyes with an angry flash and a vicious drawing down of the corners of her fine, contemptuous lips. She had been at the point of speaking and restrained herself with a muscular effort. Sir Reginald missed the look but he saw the hardening of the muscles of the cheek which was turned towards him, and he knew that a storm was close. He usually kissed his wife when meeting her after an absence of hours, but he decided to omit the ceremony on this occasion. He walked up to the fire rubbed his hands cheerfully, and said with a perfectly jovial and easy air.

"Now Ethel, guess where I've been this afternoon?"

"There is no need for me to guess, I *know*."

The words were delivered in such a well restrained *staccato* voice, and the passion beneath them was so well concealed that for a moment he really believed that someone had seen him in Curzon Street and had told his wife, who had jumped to true conclusions.

"The deuce you do," he said, "then you don't seem very well pleased at it; my dear."

His tone was so entirely genuine that Lady Hastie saw that her shaft had somehow missed the mark. If he had anything interesting to tell he might as well tell it before she fired again, she thought.

"Where have you been?" she asked.

"Ah, I thought you didn't know – I've been to Branstock's – he sent for me."

This was unexpected – she rose from the sofa, adjusted the pink shade on a candle which stood upon the mantle-shelf and said, putting as little curiosity into her voice as possible,

"What does Branstock want with you? Are you to have something to hold your tongue?"

The slight sneer in her voice and on her lips was a mean one, as a good deal of Sir Reginald's obstructive criticism in the house had been made at his wife's instigation.

"No," he answered, still good humouredly, "on the contrary I'm to have something to use it."

"Well, what is it Reginald? Don't be childish, I think I have some right to know at once without all this mystery."

"My dear, you've every right to know and you would have known some minutes ago, only you more than suggested that you knew already – I'm to have the Exchequer."

Lady Hastie's eyes danced for a second and the black look on her face almost cleared away.

"The Exchequer," she repeated, "what, in the Cabinet?"

"Ah, your omniscience didn't run to that, did it, my Ethel? And there's more to follow, I'm to lead."

"To *lead*! When? – Oh, until Mr. Smeeth is better I suppose."

"Yes, dear, quite so – until then. And as poor Smeeth gave up the ghost some hours ago, that is likely to be for some time to come. But really Ethel, it is time for me to inquire where *you* have been to-day, that you have not heard news which is all over London."

She walked slowly to the end of the room, her head bent low; as she turned again she said in a low voice,

"You're a lucky man, Reginald."

The adjective didn't please him. He stepped towards her. "Yes," he said. "The stars in their courses, and so on of course. But I think you must credit something to my own brains – to *our* brains at any rate. Come, let us kiss and congratulate, and then go down and drink to the coming premier – and his charming wife."

He was going to embrace her, and one hand had already touched her shoulder. As it did so she drew herself up suddenly. He dropped his arms and stepped half a pace back. "What on earth *is* –" he was beginning.

"How dare you touch me –?" she cried with an imperious gesture of contempt. "How dare you come here at all? You have no right even to come near me."

This had been a day of startling events to Sir Reginald Hastie, but the very genuine look of surprise with which he greeted this outburst shewed that this was the most startling of them all.

"What *do* you mean, Ethel?" he asked rather feebly. Meeting with no answer but a vicious look, he added in an angrier tone than any in which he had yet spoken. "Let us have an end of this. You've been damnably enigmatical altogether lately. What is there in the background? Has my news to-night entirely turned your brain, or *what* is it?"

"Let us have an *end* of it, by all means," she answered, drawing herself up to her full height, clenching her fists and holding her arms stiffly at her sides. "There *shall* be an end of it. You either give me up, and you know what else that means, or *her*!"

A good deal of Sir Reginald Hastie's success in politics was owing to the rapid, indeed, the almost instantaneous manner in which he grasped every side of an opponent's case at once. When older and more sophisticated politicians fenced and dodged and beat about the bush, pretending not to see the strong points in an argument, replying only to the weak ones, he always addressed himself at once to the real difficulties, and incontinently withdrew from really indefensible positions directly they were threatened. This faculty of taking in the situation at a glance failed him as little in domestic as in public difficulties. He now saw at once that his wife was not merely "bluffing," and assuming a knowledge which she didn't actually possess. He dropped the offensive and his face immediately assumed a business-like expression. He turned away from her, leaving her standing in the middle of the room in a dramatic pose, sat down, crossed his legs, and leaning forward, asked in the tone of one addressing a hostile solicitor's clerk,

"Well, and now what are your exact terms, Ethel?"

Although Lady Hastie had quite made up her mind to impose terms, and not very easy ones, she had by no means come to a decision as to their exact nature. Like most women she had hesitated to take a final position from which no retreat was possible. She had meant to have a "row," a great "row," and she had meant to come well out of it, for she felt she had the whip hand. But she had looked at the whole matter from the emotional and not at all from the business point of view. Her unreadiness showed itself in her face, and her husband felt he had scored the first point. He had, but it was a very small victory. His coolness and her own sense of being baffled acted upon her as would a smart blow from a cane upon a man whose weapon was a sword – it only made her angrier and more determined to use her advantages unsparingly.

She dropped her tragedy queen manner and tried to imitate the tone and expression of her husband. She came and stood in front of him, he pointed to a chair but she took no notice of the gesture –

"Understand then," she said, much more quietly, although her voice trembled "that this woman must be given up. Given up!" Getting passionate again, "no, I'll take no promises – she must leave London, leave England altogether – and leave at once. Stop, let me finish," seeing him sit back in his chair and apparently about to interrupt. "Don't tell me you *can't* do it, you can have money, you know that, I can pay for it as I pay for everything else."

"That you want," he added as though to complete something she had left unsaid. "You are quite right, of course I can do it if I like. I am glad to note that your estimate of my power has risen. You once doubted my ever being in the Cabinet, you may remember. But what I *can* do is not the point. Do sit down," glancing at his watch, "dinner will be ready almost directly. But now, what if I decline your terms, my dear Ethel? You have considered that possibility, of course. What are your alternatives? You won't leave the youthful statesman, surely?"

"I shall write to my brother to-night," she said, making as though to go towards the door, "and I shall see Mr. Dunlop to-morrow. I will have a separation, and every one shall know how I've been treated." The last words with a passionate sob.

He rose and stood between her and the door. "I see the point exactly," he said rather excitedly, "a public scandal, as fools will call it, will drive me out of the Cabinet and the House, too, for that matter. Oh yes, I see it all, but remember, if I am not a Cabinet Minister you won't be a Minister's wife. Stop, Ethel," he raised his hand seeing that she was about to interrupt. "Think what you're about, I'm not going to lie or pretend that you haven't got hold of the truth, but you're no worse off than any of the women you know. Even if people do get wind of this business, it doesn't matter to you, no one will think any the less of you. Isn't it worth while to be a Prime Minister's wife, even if I am like all other men?"

She made a few steps towards the door and he made a few steps back. "What do I know about 'other men' and 'other women,'" she cried with a shrill note in her voice. "I tell you *you* must give the woman up. *Other* women! Other women haven't made their husband's careers as I have made yours. Do you suppose I am going to have you coming from her to me, and going from me to her? No, I would rather go back to the States and leave England altogether, and let you fall back into the insignificance my money saved you from."

The injustice of the taunts as to making his career and saving him from insignificance irritated him even more than the vulgar shrillness of tone in which they were uttered, though that was bad enough. Lady Hastie's "money" was the accumulation of a Yankee hotel keeper (on a very large scale) and some traces of her early environment were apt to shew themselves in her voice when that voice grew angry. Those who have anything to hide in the way of social antecedents should learn to keep their tempers, especially if they happen to be women. The more delicate the material, the sooner the spots show themselves.[14]

He made a desperate effort to keep his own voice down to the conversational pitch and succeeded. The effort also suppressed to some extent his rising temper. Six years hard fighting in the House of Commons had taught him that even ten seconds consideration before retort is better than nothing.

"Well," he said, "if this is your ultimatum I suppose I must consider it. I suppose you must feel the matter keenly if you are ready to give up your own position as well as ruin mine. You shall have your answer to-morrow."

She was going to reply, but a voice from the door behind him stopped her.

"Dinner is served," it said.

He offered her his arm which she did not take, and they left the room side by side. The silence during that meal, Lady Hastie's want of appetite, and Sir Reginald's evident thirst caused some interested speculation below stairs.

A couple of hours later Sir Reginald was once more standing at the front door of No. 118A, Maida Vale, nervously pulling at his moustache, and with a worried, haggard look on his pale face.

[April 1888]

Part III.

The mistress of 118A Maida Vale, known to local tradesmen as Mrs. Reginald Blythe, shewed as little appetite for her dinner that evening as did Lady Hastie at Cathcart Place. She got through it with the rapidity of a city clerk over his mid-day chop, and going back to the drawing-room, turned down the lamp and settled herself once more before the fire to think.

The old-fashioned clock on the mantel shelf had ticked away as many seconds as to make an hour before she even changed her attitude. Then she rose and paced slowly up and down the room, her hands clasped behind her and her head bent forward. After a few minutes of this exercise she stopped with a gesture of impatience. "Bother!" she said aloud, "I *must* do something. Ah, if I only had Reginald's brain – he would have come to a decision before he sat down to dinner." She went over to a little carved black oak secretaire,[15] took out a sheet of note paper. She tore off the half sheet which bore the embossed address 118A, Maida Vale, N.W., and on the other half wrote in a large round school-girl hand: "Your intrigue with Lord Amersford is known to more than one or two and is getting talked about. Your husband," here her pen spluttered and the word was half obliterated by a little archipelago of blots "*must* hear of it soon. If you want to save his career and your own name *stop!* Don't *be careful*, but stop altogether." Where the signature should have come she made a bold flourish, pushed the paper away from her with an expression of bitter contempt on her face, and getting up again took another turn across the room.

"I had better do the thing in the orthodox way while I'm about it," she said, "and sign the accursed thing 'a friend' ... No, I can't do that. After all I haven't lied in my anonymous letter ... And yet I am her friend in this."

She caught up a little velvet frame from a table covered with nic-nacks, and held it out at arm's length in front of her. It contained a cabinet portrait[16] of Sir Reginald Hastie. "Ah, you're a clever man Reginald," she said in a theatrical tone, "but the biggest thing you've ever done is to get one woman to do a thing like this for another woman she hates. And the people," with a curve of the lip, "will never know this, my dear," she went on, bringing the portrait nearer to her face. "And half of them wouldn't know what it meant if they did, but the other half would though," with a hysterical laugh. "Oh yes, any woman would know that after this the Treasury Bench is a small thing to compass." She pressed the portrait against her lips so hard that the class was blurred for the next five minutes. "*You* don't hesitate when a thing has to be done Rege," she spoke again, "and neither will I." She put the portrait back in its place and sat down at the secretaire again, took out an envelope and addressed it "Lady Hastie, Cathcart Place, W.," in the same round hand in which she had written the letter. Then she went towards the bell but stopped as her hand touched it. "No, I'll post it myself and I'll leave it until the morning. It will probably be delivered when he's out, then; he might guess at the handwriting if he happed to see it, he's awfully sharp." She locked the letter in the secretaire, picked up an evening paper which lay on a chair and read through it mechanically from Editorial to Theatrical announcements.

A couple of hours later she was sitting at her toilet table, half undressed, looking through a little pile of letters, when she heard a sharp hurried rat-tat at the front door. The sound seemed familiar, for she rose, went swiftly to the wardrobe, scrambled into a grey dressing-gown and was making for the door when it burst open, almost striking her in the face, and Sir Reginald Hastie, his hat still on his head and umbrella in hand, came into the room.

She gave one rapid glance at his face then shut the door behind him.

"Oh, Rege! back again at this time, what is the matter? You look frightful, my dear boy; tell me, tell me at once," she said going to him and putting her hands on his shoulders.

"I can't yet; wait a moment," he answered, "my mouth feels parched, let me get some water."

He turned from her, went to the washstand and took a long drink from the carafe, not stopping to pour the water into a glass. Then he threw his hat and umbrella on to the bed and sat down in a low wicker chair.

"Come here, little woman," he said, "come to me."

Without speaking she dropped on to her knees at his feet, again put a hand on each of his shoulders and looked eagerly into his eyes. For a few seconds he returned the look in silence, the he spoke.

"Katie, she knows," he said.

She passed her hands round his neck, interlaced her fingers and bending her head so that he could not see her face, spoke almost in a whisper.

"Well, and then what, eh?"

"She says ... Oh my God! why should I tell what she says? My whole game's at an end, I shall have to refuse the Exchequer, chuck up my seat, everything."

"Nonsense, why, what can she do?" without looking up.

"She's going to leave me, go for a separation, make a scandal."

She withdrew her arm from his neck, rose to her feet and stood at his side looking across the room.

"Is that all?" she said, "Good heavens you can defy that. Does the public demand conjugal fidelity in its financiers?"

"You know it does," he returned, leaning forward with an elbow on each knee and tugging at the ends of his moustache with each hand, "look at White, quite as big a man as I am, and has had to go; and if the public doesn't, the Queen does, damn her!"

"You're talking nonsense, Reginald," she said, giving his coat collar an impatient shake, "White was very different, he was a beast and deserved all he got. I don't believe Branstock will care a bit, and she can only get a separation anyway – you've not been beating her I suppose[17] – besides, she'll change her mind, you'll be able to keep it all quiet."

There was a silence of half-a-minute, then she said –

"Come now, it'll be all right, won't it? I dare say you'll have to alter your domestic arrangements a little," with a scornful twist of the under lip, "but you'll be able to bear that."

He still did not answer or change his attitude. She was just on the point of speaking again when he said –

"Katie, come and kneel down again." She stepped to the front of his chair and sat at his feet, throwing her arm across his knee and catching one of his hands in hers, but keeping her face turned from him and not speaking.

Again there was a long silence and he sat passing his gloved fingers through her hair which she had let down, and which covered her back and shoulders. At last he cleared his throat and speaking as though his tongue and lips were parched with fever, said with a slight pause between each phrase.

"I haven't ... told you all ... Lady ... she has offered terms ... but I ... can't accept them. She means to make a scandal ... on purpose to ruin me."

Then he stopped and threw himself back in the chair fiercely champing at his moustache.

She turned round and gave him a swift, searching, half-suspicious look.

"That's not *terms*, Reginald," she said, with a strong emphasis on the last word.

"No, I know. Come here, come closer Katie." He leaned forward put both his arms about her and drew her head tightly on to his breast. "My darling," he went on speaking much more rapidly, "she says, she ... I must answer her to-morrow, and I ... she says she will sue for a separation and put an end to all my chances ... Oh, it's no use, the public won't stand it now ... or else I must ... never come here any more, and you must go away – Oh, my God if I'd had the pluck of a louse, I should have strangled her as she spoke."

A kind of stifled gasp came from her lips as he finished. She wrenched her head from his arms and sprang upright. "And what did you do?" She asked in a low, clear, cutting voice.

He rose too, "I ... did nothing, I said I'd consider," he answered.

She stepped back a pace from him, "Yes, and you came here to consider. Well, decide Reginald, it's easy enough. Oh, you know, *I* won't spoil your future if your wife would. You *have* decided. That's what you *can't* tell me, isn't it? Come, speak ... be a man," she said, again retreating as he made a slight motion of coming towards her. Her voice trembled a little, and her cheeks flamed with excitement.

There was the very slightest suspicion of irresolution, not in his face, but in his pose, as he stood looking at her for an instant. Then he sprang towards her and in spite of her violent struggles, folded her tight in his arms.

"No, by Christ," he hissed in a voice throbbing with passion, "My darling, you know. She, Branstock, the Cabinet, and the country, too, may go to the devil for aught I care. What are they, what is anything beside you? *Yes*, I *have* decided, and this is my decision." His arm was round her neck, and turning her face upwards he covered it with dry, hot, fierce kisses. She did not resist him now. A shiver passed through her whole frame, and she leaned supine in his arms with closed eyes, lost to everything but the sensuous emotion of the moment. When the spasm of passion had passed and his arms relaxed their iron grip of her, she stood upright again and walked in a weary dazed way to the bed. She sat down on it, and buried her face in her hands for a moment. He poured himself out a glass of water and drank it like one suffering from burning thirst.

When he turned round again she was standing with blazing eyes and cheeks, and with swift nervous hands was unfastening her dressing gown. She flung it off and threw it from her.

"Reginald," she said, "take me to that woman, take me at once."

He stared at her as though he thought she had suddenly been bereft of reason.

"Katie," he said, "What do you mean? What madness, you *know* I cannot."

"Then let me go by myself. Oh! I'm not going like this," running her fingers through her hair, "I'm not mad." She walked towards a wardrobe and he fell back a pace or two towards the door.

"Do be reasonable, dear," he said, "what good could it do. It would only be throwing oil on the flames. No, no, it's all no go. My mind's made up, I must give up everything but you."

She was putting a walking dress over her head as he spoke the last words. She dragged it off, threw it on to the bed and came towards him.

"Rege," she said, "you're not humbugging me are you? And you don't mean to try deceiving her and keeping on with ... us both? Do you really mean that you're going to give up all your chances just now, all your life, for me?"

Sir Reginald gave a half-hysterical, half-ironical laugh.

"Yes, yes," he said, "just about that, if you like to put it that way – No, I'm not humbugging. I shan't even try it on with her. By God, I don't care enough about her to humbug her – not about anything for the matter of that, even the Treasury. Come little woman, it's all right, let's sit down and be quiet a bit, let's talk of something else."

She came close up to him. "Kiss me, my darling," she said.

He caught her in his arms, looked curiously and a little puzzledly in her face, and kissed her twice on the mouth. "There, what now –?"

Then she held him by each elbow and looked up straight into his face – intensely, as though to watch on it the expression of every emotion to which her words might give rise.

"Listen, Reginald," she said, "that beast at Cathcart Place shall not spoil your career, ruin your life, or at least she shall smash up her own if she does. *She* dare to try to drive me from you! *She* play the outraged wife, make terms! Listen, Rege – the whip hand's mine, and now it's going to be yours. The married woman's in the thick of an intrigue. Ah! I thought you didn't care –?" He had started violently and raised both hands to his mouth, but her sharp change of tone recalled him to self-command. He dropped his hands again.

"Well, I don't," he said, "I only think you're wrong, that's all?"

"Oh, you hope I'm wrong!"

"N ... no ... I don't know ... no, I don't think I do ... I'm not sure ... go on."

"Well, whether you care or not, listen now. Go home ... go back to her now at once – go quietly and calmly, and accuse her of adultery with Lord Amersford. Tell her that she was with him at the Railway Hotel, Peterboro', on the 8th of last month, the night you were speaking at Ralston; and at Farningham, down in Kent, once last September when you were at Glevering, shooting. Tell her just that, and then dictate terms – now stop – if you can't, then make any terms you like, never come near me again – I mean it. Oh, Rege, Rege, *that* will convince you I know what I'm talking about."

While she had been speaking he had kept control of his body and had given no more violent starts, but of his tongue he hadn't quite the mastery and had interjected "Amersford," "that boy," "I never thought," "Why she was at Brighton with Mary."

When she had finished and stepped back from him, watching him keenly the while, he remained quite silent, twisting the ends of his moustache, moving his lips a little and apparently piecing certain things together in his mind. When at last he spoke, he spoke as calmly as he had done in that last interview with Lady Hastie.

"I daresay you're right," he said, "I had a row with her about Amersford last autumn, I remember, but she has always seemed quite cool to him since then. Oh, yes, you needn't laugh. I don't attach any importance to that now, that's rather evidence the other way, I know. But I can hardly go and make these circumstantial accusations without knowing one thing. You must tell me how you know it all, Katie."

"Well," she said after a second's hesitation, "I suppose I must, I've broken promises before for you – so here goes one more – Lord Camelot told me."

Sir Reginald brought his hand down with such a bang on a small marbled-topped *table de nuit*[18] which stood beside him that he knocked several pieces of skin from his knuckles, and sent a small cut-glass bottle dancing on to the floor. "Camelot," he cried, almost in a shout, "promises – damnation, what does he mean coming to you and talking like that?"

She gave her head a little jerk, half of amusement, half of irritation, and caught hold of the hand he had just injured.

"Oh *don't* be ridiculous, just at a moment like this," she said, pressing her handkerchief on to the ill-used knuckles, "Camelot told me because he knew that I was the best friend you had in the world, and that he was the next and –"

"When did he say this?"

"To-day, just before you came."

"Why didn't you tell me at once? I thought there was something wrong about you. But stop, how did he come to know it? How does he know she was at Peterboro' and all that?"

"Because he saw her there, but he –"

"And kept it all this time. Good –"

"Rege, do for heaven's sake be quiet and listen patiently, I'll tell you every-thing. Can't you sit down and be quiet?"

She pushed him to the edge of the bed and sat down beside him, still keeping hold of his hand and dabbing it with her handkerchief from time to time as she spoke.

"Now don't interrupt me – or I shall tell lies – my brain's all in a whirl. Camelot only told me because he didn't know what else to do. He *was* nearly going straight to you, but thought he'd ask me first. On the 8th or 9th of last month he was coming up from somewhere and had to change at Peterboro' about 10 o'clock in the morning. He went out of the station to stretch his legs, or get a drink, or something. You know the Great Northern Hotel is just oppo-site the station, and as he was standing close to the porch, that woman came out with Amersford, carrying a bag, and they went to the London train. He met her almost face to face and was nearly raising his hat, but they turned their heads sharply away and, of course, he did the same. He actually waited there for the next train because he was afraid of running up against them again at King's Cross. Well, only the other –"

"But why did he keep it? Why did he keep it?" he cried standing up again.

She pulled him down. "Sit down, sit down, and I'll try to tell you. How could he tell anyone? Would you tell a man if you had seen his wife like that? Of course he'd never have told – and you can't blame him – but the other night. Oh! when was it? The night before last he was at the Cecil,[19] Amersford was there, beastly drunk; he was talking and boasting to a lot of young fools about all sorts of women, and suddenly he said something about your wife. Directly Camelot caught her name he went up to him and dragged him out of the club. He tried to put him in a cab, but he wouldn't be put, so Camelot had to walk home with him; going along he lost his temper, and began to bully Amersford about men-tioning her sacred name. Then Amersford came out with the whole story, and shouted out all about Farningham, told Camelot to go to the devil, and said he should say what he liked about a damned whore, and all that sort of thing. Camelot hit him in the mouth, and threw him down on to some steps in Clarges Street, and left him wailing there. But then he made up his mind that you must know somehow, as probably Amersford would do this kind of thing again, and it would get to your ears and everybody else's, and so yesterday he came to me."

He was quite quiet and still now, but his face was deadly white with greenish streaks about it, and his rather prominent eyes seemed to have sunk an inch into his head.

He withdrew his hand from hers and put it, trembling violently, round her waist. "Why didn't you tell me all this to-day, Katie?" he asked.

"Oh! how could I? I hadn't made up my mind what to do. And you were so happy and jolly about your talk with Branstock. I *couldn't*. I was nearly telling you when I asked you if you could do without the married woman, don't you remember. But look Rege, don't make a scandal. You can't divorce her you know, because she knows about ... you and ... about me. You can easily stop her game with Amersford now, and you can make your own terms about the future. Go to-morrow and do it, and bear it dear, you'll be Prime Minister when Branstock dies, or at any rate some day. You must, for my sake."

"I must do it to-night, at once," he said getting up, "or I shall never do it."

"No, not to-night ... Well, perhaps you had better. Let me get you some brandy first, you look as though you'd drop dead."

She put on her dressing gown again and ran down stairs. She was some time gone, for she unlocked her secretaire took out the letter addressed "Lady Hastie," tore it across and burnt it in the grate. Then she came back with a wine-glass nearly full of brandy. He drank it off in two gulps.

"There," he said, smacking his lips, "now I think I can face her. The ultimatum's mine this time, and the whip's in my hand I fancy. Goodbye my sweet," taking her in his arms and kissing her a dozen times, "I must go at once or I shan't go at all, you little rogue. Come down to the door with me." He caught up his hat and umbrella, and they went down the stairs, his arm still round her waist, her hand on his shoulder. As he opened the door and kissed her again, "Goodbye," she said, "don't think me cruel, but I've never let you go with less unhappiness. I know it's awfully hard for you, poor old boy. I shan't mind your going away at night quite so much for the future, shall I? and you won't have to go quite so often. Goodbye."

* * *

That night Lady Hastie's maid heard what she called a "rumpus" going on in her mistress' room, and told her fellow servants to prepare their minds for a break up of the establishment. For the next few days, certain ugly rumours were whispered about in the Clubs as to a coming *éclat* in the world political, and more than one "Society" journal published prophetic paragraphs. But a fortnight later Messrs. Gilbert and Sullivan produced their new opera at the Savoy, and all the world knew next morning that Sir Reginald and Lady Hastie had sat together in the third row in the Stalls, and looked over one programme.

No one had anything but praise for the brilliant speech with which Sir Reginald introduced his first Budget.

John Law, 'The Gospel of Getting On. (To Olive Schreiner.)' (1888)

I saw a mother teaching her little son. Two books lay on her knee open. The one was the Gospel of Christ, the other the Gospel of Getting On.

She read from the Gospel of Christ the following lesson. "Thou shalt love they neighbour as thyself. This is the whole law and the prophets."

She closed that book and read from the Gospel of Getting On.

"Thou shalt get fame, and heap up riches. This is the law of the Nineteenth Century and the Political Economist."

I saw the boy leave home for school, carrying with him the two gospels.

"Be a good boy," his father said, "and get on."

"Don't forget to say your prayers," whispered his mother, "and get on."

* * *

The boy came home for the holidays, bringing a prize with him. He had got on. And his friend Lord Tom Noddy,[1] was made much of by his father and mother; for Lord Tom Noddy could by-and-bye help him to get on. Smith and Jones, who had won no prizes, were quite forgotten; although they were poor, and had no homes to go to. But Lord Tom Noddy was introduced to everyone as "such a good friend for our son."

* * *

I saw him at college, getting on. Sometimes he fell asleep in chapel, while a Don read "Thou shalt love thy neighbour as thyself; this is the whole law and the prophets." But out of chapel he carried everything before him; he got on.

One evening I saw him rowing on the Cam.[2] He looked full of hope, young, handsome! And with him was one who could never get on; a little thing weighted by ignorance, tethered by poverty, with just enough sense to love and worship.

She was singing a song, and this was the chorus.

"Oh talk not to me of a name great in story.
The days of our youth, are the days of our glory."[3]

The waters rippled the music. The girl's voice has a sickening sound of pain in it. His face was full of eagerness. He rested on his oars; and I watched the boat – drifting.

* * *

He left college, and entered his father's business. Every morning he went to the office; and people said the junior partner was sure to get on. He gave donations to charities, money made by the long hours and low wages of men and women who worked on his premises. He read the lessons in Church, the Gospel according to Jesus of Nazareth.

Later on he married.

"My dear," his wife said, "you must be a Member of Parliament. I will start a new charity, with a Royal Princess as President. A charitable institution helps a man get on."

* * *

Then I lost sight of him.

But one night I saw him again.

He was standing by a grave near the Cam.

A voice asked, "Who murdered this woman?"

Answer came, "This man."

"Why did he do it?"

"To get on."

"Who taught him that doctrine?"

"His mother."

"Where did she find it?"

"In a spurious gospel."

"What is it called?"

"Getting On."

"How old is it?"

"One hundred and fifty years old."[4]

"Who are its priests?"

"The Political Economists."

The voice said:

"Bring that gospel, and spread it out before me."

A roll fell from the man's hand. The pages were covered with black letters. The capitals were written in blood. The stops were curses. There was the trail of a dying crofter's finger[5] upon it, and blots – the sweat of Irish peasants.[6] Strong men weeping because they had no bread to give their children were drawn upon it, also pale-faced girls, and mothers groaning over their stunted babies.

It lay open on the grave by the Cam.

The voice asked, "Are there none left that follow Jesus of Nazareth?"

Answer came, "A few Socialists."

Then I saw a small group of men and women. They had crowns of thorns on their foreheads; and they pressed the thorns down into their flesh.

Saying,

"Love thy neighbour as thyself. This is the whole law, and the prophets."

H. Bellingham, 'Chips' (1888)

It was a very strange world for Chips. He had made up his mind long ago that he, Chips, was a mistake in it. Chips' world was a very small one; it reached only from the cellar where he slept to the crossing that he swept, but he found no room in it for him, he was elbowed out of it. Had he known how big the world really is, he might have wandered away to find the place in it that he was intended to fill. But he would not have found it, for the grown men had not yet made up their mind about Chips's place, and until they could do so, Chips must live and die in any out-of-the-way corner. Chips had at one time thought it not unlikely that some one might make room for him, but he knew better now: clearly he was one too many in the world, for the people who had a right to the places in it paid a policeman to keep him away from them. He had his crossing, but he had had to fight for that, and now his broom was worn to the stick, and the weather was often dry for weeks together. When it was not he made a few more halfpence, but he got soaked through and this made him ill, and now he was very ill indeed with a deadly fever and could not go out at all. Another boy, as wretched as he, had stolen his broom and taken his crossing, so that Chips if he could have got out would have found still less room left for him. There was nothing for Chips but to stay where he was, and to this he was reconciled by the companionship of his friend, the frog.

His friend, the frog, had been brought out of the green lanes by the big boys who went out on Sunday mornings to snare birds, and finding its way into Chips' cellar it had become the only plaything of the sick boy.

"Froggie," thought Chips, "is as much out of place as I am." And he felt for the frog the same pity he had always felt for himself.

Chips and Froggie had exchanged confidences, and in the saddest fashion they came to know that for neither of them could there by any more a place in the world.

And one bright morning when the good sun was struggling to send a broken ray down into the dim cellar to cheer the sick boy, Froggie who was lying panting painfully in the hot hand of Chips said on a sudden: –

"Dear little boy, I am very sorry to leave you all alone, but I feel as I did when I changed from a tadpole to a frog, and I know that I am going to leave my frog's body and go away out into the bright air."

And then Froggie's legs went very shaky and all in a minute he turned over on his back and lay very quite, and Chips knew he was dead.

Chips would have cried over the loss of his companion, but just at that moment he felt as it were an icy hand at his heart which made him shut his eyes in pain, and when he re-opened them he found that he held in his hand instead of the frog a quivering beam of light. And the hand itself was not the poor thin grimy hand he knew, but bright, transparent, and shapely, and all his body had undergone a similar change. The pain was all gone too and he could stand up, and he felt a strange desire to float or fly. Then he became aware of the presence of a beautiful boy, who glittered like a sunbeam and who held out his hand to him, and kissing him on the cheek led him out of the dim cellar. But instead of climbing the broken ladder they floated out into the sunny street, and instead of walking along on the hot pavement they went up high in the air above the heads of the people. But strangest of all, the air, so far as Chips could see, was peopled with a host of bright beings like himself who came and went hither and thither, in and out of the houses, and hovered round the passengers in the streets.

Said Chips, "Pretty boy, I have lived ten years in the world and I never saw anything like this."

"How could you when you were alive?" said the pretty boy, laughing a soft silvery laugh that was like a forest of silver bells ever so far away.

"Pretty boy," said Chips again, after he had thought for a minute or two, "am I dead?"

At this the pretty boy laughed again and still holding Chips's hand drew him swiftly back to the cellar door. And Chips looking in, saw himself looking very white and motionless, and understanding that he was dead, said very solemnly: –

"Poor little boy! He has got out of the way at last. There never was any room for him – And Froggie?" he asked.

"Its spirit is in your hand," said the boy. "No life perishes, but when it quits its earthly being, it roams the wide universe as a tender thought of the great God. Let it go, to do its appointed work.

Chips loosed the spirit of the frog which rapidly sped away.

"What is God?" said Chips.

It had been nobody's business to teach him anything, and Chips in seeking that place in the world which he never could find, and in thinking what mistake he must be altogether, had not got so far as to imagine Who had put him there. He knew what churches were, but of their purpose nothing. Hard-pressed for a night's lodging he had sometimes looked longingly at the deep-vaulted porches, but the iron rails kept him out. Churches were not for Chips. Of Book and Priest and what they wonderfully taught, he knew nothing. Ancient Record and adored Mystery, which were lights to the groping soul of Man, had not penetrated the crowd that wedged in Chips, else might he have caught a faint glimmer of the truth that flows there, reflected in all distorted fashions by men's vain fancies.

"God is Love."

"And what is Love," asked Chips.

Have you never heard men of soft lives with gracious women and sweet children round you, have you never heard the agonised cry of hundreds of thousands of yearning for the hand and voice and the kiss of love? The cry of these desolate, of poor women, of poor children! While you sit with your pockets buttoned polishing some rough poor law, content to be ruled by a demon called Expediency, these are wading though the sloughs of infamy and misery, fainting for a word of sympathy, lost for want of an outstretched hand. Are they nothing to you, these gloomy men and these hollow-cheeked women, the sisters of despair, these white-faced children born into hell?

"What is Love?"

His glittering guide drew him gently downwards till they hovered only a few feet above a crowded thoroughfare.

"Why, there's my crossing," cried Chips, "and there – there's that Bob that stole my broom."

And stooping he kissed the dirty cheek of the wretched Bob.

"Ah!" said Bob, turning up a grateful face towards the sun, his cheek flushed with Chips' kiss, "we do get the sun for nothink."

That was Chips' first love-lesson in God's other world.

EDITORIAL NOTES

Clarke, 'What a Christmas Carol Wrought'

1. *streetling*: one whose life is spent on the streets, living and/or working. In modern slang it is restricted to one who sells drugs on the streets, but here it is used to refer to the sale of general goods.
2. *fusees*: a fuse or match, tipped with brimstone, that is ignited by friction. Also known as a lucifer or a vesuvian; *OED*. The plight of the matchbox makers for Bryant and May had been recognized by Henry Hyde Champion and presented to a Fabian Society meeting in June 1888. This led to the organization of the Bryant and May matchgirls by Annie Besant and Herbert Burrows and their successful strike in 1888, which in turn began the New Union movement and the organization of previously unorganized unskilled workers. See also p. 317 n. 11 below.

Ashton, 'Heaw Bill Spriggs Leet New Yer In'

1. *Deansgate*: one of the main streets in Bolton city centre which runs along the left of the Town Hall Square (Teaun Haw Square).
2. *Wild Beast Show*: The travelling menagerie was a popular entertainment that brought ordinary people the only opportunity to see live wild animals. The menagerie would parade into town, and the animals would be displayed in open-sided wagons set in a square with an advertising hoard, a balcony from where the public would hear tales of the dangers of the animals inside, and a paybox where customers could pay for entry.
3. *bustles*: a stuffed pad or wire frame worn under a woman's skirt to give volume at the back; *OED*. Bill is likening the camel's hump to a woman's bustle.
4. *parashoots*: parachutes, used here to describe the size and form of an elephant's ears.
5. *menadghery*: menagerie.
6. *nussin ... warm*: from Robert Burns's (1759–96) poem *Tam O'Shanter* (1790), as Tam and his friends – like Bill and his Menociation – sit in the pub and think about their wives waiting for them at home: 'We think na on the lang Scots miles, / The mosses, waters, slaps and stiles, / That lie between us and our hame, / Where sits our sulky, sullen dame, / Gathering her brows like gathering storm, / Nursing her wrath to keep it warm'.

H. S. S., 'A Dream of Queer Fishes (A Modern Prose Idyll)'

1. *Theocritus*: Greek poet (300–260 BC), author of pastoral poetry termed idylls, which were criticized for assigning peasant characters with a greater capacity for language and sentiment than was deemed realistic.

2. *Salisbury and Co.*: a reference to Robert Gascoyne Cecil, Lord Salisbury's (1830–1903) Conservative government (1886–92). The story is a thinly disguised criticism of Joseph Chamberlain's (1836–1914) retreat from Home Rule support for the Irish Unionists after the 1886 general election.

3. *Billingsgate*: Billingsgate market in London, the largest fish market in the United Kingdom. Fish trading on the site dates back to 1699, when an act was passed allowing the general business market of Billingsgate to trade in any kind of fish. The porters working at the market had a reputation for swearing and bad language.

4. *three acres ... and a sea-cow*: 'Three acres and a cow' was a phrase coined by Jesse Collings (1831–1920), friend and political ally of Chamberlain and mayor of Birmingham, 1878–80. The phrase was used in Chamberlain's radical programme for the general election in 1885 after the franchise was extended in the 1884 Third Reform Act. Part of the programme was to distribute small portions of land to Irish tenants to encourage partial self-sufficiency, and this was seen as a poor alternative to the Home Rule he supported prior to the election.

D., 'Scaring the Capitalists'

1. *Auberon Herbert ... Charles Bradlaugh*: Herbert (1838–1906) was the son of the third Earl of Carnarvon and promoted what has been termed libertarian anarchism; he believed that a government's only function should be the defence of individual and personal property. Bradlaugh (1833–91) was also a libertarian individualist and a critic of socialism. These men have been singled out as proponents of the defence of personal property and the antithesis of the workers' delegates in the story.

2. *Earl of Wemyss ... Mr. Bradlaugh*: Francis Wemyss-Charteris-Douglas (1818–1914), eighth Earl of Wemyss and a Tory politician, had opposed the 1867 Reform Bill but lent his political weight to the Master and Servant Amendment Act of 1867, which reduced employee breach of contract from a criminal to a civil offence. He had a paternalistic view on employer/employee relations, and he helped form the Liberty and Property Defence League in 1882 to resist socialism and trade unionism. Arthur James Balfour (1848–1930), Conservative politician and Prime Minister in 1902–5, was made Secretary of State by his uncle, Lord Salisbury, in 1887. During this post, he locked horns with the Irish Unionists, broke up the National League, and in 1888 prosecuted Charles Stewart Parnell (1846–91) and other Irish nationalists on what was later revealed to be forged evidence. Auberon Herbert (1838–1906) was a Conservative Member of Parliament who crossed the floor to be returned as a Liberal MP in 1870. He retired from politics in 1874 and published widely on an extreme form of individualism he termed voluntaryism, advocating the removal of state interference in property, education or contracts and the introduction of a voluntary taxation system. George Howell (1833–1910) was the son of a self-employed stonemason who became a Liberal MP. Howell opposed socialism and the development of independent labour politics. On Bradlaugh, see previous note. All of these men held opinions and politics antithetical to socialism.

Maubourg, 'A Mournful Fate'

1. *duds*: a derogatory term for coarse clothing.
2. *faubourg*: an old French term for a city suburb. The rebuilding of much of Paris in the nineteenth century demolished most of the faubourg, and the seamstress's use of the term suggests that she lives in one of the old, unmodernized areas of the city, possibly a slum.

Anon., 'Archie Cameron's Success'

1. *Brobdingnagian*: the race of giants encountered by Gulliver in *Gulliver's Travels*. Archie Cameron has 'failure' writ large upon him.
2. *Hope deferred ... grow sick*: 'Hope deferred maketh the heart grow sick: but when the desire cometh, it is a tree of life'; Proverbs 13:12. Perpetual endeavour without success is dispiriting; endeavour deserves reward.
3. *The Lady of Lyons*: *The Lady of Lyons or, Love and Pride* (1838) by Edward Bulwer Lytton (1803–73). Pauline Deschappelles, a merchant's daughter, is tricked into marrying Claude Melnotte, a wealthy and talented son of a gardener, but eventually realizes that she is in love with him. It is a story of inter-class relationships.
4. Claude: Claude Melnotte. Claude is talented and successful, the opposite of Archie.
5. *Mr. Horace Bowdler*: possibly a reference to Thomas Bowdler (1754–1825), author of *The Family Shakespeare* (1818), which censored the works of Shakespeare.
6. *gun in hand*: Claude Melnotte is first seen after winning a shooting match.
7. *Campbell*: a misprint.
8. *paletot*: a double-breasted overcoat with peaked lapels.
9. *mun*: must.

Hannigan, 'Aristos and Demos'

1. *St. Michael*: an archangel charged with fighting Satan. Daniel 12: 'At that time [the end of the world] shall Michael rise up, the great prince, who standeth for the children of thy people'. Demos is taking the same role in an earthly fight.
2. *myrmidons*: a warlike people, from Homer's *Iliad*. Hannigan is aligning pre-Christian imagery with the aristocracy and Christian imagery with the workers to create a hierarchy of morality in line with Biblical teachings.

Bramsbury, 'A Working Class Tragedy'

1. *Cranston's ironworks ... throughout the country*: The industrial factory in the rural environment and its growing importance is a trope emphasizing Hyndman's (and many other socialists') idealization of pre-industrial society. Cranston's rural setting symbolizes the destruction of traditional rural life and work by the introduction of machinery for the increase of profit at the expense of the worker.
2. *a sight worse for some of you others*: Frank declines to take part in collective action twice in the fiction. His individualism is both his downfall and his tragedy.
3. *Young, energetic ... a capitalist*: Frank's enthusiasm and dedication to work are emphasized to assert the socialist argument that those out of work are not unemployed through their own laziness, or through a preference for criminal activities, alcoholism or fecklessness,

but through greed for profit and often arbitrary decisions by employers. Frank's desire to place himself in the role of capitalist suggests the perpetuation of capitalism through the focus on aspiration for individual gain rather than for social good and the necessity of redirecting the goals of aspiration towards socialism before any change can be effected.

4. *out of his time*: by the time he had completed his apprenticeship. Apprentices were bound to their master for around seven years during training and were paid very little for their services – often only enough to pay for food and board. The fact that Frank could save enough from his apprentice wages to get married is testament to his thrift.

5. *Will Shakespeare ... moonlighting himself sometimes*: The story of Shakespeare being caught poaching deer on Sir Thomas Lucy's land and being whipped and beaten as punishment was a popular myth in the nineteenth century. Later critics have doubted the veracity of the story, and Joseph Pearce asks, 'isn't it likely to be a romanticized memory of the local hero, casting him into the role of a latter-day Robin Hood, stealing from the rich to give to the poor?'; *The Quest for Shakespeare* (San Francisco, CA: Ignatius Press, 2008), p. 92.

6. *coverts at the Park*: thickets and shelters for wild animals. The head keeper's role was to protect the wild animals on the landowner's ground from poachers, and Frank proceeds to recognize that poachers will know as much about the enclosed land as anyone. The public ownership of land was one of the crucial goals for socialists, and H. M. Hyndman, in his book *England for All*, published for the inaugural conference of the Democratic Federation (later the Social Democratic Federation), opened the argument with a chapter on 'The Land' that began: 'Possession of the land is a matter of such supreme importance to the liberty and well-being of Englishmen, that the only marvel is not that there should be a growing agitation on the subject to-day, but that the nation should ever have been content to bear patiently the monopoly which has been created during the past 300 years'; (London: E. W. Allen, 1881), transcribed by T. Crawford, *Marxist Internet Archive*, at http://www.marxists.org/archive/hyndman/1881/england/chap01.html [accessed 1 November 2012].

7. *Red Lion*: The issue of alcohol and its consumption by the working classes was debated strenuously by socialists. On one side, temperance advocates and Liberal-socialists such as the leader of the Independent Labour Party, James Keir Hardie, encouraged workers to drink no alcohol at all; see 'Nigel Grey' by Lilian Claxton in Volume 2, serialized in Hardie's *Labour Leader*. On the other, Tory-socialists such as Hyndman and Robert Blatchford drew the Tory appreciation of recreation and leisure into their socialism, and this included the enjoyment of British beer. In this fiction, Bramsbury makes a distinction between the enjoyment of alcohol and the conviviality of the pub through the banter of the mechanics and labourers in Benton's Red Lion and the discussions of Wright and his socialist friends in the London public house (see Chapter XXIV) and the dissolution caused by excessive drinking (see, for instance, the fight in Beulah Place overheard by Frank in Chapter XXV).

8. *Il Trovatore*: an opera by Giuseppe Verdi (1813–1901) first performed in 1853. This was, and continues to be, a popular opera with a complex story of inheritance, kidnap and revenge. Mr Gray's applause for Louisa's recital of popular music demonstrates both his sycophancy and his preference for the material over the spiritual – evidenced in his attendance at the 'best London performers' when he should have been attending to church business at 'the May meetings'. The May meetings Mr Gray mentions probably refer to the Protestant Missions of the World conference, which held its centenary conference at Exeter Hall in May 1888. The report of the proceedings lists lectures on

a range of non-Christian and non-Protestant religions and Protestant missionary work across the globe, but there is no record of a lecture on the condition of London match-makers.

9. *Liszt*: Franz Liszt (1811–86), Hungarian composer and pianist, considered the greatest pianist of his period.

10. *Exeter Hall*: a large hall on the Strand in London that was used for large meetings, religious conferences, sermons and lectures; it was also the headquarters of the Young Men's Christian Association (YMCA).

11. *matchbox makers living in garrets*: In June 1888 Henry Hyde Champion (1859–1928) attended a Fabian meeting on 'Female Labour', and in the discussion following Clementina Black's (1853–1922) lecture, he drew attention to the conditions and low pay of workers for the match manufacturers Bryant and May. Champion had visited a woman who made matchboxes for the company; she was working with the body of her dead baby next to her as she tried to earn enough to pay for the burial. It was from this meeting that Annie Besant (1847–1933) and Hubert Bland (1855–1914) became involved with the matchgirls and organized a successful strike for better pay.

12. *I'm hanged ... as we do*: Vernon's claim has echoes of Charles Dickens's Bounderby and his belief that the Coketown workers 'expect to be set up in a coach and six, and to be fed on turtle-soup and venison, with a gold spoon'; see *Hard Times* (1854), ch. XI.

13. *paying them more ... now*: another instance supporting the theory that the author of this fiction is Henry Mayers Hyndman. Mr and Mrs Cranston outline the capitalist economics of buying labour for the lowest rate and selling the product for the highest. Hyndman was, at this point, in the process of translating Marx's *Das Kapital* into English and serializing the translation in his other periodical, *To-Day*, between 1885 and 1888. The translation was published under the pseudonym 'John Broadhouse'. In the issue for December 1886, Hyndman had published his translation of 'Chapter VI: The Buying and Selling of Labour Power', which considers the necessity of exchanging labour power for subsistence:

> The *quantum* of labour required for its daily production fixes its daily value. Suppose, now, that the average quantity of gold produced in a half-day of six hours equalled three shillings; then three shillings expressed the daily value of the labour-power. If the owner of the labour-power offered himself for three shilling per day, he would sell his labour at its proper value, and, according to our supposition, the holder of money, eager to turn his shillings into capital, would pay that sum. (p. 217)

In the March 1887 issue of *To-Day*, Hyndman begins his translation of 'The Production of Surplus Value', and in the April issue he translates Marx's calculation:

> The workman thus finds in the workshop the means of production necessary for a day's labour, not of six, but of twelve hours. Seeing that 10lbs. of wool have required six hours' labour to covert them into ten yards of cloth, 20lbs. of wool will require 12 hours' labour to convert them into 20 yards of cloth. Let us now consider the product of this labour, of which four were realized in the wool and the wear and tear of the loom, and one by the wool in the operation of weaving. But the money expression of the five days' labour is 30s. or £1 10s., which is therefore the price of the 20 yards of cloth. A yard

of cloth costs 1s. 6d. now as before, but the total value of the commodities employed in the operation do not exceed 27s. while the value of the cloth is 30s. The value of the product thus exceeds by one-ninth the value advanced for its production. The 27s. advanced are thus transformed into 30s., – they have begotten a surplus value of 3s. The conjuring trick is accomplished. Money is metamorphosised into capital.

Bramsbury, by setting out the capitalist arguments of the Cranstons, appears to assume a basic knowledge on the part of the reader of the theory of surplus value. Hyndman was criticized by other socialists for his adherence to Marx's theories as set out in *Das Kapital,* as many criticized Marx for inconsistency. See the letters of Hyndman, Shaw and Besant on the subject in the *Pall Mall Gazette*, May 1887: 'Bernard Shaw – Henry Hyndman – Annie Besant – 1887. Exchange of Letters on Value Theory in Marx', transcribed by T. Crawford, *Marxist Internet Archive*, at http://www.marxists.org/subject/economy/authors/fabians/earlyenglishvalue/lettersonvalue.htm [accessed 17 November 2012].

14. *greatest good of the greatest number*: Jeremy Bentham (1748–1832) set out his theory of utility in *Introduction to the Principle of Morals and Legislation* (1789), which proposed that governments and individuals should act on the principle of actions and decisions being taken to produce the greatest amount of pleasure and the least amount of pain for others. Frank's 'sententious' repetition of this principle, after being presented with evidence refuting his claim, illustrates the socialist argument that this philosophy was used not to ensure the greatest happiness for the greatest number, but to maintain Liberal *laissez faire* policies that simultaneously withdrew support for the poorest and most vulnerable and removed any sense of responsibility by the rich for those who produced the country's wealth. At this point, Frank is oblivious to the difficulties this principle will pose him in finding alternative employment.

15. *coddem*: a game where an item is hidden in the hand of one player and the other player/s must guess which hand it is in. The game is better known as Tip-it.

16. *Thou speak'st ... night*: the introduction of Puck to one of Titania's fairies; Shakespeare, *A Midsummer Night's Dream* (c. 1595–6), Act II, scene ii. Puck, or Robin Goodfellow, is a mischievous sprite who claims, 'I jest to Oberon and make him smile'; Ben, the local poacher, identifies himself with Puck's democratic lawlessness. Ben's knowledge of Shakespeare shows the intelligence of the working class and suggests that their interest in culture extends beyond 'low' music halls. His choice of quotation also alludes to his night work as a poacher.

17. *law clerk*: The magistrate is a local citizen who volunteers time to pass judgment on summary cases that can be resolved in the magistrates' court or to pass more serious (indictable) cases on to the crown courts. Because of George Cranston's injury, which law defines as bodily harm calculated to cause hurt or discomfort, the charge against Ben would be Assault Occasioning Actual Bodily Harm, contrary to section 47 of the Offences Against the Person Act, 1861. This charge is called an 'either-way' case because it could be heard in either the magistrates' court or the crown court, where a harsher sentence could be passed. This is why Mr Gray proposes sending the case to trial. Because magistrates are not trained in law, they are advised on legal issues by a justice's clerk, and it is he who brings some calm and reason to the hysterical and vindictive reactions of Mr Cranston and Rev. Gray.

18. *prisoner's antecedents ... snaring hares*: Until the 2003 Criminal Justice Act relaxed the rules, the prosecution could not disclose a defendant's previous convictions. Even after

the 2003 Act, those previous convictions disclosed to the court must be relevant to the case. Ben's convictions for poaching are not relevant to a case of actual bodily harm and are used by Gripper against due process (which states that justice should not be arbitrary or unreasonable) to ensure an unfavourable outcome for Ben.

19. *seven years penal servitude*: an example of the hysterical reaction from a biased Bench. Under the 1861 Offences Against the Person Act (which is still current in the British legal system), magistrates are restricted to a maximum sentence of six months' imprisonment, and a crown court would be restricted to a maximum sentence of five years' imprisonment. Elder Cranston simultaneously shows his lack of legal knowledge and his lack of respect for justice.

20. *fall to the husband of Miss Eva*: Under the Married Woman's Property Acts of 1870 and 1882, women were allowed to hold property inherited after marriage (1870) or before and after marriage (1882). Before these acts were passed, everything a woman possessed legally became her husband's property under the law of coverture when, at marriage, a woman and man became one person in law. Before the 1857 Divorce and Matrimonial Causes Act, a man was legally entitled to his wife's property and earnings even after desertion. The assumption that Eva's future husband will become the owner of the Ashville property is presumably based on tradition rather than legal right.

21. *Infinitely better … Her Majesty's dominions*: Lieutenant Vernon is, presumably, the younger son of a member of the landed gentry. Eldest sons would inherit their father's property, while younger sons would have to support themselves by entering one of the 'honourable' professions: clergy in the established church, a commission in the army (which before 1870 could be bought) or a place at the bar practising law. Vernon's enthusiasm for empire and expansion is not entirely antipathetic to Hyndman's socialism. Hyndman envisaged the expansion of socialism being enacted through the British Empire, as the colonies would form 'a united democracy of English-speaking peoples'; see *England for All*, ch. 7 'The Colonies'.

22. *unnecessary violence*: Under British law, both the public and the police must exert reasonable force to either defend property or carry out the law. Gripper is not abiding by this aspect of the law, and Frank shows knowledge of the law by being aware that he is arrested with unnecessary violence.

23. *cresses*: Watercress is a common plant to British freshwater and one of the oldest known plants to be consumed by human beings. The plant grows wild and in abundance and is in season between April and October. Frank's handful would help feed his family without depriving anyone of cultivated crops.

24. *carneys*: to act in a wheedling or coaxing manner; *OED*. Gripper still craves the attention of George Cranston.

25. *gets his monkey up*: to get angry or annoyed.

26. *dutch clock*: an ornate wall clock with external weights.

27. *relieving officer*: an official administering the 1834 Poor Law Amendment Act and the person to whom claims for financial help would be directed. Frank's wife would have applied for outdoor relief – financial help while living in their own home – as she later states that the Board of Guardians, to whom her application is passed, advised her to enter the workhouse.

28. *the house*: the workhouse. The shame attached to being admitted to the workhouse was felt keenly by all people who had worked and striven for financial independence. Frank and his family are trapped by Mr Cranston's hold on all aspects of local power held over the workers – employer, magistrate, Poor Law guardian.

29. *I've never ... altogether*: Ben Green recognizes the difference between poaching and theft under British law. The Night Poaching Act of 1828 and the Game Act of 1831 (both of which are still in force today) separate the taking of game and rabbits from the appropriation and taking without consent, which are embodied in the Theft Acts and related statutes. His point raises the issue of the theft of land and refocuses criminality onto landlords, whose private ownership of land, and capitalists, whose stranglehold on employment, both forced workers into acts deemed criminal under capitalist law but which are understandable and humane acts for the survival of the self and others. See D. Mutch, 'Re-Humanising Marx: Theory and Fiction in the *Fin de Siècle* British Socialist Periodical', in A. Mousley (ed.), *Towards a New Literary Humanism* (Basingstoke: Palgrave, 2011), pp. 197–212.

30. *Furious as ... Frank's mind*: Frank has no murderous feelings towards Gripper and is using reasonable force – having dropped his gun – to repel his attacker in order to escape, which the law states is justifiable for self-defence.

31. *gin and snare*: the tools of the poacher's trade. A gin is usually a spring-loaded mechanical trap for catching wild animals; a snare is a trap using rope to catch an animal by the foot.

32. *remand*: In general terms, to remand means to send back or return (*OED*), but in this legal sense it means to return the accused to prison to await trial. For less serious charges than murder, the accused would be awarded bail and allowed to return home to await trial. Any reason to suspect the accused will abscond before trial, interfere with witnesses or commit further offences might result in the accused being remanded (returned) to custody until the trial verdict. After the verdict, the accused is either released (in the case of a not-guilty verdict or if a suspended sentence is imposed) or begins a jail sentence.

33. *They will kill him*: meaning he will be found guilty and hanged for the crime.

34. *Pecksniffian charity*: Seth Pecksniff is a lawyer and architect in Dickens's *Martin Chuzzlewit* (1843–4). This character is the epitome of sanctimonious hypocrisy, in the same manner as those who declare the poor, unemployed, sick and disabled to be deserving of their place in the workhouse. The rich benefit from the profits of the workers and then consign them to the harsh regime of the workhouse when they are no longer needed, all with a sanctimonious air of charity.

35. *that wicked Land League*: The Land League was an Irish movement founded by Michael Davitt (1846–1906) in 1879, which aimed to remove land ownership in Ireland from English landlords and redistribute to occupying owners who were formerly tenant farmers. The movement was the beginning of Irish independence from British colonial rule. Mrs Cranston's sympathy is given to the comparatively rich who acquire money by the means of non-productive rent, while dismissing as greedy those who seek to earn a little more than subsistence rates.

36. *too lenient ... the present agitation*: Some Irish landlords were progressive in their attitude to the land and their tenants, but many of them were exploitative and greedy. While some landlords agreed to the demands of the Land League for reductions in rents, those who refused were denigrated in the press and subjected to incendiary attacks by tenants. The Land Acts of 1881 and 1885 enforced the reduction of rents by around 20 per cent and forced many landlords into bankruptcy. Jack Somers sees a similarity between the collective demands of the Irish Land League and the English trades unions and argues for a less flexible attitude than that shown by the Irish landlords.

37. *disestablishment of the Irish Church*: In 1869 William Ewart Gladstone's (1809–98) government passed the Irish Church Act, which separated the Irish Protestant Church from the Church of England. This act created an independent Church of Ireland, which

had autonomous powers, including its own constitution and the ability to appoint its own bishops. There were protests from the Catholic population that a Protestant church should not hold the title 'Church of Ireland'. Rev. Gray holds a materialist view of the role of the church as a form of control wielded over the population.

38. *committing the prisoner to trial*: The charge of murder is outside of a magistrate's jurisdiction and must be sent to crown court for trial by judge and jury. Cranston's following statement on his opinion of Frank's guilt overreaches his remit and reveals his biased attitude, which is given in contradiction to the legal statement of all being innocent until proven guilty.

39. *in durance vile*: meaning to be imprisoned, confined or constrained against one's will. Ben uses the term here to refer to the prison to which Frank was committed, but Robert Burns (1759–96) uses it in relation to the workhouse in 'Epistle from Esopus to Maria' (1794): 'A workhouse! ah, that sound awakes my woes, / And pillows on the thorn my rack'd repose! / In durance vile here must I wake and weep, / And all my frowsy couch in sorrow steep'.

40. *chaff bed*: a mattress stuffed with husks of corn or grain rather than with feathers or down. The children have a bed, but one that would have been made from the stray heads of wheat collected by the children and their mother, which Ben later laments is now unavailable to them.

41. *peelers*: policeman. According to the *OED*, this is a corruption of the name of Sir Robert Peel, who created the official full-time professional police force in 1829. Bobbies and rozzers are other colloquial names for policemen also derived from Peel's name.

42. *the missus and the kids ... too devilish clean*: Women and children had for centuries been employed in the harvest field, but the 1867 and 1873 Agricultural Gangs Acts restricted the use of children in agriculture. The 1873 Act made it illegal to employ children under the age of eight and restricted the hours children over the age of eight could work. Ben's children are described as four and five years of age and therefore would have been significantly underage when previously employed. Improved farming practices mean that there is less waste and less opportunity for workers to gather wheat for their own use.

43. *stranger in a strange land*: Moses fled Egypt for killing an Egyptian who beat a Hebrew; Genesis 2:22. In Midian, Reuel gave Moses his daughter Zipporah in gratitude for helping his daughters water the flock. Zipporah gave Moses a son whom he named Gershom, 'for, said he, I have been a stranger in a strange land'. As Moses is in Midian, so Frank is in London.

44. *New Cut*: a street in Lambeth and Southwark now known as the Cut. The market held in the New Cut every Friday and Saturday was one of the largest in Victorian London and was noted by Henry Mayhew (1812–87) in *London Labour and the London Poor* (1851, 1861–2) as having been reduced in size by the imposition of police regulation.

45. *hobbledehoy*: a youth between boyhood and manhood, a clumsy or awkward youth; *OED*. The market is full of people of all ages.

46. *cag mag*: unwholesome, decayed or loathsome meat; offal; hence anything worthless or rubbishy; *OED*. The shoppers at the market are fighting to buy and consume scraps of rotten meat and presumably paying a premium for it, as the demand for scraps will inflate the price.

47. *broiled bloater ... gingerette*: A bloater is a smoked herring, which is cured whole rather than opened and cured like a kipper; the bloaters in the lodging house are being grilled before being eaten. Gingerette is a carbonated cordial similar to ginger beer. The food

bought and consumed by the working-class inhabitants of London has few health-giving properties.

48. *coverts*: see above, p. 316 n. 6.

49. *Parisian Communard*: a member of the Paris Commune of 1871. The French government's attempt to remove the arms from the Paris militia brought about the overthrow of the government in the city, and the Parisian working class took power. The revolution lasted only seventy-two days (between 18 March and 28 May 1871) before the national government took control of the city again. Eva's education in socialist theory has been gleaned from one who had practical experience of implementing socialist policies.

50. *Madame Roland ... Louise Michel*: Madame Roland (1754–93) was born Marie-Jeanne Philippon and, along with her husband, Jean-Marie Roland de la Platière, was a prominent supporter of the revolution to remove the monarchy and a member of the Girondist faction. Both she and her husband spoke out against the excesses of the revolution, and she was guillotined on fabricated treason charges. Louise Michel (1830–1905) was a teacher with socialist ideals who became a nurse and soldier during the Paris Commune, and who was transported for her part in the Commune. She returned to Paris in 1880 and became involved in the struggle for the social revolution, spending the next ten years attending meetings and being arrested. She moved to London in 1890 and became involved with the anarchist movement. Vernon is not being complimentary by likening Eva to these female revolutionaries.

51. *unemployed meeting ... Thames Embankment last year*: the large meetings of the unemployed organized by the SDF from January 1885, which included meetings at the Royal Exchange and Hyde Park as well as the Thames Embankment. Eva has either attended the meetings or has studied the reports.

52. *Chop down trees ... Grand Old Agitator*: a reference to William Ewart Gladstone, four-time Liberal Prime Minister between 1868 and 1894, later known as the Grand Old Man. Gladstone's hobby and exercise was felling trees on his estate at Hawarden in north Wales, and this created his image as a proactive politician.

53. *old feudalism ... "For God, Queen and Country"*: Colonel Ashville was a supporter of the Tory Young England movement, which had been the idea of young Tory politicians George Smythe (1818–57), Lord John Manners (1818–1906) and Alexander Cochrane-Wishart-Baillie (1816–90) to revive a romanticized version of feudalism, paternalism and orthodox religious practices. Benjamin Disraeli (1804–81) adopted some of the ideals under the banner of Young England and drew them into his novels *Coningsby* (1844), *Sybil* (1845) and *Tancred* (1847). The basis of the Young England ideal was the traditional Tory trinity of Alter, Throne and Cottage – the church, the monarchy and the people working in harmony. It is Frank's sense of security under the paternal Ashville that leads to his downfall, as he turns to the landowner and away from the socialists.

54. *Your Queen ... certain conditions*: Somers argues that the Colonel's politics are as romantic and sentimentalized as Eva's socialism and that even those who profess loudly their patriotism – such as the northern Irish Protestants – will do so only so long as it benefits them to do so.

55. *Tarter*: one who resembles a Tartar in disposition; a rough, violent or intractable person; *OED*. Vernon feels Eva will make an unmanageable wife.

56. *New duties ... nonsense*: George Cranston's view of the married woman may seem unregenerate even for 1888, as the New Woman and socialist movements had begun to debate and demand female emancipation. However, Eva does voluntarily distance herself from her earlier politics after her marriage and on the advice of her husband. If Brams-

bury is a pseudonym for Hyndman, then this would reflect his attitude towards women
– an attitude that Karen Hunt argues has been applied to the SDF generally, despite its
radical female members. She quotes Hyndman on the fight for women's right to work:
'He argued that "it is absurd to strive for freedom under present economical conditions.
Such false freedom could lead to deeper degradation. She must work with the Socialists
for a complete reconstruction of society"'; Hyndman, *Justice*, 5 April 1884, quoted in
Hunt, *Equivocal Feminists*, p. 122.

57. *Federation*: The conversation between Somers and Blake sets out the divisions in the
SDF at the time of publication. The setting for the conversation in the Radical Club
recognizes the group's original political incarnation as the Democratic Federation, which
included Radical members and policies before adopting a wholly socialist manifesto in
1884. The conversation between Somers and Blake in this chapter works through some
of the arguments over the methods of attaining socialism aired by members of the SDF
in the mid-1880s. Blake's support for socialist candidates for the 'London School Board
and similar bodies' voices the opinion of *Justice*'s working-class editor, Harry Quelch
(1858–1913); and, if it is assumed this fiction was written by Hyndman, Blake's positive
characterization might be read as a fictional representation of Quelch, who had a close
working relationship with Hyndman. The SDF fielded candidates in the 1885 general
election – John Burns (1858–1943) at Nottingham, Jack Williams (n.d.) at Hampstead
and John Fielding (n.d.) at Kensington, polling 598, 27 and 32 votes respectively – but
the process was mired in accusations of the SDF taking 'Tory Gold' to support their candidature. Both Hyndman and fellow SDF member Henry Hyde Champion were accused
of accepting money from the Tory agent Michael Maltman Barry (1842–1909). George
Bernard Shaw (1856–1950) lamented that 'The Federation are convicted of offering to
sell their fictitious numbers to the highest bidder (in money, not in reforms)'; Shaw to
A. Scheu, quoted by Bevir, *The Making of British Socialism*, pp. 163–4. Hyndman denied
the accusation and blamed Champion, claiming in his autobiography that Champion
'set to work to try to make twelve o'clock at eleven by carrying on an intrigue with the
Tories in order to bring about some reforms in his own day'; *The Record of an Adventurous Life*, p. 309. John Barnes, Champion's latest biographer, found no solid evidence
that Champion was a puppet of any political party but suggests that Barry's embolden-
ing influence combined with Champion's enthusiasm makes it likely that money was
accepted. Neither Hyndman nor Hyndman and Champion's biographers suggest that
Champion had ambitions to stand for Parliament himself at this election. He did stand
as a Labour candidate at the Deptford by-election in 1888 but withdrew before the election and again in 1892 for Aberdeen South; this tendency might have made him a basis
for the character of Somers. Champion had begun to separate himself from the SDF at
the time of this serial, publishing *Common Sense* in 1887 and the *Labour Leader* in June
1888 after *Common Sense* had ended in March of the same year. Somers's description of
'Phillips' might be a reference to Hyndman's own reputation as dictatorial, that being
one of the reasons for the departure of Morris and the nine other members of the SDF's
executive council to form the Socialist League in December 1884. For further reading,
see Barnes, *Socialist Champion*; Tsuzuki, *H. M. Hyndman and British Socialism*; Crick,
The History of the Social-Democratic Federation; and Hyndman, *The Record of an Adventurous Life*.

58. *fair traders*: Fair trade was a market-based economic principle that sought to place limita-
tions on the export and import of goods into and out of Britain according to economic
or trading necessity. Fair traders argued that by creating some protectionism for British

goods, British employment would be made more secure. Socialists warned that this was just another version of capitalist economics and would benefit only the merchant and upper classes.

59. *old college chum*: If the character of Somers is read as a fictional representation of Champion, then this might refer to his close relationship with Robert Percival Bodley (Percy) Frost (n.d.), whom Champion had known since their schooldays at Marlborough. Frost and Champion were particularly close during their early years in the SDF, and Frost's family home was in Russell Square.

60. *Plimsoll water-line*: the internationally agreed gauge as to the maximum load a ship can safely carry; devised by Samuel Plimsoll (1824–98), MP for Derby in 1868–80 and an advanced Liberal with a strong sense of social justice. His concern for the loss of thousands of merchant seamen through the sinking of overloaded ships led him to bring a motion before Parliament to require all ships to show and adhere to the water line, and this was brought into law in the 1876 Merchant Shipping Act. The fishing vessels in the docks are in breach of this law and the Lloyd's shipping register, which made the Plimsoll line mandatory in 1885.

61. *thirty hog*: 'Hog' is slang for a shilling, as is the term 'bob' a little further on. The fishmonger paid the equivalent of one pound and fifty pence for a poor catch.

62. *Everyone who wanted a job … better luck tomorrow*: Frank's sympathy for the unsuccessful workers undermines his declarations of individualism. Jack Mitchell has read this scene as 'anti-naturalistic' in 'the way "jungle law" operating on the labour market of the docks is shown as something *unnatural* and not in terms of Social Darwinism'; Mitchell, 'Tendencies in Narrative Fiction', p. 61.

63. *A dollar … a cent*: A dollar in British currency is slang for a five-shilling piece; the word cent usually refers to something that is one-hundredth of the whole. Frank does not have even a hundredth of what is needed for the licence to work.

64. *twelve-hour-a-day class*: The length of the working day for the average labourer was debated by many, and socialists called for a reduction to an eight-hour day. Foremost among those arguing for a reduction was Tom Mann, at this point still a member of the SDF but soon to be influential in the development of the New Union movement. Hyndman had argued that labour could be reduced if British industry concentrated on the necessities and forewent sweated labour in the production of irrelevant goods.

65. *language of flowers … forget-me-not*: The Victorians assigned sentiments to certain flowers, and the exchange of flowers carried meaning with the gift, the best known being the red rose meaning love. The forget-me-not meant true love and remembrance; the water-lily represented eloquence and purity of heart.

66. *Doss money … 'Lump' … fruz*: The carman recognizes Frank's homeless state and his inability to afford lodging – having no 'doss money' – his unwillingness to enter the workhouse – the 'Lump' – and his incapacitated state being caused by sleeping outside in the freezing temperature – being 'fruz', meaning frozen.

67. *a brown*: a penny. For more on the London coffee stalls, see A. Neil Lyons, 'Little Pictures of the Night' (1903–4) in Volume 3.

68. *crock's head from my dickey*: The crock's head is presumably referring to the horse and inferring that it is old and broken down; the dickey is the seat where the cab driver would sit. The fog was so dense that the cab driver had to leave his seat on the cab because he could not see the horse in front of him.

69. *ganger's box*: A ganger is someone in charge of a group of workmen; in order to select the workmen for the job, the ganger would stand on a box in order to better see the men and choose those he deemed best for the work.

70. *Whether 'tis ... end them?*: Shakespeare, *Hamlet*, Act III, scene i. Frank, like Hamlet, considers and rejects suicide.

71. *told off*: counted. The men are being divided into groups to carry out the work.

72. *house-jobber*: the owner of houses held to rent at high prices. The term 'jobber' is usually used to mean someone who rents out horses and carriages, but in this case it is used to refer to someone who does the same with houses.

73. *Beulah Place*: an ironic reference to John Bunyan's Land of Beulah in *The Pilgrim's Progress*, 'where the sun shineth night and day'. The issue of healthful and affordable housing was central to the socialist vision. See Robert Blatchford's vision of a socialist city in Chapter IV of 'The Sorcery Shop. An Impossible Romance' (1906–7) in Volume 4.

74. *stived*: deprived of fresh air. Wright's apartment is larger than many others in the court because he chooses not to live in cramped conditions.

75. *in quad for priggin'*: Quad is slang for prison, presumably referring to the four sides of a prison surrounding a quadrangle inside; prigging is slang for stealing, usually petty theft. The woman's family is accused of being thieves and jailbirds.

76. *stand Sam*: to pay expenses, especially for food and drink; *OED*. Frank is offering to reciprocate Wright's purchase of the meal for both the day before.

77. *Boro'*: an area of south-east London at the southern end of London Bridge. This area is also featured in A. Neil Lyons's 'Little Pictures of the Night' in Volume 3, and Hugh Derrick's 'The Making of a Red' (1913–14) in Volume 5.

78. *But a drop ... do you good*: Early temperance advocates focused on encouraging the refusal to drink spirits while allowing beer, but later advocates promoted total abstinence (teetotalism). On 1 September 1832 the 'Seven Men of Preston' who formed the Preston Temperance Society, including the working-class journalist and reformer Joseph Livesey (1794–1884), pledged to abstain entirely from drinking alcohol, except for medicinal purposes. There were other, earlier temperance societies, but Preston was the first to abstain entirely. There is an unsubstantiated story that claims the term 'teetotal' was coined by Richard Turner (1790–1846) of Preston, whose stutter when taking the temperance pledge became the word used for abstinence from alcohol. Turner's *Dictionary of National Biography* entry points out that Irish labourers had used the term to mean complete or absolute, but Turner's use gave it a specific meaning that has lasted for almost two centuries. Even so, there was often an acceptance of alcohol as medicine, hence the jocular justification of indulgence: 'it's for medicinal purposes'.

79. *at the corner ... little or no traffic*: The description of this street corner could be a reference to Dod Street in Limehouse. This position was a favourite site for SDF open-air lectures until 9 August 1885, when the speaker, W. B. Parker, was arrested and charged with obstruction. The SDF, Socialist League and Fabians combined forces in what was seen as a battle for free speech and defied the ban on meetings at the site. A number of arrests, including of William Morris, who had been protecting Karl Marx's daughter, Eleanor Marx Aveling, from assault by a policeman, brought the cause to the public's attention. The socialists eventually won their right to speak at Dod Street when a giant rally was held without any police interference or arrests.

80. *palliative measures advocated by the Socialists*: The content of this lecture adds weight to the reading of Somers as Champion. The unemployed demonstrations of 8 February 1886 (known as Black Monday) and those of October and November 1887 (culminating in Bloody Sunday on 13 November, when bystander Alfred Linnell was run over by

a police horse and subsequently died) had convinced Hyndman that protest and direct action were now the best way of achieving the socialist revolution. Champion's military experience did not give him confidence that a group of starving people, no matter how large, could overthrow the British army and establishment. Although Champion took part of the 1886 demonstration that ended in the West End Riot (see Chapter XXXIV) and was subsequently charged and acquitted of sedition, along with Hyndman, John Burns and Jack Williams (n.d.), he did not take part in the 1887 demonstration that attempted to break the police cordon which closed Trafalgar Square to public meetings. At this point Champion was advocating parliamentary representation and would go on to help organize the 1889 London dock strike with John Burns and Ben Tillett – both methods of improving the working-class position that Hyndman, at this point, dismissed as palliatives to capitalism.

81. *Gatti's*: a coffee house and dining-place in the Strand. It is described as 'a fine, striking, and fairly inexpensive dining-hall, where a moderate meal may be had at a moderate price'; C. E. Pascoe, *London of To-Day: An Illustrated Handbook for the Season* (Boston, MA: Roberts Brothers, 1890), p. 70.

82. *a girl of that sort ... Jack Somers*: the point where the character of Jack Somers diverges from Champion. Champion had married a working-class woman four years his senior, Juliet Bennett, in 1883. Champion's biographer, John Barnes, notes the obscurity surrounding this part of Champion's life but also the close relationship between Champion and the eponymous character in *George Eastmont: Wanderer* (1905) by his close friend Margaret Harkness (1854–1923). Eastmont's wife is a part of his socialist experiment, is addicted to drink and drugs, and dies while he is on trial for his part in a socialist demonstration in London. As Barnes claims, 'In the absence of evidence one cannot say how accurately Margaret Harkness represented the Champion marriage, but there seems to be no doubt that she did represent it'; *Socialist Champion*, p. 31.

83. *trapsing*: traipsing, meaning to move in a slovenly manner; *OED*. Mr Steggles suspects his daughter of acting in an unseemly way.

84. *marndering*: meaning either to grumble discontentedly or to fritter away; in this instance the workers fritter their time and their lives away in employment that hardly allows them to live the lives of human beings.

85. *Isaacs and Molley*: presumably fictional representations of Peters and Kelly, leaders of the Fair Trade League and organizers of the demonstration in Trafalgar Square on 8 February; see above, pp. 323–4 n. 58.

86. *Trafalgar Square next Monday*: Trafalgar Square is a public space owned by the Crown at the heart of the city of London which, during this period, was used for public demonstrations and by the homeless for sleeping at night. The meeting discussed here was held on Monday, 8 February 1886, and was subsequently known as 'Black Monday' or the 'West End Riots'. Hyndman and the SDF organized a counter-demonstration against the Free Trade meeting that was due to be held in Trafalgar Square on that day. The subsequent disturbances caused the destruction of property in Pall Mall, directed primarily at the Liberal and Conservative private members clubs, and panicked middle- and upper-class Londoners. SDF members Hyndman, Champion, John Burns and Jack Williams were arrested and tried for sedition. Metropolitan Police Commissioner Sir Charles Warren subsequently ordered the clearing of the homeless sleepers during October and November 1886 and closed Trafalgar Square to public meetings after the demonstrations in 1887, which culminated in 'Bloody Sunday'.

87. *Waterside Labourers' Association*: There had been difficulty organizing a trade union to cover the casual employees at the London docks, a difficulty that had been exacerbated by the bogus unions founded by Thomas Kelly and Samuel Peters – similar activities are hinted by the reference to Molloy as a 'scamp'. At this point, only the specialist workers – the stevedores, crane-drivers, watermen and corn-porters – were unionized.

88. *The colonel ... boiled pork*: Colonel Ashville is a traditionalist, taking only the historic accompaniments to the meats found on an English table. Despite his tolerance of Eva's attitudes towards class relations, the Colonel is neither comfortable with nor open to change; even his port is from an era before Chartism and the demand for the working-class vote.

89. *slop*: an outer garment, as a loose jacket or tunic; *OED*. Ben wears loose clothing to hide his poached game.

90. *Village Blacksmith*: Henry Wadsworth Longfellow's (1807–82) poem, which was set to music by Willoughby Hunter Weiss (1820–67) and became a popular parlour song in the mid-century.

91. *It's my Delight on a Shiny Night*: a traditional folk song entitled 'The Lincolnshire Poacher', which celebrates the act of poaching game.

92. *For men must work and women must weep*: a line from the Charles Kinglsey (1819–75) poem 'The Three Fishers' (1851) about the loss of three fishermen and the mourning of their wives. The poem was set to music, and the line repeated by Frank became a well-known phrase.

93. *four-half*: half ale, half porter sold at fourpence a quart; *OED*.

94. *bit of a lead*: usually referred to as a friendly lead, where a collection is held for someone in financial trouble. The image is that of people with little to spare acting collectively to help those in worse difficulties than themselves.

95. *Stevedores*: Although the term 'stevedore' can be applied to men employed to unload cargo on the dockside or to the overseers of the men, in Britain unskilled men are usually referred to as 'dockers', while 'stevedore' is used to refer to the skilled ganger who is in charge of the dockers.

96. *wharf manager ... accept this offer*: The cavalier treatment of injured workers and the families of those killed at work because of poor working practices was a concern to socialists. See also 'Citizen', 'The Blackleg' (1893) in Volume 2.

97. *useless coffin*: a quotation from the Rev. Charles Wolfe's (1791–1823) elegy 'The Burial of Sir John Moore' (1817). Sir John Moore was an army officer killed during the Spanish war of 1808–9. He wished to be buried on the battlefield rather than carried back to England and so was buried wrapped in his military cloak rather than the 'useless coffin'. Wolfe's poem became one of the most popular poems in English.

98. *ride back with them*: A carriage for the grieving relatives as well as for the coffin was seen by the working classes as a necessary part of a respectable funeral. The working classes would spend a great deal on the funerals of relatives, vying for the best, most elaborate forms of mourning. Many working-class families would pay into a Burial Club to save for their funerals, and the more lavish the funeral, the more highly that family and their dead would be regarded. Commentators and philanthropists denounced this form of saving, as often the money spent on the funeral was needed to support the bereaved family. Mrs Wright and Nelly have been saved this expense by the dock proprietors paying for the funeral as a form of compensation.

99. *Square*: Trafalgar Square.

100. *Natal*: later Durban, a port town in South Africa. Britain had long had a tense relationship with the earlier Dutch Boer settlers on the Cape and the South African interior and had captured Natal from the Boers in 1842. The discovery of diamonds at Kimberley and gold in the Rand were the causes of the First (1877–81) and Second (1899–1902) Boer Wars, as Britain wrested control of the rich land out of the hands of the Boers. The Cranston establishment of a branch of their machinery-manufacturing business there will take advantage of the need for heavy mining machinery.

101. *Government ... Tory ideas*: The British Empire was the largest in the world at this time, and all political parties believed in the importance of British overseas rule; even socialists such as Hyndman and Blatchford argued that British rule in India should be maintained for paternalist purposes. Conservative politician and Prime Minister Benjamin Disraeli thought the possession of India crucial to British global power. In the 1870s Disraeli's policy was 'proud reserve', as foreign policy concentrated on preserving the might of the British Empire and stood apart from European affairs until the German suggestion of an invasion of France in 1875. Disraeli, siding with Russia in the condemnation of Germany, brought Britain out of 'reserve' and into European alliances. The Colonel is maintaining a traditional Tory preference for foreign affairs focused on the Empire and the international power the Empire conferred on Britain.

102. *Square*: Trafalgar Square.

103. *well-built man*: The description and actions of this unnamed character suggests a fictional representation of John Burns. Burns was at this time an SDF member who left to organize the 1889 dock strike with Tom Mann and Henry Hyde Champion; he later became a Liberal MP.

104. *navvy*: an abbreviation of navigator; a construction worker employed in the building of roads or canals; *OED*

105. *precious artful one too*: Hyndman had complained of the planting of agent provocateurs within the crowd to cause violence and therefore discredit the socialist cause; see H. M. Hyndman, 'Starving Men Refuse to Wait', *Justice*, 13 February 1886, p. 2. This claim is given credence by the presence in the crowd of Sir Edward Henderson, Commissioner of the Metropolitan Police, in plain clothes.

106. *Fair Traders*: see above, pp. 323–4 n. 58.

107. *a pale-faced individual ... waterproof coat of the middle-class*: Henry Mayers Hyndman, founder and sometime chairman of the SDF. Hyndman describes the appearances of himself and his fellow socialists in the first volume of his autobiography: 'It was a curious scene. Morris in his soft hat and blue suit, Champion, Frost and Joynes in the morning garments of the well-to-do, several working men comrades and myself, wearing the new frock-coat in which Shaw said I was born, with a tall hat and good gloves, all earnestly engaged in selling a penny socialist paper'; *The Record of an Adventurous Life*, p. 334.

108. *Pall Mall*: the road running between Buckingham Palace and Admiralty Arch in London.

109. *to the Park*: It was the intention of the SDF to lead the crowd to Hyde Park to complete the demonstration, but the people's increasingly ugly mood meant that Hyndman, Burns, Champion and Williams were unable to control the actions of the multitude, which led to the charges of sedition.

110. *three or four rough looking fellows ... standing near*: Hyndman, in his autobiography, distinguishes between the socialist demonstrators and the paid participants of the Fair Trade meeting. On the looting of the West End during the disturbance:

It was a funny enough scene to observe these people from the East End of London, brought up from their poor quarters at five shillings a head by the funds of the Fair Trade League, freely helping themselves to new garments and then putting them on in the Green Park. In South Audley Street matters got worse still, and some of us saved a barouche-full of ladies who were being roughly threatened by some of the fellows from what seemed likely to be a very ugly encounter. (*The Record of an Adventurous Life*, p. 402)

Hyndman's concern to separate the socialist demonstrators from those he claims to be in the pay of the Fair Trade League is not shared by the *Times*, who describe the whole crowd as 'roughs' ('The Rioting in the West-End', 10 February 1886, p. 5) and 'ruffians' ('The Riots in London', 11 February 1886, p. 6). The truth of the matter is that no one knows who in the crowd were socialists, fair traders or troublemakers.

111. *defending the Fair Traders' platform*: There was some horseplay in the crowd as supporters of each side attempted to overturn the platform of the opposing speakers. Frank's recognition of them as defenders of the Fair Trade speakers positions them as troublemakers, based on the opinions of Hyndman and the SDF participants and journalists covering and commenting on the event.

112. *Langham*: The Langham Hotel on Portland Place in London's West End was opened in 1865 as Europe's first 'Grand Hotel' and was popular with London's high society. That this hotel is the Ashvilles' residence while staying in London for the season illustrates the immense wealth of the family.

113. *the Circus*: Oxford Circus on Regent Street. The carriage would have to pass over Oxford Circus to reach the Langham Hotel from Hyde Park.

114. *rumours of rioting were rife*: In the days following the disturbances of Black Monday, London was covered in a blanket of fog, and this fuelled the fears of the wealthy of another impending attack by the unemployed.

115. *slumming expedition*: sightseeing by upper- and middle-class men and women in the poverty-stricken areas of the large cities. Some sightseers went with the sole intention of indulging their own prurient fascination with the poor and the slums – as does the 'dainty young creature' later on – but others, Blatchford and Champion for instance, recall the effect of their witnessing the degradation of the British poor as the origins of their socialism and the beginning of their political agitation.

116. *8th of last month*: Black Monday or the West End Riots; see above, p. 328 nn. 102–9.

117. *Tooley Street ... Horsleydown*: poor south London dock areas. Tooley Street housed the 'kip' (lodging house) that George Orwell (1903–50) stayed in while living as a tramp during his research for *Down and Out in Paris and London* (1933).

118. *arrears ... Ireland*: The Land Act of 1870 gave councils of tenants the opportunity to protest against unfair evictions as well as provided loans of up to two-thirds the price of the land farmed by a tenant for them to buy the land. Somers is insinuating that since the introduction of some legal protection, Irish tenants have an easy time.

119. *a pane of glass in your eye*: Somers is wearing a monocle, one of the visual signifiers of his upper-class position.

120. *What I want ... proved yourself worthy*: Colonel Ashville sets out a feudal vision of the landowner's paternal responsibility for his tenants in opposition to the present capitalist system. Frank's downfall is looking back to this unachievable past when he should be moving into the future with socialism.

121. *mangel-wurzel from a pheasant*: A mangel-wurzel is a root vegetable similar to a beetroot. Markham's assumption is that Frank will be unable to distinguish animal from vegetable.

122. *people working … teetotallers may say*: see above, p. 325 n. 78 on temperance and teetotalism.

123. *allotments*: a portion of land cultivated by an individual. The idea of allotments dates back to before the Norman Conquest, when an area of cleared ground would be held as common land. The Enclosure Acts of the eighteenth and nineteenth centuries took common land into private ownership and removed the benefits of being able to cultivate crops or keep animals, which allowed people independence; the enclosures forced many people into the dependency of employment. The Allotments Act forced local authorities to provide allotments for people if there was a demand, and allotment owners would pay a rent for the land.

124. *associated farms*: meaning the collective farming of land and the collective benefit of the harvest and profits. The development of an ideal society with land and agriculture at its basis had been attempted by Feargus O'Connor (*c.* 1796–1855) with the Chartist Land Plan, which had collapsed by 1851. Similarly, Charles Allen Clarke's Daisy Colony also collapsed amid arguments between the tenants in 1907. Frank's development of associated farms may be read as a criticism of quixotic ideals in the midst of capitalist greed; the only way to change society is to change all of it and not create pockets of socialism that will inevitably be overwhelmed by capitalism.

125. *thick black fall*: a veil attached to a bonnet, covering the face of the wearer.

126. *Burton*: presumably a misprint that should say 'Benton'.

127. *cross buttock*: The cross buttock throw is a move used in some bare-knuckle fights that allowed such throws. In this move, the fighter grabs the wrist of his opponent, turns his back to his opponent, and pulls him over his back to throw him to the ground. This move had been legal under the London Prize Ring rules but had been outlawed by the 1853 Revised London Prize Ring rules and the 1867 Queensberry rules. Frank is a skilled fighter, but the poacher was even more so.

128. *hollow square … summer evenings*: This description of the village green at the centre of the associated farm houses is reminiscent of William Blake's (1757–1827) 'The Echoing Green' from *Songs of Innocence* (1789). Where Blake's poem ends on a sense of mortality as the night draws in and the elderly are left on the green as the children go home to bed, so the inevitable end of Frank's socialist project is anticipated as the vision moves from the scene, through the patrician landowner, and to the church and the capitalist in the characters of Rev. Gray and Mr Cranston.

129. *sportsman*: in this sense, the shooting of game animals and birds.

130. *Eva's patrician pride … her lips*: Eva, despite her supposed attachment to socialism and equality, cannot put into practice for herself those ideas she promotes to others. She prefers to play the benefactor than to place herself on an equal footing with those she regards as inferiors. Her attitude to Frank's declaration is no different to that of her patrician father and demonstrates the impossibility of practising socialism within a capitalist society.

131. *his word would be law to her*: see above, pp. 322–3 n. 56 on the SDF and women.

132. *He often wondered … fully occupied*: see above, pp. 322–3 n. 56 for the SDF attitude to women. If Bramsbury is assumed to be the pseudonym of Hyndman, then the marriage of Eva to Cranston might be read to reflect his own attitudes towards the role of the woman in a marriage. Hyndman was married twice: to Matilda Ware, who died in 1913, and then to Rosalind Travers, who outlived him but died of an overdose after publishing her memoirs of him. Both appear to have been as devoted to Hyndman as Eva is to

Cranston; Matilda is recorded as working as tirelessly as her husband for the cause of socialism.

133. *tenour*: the Middle English spelling of tenor, a spelling that would have been deemed historical when the fiction was published, but which emphasizes the contrast between the sedate and dignified Colonel and his feudal attitudes of duty and responsibility and those of Cranston's capitalist greed and self-indulgence. Eva's nature is defined by the powerful males in her life – first her father and then her husband.

134. *His new master ... his own profits*: In *A Summary of the Principles of Socialism* (1884) by William Morris and Henry Mayers Hyndman, available online at *Marxists.org*, http://www.marxists.org/archive/morris/works/1884/principles/flippy.htm#page/48/mode/2up [accessed 24 January 2013], they denounced the use of machinery for profit, arguing that with the 'introduction of machinery, this complete domination of the capitalist class and sweeping expropriation of the labour of the workers, piled up the wealth for the few' (p. 33). Cranston returns the farms to the capitalist mode of profit through the application of machinery to farming and the exploitation of the labourers. Frank had attempted to use the machinery for the good of all in the form argued by Morris and Hyndman: 'Were machinery properly applied, far less than two hours labour a day for each male above twenty-one would suffice for all to live in comfort, if none lived in excessive luxury on the labour of others' (p. 47).

135. *battue shooting*: game bird shooting where beaters frighten the birds out of cover and into flight in the direction of the shooters. Cranston and his friends are either unwilling or unable to shoot the birds freely, and instead need the game to be directed to their guns by others.

136. *pangs of despised love*: Hamlet's soliloquy, Act III, scene i. Frank has experienced many of the sufferings in Hamlet's list of the pains of life, as well as the 'pangs of despised love', including 'The oppressor's wrong, the proud man's contumely' and 'the law's delay'.

Anon., 'A New "Labour" Paper'

1. *Metropolis Liberal and Radical Association*: a reference to the Metropolitan Radical Federation and the London Liberal and Radical Union, which were both founded in 1886. The reorganization of metropolitan Liberal and Radical clubs was seen by the Fabians as an opportunity to permeate this political network with socialism. By 1890 the Fabians Stewart Headlam (1847–1924) and Sidney Webb (1859–1947) were elected representatives on the London Liberal and Radical Union, hence 'G. A.'s' following comment.

2. Absit omen: Latin, literally 'may the omen be absent'; the wish that an undesired event may not happen. The Grey-haired Agitator is gently mocking the Youthful Enthusiast's attempts to encounter no difficulties.

3. *Mr. MALTMAN BARRY*: Michael Maltman Barry is described by the *Oxford Dictionary of National Biography* as a 'journalist and Tory-Marxist'. Barry had a working relationship with Champion and was partly responsible for tarnishing Champion's reputation after the 'Tory Gold' scandal that claimed Champion had accepted Tory money from Barry to support the SDF candidates standing for election in 1885 in order to split the Liberal vote.

4. *the PARKE case*: Ernest Parke (1860–1944), appointed editor of T. P. O'Connor's (1848–1929) *Star* in 1891, simultaneously edited the *Morning Leader* and, in 1912, the *Daily News*. In 1889, while sub-editor of the *Star* and editor of the *North London Press*, Parke

had named the Earl of Euston as one of the aristocrats who had avoided charges after the raid of a male brothel. Parke contested Euston's claim for criminal libel but lost and was given a twelve-month custodial sentence. The *Labour Elector* was highly critical of Parke, despite his cause being supported by many socialists, and an article ('that paragraph' mentioned by 'G. A.') that advocated Euston 'wringing' Parke's neck was published twice despite strong censure from papers and socialists. The piece was written by Maltman Barry, but Champion took full editorial responsibility, and it was Champion who republished it.

5. *Mr. WILFRED BLUNT*: Wilfred Scawen Blunt (1840–1922), poet and sometime politician. Maltman Barry had tried to persuade Blunt that the Conservatives would support Irish Home Rule when Blunt stood as the Conservative candidate in 1886 and as the Liberal candidate in the Deptford by-election in 1888. Blunt was imprisoned between 1887 and 1888 for chairing a banned anti-eviction meeting in Ireland.

6. *Mr. T. R. THRELFALL*: Thomas Robert Threlfall (n.d.), president of Southport Trades Council, secretary of the Trade Union Congress in 1885 and of the TUC's Labour Electoral Committee for parliamentary representation formed in 1886. The Committee supported Liberal-Labour representation rather than the formation of a distinct Labour party, despite the claim by 'G. A.'. Threlfall unsuccessfully stood as Liberal candidate for Sheffield Hallam in 1886 and as Liberal-Labour candidate for Liverpool Kirkdale in 1892, but the Committee also supported Keir Hardie's independent candidature at the Mid-Lanark by-election in 1888.

7. *LORD COMPTON*: Spencer Compton Cavendish (1833–1908), eighth Duke of Devonshire and Marquis of Hartington. A Liberal politician, Cavendish was elected Liberal leader in 1875 after Gladstone resigned. He led the Liberal Party to success in the election of 1880 but allowed Gladstone to return as Prime Minister after his successes with the Midlothian speeches.

8. *GAINSFORD BRUCE*: Sir Gainsford Bruce (1834–1912), High Court judge and Conservative politician. 'Y. E.' believes the Liberal Party will be of greater benefit to the workers than the Conservative Party and therefore a socialist party is unnecessary.

9. *Representation of the People Act*: The 1884 Third Reform Act had extended the franchise to the counties as well as the towns covered by the 1867 Second Reform Act, but still one-third of men were ineligible to vote. One reason was that the registration process was bureaucratic and complex, which deterred those with lower levels of literacy. Another was that the franchise was still linked to the £10 p.a. property. Although Champion came from a wealthy family, his business affairs at this point are unclear, and his biographer records Champion's financial problems after the 1886 West End Riots, as creditors refused to lend him money, anticipating him being sentenced for his part in the riots. It may be that Champion's disenfranchisement is due to his poverty, and his rent may have fallen below the £10 p.a. threshold.

10. *Eight Hour Day*: Champion supported the campaign for the maximum eight-hour working day and worked alongside Tom Mann and Robert Cunninghame Graham in the demand. Champion's company the Modern Press published Mann's pamphlet *What a Compulsory Eight Hour Day Means to the Workers* in 1886.

11. *Mr BROADHURST*: Henry Broadhurst (1840–1911), stonemason, trade unionist, leader of the Trade Union Congress parliamentary committee, and secretary of the Labour Representation League – which supported trade unionists in Parliament – until its demise in 1874. He successfully stood as a Liberal candidate for Stoke on Trent in 1880.

Champion had castigated Broadhurst for benefiting from shares in Brunner-Mond at the expense of the workers while maintaining his trade union associations.

12. *Protection*: Champion, and many other socialists, rejected the arguments for the protection of British goods and production because they perceived it as a 'fraud' that would benefit employers and manufacturers, allowing them to reduce wages, rather than benefit the workers by allowing employers scope to raise wages.

13. *Mr. MAPLE*: Sir John Blundell Maple (1845–1903), furnishing and drapery businessman and, from 1887 until his death, Conservative member for Dulwich. The 'G. A.'s' greater sympathy for the Conservative employer relates to Champion's associations as a Tory-socialist and his acceptance of paternalist approaches to industrial relations.

14. *BRYANT, MAY & Co.*: Bryant and May's match factory was the site of the matchgirls' successful strike and the beginning of New Unionism; see above, p. 313 n. 2.

15. *Mr. WHITELEY*: William Whitely (1831–1907), department store owner whose claim was that he could supply everything 'from a pin to an elephant'. He also built factories for food production and developed a model housing estate for his workers.

Tourgeneff, 'Only a Dog'

1. *two arshines and twelve vershoks*: An arshine is a Russian measurement of length roughly two and a half feet; a vershok is roughly one and three-quarters of an inch. Gerassim is around six feet nine inches, or eighty-one inches, in height.

2. *besom*: a type of broom made from twigs attached to a long wooden handle. Gerassim is presented with the tools of his manual labour.

3. *pouds*: a Russian measure of weight, the equivalent of just over two and a half stone, thirty-eight pounds or 16.38 kg. Gerassim's bed can take up to twenty-six stone, 359 lbs or 164 kg.

4. *rouble*: Russian currency. The silver rouble was the lowest denomination of rouble, worth less than the gold and platinum roubles.

5. *Minin or Pozharsky*: Kuzma Minin (d. 1616) was a meat trader who was ennobled for his bravery in leading a volunteer corps against the Polish invasion of Moscow in 1612. Dmitry Posharsky (1577–1642) was an aristocrat who similarly distinguished himself during the struggles against Polish aggression. The two are held as national heroes and are commemorated in a joint monument in Moscow's Red Square.

6. *an idol – nay, worse than an idol*: 'Idol' here is used in the sense of an 'inert inactive person' (*OED*) rather than something to be worshipped.

7. *Tanusha*: according to the footnote in the original, this is a diminutive of Tatiana.

8. samo-var: an ornate metal receptacle, usually suspended over a fire, used to heat water for tea.

9. femme de chamber: lady's maid, chambermaid.

10. *ten copeks*: Russian currency worth one hundredth of a rouble.

11. *India-rubber soles*: Natural rubber was first cultivated on an industrial scale by British planters in India. The first commercial plantation was established in Kerala in 1902, and thus the name 'India rubber' was coined in reference to farmed rubber plants. The doctor's soles differentiate his footwear from the bast shoes of woven bark traditionally worn by Russian peasants or the leather shoes worn by the urban Russian. His shoes suggest modernity, but his treatment is primitive.

12. *the odour of burnt feathers*: The smell of burning feathers was traditionally used to bring people out of faints and again suggests the doctor's primitive methods.

13. *versts*: a unit of length measuring just over a kilometre. The village is, therefore, a little more than 25 kilometres or 15 miles from the highway.

'Bauer und Dichter', 'Eros or Erin. A Tale of an Irish Conspiracy'

1. *Coercion Act*: a reference to a number of acts passed to suppress and control agitation in Ireland against British rule. In 1881 the Protection of Person and Property Bill suspended *habeas corpus* in parts of Ireland; see also n. 3 below on the Peace Preservation Act. Fred Oakhill hopes for the same controls to be extended to Britain to punish those promoting or publicizing Irish nationalism.

2. *Newgate or Portland*: Newgate Prison in the City of London stood in Newgate Street. There had been a prison on this site since 1188, and it had been extended and rebuilt a number of times due to fires and the expansion of the prison's population. The conditions of Newgate were appalling, and it was notorious for being rife with disease. The prison was closed in 1902 and the Old Bailey was built on the site. Portland Prison is located on the isle of Portland in Dorset. This prison was opened in 1848 and is still in use as a young offenders' institution. In the mid-nineteenth century the prison held a large number of Roman Catholic Irish political prisoners, hence Oakhill's prediction for Lutterell.

3. *Peace Preservation Act*: There were a number of Peace Preservation Acts passed during the nineteenth century (1814, 1856, 1870, 1871, 1875, 1881, 1882), each designed to quash disturbances against British rule of Ireland. The reference here is presumably to the 1881 Act, passed by Gladstone's government, which was intended to control the use of arms by Irish nationalists.

4. *Erin's*: Erin; poetic, romantic name for Ireland derived from the Gaelic *Éirinn*.

5. *bitter cry ... shut him out*: Luttrell has considered all the options for employment open to a man of money: the law, medicine, the church and the military. His fears for the employment of barristers is expressed in terms of the 1883 study of poverty in London, *The Bitter Cry of Outcast London*, attributed to Andrew Mearns but now believed to have been written by W. T. Stead, editor of the *Pall Mall Gazette*, where the study was first published.

6. *stone jug*: slang for prison.

7. *Commissioner to Administer Oaths, &c.*: an official who administers the swearing of oaths, affidavits, etc. Commissioners for Oaths are usually members of the legal profession: solicitors, barristers or notaries. O'Hara is asking Luttrell to take an oath that he is who he says he is before any further details of the group are given to him.

8. *the Bank*: the Bank of England. Revolution is being planned at the heart of the British financial district.

9. *stephanotis*: *stephanotis floribunda*, also known as Madagascar jasmine, is a white scented houseplant with waxy leaves.

10. *dynamite and the knife*: a reference to the Fenian dynamite campaign undertaken between 1881 and 1885, during which dynamite was used by members of the Irish Republican Brotherhood to cause explosions in a number of British cities, including Manchester, Liverpool and London.

11. *St. Pancras ... Manchester*: Manchester trains do not run out of St Pancras, which serves the north-eastern side of the country. Trains to the north-west of the country would depart from Euston station.

12. *Gaiety stalls*: Arthur Lowrie could be referring to either the Gaiety Theatre at Aldwych, London, or the one at South King Street, Dublin, but his point is that he does not spend all his money on his own entertainment.
13. *national*: presumably meant to read 'natural'.
14. *Crystal Palace excursionists*: The Crystal Palace was originally sited in Hyde Park and built for the Great Exhibition of 1851. When the exhibition closed and Hyde Park was returned to its former state, the Crystal Palace, which had become a popular tourist attraction, was relocated to Sydenham and reopened in 1854. By the end of the nineteenth century, the popularity of the Crystal Palace had waned and the owning company was heading towards bankruptcy. George Gissing (1857–1903) includes a description of the return train from the Crystal Palace to Holborn Viaduct in the chapter 'Io Saturnalia!' in *The Nether World* (1889):

> A rush, a tumble, curses, blows, laughter, screams of pain – and we are in a carriage. Pennyloaf has to be dragged up from under the seat, and all her indignation cannot free her from the jovial embrace of a man who insists that there is plenty of room on his knee. Off we go! It is a long third-class coach, and already five or six musical instruments have struck up. We smoke and sing at the same time; we quarrel and make love – the latter in somewhat primitive fashion; we roll about with the rolling of the train; we nod into hoggish sleep.

Although Gissing's vision of the working classes in this novel is particularly bleak, Lawrence Luttrell would be surrounded by working-class excursionists on his journey home.
15. *John Mitchell's "History of Ireland"*: John Mitchell (1815–75) was an Irish nationalist from Camnish, Londonderry, who published his *History of Ireland* in 1867 while living in America. Mitchell was a member of the Irish Republican Brotherhood who held and published revolutionary ideas on the ending of British rule over Ireland.
16. *other side of the herring pond*: a reference to Irish emigrants in America who formed Fenian groups in the United States; after the American Civil War, these boasted 40,000 members. Waring hopes for British and Irish leadership in the Irish revolution they are working towards, as well as Irish-American paramilitary men.
17. *navvy*: see above, p. 328 n. 104.
18. *Don Quixote*: *The Ingenious Gentleman Don Quixote of La Mancha* by Miguel de Cervantes (1547–1616) was published in two volumes, 1605 and 1615, and is agreed by scholars to be the first of the novel genre. Cervantes's eponymous hero has a naively exaggerated sense of chivalry, and his name is the root-source of the word 'quixotic', meaning something idealistic, unrealistic and impractical; *OED*. Fred Oakhill is placing Luttrell's rescue of the young boy in the same idealistic sense.
19. *hodmen*: one who carries the hod used to transport bricks around a building site. Alice's point is that she rarely sees Irishmen in skilled trades.
20. *worthy to fight ... lead her armies*: a number of regiments of the British Army were Irish, including 'The Irish Regiment', which was founded in 1674.
21. *middle-class Conservatism*: The British Conservative Party was also known as the Unionists and fought to keep the union of England, Ireland, Wales and Scotland intact.
22. in propria persona: in person or in one's own character. The phrase is a legal term meaning to represent one's self in court without representation by a solicitor or barrister, and

its use here may suggest that O'Hara announces his own arrival, rather than one of the servants.

23. *Kate*: from here until the end of the fiction 'Alice' becomes 'Kate'.
24. *Newgate*: see above, p. 334 n. 2.
25. *Consols*: Consolidated Annuities, British government bonds. First issued in 1751 and paying a dividend of 3 per cent, this was reduced to 2.75 per cent in 1888. Consolidated Annuities are still a part of the British national debt today.
26. *Greuze*: Jean-Baptiste Greuze (1725–1805), a French artist whose paintings are described by his entry in the National Gallery as being 'related to the cult of "sensibility" ... and to the rise of the bourgeois novel and drama'. In Arthur Conan Doyle's *The Valley of Fear*, Sherlock Holmes explains that 'in the year 1865 a picture by Greuze entitled La Jeune Fille a l'Agneau fetched one million two hundred thousand francs – more than forty thousand pounds'. Thus a Greuze painting would appeal to both the bourgeois sensibility and the display of personal wealth of the owner.
27. *marchal's bâton*: symbolizing the possibility of each man rising to the rank of Marshall, but Luttrell realizes that not all men can be leaders and the fight to make the rank of leader is aided by wealth.
28. *"Songs before Sunrise"*: a series of poem by Algernon Charles Swinburne (1837–1909), published in 1871 and addressing the issue of Italian unification and republicanism. The radical sentiments of Swinburne's poetry in this collection would chime with Luttrell's Irish republicanism.
29. *peached*: meaning to impeach, to accuse. Delaney claims one of the group has given evidence against the others.
30. *screen*: an ornamented board used to protect the face from the direct heat of a fire. A screen could either be large enough to stand independently in front of the fire, or small enough to be hand-held, as is Kate's.

Bland, 'Blood'

1. *Shepherds Bush ... together at Guy's*: Shepherds Bush Young Gentlemen's Preparatory School, London, an independent school for children up to the age of eleven or thirteen that prepares children for secondary education. Rossall is a private boarding school in Fleetwood, Lancashire, founded in 1844. Guy's Hospital, London, is where the narrator and his friends trained in medicine. Guy's Campus, housing the School of Biomedical Science, the Dental Institute and the School of Medicine, is now next to Guy's Hospital and is part of King's College London. Wicksteed has known Roland Ker for most of his life, and they grew up together.
2. *fusee*: see above, p. 313 n. 2.
3. *Rothschildian*: from Rothschild, a German-Jewish family dynasty, whose wealth was made through banking in the eighteenth, nineteenth and twentieth centuries. The term 'Rothschild' denotes huge wealth; Wicksteed's inheritance is not comparable.
4. *greenest of things blue – the bluest of things grey*: Algernon Charles Swinburne's 'Felise' (1866), in which the poet-narrator muses on the inconsistency of his lover as they part.
5. blond cendré: ash blonde, a very light shade of blonde.
6. contralto, *bull and* vibrante: Contralto is the lowest pitch for a female voice in music; to be bull-voiced means to have a powerful voice; vibrante means both to quiver and throb, and something that is exciting and colourful. Mrs Ker's voice is beautiful and unusual,

set apart from her contemporaries who are reduced by apostrophes to 'singers' in comparison.

7.   *Darby and Joan*: an apocryphal elderly couple epitomizing lasting love into old age. Wicksteed views Ker and his wife's love to be more vital and youthful than the quiet but devoted relationship of Darby and Joan.

R. G. B., 'Birds of a Feather'

1.   *John Stuart Mill … Sinnett*: John Stuart Mill (1806–73) was an advocate of women's rights; he maintained a relationship with the married Harriet Taylor for nineteen years before her husband's death. Immanuel Kant (1724–1804) remained unmarried, and his philosophy on marriage, from *The Science of Right* (1797), was that it should be monogamous and for the benefit of procreation:

> For, this natural employment – as a use of the sexual members of the other – is an enjoyment for which the one person is given up to the other. In this relation the human individual makes himself into a thing, which is contrary to the right of humanity in his own person. This, however, is only possible under the one condition, that as the one person is acquired by the other as a thing, that same person also equally acquires the other reciprocally, and thus regains and reestablishes the rational personality.

Auguste Comte (1798–1857) frequently visited prostitutes and conducted an affair with married Italian pianist, Pauline, with whom he had a daughter. Alfred Percy Sinnett's (1840–1921) work *Esoteric Buddhism* (1883) outlined the teachings of theosophy, and he published the play *Marriage by Degrees* in 1911.

2.   *George Eliot and Mary Wollstonecraft*: George Eliot (1819–80), born Mary Anne Evans, lived with the married George Henry Lewes from 1853 until his death in 1878, as Lewes was unable to divorce his wife. Mary Wollstonecraft (1759–97) had become infatuated with the married Henry Fuseli in 1788; she lived with Gilbert Imlay between 1793 and 1796, having a baby, Fanny Imlay, with him; she then met William Godwin in 1796 and married him before their child, Mary Wollstonecraft Godwin, was born in 1797.

3.   Punch: *Punch, or the London Charivari* was a popular weekly satirical magazine established in 1841 by Henry Mayhew and eventually ceasing publication in 1992. *Punch* was extremely popular but would not be considered intellectual.

4.   Family Herald: The *Family Herald: or, Useful Information and Amusement for the Million*, another weekly periodical published in 1843–1940, which carried a high volume of serial and short fiction. Both *Punch* and the *Family Herald* would be considered popular literature without any intellectual base.

5.   *Much Darker Days*: a novel by Andrew Lang published in 1884 under the pseudonym 'A. Huge Longway'.

6.   *devilled*: meaning both food that is grilled and possessed by a devil.

7.   *the devil walking about as a roaring lion*: from 'Be sober, be vigilant; because your adversary the devil, as a roaring lion, walketh about, seeking whom he may devour'; 1 Peter 5:8. George Eliot craves a final death at the hands of the devil, it being preferable to the eternal boredom inflicted on her and Mary Wollstonecraft.

8.   *Potipahr's wife, Messalina, and Madame de Pompadour*: In Genesis 39, Joseph refused sex with Potiphar's wife after Potiphar had entrusted him with his household. Potiphar's

wife falsely accused Joseph of attempted seduction, and he was imprisoned. Valeria Messalina, wife of Emperor Claudius and cousin of Nero, had a reputation for promiscuity, and Pliny recorded the tale of her sex competition with a prostitute. Jeanne Antoinette Poisson, Marquise de Pompadour (1721–64), was the mistress of Louis XV of France. These names imply that Hell is populated by sexually free and promiscuous women.

9.   *Salvation Army*: A Christian-based movement, the Salvation Army would not countenance occult practices such as mesmerism, and they were influential in the rescue of prostitutes from their lives of sin. The Salvation Army sent men and women into the urban slums to convert the inhabitants to Christianity. They also conducted relief work to alleviate some of the sufferings of poverty, but generally the socialist movement was critical of the Salvation Army for elevating the soul above the body's material sufferings and therefore distracting the poor from working towards social, political and economic change. See, for instance, the exchange between Hyndman and John Law [Margaret Harkness] in *Justice*, March 1888, after the publication of her novel *Captain Lobe: A Story of the Salvation Army* (1888; republished 1890 under the title *In Darkest London*).

Broadhouse, 'How He Lost his "Strad"'

1.   *swound*: an archaic word for a swoon or fainting fit.

Katte, 'The Whip Hand. A Political Story – in Three Parts'

1.   *Chancellor of the Exchequer*: The second Lord of the Treasury in the British government, the Chancellor is the minister responsible for the finance and economics of the country. At the time this story was published, the Chancellor of the Exchequer was George Goschen, Viscount Goschen (1831–1907), MP in Lord Salisbury's government.

2.   *Curzon Street*: In the wealthy London district of Mayfair, Curzon Street runs between Berkeley Square and Park Lane. The street has been home to many rich and powerful people, including Benjamin Disraeli and Alfred de Rothschild (see above, p. 336 n. 3). Sir Reginald's wealth and standing are signified by his house.

3.   Punch: see above, p. 337 n. 3.

4.   *under secretaryship*: Permanent Under-Secretary of State is the title of the civil servant in charge of a parliamentary department – ministerial and non-ministerial – and is the highest rank in the service. Sir Reginald will overstep this position in his promotion to the most important ministerial role in the government.

5.   *South Audley Street*: runs between Grosvenor Square and South Street in the district of Mayfair and abuts Curzon Street.

6.   *go up to the Peers*: given a title and made a member of the House of Lords. Although the Lords had the power of veto over bills passed by the House of Commons, this promotion was deemed to be giving an easier life to those who had served their time in the Commons.

7.   *Maida Vale*: a residential area of London to the north and west of Mayfair. Respectably wealthy, the area is not the same signifier of huge wealth as Curzon and South Audley streets.

8.   *pocket borough*: or 'rotten borough', a parliamentary district controlled by a single person or family. Sir Reginald was gifted the parliamentary seat by his uncle and was not elected on his own merit.

9. *the followers of Irish leader himself*: the Irish Parliamentary Party, also known as the Home Rule Party. At this time the party leader was Charles Stewart Parnell (1846–91), who led the party from 1882 to 1891.

10. *art fabric*: patterned silk, presumably the hand-printed Liberty Silk manufactured by Arthur Liberty for his famous Regent Street shop.

11. *lappet*: a loose or overlapping part of a garment, forming a flap or fold; *OED*.

12. Standard: The *Standard* was a London newspaper founded by Charles Baldwin (1774–1869) in 1827, with the *Evening Standard* (which is still published today) founded in 1859. The paper originally had Tory leanings, and proprietor James Johnstone (1815–78), who bought the paper from Charles Baldwin, accepted Tory funds to keep the paper afloat in 1858.

13. *Egypt*: a pet name emphasizing the class difference between Sir Reginald and Kate, as recognized in the 'absence of fine shades'.

14. *Lady Hastie's "money" ... show themselves*: His wife's money was earned and not inherited; therefore she is deemed not as refined as Sir Reginald, whose family is not tainted by trade. However, in the second half of the nineteenth century a number of British aristocrats married wealthy American heiresses to bolster the dwindling wealth of their families.

15. *secretaire*: a cabinet or desk where private papers would be kept.

16. *cabinet portrait*: a photographic portrait.

17. *only get a separation ... beating her I suppose*: The 1857 Matrimonial Causes Act had allowed women to petition for divorce for the first time. The act created the magistrates' court, which allowed divorce to be applied for without the necessity of an Act of Parliament. Husbands could sue for divorce on the grounds of adultery alone, but women had to prove adultery as well as another offence such as cruelty, desertion, bigamy or incest. Had Sir Reginald been beating his wife, she would have been able to divorce him.

18. table de nuit: a bedside table.

19. *the Cecil*: a large and lavish hotel on the Embankment.

Law, 'The Gospel of Getting On. (To Olive Schreiner.)'

1. *Lord Tom Noddy*: 'Tomnoddy' is defined by the *OED* as a stupid or foolish person.

2. *rowing on the Cam*: The boy is now a Cambridge student, a level of education impossible to achieve without considerable wealth, but one where the network of contacts would help students to 'get on'.

3. *Oh talk not to me ... our glory*: the first two lines of Byron's 'Stanzas Written on the Road between Florence and Pisa', rather than the chorus. The poem was set to music by Ernst Eberhard (1839–1910) in New York in 1881.

4. *One hundred and fifty years old*: Harkness is referring back to the political economists of the past who had argued for individual gain and free trade as the basis for exchange. One hundred and fifty years before the publication of this story places the development of this 'Gospel' between Sir Dudley North's (1641–91) *Discourses upon Trade* (1691) and Adam Smith's (bap. 1723, d. 1790) *Wealth of Nations* (1776), at the period of the French physiocratic school led by François Quesnay (1694–1774) and Jean Claude Marie Vincent, seigneur de Gournay (1712–59), who argued for 'natural rights' and a *laissez faire* government.

5. *a dying crofter's finger*: a reference to the Highland Clearances of the late eighteenth and early nineteenth centuries, when the centuries-old ways of crofting – individual farming and small-scale land ownership within crofting townships – were ended by the eviction

of crofters from their land by the Scottish aristocracy to claim the land and use it for large-scale arable and cattle farming.

6.   *the sweat of Irish peasants*: The removal of Catholic landlords after the Act of Union in 1801 brought Ireland under the control of Britain and brought landownership under the control of the English aristocracy and gentry. The Irish peasant worked the land for the enrichment of the English landowner.

SILENT CORRECTIONS

Maubourg, 'A Mournful Fate'

p. 28, l. 12   Shorthly] Shortly

Bramsbury, 'A Working Class Tragedy'

p. 90, l. 12   of] of the
p. 99, l. 18   me] me who
p. 133, l. 13   But] But he
p. 135, l. 3   waive] wave
p. 135, l. 34   Anything] Anything was
p. 163, l. 5   cherry] cheery
p. 164, l. 9   raddish] radish
p. 171, l. 22   signs] signs of
p. 171, l. 23   speak] speak to
p. 173, l. 3   ane] one
p. 174, l. 2   sooner] sooner than
p. 185, l. 40   preferred] proffered

'Bauer und Dichter', 'Eros or Erin. A Tale of an Irish Conspiracy'

p. 251, l. 23   its] it's
p. 251, l. 27   Laurence] Lawrence
p. 252, l. 7   Laurence] Lawrence
p. 252, l. 9   Laurence] Lawrence
p. 262, p. 2   two] three

Katte, 'The Whip Hand. A Political Story – in Three Parts'

p. 289, l. 33   stolidy] stolidly